Protecting Motherhood

Protecting Motherhood

Women and the Family in the
Politics of Postwar West Germany

Robert G. Moeller

UNIVERSITY OF CALIFORNIA PRESS
Berkeley • Los Angeles • Oxford

University of California Press
Berkeley and Los Angeles, California

University of California Press, Ltd.
Oxford, England

Material in this book appeared earlier in journal articles and is
used with permission: "Protecting Mother's Work: From Production to
Reproduction in Postwar West Germany," *Journal of Social History* 22
(1989): 413–37, and "Reconstructing the Family in Reconstruction
Germany: Women and Social Policy in the Federal Republic, 1949–
1955," *Feminist Studies* 15 (1989): 137–69.

Library of Congress Cataloging-in-Publication Data

Moeller, Robert G.
    Protecting motherhood : Women and the family in the politics
of postwar West Germany / Robert G. Moeller.
        p. cm.
    Includes bibliographical references and index.
    ISBN 0-520-07903-5   (cloth : alk. paper)
    1. Women—Government policy—Germany (West) 2. Motherhood—
Government policy—Germany (West)   3. Family policy—Germany (West)
4. Women's rights—Germany (West)   I. Title.
HQ 1236.5.G3M64   1993
305.42—dc20   92-6622
                                                                     CIP

Printed in the United States of America

9 8 7 6 5 4 3 2 1

For Lynn Mally

Contents

Illustrations

Acknowledgments

Without much help from many friends and colleagues, I never would have written this book. I welcome the opportunity to acknowledge my debts, though I know that I can never fully repay them.

I have benefited enormously from the friendship, encouragement, intelligence, and wit of Temma Kaplan. Perhaps more than anyone else, she first convinced me that I had something worth saying about women, families, and social policy in postwar West Germany. During four years in New York in the early eighties, I became acquainted with the German Women's History Group. I remain grateful for the responses, reactions, critical readings, and friendship of Renate Bridenthal, Jane Caplan, and Claudia Koonz, who offered me an intellectual and social community that still sustains me and that constituted a major reason for finishing the project. In addition, Atina Grossmann, Deborah Hertz, Marion Kaplan, and Molly Nolan consistently provided support and enthusiasm for my work. Individually and collectively, the scholarly efforts of these historians have profoundly influenced my research.

The years in New York also allowed me to become friends with David Abraham, Victoria de Grazia, Ellen Ross, Ioannis Sinanoglou, and Marilyn Young. Along the way, all took time from their own work to read and comment extensively on mine. My friendship with Carroll Smith-Rosenberg greatly enriched my scholarship; she continues to offer me a model of intellectual integrity and generosity that would be difficult to match. At key points, I have received additional assistance and guidance from James Diehl, Gerald Feldman, Geoffrey Field, Estelle

Freedman, Ute Frevert, Karin Hausen, Susan Mann, Gwendolyn Mink, Karen Offen, Robert O. Paxton, Susan Pedersen, Reinhard Rürup, Christoph Sachsse, Sharon Ullman, Judith Walkowitz, Steven Welch, and Linda Zerilli. Alvia Golden, Sara Krulwich, and Jane Randolph heard many of the stories that went into this book and reminded me to laugh.

Several years ago, Geoff Eley, Vernon Lidtke, and Volker Berghahn did much to convince the University of California Press that an outline might actually become a book. Their perceptive responses, both then and subsequently, their early vote of confidence, and their continued critical engagement with the project have helped to keep me going. Eley and Berghahn have commented on the work in progress, and their responses have always been valuable. Cornelia Dayton reassured me that even an historian of colonial America might find this book interesting. And James Cronin labored through an early draft, offering many good ideas for making it better.

Sheila Levine, my editor, has been much more than that from the beginning. She saw this project through from hazy start to finish. I think she was always far more certain than I that I would actually write this book. I also appreciate the considerable efforts of Ellen Stein, who did much to improve my prose, and Rose Vekony, who expertly guided the manuscript through its final stages. Their enthusiasm for my work came at exactly the right moment.

Heidrun Homburg and Josef Mooser greatly eased the trials and tribulations of research in Germany. They made Bielefeld an idyllic retreat, always providing a rare mix of intellectual camaraderie, friendship, and good food. In Berlin, Marlene Müller-Haas and Hansjörg Haas offered the same.

I came to the University of California, Irvine, in the summer of 1988. Since my arrival, Jon Jacobson and Patricia O'Brien have been truly exceptional colleagues and friends; they have seen me through the ups and downs of writing. Joan Ariel, women's studies librarian, and Ellen Broidy, history librarian, have given of their time and expertise as critics, researchers, and friends. Lynn Hammeras and Kathy White shared generously of their extensive knowledge of early childhood development. For more than forty hours a week they also cared for my daughter, Nora Mally, better than I could ever have hoped to, giving me the space and emotional energy to write about families *and* to be part of one.

Throughout my research, the staffs of many German archives helped lead me through the documents and uncomplainingly filled the massive photocopying orders I left in my wake. Just as patient and professional were the interlibrary loan departments of Columbia University, the University of California, Santa Cruz, and the University of California, Irvine. Hans-Dieter Kreikamp of the Bundesarchiv (Koblenz) deserves particular mention. Only thanks to his considerable efforts was I able to dip so deeply into such a range of archival materials, never before open to historians.

I was extremely fortunate to receive ample funding for my work at two crucial points. A short-term travel grant from the German Academic Exchange Service (Deutscher Akademischer Austauschdienst), a grant from the Spencer Foundation of Teachers College at Columbia University, and a summer stipend from the National Endowment for the Humanities allowed me to photocopy massive amounts of material during an initial foray into German libraries and archives. Support from the German Marshall Fund of the United States permitted me a luxurious year to sort through it. In the final stages of the project, funding from the Gender Roles Program of the Rockefeller Foundation gave me nearly as much time to write. Support from the Rockefeller Foundation, supplemented by a travel grant from the American Council of Learned Societies, also made it possible for me to participate in an international conference, "Women in Hard Times," in August 1987. There I received extensive responses to my work and shared in a truly exceptional intellectual experience organized by Claudia Koonz. Along the way, support from the academic senates, committees on research, and deans of humanities at the University of California, Santa Cruz, and the University of California, Irvine, and from the Focused Research Initiative, "Woman and the Image," at Irvine have funded research assistants and facilitated accumulation of even bigger piles of photocopies. Ann Rider spent many hours in the library chasing down references, allowing me to stay home and write.

The death of my father, H. G. Moeller, my daughter's third birthday, and final word from the University of California Press that it would publish this book all came at about the same time in July 1991. Historians love paradoxes, but I will not dwell on this one. My father, my mother, Marian Moeller, and my sister, Patricia Steimer, offered unqualified support and acceptance. Nora challenged all my assumptions about parents, children, and families, and kept things in perspective.

This long list of thanks only begins to suggest how extraordinarily fortunate I have been over the years it has taken me to complete this book. Lynn Mally has lived with this project from the start, and she has had to hear enormous amounts about every stage of it along the way. Without her critical intelligence, patience, good humor, and friendship, I doubt that I would ever have finished.

Introduction

Writing in 1946, Agnes von Zahn-Harnack observed:

> Hardly any other question will be so important for the future shape of German domestic life, for German culture and morals, and for [Germany's] reintegration into world culture as the question of the relation of the sexes to each other. [This question] will be raised in the arena of politics as well as economics, and in the specifically sexual arena as well. Every war and postwar period brings serious devastation and crisis, but defeated peoples are doubly endangered. They must fear the internal dissolution of many bonds that the victor can more easily maintain. The defeated party runs the risk of self-hate that allows it to throw away even what might be maintained.[1]

Zahn-Harnack's credentials qualified her as a keen observer of sexual politics. Cofounder of the German Association of Women Academics, author of a major history of the German women's movement, and the last president of the League of German Women's Associations (Bund deutscher Frauenvereine), the national umbrella organization that had brought together various strands of the bourgeois women's movement before its dissolution in 1933, she was also active in the political organization of middle-class women in Berlin in the late forties.[2] But no such qualifications were required to realize that a reassessment of gender relations would be a crucial part of rebuilding Germany after 1945.

Indeed, in many respects Zahn-Harnack expressed the obvious. Wars throw into disarray the domestic social order of the countries they involve. Particularly in the twentieth century, wars have been fought with

1

the massive mobilization of society by the state; the war at the front finds its counterpart in the war at home. While some men put on uniforms and try to kill those identified as the enemy, other men and even more women take on expanded responsibilities as workers, as single parents, and as sustainers of the domestic social and political order. Consequently, wars rupture boundaries that do not appear on maps—the boundaries between women and men. Unlike the boundaries between nations, these borders are never fixed; they are constantly challenged, questioned, and negotiated, though most people remain largely unaware of that process and live it without consciously participating in it. During wartime, however, state intervention into virtually all aspects of social and economic life alters the relations between women and men; the process is explicitly political, and its effects are immediately apparent. From the start, wartime changes are seen as temporary, extraordinary responses to extraordinary circumstances. At war's end, the social and political process of renegotiating boundaries commences, and again, the state's direct involvement makes explicit efforts to reestablish normalcy, to rebuild what has been destroyed, and to determine where the past can no longer provide direction. The politics of the family and women's status is essential to this general passage from war to peace.[3]

After 1945, the "political reconstruction of the family"[4] took place in all countries that participated in the Second World War, but the salience of gender as a political category in postwar West Germany was particularly striking. On the most basic, immediately recognizable level, relations between the sexes commanded attention because postwar Germany was a society in which women far outnumbered men. As the journalist and political activist Gabriele Strecker observed, in purely visual terms the high rate of male casualties in the war and the large number of soldiers detained in prisoner-of-war camps meant that in 1945 Germany was a "country of women."[5] This lasting demographic legacy of the Nazis' war of aggression combined in the late forties with the social dislocation and economic instability of the immediate postwar period to prompt widespread fears of a "crisis of the family." In a society where adult men were in short supply, this was a crisis of the status of women and gender relations.

Unlike the situation in Britain, France, and the United States, the problem for German women was not how to adjust to their postwar demobilization from nontraditional occupations; they faced challenges of a very different sort. Until the late forties under Allied controls, shortages of all necessities became worse than they had been before the war's end, and the gradual release of men from prisoner-of-war camps, which continued into the fifties, delayed family reunions. War deaths meant that many families remained "incomplete" (*unvollständig*)—without adult males—and many marriages collapsed under the strains of long separations. The end of the war meant no end to the war at home.

Women's hardships and the perceived disequilibrium of gender relations caused by women's altered status in the war and postwar years became central concerns of politicians and public policy-makers. For women and men, from the Social Democratic Party (SPD) to the conservative Christian-Democratic/Christian-Social (CDU/CSU) coalition, there was a broad political consensus that the war had placed particularly great strains on the family, and that "more than any other societal institution, the family had fallen into the whirlpool created by the collapse." This made the family "the central problem of the postwar era."[6] Everyone could agree that after the hard times of the war and its aftermath, the needs of women and the family deserved special attention.

This book explores how postwar West Germans approached these issues in the first decade of the Federal Republic's history. It focuses on public-policy debates over the definition of gender equality in the new West German constitution, family allowances, protective legislation and women's participation in the wage labor force, and family-law reform. Here, West Germans outlined blueprints for reconstructing gender in reconstruction Germany. Debates over these policies provide an exceptionally rich source for examining postwar Germans' attitudes toward gender relations because they engaged such a wide-ranging variety of witnesses and experts; employers, trade unionists, party politicians, ministers of religion, organized women's groups, lawyers and judges, medical practitioners, sociologists, and civil servants were all brought onto the stage, into newspapers and journals and before parliamentary commissions. In remarkably explicit terms, they voiced their opinions on women's work, family life, and motherhood. By exploring the extensive discussions and the implementation of specific measures, this book seeks to illuminate how established conceptions of gender difference influenced public policy and how state policy in turn shaped the conditions of women's social and economic status during West Germany's "economic miracle" (*Wirtschaftswunder*).

It would be possible to pursue other thematic paths to the same end. The process of redefining "woman's place" in postwar West Germany occurred not only in social policies that expressed how families *should* be but in the lived experiences of families as they *were;* not only in the sometimes arid debates of policy-makers but in novels, movies, and pop-ular magazines;[7] not only in the halls of parliament but in the dance halls, where young Germans discovered the lures of rock and roll, along with new languages for expressing their sexuality and articulating gen-erational conflicts; not only in debates about nuclear families but in women's organized protests against the threat of nuclear annihilation; not only in policies formulated at the national level but in measures af-fecting housing, education, and public assistance carried out at the re-gional and local level; not only in discussions of how to defend women and the family but in discussions of how to defend the nation from the perceived threat of communism; not only in laws designed to protect women workers but on the shop floor where women workers protected themselves.[8]

By focusing on one part of a more complex process, this book seeks to identify a set of questions; it does not exhaust possible means to find answers. In this sense, it is part of a history of women in the postwar period that is still very much in the making. Although this history is now being written, the post-1945 historiographic landscape still looks ex-traordinarily barren compared to the substantial literature on German women in the Kaiserreich and Weimar and under National Socialism.[9] In the few general treatments of the late forties and fifties that exist, the problems of reconstruction are the problems of Germans without gender.[10] This book insists that in any adequate account of postwar Ger-man history, gender must be a central analytic category. It analyzes key elements of the national politics of *Frau* and family in the postwar years and the forces shaping the political rhetorics available for describing relations between women and men. Debates over these concerns con-stituted a crucial arena where women's rights, responsibilities, needs, capacities, and possibilities were discussed, identified, defined, and re-inforced.

Political responses to the "woman question" (*Frauenfrage*) in the late forties and fifties drew on an already well-established repertoire. In pushing for women's equality and for a reform of family law in the fif-ties, Social Democrats and liberal middle-class women political activists returned to an agenda that originated in the late nineteenth century, when the Bourgeois Civil Code (Bürgerliches Gesetzbuch) established explicitly patriarchal provisions governing marriage and family life as the law of the land. Demands for revising the law were as old as the law itself.[11] Concerns about structuring the wage workplace to meet the par-ticular requirements of women's bodies, psyches, and souls were also well-established aspects of the state's attempt to provide women workers with special treatment, trade unionists' and Social Democrats' struggle to improve women's working conditions, and the acknowledgment that most women wage earners worked a second shift at home.[12] Pressure in the fifties for family allowances to supplement the wages of the fathers of large families evoked long-standing working-class demands for the "family wage," conservative pronatalist enthusiasm for state support of families "rich in children," and anxieties, long predating the demographic impact of the Second World War, that family-size limitation would lead to population decline. At least since the late nineteenth century, the German system of social insurance, the foundation of the welfare state, aimed not only at addressing the crisis of democracy—the challenge to the Kaiserreich presented by the emergence of an organized working-class movement—but also at resolving the perceived crisis of *demography*—the falling birthrate. Policies tailored to meet the needs of male productive wage workers and their dependents also embodied a conception of women's essential unpaid reproductive work. Men's claims on the welfare state were based on their contributions as workers in the market economy; women's claims on the welfare state were based on their relations to others, as wives and mothers, as workers in the home.[13] When these political projects reemerged in the fifties, they were by no means entirely new.

Still, this book argues that when familiar themes surfaced in postwar West Germany they carried additional layers of meaning. In particular, they became part of a direct confrontation with the ideological legacy of National Socialist attitudes toward women and the family. In the categories of postwar West German politics, the Nazis had attempted to reduce women to breeding machines for the *Volk*, erasing the boundary between private families and public policy. For West Germans, restoring women to an inviolable family, safe from state intervention, was a shared objective. They renounced a past in which they had sought political stability in *Lebensraum* (living space) in eastern Europe; they replaced it with a search for security in the *Lebensraum* of the family, where a democratic West Germany would flourish. At the center of this construction was the German woman. In describing the debates over national policies affecting women in the fifties, this book emphasizes that by grounding conceptions of postwar security so solidly in specific conceptions of the family, social policy-makers articulated a narrowly circumscribed vision of women's rights and responsibilities.

For the political definition of women and the family, communism was just as powerful a negative point of reference as fascism. In her perceptive study, *Homeward Bound: American Families in the Cold War Era*,

Elaine Tyler May effectively documents how metaphors of "containment" influenced not only United States foreign policy in the fifties but also perceptions of gender relations and the family. "In the domestic version," she writes, "the 'sphere of influence' was the home."[14] In the Federal Republic of Germany, the context of the Cold War was even less subtle and more significant than in the United States, because West Germans were forcefully confronted with the example of their German-speaking neighbors to the east; the discussion of women's rights and responsibilities was frequently informed by a comparison with the status of women in the German Democratic Republic.

Debates over measures affecting women and the family constituted a particularly important arena for political self-definition in the Federal Republic because the family was among the few institutions that West Germans could argue had survived National Socialism relatively unscathed, a storehouse of uniquely German values that could provide a solid basis for postwar recovery. Helmut Schelsky, one of the founders of postwar West German sociology, published a much-cited study of the German family in the early fifties in which he expressed a widely held conception that in the wake of the "sudden and complete collapse of the state and economic order, as it took place in Germany, [the family] was able to prop up the individual person and was capable once again of carrying out total societal functions that the modern economic and state system seemed to have taken from it long ago." The family was a "vestige of stability in our social crisis."[15] This was a highly idealized vision, but in articulating this ideal, Schelsky and many other postwar West Germans demarcated a terrain where they could begin to shape not only policies affecting women and the family but also their vision of a democratic political order.

The urgency of this task was self-evident; the need for legitimate political identities was pressing in a country whose creation was the outcome of defeat in war and which was the product of another in a long series of revolutions from above, this time imposed from outside. The victorious Allies determined de facto that there would be two geographic and political areas called Germany, but in the fifties it was left to Germans—East and West—to create themselves. Much of this book is devoted to analyses of men's descriptions of women. Men—vastly overrepresented in parliament, in the government, in political parties, in trade unions, and in the medical, legal and academic professions—dominated debates over national policies affecting women and the family. In this book, however, I argue that when men specified their conceptions of women's rights and needs they were also defining themselves and their vision of a just society; thus, this book attempts not only to examine the impact of postwar reconstruction on women but also to suggest what the politics of gender can tell us about the larger process of framing political identities in the first decade of the Federal Republic.[16]

The study of state social policies affecting women and the family in the past can provide a useful perspective on the problems of defining a feminist social policy in the present, which is another purpose of this book. It directly addresses many issues—the tensions between demands for women's equality and women's special treatment, the contradictions for women in many self-proclaimed profamily doctrines, and the difficulties of formulating a language of political equality that allows for a recognition of difference—that are of primary interest to feminist scholars and legal experts and that are central to discussions of social policies shaping women's lives. The interpretation of the West German experience offered here is a reminder that democratic welfare states can be both "friend and foe" for women.[17] Measures intended to "protect" women and to acknowledge the significance of their "natural" tasks are often responses to genuine social needs, but once in place they may limit the ways in which certain problems are perceived and the areas where solutions are sought, obscuring alternative conceptions and other potential solutions.[18] The historical study of the state's attempt to specify women's status, to delimit women's equality, to define families, and to reinforce conceptions of gender difference can thus alert us to the ways in which the identification of women's needs can all too easily lead to the limitation of women's rights.

CHAPTER ONE

Emerging from the Rubble

"No more bomb attacks . . . but nothing more to eat"

January 1933, the Nazi seizure of power; September 1939, the German invasion of Poland and the start of the Second World War; May 1945, the German defeat and surrender—these are dates familiar to everyone, events that frame most accounts of the history of National Socialist Germany. They define the chapter divisions in standard histories; they constitute a convenient periodization that describes the beginning and end of the Thousand Year Reich. May 1945 marks a "zero hour" (*Stunde Null*), a new beginning, which will ultimately bring West Germans to the Federal Republic and the economic miracle. Can this periodization adequately make sense of German women's experience in the thirties and forties? Consider the story of Frau F., told to a social worker more than four years after the war's end:

In 1939, Frau F.'s husband was drafted. He went off to war, leaving her in Darmstadt with their three-year-old daughter, Gisela, and their son Willy, only a year old. At first, Frau F. and her children managed to survive his absence quite successfully. She found work as a postal carrier; her income, supplemented by the separation allowance paid to her as a military wife, allowed her to open a savings account and to indulge her children's food fantasies. Gisela could eat her favorite fruit and a sausage sandwich almost daily, and Willy stuffed himself with pancakes and fruit. Occasionally Frau F. had to work until midnight to maintain an orderly household, but she got some assistance from her mother, who lived in the neighborhood and helped with childcare.

In 1944, Frau F.'s hopes for an even brighter future ended. By then, Allied bomb attacks had extended farther and farther into Germany, and frequent alarms drove her and her children into basement shelters. On 11 September 1944, their apartment building was hit directly. Fleeing with her children from one shelter to another, Frau F. looked on horrified as Willy's clothes caught on fire. She extinguished the flames, but in the commotion Gisela vanished; no one knew what became of the child, and she was never found. With their burned clothes and flesh, mother and son struggled through Darmstadt to the home of Frau F.'s sister-in-law, whom they found sitting in front of her apartment, which also had been bombed out. She had escaped with only two suitcases and some linens. Joined by Frau F.'s mother, the two women and Willy spent several days outside in the ruins, sleeping in bomb shelters, before Willy and his grandmother were sent to relatives in the countryside. Frau F. and her sister-in-law found a room in the home of a doctor, a former employer from Frau F.'s past as a domestic; the doctor had been drafted, and his wife gave them shelter.

The village to which Willy and his grandmother fled became a battleground, leaving them homeless once again. Only after lengthy disputes with local authorities in Darmstadt did Frau F. obtain the official authorization for them to return to the city; reunited, they all shared a room with Frau F.'s sister-in-law. American troops seized Darmstadt, and black GIs occupied the building in which Frau F. and her family had found refuge. The three women took their things, and after a day-long search they found an empty basement that was still habitable. Willy became quite proficient at securing food from the soldiers; when his begging act failed, his growing expertise as a thief succeeded.

The return of Herr F. in 1945 made things no better. Though not injured in the war, he bore other less visible scars. Nervous and irritable, he was a chain-smoker in a society where ample supplies of cigarettes were available only on the black market. He flared up at the slightest provocation, and it was impossible to escape his wrath in the cramped basement. Frau F. found employment with the Americans right after the war's end, but she quit her job once Herr F. found work. Nevertheless, his ration card did not cover his appetite, and Frau F. could meet his demands for meat only by cutting back on what she consumed.

After nine months in the basement, local housing authorities assigned the F. family to three small attic rooms and a tiny kitchen, which they shared with Frau F.'s mother and Herr F.'s sister, who had been left a widow by the war. Their quarters became only more crowded; within three years after the war's end, Frau F. gave birth to a daughter and a son. Her attempt to abort a third pregnancy by taking large doses of an over-the-counter drug was unsuccessful; another son joined the family.

Although thoroughly exhausted by her household labors and her responsibilities for her children, Frau F. feared going to bed before her husband had fallen asleep; she wanted to avoid his sexual advances. Her reluctance provoked his ire: Why, he asked rhetorically, should he work, if he was denied sexual pleasure? Her pleas that he might use a condom prompted only the response that prophylactics were harmful; when she refused him, he masturbated and complained the morning after that she was responsible for his headaches. Only the intervention of Frau F.'s mother and sister-in-law prevented her husband's verbal abuse from becoming physical. Although she proposed divorce, her husband would not accept this alternative. Economically dependent on him and tied to her children, she had little choice but to remain in the marriage.[1]

"Collapse" or "liberation"? According to one set of scholarly reflections marking the fortieth anniversary of the Nazi defeat, these were the two conceptual frameworks available to Germans for understanding 8 May 1945, the day of German capitulation.[2] German women who had suffered under National Socialism because of their religious or political beliefs, or because of their failure to fulfill racist Aryan standards, doubtless experienced May 1945 as a liberation. The end of the war also was the end to oppression for many women in Nazi-occupied territories and for women forced from their homelands to perform forced labor in Germany during the war. Unlike the sufferings of Frau F., the hardships of these women had been caused not by Allied bomb attacks but by the policies of the German government during the Third Reich.[3]

For those who had embraced the Nazis' policies, the war's end marked a depressing and disillusioning conclusion to a grand experiment. Doris K., born in 1924, an enthusiastic Nazi and member of the League of German Girls (Bund deutscher Mädchen), recorded her memories of the war's end in a poem:

> The blue, sun-filled days
> are lost and scattered—I hardly know how.
> I barely carried their touch in my heart.
> We loved them. And we do not shed tears over them.
>
> The star-filled nights, full of love,
> are dreams from another time.

And if it were to stay spring outside forever—
they are far away—God only knows how far.
. . . .
Yes, it is day—but gray surrounds the earth.
Oh, it is night—but there are no stars.
And God, with his inscrutable mien,
is as far from us as he once was near.[4]

Day turned into night. A distant God. Though not necessarily in such adolescent, maudlin terms, 1945 represented a decisive turning point, a complete collapse, for Doris K. and others who had believed they were the promise of a new Germany. A sudden twilight had also arrived for the zealous, ideologically committed, and often completely unrepentant leadership of Nazi women's organizations.[5]

However, for the majority of German women who met the racial and political criteria of National Socialism but for whom the politics of the Nazis had been of little or no direct interest, the war's end constituted no such clear break, neither liberation nor collapse. The defeat of the Nazi regime represented not a rupture with the past but rather a moment in a continuum of hardship and privation that had begun with the Soviet Army's victories in the east and extensive Allied bombing of German cities in 1942 and 1943.[6]

Stories like Frau F.'s, recorded by social workers and sociologists in the late forties, provided the basis for an extensive investigation of the perceived crisis of the family in Germany after the war. Allied bomb attacks had leveled cities, decimated housing stock, and disrupted the transportation network. In areas of heavy industrial development, such as the Ruhr, the destruction was particularly extensive, and in some areas, as few as four percent of all apartments remained undamaged.[7] "Women of the rubble" (*Trümmerfrauen*) assumed a mythic status in accounts of the postwar period, as they literally cleared away the ruins of German cities to make way for a new beginning.

Social observers also described the "rubble of families" (*Familientrümmer*) and the "broken souls" of men. Removing these social and psychological ruins and "rebuilding men" (*Wiederaufbau der Männer*) was essential, and as accounts of this devastation made apparent, this too was women's work.[8] Hilde Thurnwald, who spent much of 1946 and 1947 studying 498 Berlin families, anticipated the criticism of those who might argue that she had paid inadequate attention to men. An emphasis on women, she explained, captured social reality because "at present in these families women have moved into the central position as providers."[9]

From the perspective of contemporaries, the war and its aftermath left women in positions of great responsibility; they played a crucial role in sustaining Germany in the last years of the war and in the rocky transition to peace. Forty years after the German surrender, Richard von Weizsäcker, the West German president, reflected: "If the devastation and destruction, the barbarism and inhumanity, did not inwardly shatter the people involved, if, slowly but surely, they came to themselves after the war, then they owed it first and foremost to their womenfolk."[10] The image of women as peculiarly equipped to overcome "barbarism and inhumanity" was not created from hindsight; rather, the president of the Federal Republic described a popular consciousness that already existed in the late forties.

Postwar social observers, however, who repeatedly remarked on how women had revealed enormous capacities by meeting the challenges of the last war years and the postwar crises, also emphasized that these stressful times had put women and the family at risk. The war had forced women to assume extraordinary burdens, and the war's end had only intensified their labors. The postwar accounts that articulate these perceptions correspond strikingly with reflections recorded in a number of recent oral history projects and first-person accounts that illuminate how West Germans recall their exit from National Socialism. From both sources there emerges a picture of women as strong, yet threatened, self-reliant, yet vulnerable.[11]

Sociological investigations of the late forties designate women as victims of circumstances beyond their control; in oral histories conducted over three decades later, German women define themselves in the same way. Their stories focus on women's difficult times in the war and the scarcities and hardships of the postwar period, not on the economic recovery under the Nazis in the thirties or the years of stunning victories in Hitler's Blitzkrieg.[12] By identifying themselves as victims, women, even more readily than men, allowed themselves to avoid any direct confrontation with the horrors of the Thousand Year Reich. In addition, the Nazis' outspoken declaration of politics as a male preserve made it possible for women to claim that the regime's excesses were products of a state controlled exclusively by men.[13]

The circumstances of the postwar period hardly created an opportune moment for the large-scale entry of German women into public political life or for coming to terms with the ambiguities of the National Socialist past. A British observer, assigned to the Women's Affairs section of the forces of occupation, remarked in the summer of 1947: "The German housewife is facing a daily crisis which at any moment may turn to disaster in the form of illness, unemployment, failure of rations, or, in a vast number of cases, the crowning calamity of motherhood. Facing these facts squarely, what inducement is there for women to exert themselves beyond their daily routines, much less to participate in anything as vague and complicated as politics or as burdensome as public affairs and civic government?"[14]

Frau Ostrowski, a Berliner born in 1921, restated this rhetorical question over thirty years after the war's end. Recalling a political meeting in Berlin in the late seventies, she had only disdain for

> a historian who wanted to tell us that we should forcefully confront our past and that we should have started in 1945. I asked him, "When were *you* born?" "Well, '46." I say only someone who hasn't experienced that time can utter such nonsense. I mean, after '45 no one thought about confronting the past. Everyone thought about how they were going to put something in the pot, so that their children could eat something, and about how to start rebuilding and clearing away the rubble. In short, women had . . . no time at all to think about such things.[15]

To be sure, there were important exceptions to this rule. Particularly for women who had been politically active in Weimar, who had seen their organizations either disbanded or totally transformed under Nazi leadership, the end of the Thousand Year Reich marked a renewal of public political life.[16] But in the postwar years, politically active women were rare, especially among those who had come to adulthood during the Nazi dictatorship and had virtually no experience of democratic politics. Like Frau Ostrowski, many women were primarily concerned with "put[ting] something in the pot." They did not try to assess their share of responsibility for the bombs that had fallen or demand a political role in shaping a new Germany. Instead, most sought to reconstruct what the bombs had destroyed, to return to an imagined past of prosperity, peace, and security, and to maintain one source of constituted authority—the family—which the bombs had not leveled.

The language of "collapse" (*Zusammenbruch*) to describe 1945 drew on the same vocabulary employed by Hitler in his analysis of 1918. In Hitler's metahistorical imagination, collapse was the product of long-term cultural decline, materialism, and the growing influence of the Jews. In May 1945, collapse conjured up nothing so grandiose; rather, it described the war's end without assessing responsibility for the war's beginning.[17]

There is no question that the suffering of many Germans, both during the war and after, was real. Jürgen Habermas, writing of the experiences of German prisoners of war, war widows, bombed-out evacuees, and refugees during and after the war, reminds us: "Suffering is always concrete suffering; it cannot be separated from its context. And it is from this context of mutual experiences that traditions are formed. Mourning and recollection secure these traditions."[18] But Habermas also questions the motives of "whoever insists on mourning collective fates, without distinguishing between culprits and victims." To paraphrase Max Horkheimer, she who would speak of shortages and suffering must also speak of fascism. Immediately after the war, speaking of shortages and suffering or of families at risk was a way *not* to make this connection, a way not to speak of fascism. Rather, it was part of the stuff from which Germans constructed a shared past and an identity as victims.

For Germans engaged in this project, the "war and postwar years" (*Kriegs- und Nachkriegszeit*) were fused, a strangely depoliticized episode in which the culprits were bomb attacks, extreme shortages, fears of starvation, and a victor's peace that left many men removed from their families. From the perspective of the postwar years, it was this combination of events that placed enormous strains on women and threatened the family's future. According to this scenario, preserving and restoring the family was not only the responsibility of individual women; it was a central part of a larger agenda for social and political reconstruction as West Germans moved from a troubling past toward an undefined future.

After May 1945, memories of the years of National Socialist rule before the Germans began experiencing reversals in the Nazis' war of aggression were as close to a vision of prosperity and stability as many German women could get. Thurnwald, writing in 1947, found it "remarkable" that

> a growing number of families are looking backward—the flight into the past and better days, with which they mainly mean the Hitler years. The difficulties of the present make the past seem even rosier, not just for former party members but for other men and women as well. They forget the horrors of the war and hold onto [the memory of] what they had . . . then. Overburdened mothers, who without any significant help from others feel themselves almost crushed by elemental forces in their cold, frequently half-destroyed abodes, are particularly visible in this group. . . . Statements like "If Adolf were there, then there would be order at home" or "We had it better with Adolf" . . . can frequently be heard.[19]

Imagining a past in which "we had it better with Adolf" was indeed "remarkable," but it was not surprising. Seen from the forties, the thirties constituted a vision of normalcy that could look quite appealing. The past in which "we had it better with Adolf" was certainly not that of bomb attacks and the declaration of total war in 1943. Rather, it was a past in which the Nazis had apparently been able to overcome the repeated crises of the 1920s, to get Germany out of the depression, to put the unemployed back to work, and to introduce other measures that eased the burdens of women whose primary workplace was the home. Both Nazi propaganda and practical economic policy assured Germans that things would get better and better; in the 1930s, there were many indications that for politically acceptable Aryans—by no means all Germans but still the overwhelming majority of the population—promises would become reality.[20]

It is difficult to chart the boundaries between acquiescence, accommodation, acceptance, and support; there is no accurate gauge of women's attitudes toward Nazi ideology and policies that elevated the status of those women, judged fit according to the regime's racialist criteria, for whom children and housework constituted the most important employment.[21] The Nazis did not conduct public opinion polls to assess whether women accepted the ideological wrapping that surrounded material benefits or whether they might welcome the regime's support for their work without accepting identification as "mothers of the *Volk*" (fig. 1). However, such measures as marriage loans, family allowances, and tax advantages for families with children probably did much to increase the popularity of the regime among women, at least among those women whose families received these benefits.[22]

When they were first introduced, marriage loans were designed to bar married women from the wage labor force; eligibility depended on a wife's ending work outside the home. The loan was typically issued to the husband, not the wife. Young couples used the loans—roughly the equivalent of four to five months' wages for industrial workers—to furnish their homes. Beneficiaries could pay off one percent of the principal of the no-interest loans each month over a period of a number of years. Moreover, a woman's entry into reproductive labor cut the loan by one-fourth for each birth. Although many women continued to limit their families to one or at most two children, the woman who bore four children could close her family's account.

Some 700,000 couples met the economic, racial, and eugenic criteria to receive the loans—more than one-fourth of all couples who married between August 1933 and January 1937. In 1937, an economy at nearly full employment and continued economic expansion fueled by the

Nazis' armaments drive led the government to suspend the requirement that the new bride quit her job in order to qualify. In 1939, 42 percent of all marriages were aided by the loans.[23]

All families with children were given additional advantages through income-tax reforms that increased allowable deductions for children while placing a heavier tax burden on families with only one child and individuals and couples with no children. By March 1938, some 560,000 families, including in particular those with five or more children, received additional direct grants.[24]

At least in part, the rise in the marriage rate after 1934 may have reflected the impact of the marriage-loan program; for women and men who had postponed marriage during the years of economic crisis, loans of up to RM 1,000 could do much to make easier the early stages of married life. There is no evidence, however, that women who married were volunteering to become the combat troops in the Nazis' pronatalist campaign, the "battle for births." An increasing birthrate after 1933 probably resulted more from a return to trends disrupted by the economic crisis of 1930 to 1932 and the intensified prosecution of those seeking and performing abortions than from paeans to Aryan motherhood. Even coercive measures could not dramatically raise the birthrate above the level it had reached in the twenties before the onset of the Great Depression.[25] The thirties witnessed no convincing reversal of the demographers' downward curves that proved that Germans were "dying out."

The memories of some working-class women suggest how marriage loans and other forms of direct financial assistance to families had other consequences. Babette Bahl, a Ruhr miner's wife, recounted forty years later how she used her marriage loan to outfit the kitchen in her new home. When she gave birth to her first child, Frau Bahl purchased a bedroom suite with a small down payment. When the third child came, she bought a washing machine, then a bicycle and a sewing machine. She remembers the birth of her fourth child: "And so the little one arrived, and once again we got 250 marks from the state, in other words, from Hitler. . . . No debts, that's what my husband said, now we can really live." Frau Moritz, also a Ruhr miner's wife, was a member of the National Socialist women's organization, the NS-Frauenschaft. On the birth of her fourth child, she recalls receiving a shower of presents and coupons that she exchanged for shoes and a "bed, an entire bed for me . . . a white, wooden bed with a mattress, a new bed. We got a coupon: I couldn't believe it, that my husband and

I would be sleeping in a bed."[26] As the Nazis had hoped, the purchase of consumer durables contributed to Germany's economic recovery in the thirties; it also marked Frau Bahl's and Frau Moritz's memories of their children's births.

In the 1930s, the promise of a vacation for workers did not guarantee all workers a vacation any more than saving for the "People's Car" meant ownership of a Volkswagen. Nonetheless, such measures solidified support for the regime by previewing a better future; they indicated that the pledge to construct a new order was more than rhetorical.[27] Similarly, though Nazi marriage loans and family allowances neither benefited all Germans nor covered the cost of raising children, they did provide evidence that the elevation of hearth and home, motherhood and family, was not just symbolic. Policies that reminded women that "biology was destiny" reinforced patriarchal families; they ultimately most benefited men. But the sexual division of labor that designated housework and child-rearing as women's work was not created by National Socialist family policy, and the Nazis *did* consistently acknowledge the social significance of this work and introduced some measures to improve the material circumstances under which it was performed. This legitimation for the regime registered less in a soaring birthrate than in the construction of credibility and consensus.[28]

The Nazis did little to make attractive to women career alternatives to marriage, motherhood, and housewifery. Although many German women remained in the wage labor force in the 1930s and the absolute number of women going out to work increased, women's work opportunities and access to new jobs did not expand dramatically. The regime prohibited the employment of women in some occupations and greatly restricted their access to others, in part by limiting their entry into higher education except for such professions as teaching, which were considered appropriate for women. National Socialist rhetoric also criticized married women whose employment allegedly gave families an extra wage by taking jobs away from men. The assault on these "double-earners" (*Doppelverdiener*) was not unique to the Nazis; many others, particularly from the political right and the Catholic Center party, had called for legally restricting the employment of married women in the last years of the Weimar Republic. But National Socialists could move from words to policy, and measures like the marriage loan scheme, introduced as part of the Law for the Reduction of Unemployment of 1 June 1933, were initially intended "to send women back to the home from the workplace."[29]

In industrial and white-collar occupations, gender-specific wage differentials remained substantial, and opportunities for women to move
to better jobs were limited. The one exception was white-collar work in
sales or clerical jobs, and a growing tertiary sector continued to employ
more and more women as it had in Weimar. Still, even the attractiveness
of this work was relative; employment in retail sales might be preferred
to a dead-end job as an unskilled or semiskilled worker in industry or
domestic service, but it held no promise of advancement or economic
security.[30]

It is this set of circumstances that led Timothy W. Mason to conclude
that "the drive for domesticity," in the realms of both ideology and policy, "really did meet the needs and aspirations (and aversions) of *at least
some* of those women who had no wish to work in factories, offices and
shops, and run a household as well."[31] Although Mason's language of
women's *wishes* overstates the extent to which women were free to ex-
press desire when confronted with limited options, in this regard, Nazi
Germany had much in common with all other social orders. In the
1930s, certainly, it is plausible that housewifery and motherhood might
appear as preferred occupations for many German women. Psychologically and materially, Nazi policies rewarded women who made the
home their primary workplace.

In an interview with an oral historian, Frau B., a textile worker who had
been a trade unionist before 1933, recalls the transition from war to
peace: "In fact, everyone was enthusiastic in the Third Reich, we were in
good shape. The beginning was wonderful, everyone was provided for,
everyone was doing equally well. . . . They often said that if they hadn't
gone to Russia or moved against the Jews, then everything would have
been all right."[32] In these selective memories, *we* were in good shape;
they went to Russia and moved against the Jews. *Germans* enjoyed good
times before 1939; *Nazis* went to war and created Auschwitz.

National Socialism's "drive for domesticity" ran into the brick wall
of the exigencies of total war. Worsening conditions in the war at home
coincided with the intensification of the government's efforts to mobilize
both single and married women, the so-called silent reserve (*stille Reserve*) into the wage-labor force.[33] The defeat at Stalingrad and the extension of Allied bomb attacks into the southwesternmost part of Germany combined to ensure that things would get no better.

Even then, Germans did not starve. The Nazis did everything in their
power to avoid the severe shortages that had plagued Germany at the
end of the First World War; the memory of widespread domestic unrest

in those years haunted Hitler, and this nightmare informed Nazi efforts to maintain the supply of butter while producing more and more guns. Nazi policy sought to increase domestic agricultural production at home, to develop substitute foodstuffs, to pillage the occupied parts of eastern Europe in order to maintain food supplies within Germany, and to restructure the agricultural sectors in occupied areas to meet the needs of the German war economy.[34]

Still, reports of the secret police revealed a rapid deterioration of domestic morale during the war, as rationing extended to more and more goods and the alternative economy of the black market flourished. By 1944, the retreat of the German army from areas occupied in eastern Europe meant a further reduction in the available food supply. In order to perform their daily tasks, women had to become accomplished at evading controls, scrounging, and functioning on the black market.

The war that was to bring the German people more, not less, greatly complicated women's unpaid labor. The sphere of domesticity expanded dramatically, as shopping meant standing in endless lines and scrounging, as cleaning extended to removing the rubble in the aftermath of bombings, and as mothering included rushing children into shelters at the sound of the first air-raid alert. In their constant search for food, women did not follow the Nazi prescription to place "the common good before self-interest" (*Gemeinnutz vor Eigennutz*); their highest priority was their own survival and the survival of those dependent on them.

Waiting for hours in line for short rations, learning of the death of a male relative at the front, living in fear of Allied bombardment, leaving cities to avoid the bombs—it was in these forms that the war most forcefully and directly entered the lives of many German women. The establishment of routines under conditions of danger and uncertainty was work left largely to them. Under these abnormal circumstances, women's normally invisible work became quite visible.[35]

Although the flourishing black market graphically displayed class differences among women competing with unequal resources for dwindling supplies, the bomb shelters reduced all to the same "national community" (*Volksgemeinschaft*). As Goebbels observed, "the bomb terror spares the dwellings of neither rich nor poor."[36] The conscription of adult males to fight the Nazis' war meant that far more women than men enjoyed this artificial leveling of social distinction in the war at home. However, neither this leveling nor women's contribution to maintaining social order created a sense of emancipation. The imposition of substantial burdens on women under circumstances of total war brought immense additional responsibilities, not expanded rights.[37]

Women did not respond enthusiastically to Nazi appeals to enter the wage-labor force. In fact, at the beginning of the war, some women used the allowances granted to military dependents as an excuse to leave wage work altogether. The regime responded quickly to labor shortages by importing unfree foreign workers, at least in part out of its commitment to limit the labor-force participation of German women. Polish women and men could be compelled to do the work from which German women should be spared. Still, these surrogates were not adequate to meet the demands of the war economy.[38]

The move to total war after the German defeat at Stalingrad included a decided intensification of Nazi attempts to mobilize the silent reserve (fig. 2). By late 1943, however, the enormous difficulties that women confronted in their unpaid work made it even less likely that they would willingly seek additional work outside the home. For those women who did go out to work, access to many jobs remained restricted, and women's wages were still well below men's. Conditions of wage work became only more difficult as bombs destroyed factories and disabled urban transportation systems, as jobs included extra shifts as lookouts for Allied bombers, and as clerical tasks might entail removing rubble.[39] Nazi attempts to justify women's mobilization in terms of women's natural capacity for self-sacrifice prompted no apparent popular response.[40]

The enormity of women's second shift under the deteriorating conditions of the war economy made working-class women particularly resentful of middle-class housewives who were more successful at evading Nazi attempts to mobilize women for wage work. Perceptions of the advantages granted mothers with small children also produced strains among women across generations. A woman who had worked during World War I and raised her children in the 1920s found herself once again in a high-priority group for labor mobilization in World War II; with no small children in her family, she could not claim exemption on the basis of her responsibilities at home. She complained that "in this war the young women were well off. They got themselves some children so that they didn't have to work, and they got so much support that they could afford to have a wonderful life."[41] By 1944, Frau F., whose story began this chapter, would probably not have agreed.

The defeat of Nazi Germany was assured by March 1945, when the Red Army took Danzig and United States forces crossed the Rhine and entered Germany. By late April, Soviet troops pushing westward met

American troops coming eastward. By early May, the Red Army was in Berlin, and the German High Command had surrendered. But as Frau F.'s story makes clear, for some German women 1945 marked no radical discontinuity. Anna Peters, born in 1908, the daughter of a Social Democratic cabinetmaker, and married in 1934, remembers that spring:

> The crisis of 1945: we had no more bomb attacks, but we also had nothing more to eat. Genuine starvation only really began for us in '45. The government that ruled over us [up until then] took care that there was at least enough to eat and that you could get full. But beginning in '45 that was no longer the case: then we starved, genuinely starved. You were never full. At no meal were you full. . . . When you met women standing in long lines in front of stores, their faces were all gray, almost black—that's how bad they looked, almost starved to death.[42]

Scarcity of housing, clothing, and food and the continued absence of many adult men who were never to return or who were in prisoner-of-war camps tied the last war years to the years 1946, 1947, and 1948.

Those fleeing the forward march of Soviet troops swelled a West German population that could not cover its own most immediate needs. By 1947, together with those ethnic Germans "expelled" (vertrieben) from eastern Europe according to the terms of postwar peace settlements, refugees numbered over ten million. Another eight to ten million "displaced persons"—foreigners forced to come to Germany as workers during the war and others removed from their homelands by the Nazis for racial, religious, or political reasons, including survivors of concentration camps—had no choice but to remain in Germany while they awaited repatriation.[43]

The Big Three—the United States, the Soviet Union, and Britain—provided no clear strategy for confronting these pressing problems or for addressing the longer-term question of what was to become of Germany. Together, they had destroyed the Thousand Year Reich, but they could not agree on the form a newly constituted German political authority should take. In the absence of clearer formulations, the Allies fell back on agreements reached at the Yalta Conference of February 1945. At this meeting, Roosevelt, Churchill, and Stalin had determined that together with the French, they would divide Germany into zones of occupation, leaving to an unspecified future the definition of more lasting territorial arrangements. When Big Three negotiators were joined by representatives from France at Potsdam in July 1945, they defined provisions for establishing German local self-government and mechanisms for licensing domestic political parties and other interest groups such as trade unions, but they also made clear that it would be some time before Germans would be left alone to determine German affairs.[44]

Occupation hardly made German women's unpaid labor easier; rather, in many respects the end of the war meant that things went from bad to worse. The blessings of a mass-production capitalist economy promised by the western forces in their zones of occupation contrasted with the realities of worsening shortages. At the end of the war, the Allied decision to leave prices fixed while not reducing the supply of paper currency guaranteed a flourishing black market and hoarding, as too much money chased too few goods. The Allies maintained an official system of rationing and introduced five categories of entitlement, beginning with "heavy laborers" and ending with the "rest of the population," a broad category that included pensioners, housewives, and domestic workers. Escape from Category V, the "starvation or ascension" category (*Hunger- oder Himmelfahrtkarte*), prompted some women to enter wage labor, less for money than to improve their status for rations. Others reportedly took jobs in specific industries like textiles because they were promised partial payment in kind; textiles in turn could be exchanged for foodstuffs on the black market.[45]

Women's magazines abounded with recipes for making something out of nothing, baking with flour produced from acorns, "doing laundry without soap," but theory translated poorly into practice.[46] It was women who most immediately experienced the shortages. In the winter of 1946–47—called the "eighth winter of the war" by some—seventh-grade schoolgirls in Nuremberg who were asked to describe their wildest wishes responded unanimously: "I wish for more to eat." One added, "I wish for a cake, but my mother can't make that, because we don't even have bread."[47] Mothers needed no school-sponsored surveys to know of their children's unfulfilled desires. The report of a social worker in Duisburg from 1947 corroborates Anna Peters's memories: "The unhappy housewives get the starvation rations only after waiting, standing in front of the stores for many hours. Because of these circumstances, bitterness and unhappiness are spices that unavoidably flavor every meal."[48] "Watery soup in the morning, watery soup at noon, watery soup in the evening, do nothing to improve [peoples'] spirits," was the understated observation of a social worker in Gladbach during the "epoch of calories," years when what went on the dinner table took on extraordinarily great significance.[49]

Scrounging and organizing consumption on the illegal black market occupied even more of women's lives than during the last war years; the struggle for the most basic necessities became the chief preoccupation for many women. Women's unpaid labor took place as much in the streets as in the home. A family social worker in Duisburg regretted that "even members of respectable families go out to steal and take part in the black market. At every time of day and with complete openness, the black market is fully in operation."[50]

A mother's calculations became ever more complex in an economy in which money was the least attractive medium of exchange; price ceilings and rationing policies meant that few goods were available at official prices. On the black market, trade in kind was preferred to money of dubious value. Thurnwald captured the scene in one Berlin street where mothers saved half each month's ration of powdered eggs to trade for underwear and socks for their children. Women "compare whether it would be better for a child to be better fed or to have frozen feet."[51]

Under such circumstances, it was not surprising that a former Nazi adherent candidly admitted to Thurnwald in 1947, "Why shouldn't we have a positive attitude toward National Socialism? It created secure living conditions for us and many other people." This woman, who still quoted the speeches of Hitler and Goebbels at every possible occasion, employed an unexplained principle of selection to exclude them from other "big" Nazis to whom she attributed Germany's defeat. She and her husband praised "the good sides of National Socialism": "No one starved, no one froze, and if Hitler were to come back now, everything would fall into place in short order." Even self-proclaimed opponents of the regime might admit to Thurnwald that "Hitler was a bum, [but] nonetheless at least he made sure there was enough to eat."[52]

For women, sex had already emerged as a medium of exchange during the war. In her work on Württemberg, Jill Stephenson describes how women, left to run farms without sons and husbands, encouraged male foreign workers assigned to their farms to work harder in return for the promise of sexual relations.[53] After 1945, the foreigners who could offer benefits in return for sex were Allied soldiers, and in the sociological studies and official reports of the late forties and fifties there are frequent accounts of German women using their bodies as currency on the black market.

Fraternization became an emotionally charged symbol of the occupation of Germany. From a sympathetic perspective Thurnwald could observe: "Light, warmth, a cup of hot cocoa, the prospect of being able to spend a couple of carefree hours often brings a young woman into a soldier's apartment or prompts her to seek out a dance hall with her

friends." Not just the "material gifts of love" that soldiers could offer
but also the promise of release from the constant pressures of daily life
made relationships with the forces of occupation desirable.[54] For at least
some observers, the fraternizer was no more subject to condemnation
than other women, who found "uncles," men whom they did not marry
but with whom they set up households.[55]

Other judgments were not so generous. A health officer in Neuss regretted that "among many there is a blurring of any measure of right and
wrong," especially among "young women on their own, whose husbands are in prisoner-of-war camps, missing or dead, [who] have un-
regulated relations with men, with truck drivers, foreigners, and in any
case with those who can get them food." Even more outrageous, according to this report, was the practice of some mothers who "systematically
send their sixteen- and seventeen-year-olds (in one case, a twelve-year-
old) into the camp of foreigners, Poles, in the American-occupied zone,
to British soldiers, with the appropriate instruction on how to behave,
in order to get food and cigarettes." The health officer admitted to ambivalent feelings about the behavior of these "inhuman mothers"; he
conceded there could be no question that "today, those who are fundamentally honest [and who] only wanted to consume their rations would
suffer a horrible fate."[56]

While the fraternizer might win some sympathy, she was also
blamed; she embodied the image of a postwar woman beyond morality,
a symptom of crisis conditions. Although the victim of rape by Allied
soldiers could not be held responsible, she too indicated the inability of
German men to protect German women. Reports of rape by black GIs,
French Moroccans, or, in dramatically greater numbers, by Red Army
soldiers, were also filtered through twelve years of systematic racialist
propaganda (fig. 3). Not only had German men failed to prevent the rape
of German women; in popular consciousness, the rapist was often the
"inferior" black or the "Mongol," a code word by which all Soviets
were labeled as Asian. Contemporary commentary on rape focused far
more on its implications for the male psyche than on what it meant for
the health and well-being of women.[57]

Some observers determined the boundaries between rape and prostitution only with difficulty. Fears of rape and sympathy for rape victims
blurred with suspicion that women had failed to resist or had succumbed
to blandishments and material benefits offered by the Allies. Among
those interviewed in a Ruhr oral history project, Ernst Stecker, a politically active metalworker, forty at the end of the war, underscores one

of his most vivid memories from the spring of 1945: "A Negro said: 'The German soldiers fought for six years, the German woman for only five minutes!' That's a fact from beginning to end. I was ashamed."[58] Rape, prostitution, and fraternization became disturbing signs of German surrender and defeat, of foreign occupation in a most literal sense, of a world in which German women's sexuality was outside of German men's control.[59]

Allied appeals for women to work for wages met with even more resolute resistance than Nazi attempts to increase women's rates of labor force participation in the years of total war. Mothers also held back their adolescent children from wage work; their service as scroungers represented a potentially greater contribution to the family's survival.[60] Compared to 1939, half a million more women were working for wages fifteen months after the war's end, but at least in part this increase reflected the flood of refugees and expellees, the *Vertriebene* from the Soviet-occupied east. Without savings or goods to exchange on the black market, women in this group had fewer opportunities to avoid working for wages, though in some cases their lack of adequate clothing or shoes presented another sort of impediment to labor-force participation.[61] Beginning in the summer of 1945, women between the ages of fourteen and fifty were legally obliged by state and provincial authorities to register with labor exchanges for work, but housewives and daughters still living at home were exempt. The military government had called for an end to sex-based wage differentials, but women's wages remained about forty percent lower than men's, and even in unskilled jobs women earned twenty to twenty-five percent less than their male counterparts.[62]

The Allies also confronted the determination of German labor-ministry officials to limit and label as temporary women's access to jobs held largely or exclusively by men. West German authorities deemed totally unacceptable a mobilization of women "following a Russian model" that would force women into occupations not suited for them. They vehemently demanded the reinstitution of protective legislation suspended during the war, leading one frustrated British official to call for a revision of the "luxurious German labour protection laws necessary in respect to women." Failure to undertake such steps would represent nothing less than a violation of the Potsdam agreement, which had stipulated that "the standard of living in Germany shall not be better than the rest of Europe," making it "inappropriate for us to enforce social legislation which gives German women a more favourable position in industry than that enjoyed by other women in Europe."[63]

To no avail, the Military Government lectured German labor officials that in the United States "women chauffeurs are considered better than men, [and] in addition, women could be employed as streetcar drivers, as watch-makers or as glaziers, while in the Russian zone, women have proven themselves in particular as traffic police, and assistants in the construction industry."[64] Allied officials were repeatedly exasperated by German officials' patent unwillingness to mobilize all women into a greater range of occupations and by what a British labor ministry observer, Mrs. B. P. Boyes, identified as a "marked prejudice in Germany against the employment of women in non-traditional occupations. The general feeling seems to be that women's place is in the home and that if she must work, she should confine herself to occupations which are 'womanly' such as dressmaking, clerical work, hairdressing, etc."[65]

An even more significant barrier to labor-force mobilization remained the continued pressure on women to perform extraordinary forms of unpaid labor and the limited value of wages in the inflationary postwar economy (figs. 7 and 8). The implications were immediately apparent to an officer of the British Manpower Division, who soberly observed that "the earning of Marks which will not buy scarce commodities is not so important to the family as foraging for food, a duty which often falls upon the womenfolk."[66] Social workers in Frankfurt reported a common response among women exhorted to enter wage labor: "I can't afford to work, I have to provide for my family."[67] The labor minister of heavy-industrial North Rhine–Westphalia informed British observer Boyes in early 1948 that "at the moment, the monetary value of a ration card for cigarettes is worth more than a young woman's work for a month."[68] Boyes concluded that "the value of the currency is so low and the supply of consumer goods so scanty that the additional income to be derived from wages would be virtually worthless. Once the basic ration has been purchased there is little or nothing to be bought, except at exorbitant black market prices, or in exchange for goods."[69]

By 1948, Allied officials conceded that as long as women continued to play a crucial role as black marketeers and scroungers, attempting to mobilize those who were responsible for dependents was futile, serving only to heighten antagonism toward the forces of occupation. Allied officials realized that it would require currency stabilization and an end to the black market to increase the supply of available labor. They reasoned that the demographic legacy of the war—the fact that Germany was a nation with far more adult women than men—would restrict opportunities for many women on the marriage market, forcing them into the labor market.[70] By early 1948, with currency stabilization close at hand and German self-government in the foreseeable future, the Allies gave up on efforts to increase the number of wage-earning women and to place women in jobs typically held by men.[71]

Those women who entered or remained in the wage-labor force before currency stabilization confronted enormous difficulties. Thurnwald provides a graphic description of the double burden of working mothers in the Berlin winter of 1947: "The mothers who work during the day in unheated firms have frostbite on their feet and hands, they suffer from a catastrophic transportation system, and at home they still have to manage a household where water pipes, drains, and toilets are frozen, and where carrying water and removing waste requires an additional effort of which they're incapable. They have no time for their children and because of their anger or exhaustion, they have no warmth."[72] The dilemmas facing working mothers were inscribed in the memories of Klara Steiner, a streetcar driver in Berlin after the war. Forty years later, she was still filled with self-reproach: "I should not have looked for work. . . . Today I'm convinced that I should have gone scrounging, so that I could have fed my children. With your earnings, you couldn't buy a loaf of bread on the black market for 100 marks. And my children suffered because of that; they never got full."[73]

More than three million German soldiers were killed in the war, and in 1945 nearly two million more remained in prisoner-of-war camps. The first postwar census, conducted in October 1946, meticulously recorded that for every 100 males, there were 126 females. In big urban centers, the official ratio was as high as 146 females to 100 males, the figure for Berlin. Although the chaotic circumstances under which this census was conducted meant that its results were probably unreliable, there could be no question about the general tendency it described.[74] More than dry statistics, the 1946 census articulated the widespread sense of alarm about the demographic imbalance created by the war. Comparing numbers of unmarried men and women in the "biologically most important age group," the census determined that for every 1,000 marriageable males, there were 2,242 available women. While predicting that the return of soldiers from prisoner-of-war camps would change this ratio, the census concluded that "the men are missing for around one-third of all women of child-bearing age." Within Germany's borders, there were nearly three million more married women than men between the ages of fifteen and forty-five, one indication of the number of men missing or in

prisoner-of-war camps. As late as 1950, when many men held as prisoners of war had returned home, there were still more than 130 women
for every 100 men aged twenty-five to forty.[75]

The long-term significance of this demographic legacy found expression in a language that described a "surplus of women" (*Frauenüberschuss*) and a "scarcity of men" (*Männermangel*), abstract categories
that blurred the distinction between economic and socio-psychological
reconstruction and captured inadequately this lasting consequence of
the Nazis' war of aggression. Not surprisingly, at least some women took
exception to this linguistic condensation of their fate. Writing in *Constanze*, a popular postwar women's magazine, Helga Prollius complained of the formulation *Frauenüberschuss*: "What an ugly word!
And what an even uglier meaning! A word that is taken from the language of trade and signifies nothing more nor less than a product, and
at that a product of which there is a surplus, which is superfluous."[76]
Still, such dissenting voices were exceptions amid a general consensus
that the "scarcity of men" would have dire implications for rebuilding
the German population.

When men taken prisoner of war came home, cramped quarters became even more crowded and scarce supplies were stretched even further. Living conditions like those of Frau F. in her Darmstadt attic apartment were common, particularly in urban areas hit hard by Allied
bombing. A social worker in Duisburg described the "misery of the bun-
ker," basement apartments in which "the normal separation of sexes
and generations can hardly be realized" (fig. 9). This observer continued, "Although during the crisis period of the war people were able to
reconcile themselves to such circumstances as an unavoidable consequence of bombing, today there is no more justification available in the
normal course of daily life."[77]

Reunions with returning prisoners of war often proved difficult for
wives and children; Frau F.'s experience is recorded in unusually complete detail, but it was by no means exceptional. Hannelore König, seven
years old when her father left for war in 1942, recalls his return from
an American prisoner-of-war camp in 1948: "I hardly knew him. And
he was completely uninteresting to me; he could have stayed away. Yes,
he was superfluous for us. . . . After all, we'd done all right. . . . And the
men all came back sick from prison. Most of them did not work. My
father, for example, had lost an arm and had a stomach ulcer. Yes, he
was sick, he couldn't work, he wasn't capable of it."[78] A Berliner, Betty

Prochnow, recalled the day in October 1946 when her husband unex-
pectedly stood in front of her apartment door. Her son "didn't recognize
him, although I'd always shown him a picture. He called him 'Un-
cle.' . . . My husband had changed, it was difficult for him."[79]

Men returned home to confront children they did not know and
wives whose "forced emancipation" had increased their independence
and self-reliance. Else Köhler, another Berliner, reflects on the return of
her husband Rudi from a prisoner-of-war camp: "He thought that when
he came home, he'd be able to care for us. And instead he had to let me
take care of him. He didn't really feel like a man. He suffered because
I did everything alone and because he couldn't help me much."[80] Not
only had women established themselves as providers but they were also
experienced at deciphering the layers of postwar bureaucracies that controlled housing and the rationing system. Men resented their own ignorance and their dependence on women.

In reunited families, stretching scarce resources to sustain more bodies caused conflict. "Sometimes the children complain spontaneously,"
reported Thurnwald, "that their share of the food has been diminished
by the father or the elder brother."[81] A social worker in Wuppertal observed that family members stole one another's ration cards, and husbands of pregnant women demanded the supplemental allotments to
which their wives were entitled.[82] In some cases, hunger and scarcity
threatened to break up a family. One starving husband secretly carried
the family's precious CARE package down into the basement and in a
matter of days consumed its contents. When his outraged wife discovered his deception, she went immediately to a lawyer to file for divorce.
Although counseling prevented the dissolution of the marriage, the in-
cident revealed how struggles over food could rank alongside infidelity
as major sources of marital tension.[83]

A mushrooming divorce rate after the war indicated that the strains
of reunion sometimes proved too great. At 87,013—nearly 80 percent
above the 1946 level—the number of divorces reached a postwar high
in 1948. More divorces involved couples with children than before the
war, and gloomy statistics recorded that in 1948 alone, 80,000 children
had become "orphans of divorce."[84] In those marriages that ended, the
courts judged men solely or primarily responsible in far fewer instances
than before the war. In 1948, the courts determined that women were
"solely guilty" for the breakup of marriages in 23.9 percent of the cases
and shared blame with men in 33 percent of the cases; the corresponding

figures for 1939 were 15.5 and 26.8. The distinction was particularly important because women deemed completely or partially responsible for the dissolution of their marriages were ineligible for spousal support payments.[85] *Constanze* reported with alarm that "the divorce mills of the regional courts (*Landgerichte*) rattle along uninterrupted. The swollen river of divorce proceedings has almost flooded the banks." While this reflected a long-term increase in the divorce rate, the most important immediate causes were "living apart during long years of separation, ill-considered marriages during the war, the internal and external crisis of the times."[86]

One woman whose husband returned in 1946 remembers her circumstances: "He was afraid to go out, he didn't scrounge, he didn't do anything. I did the work that I had to do as a housewife and mother, but my husband didn't want to do his job, namely getting wood. . . . And I certainly took note of that, while I was facing difficult times and trying to make a meal out of nothing, gathering herbs just so it would have a little taste, standing for hours, keeping the apartment clean, keeping him clean, washing his dirty underpants, then I can certainly expect that he'll do his man's work! I'd rather be alone. I got divorced."[87]

Similar cases appear throughout the sociological studies of postwar German families. In Darmstadt, Frau X.'s husband, a skilled metalworker, returned from the war, but after several weeks back at work he simply stayed at home, "because," he claimed, "it's not worth it to work for that little bit of money." Frau X.'s son shared her feelings of estrangement from this man, who expected his wife to relieve him of all responsibilities. By distancing himself from his family, Herr X. only strengthened the bond between mother and son; the seven-year-old boy, who hardly knew his father, concluded that Herr X. did not really belong.

Frau X. had no choice but to seek work. Trained in retail sales, her job prospects were severely limited as long as barter was the dominant form of exchange; she could find a job only as a domestic in the homes of American families. Her workday now began at six, when she cleaned her own apartment and prepared her son for school at eight. By nine, when her other job started, she had already prepared lunch for her family. Returning home exhausted at six, she still faced washing and mending. Herr X. continued to refuse work and began to steal money from his wife. Frau X. often came home to an apartment littered with empty beer bottles. Other times, her husband made a noisy entrance when he came in late from the local tavern. He rejected his wife's appeal to re-

form for the good of the family, calling this advice "moral preaching."
When she discovered that he was also seeking solace in the company of
a younger woman, she filed for divorce.[88]

The drastic shortage of adequate housing might mean that divorce
did not lead to physical separation. Social workers feared that such living arrangements determined by scarcity could contribute to the "moral
endangerment" of women and children. A family social worker in Dortmund described a divorced couple that had continued to live together
because no other housing was available. The woman, together with her
three children, occupied one room, the man, the room adjoining. The
woman received visits from her new lover, also the father of three, and
her children "regularly experienced these visits." The man's new lover,
a streetcar driver, lived in the same apartment building. The divorced
couple's attempts to find other housing solutions proved futile.[89]

Sometimes economic exigencies ensured that former partners' lives
remained so intertwined after divorce that a marriage of sorts continued. Helmut Schelsky, who studied the family structure of expellees who
settled in northwest Germany, described the case of a thirty-seven-year-
old truck driver who was unable to find housing after his wife divorced
him. He still lived with her and their three children. His ex-wife continued to "cook and care for him," because from his earnings "after
support payments, there isn't enough left to eat in a restaurant or to hire
a housekeeper." She sued for an increase in her monthly support payments, and though she lost the court case her husband ultimately agreed
to a settlement. Schelsky concluded that "economic concerns have
proven to be more compelling than the reasons for the divorce, so that
in practical terms, a marriage exists, of course without the blessing of
state or church."[90] The woman rejected remarriage because she believed
that under these new circumstances, she and her former husband could
get along better with each other.

Delayed reunions might also result in complicated living arrangements and novel forms of survival networks. Gerhard Wurzbacher,
among those who rebuilt postwar West German sociology, supervised
a survey of 164 German families in the late forties and early fifties. In
one of the cases he recorded, a husband who returned home at the end
of the war could not find his wife. Believing her dead, he became engaged to another woman. When his wife reappeared he broke off the
new relationship, though only temporarily. He took up again with the
other woman, who gave birth to a baby boy. Despite her insistence that
he inform his wife, he refused; his wife ultimately learned of her

husband's second family from other sources. Furious at first, she reconciled herself to this development and even agreed to take in the boy during vacations. The boy's mother gave up her job when he was born, devoting her energies exclusively to caring for him and maintaining the apartment that she had long shared with another woman. Her friend's wages provided for their common household. Because she worried that her only child might grow up "spoiled and soft" were he to live only with women, she planned to send him to kindergarten as soon as possible so that he could be with other children of both sexes. The child's arrival immensely improved her standing with her relatives; common concern for the child created a strong link among them. Her roommate loved the boy like her own child and always referred to him as "our child."[91]

There is no record of how many similar family constellations developed in the war and postwar period. Of 15.4 million West German households enumerated in the 1950 census, however, 1.7 million were composed of women living alone, and another 2.1 million of women who headed households that included more than one person. In 1946, 16.4 percent of newborns were "illegitimate," and as late as 1950 the figure was still close to 10 percent.[92] These aggregate figures were deeply troubling to many West Germans and prompted lively discussions of "half-families," "incomplete families," "mother-families," and women's "forced emancipation" in the pages of postwar women's magazines and in the scholarship of some of the leading postwar West German sociologists. In the short term, contemporary accounts recorded an acceptance of a range of family forms as survival strategies and an increased tolerance for divorce, unwed motherhood, pre- and extramarital sex, and abortion dictated by economic necessity.[93] According to one survey conducted on popular attitudes about the "sphere of intimacy," these actions were viewed as understandable responses to the Frauen-überschuss. Justifying her approval of intimacy between unmarried women and men, a widow explained that "hundreds of thousands have to remain unmarried and suffer." A female metalworker added, "What are we supposed to do otherwise?"[94] Of 1,000 people aged twenty and over polled in West Berlin and the Federal Republic in September 1949, 54 percent of all men and 53 percent of all women registered their approval of "an unmarried woman [who] deliberately becomes a mother," and fewer than one in four expressed unequivocal disapproval.[95]

Still, such attitudes reflected not the acknowledgment of long-term changes or the renewal of the debates over sexual reform that had flourished in the Weimar Republic, but rather accommodation to conditions that were viewed to be exceptional. The same polls that revealed tolerance for abortion, extramarital sexual relations, and unwed motherhood recorded overwhelming support for the institution of marriage, viewed as a "factor of order, which appears to be particularly necessary and desirable precisely as a reaction to the disorder of external circumstances."[96] Despite the tremendous pressures on family relationships and the range of alternative forms of social organization that emerged in the last years of the war and the postwar period, the family—conceived of as the nuclear family—reappeared throughout these studies as an ideal for many Germans, male and female. The sociological studies of the immediate postwar years that provided extraordinarily rich descriptions of families in crisis also emphasized the family's resilience and stability after the "collapse" of 1945. Holding the family together, in turn, was the primary responsibility of the wife and mother.[97]

Interviews with women three decades after the war's end in the Ruhr oral history project headed by Lutz Niethammer also reveal how the family assumed a crucial significance in women's memories of the postwar years; it promised security to women who could locate few other sources of authority and order. In Niethammer's words, the family emerged for women as "an obligation, a phantom, and a project" that promised "warmth, understanding and help, simplicity, fairness, and protection." It was, as Niethammer emphasizes, "the product of fantasy," a "concrete utopia," but in the years after 1945 it was difficult for German women to fantasize in other directions, to envision other "concrete utopias."[98] Under the circumstances of the immediate postwar years, this utopia could not be realized; nonetheless, it was the model of social organization most readily imagined. It was a recognizable arena in which women could define for themselves a course of action and locate their contribution to reconstructing Germany.[99]

Sociological studies and oral histories provide evidence that women experienced their accomplishments in the postwar period as evidence of their abilities and their claims to social and political recognition. But even those women who cited their achievements as proof of their equality with men did not seriously question, let alone reject, the prescriptive identities of wife and mother. They did demand the assurance that they would be able to pursue these occupations under secure conditions. Reports of social workers and sociological studies resounded with the same rhetorical questions that were etched in the memories of women interviewed by oral historians in the seventies and early eighties. When bedding, diapers, and clothing were nonexistent, how could women look forward to motherhood? When there was nothing to put in the pot, how could wives and mothers feed their families? When days were spent standing in lines, attempting to cut through the bureaucratic red tape of the occupation forces, and dealing on the black market, what time remained to give children proper care?[100] Reflecting on the postwar years from the perspective of the early fifties, a Hamburg journalist, Edith Oppens, commented, "There no longer existed a social order in which women found their place and protection. . . . All protective measures for health, for life, and for honor as well had proven themselves to be illusory."[101] Reconstruction would mean a return to normalcy, when women and men would be allowed to do their jobs under normal circumstances and women would find their place in a social order that permitted them to devote their full attention to their most important work.[102]

As Germans approached 1948, a future that had been hazy at best in May 1945 was beginning to take shape. In his famous speech of 12 March 1947, President Harry Truman informed the United States Congress and the world that "every nation must choose between alternative ways of life." The choice he depicted was between a system based on the "will of the majority," freedom, and free institutions, and one "based upon the will of a minority forcibly imposed upon the majority."[103] The immediate context of Truman's remarks was shaped not by events in Germany but by American fears of Communists seizing power in a civil war in Greece. Nonetheless, it required no imagination to comprehend that the implications of the Truman Doctrine extended much farther than the Mediterranean.

In June, Truman's secretary of state, George C. Marshall, added an economic foundation to this ideological pronouncement. Although the Marshall Plan was ostensibly directed against "no particular doctrine but against starvation, poverty, uncertainty and chaos," West German leaders were fully aware that accepting assistance from the United States to battle these ills within their borders would bring with it the responsibility to battle the potential westward spread of Soviet communism. The "European Recovery Plan" was aimed at creating a politically and economically stable *western* Europe that would include a politically and economically stable *West* Germany.[104]

The creation of an Economic Council for the British-American Bizone in May 1947 paralleled these developments and represented one more step toward the incorporation of western Germany into that much larger western alliance. Staffed by representatives named by German state governments, by early 1948 this body assumed status as a shadow parliament. With larger parameters securely in place, West German administrators were increasingly charged with defining the shape of West Germany's future. In more and more particulars, Germans were in a position to make their own history, though the Allies had ensured that it would not be under circumstances of their choosing.

The reform of the West German currency in June 1948 was the response deemed essential to establish solid bases for economic recovery. Many Germans believed that a stable new Mark was the prerequisite for a fresh start, a conviction based in part on memories of how currency stabilization in November 1923 had ended the post–World War I hyperinflation and ushered in a period of relatively prosperous economic times. On 20 June 1948, every German citizen was entitled to exchange 50 Reichs-Marks for 50 new *Deutsch*marks, of which DM 40 could be claimed immediately. All other savings could be exchanged in the future at a ratio of ten to one.[105]

The new money was backed only by the continued presence of the forces of occupation and the widespread belief that an end to inflation and the black market would herald a return to normalcy. To be sure, no one expected to reinstitute the status quo ante bellum; introducing the Deutschmark was a decisive step toward dividing Germany into two independent political entities. The assurance that the Deutschmark would be the official currency in the western zones of Berlin as well as in the western Allies' zones of occupation triggered the Soviet blockade of all land transport into the former capital of the Reich. This last, unsuccessful attempt by the Soviets to register their objection to a separate West Germany, integrated into an alliance dominated by the United States, only solidified a West German and American anticommunist consensus and accelerated the movement toward the split. West Berlin and the western zones of occupation took on added symbolic and geopolitical significance as the first line of defense against Soviet communist expansion.[106]

Of more immediate consequence for most women in the western zones of occupation in June 1948 was the fact that with the currency reform, the black market vanished. In the formulation of Ludwig Erhard, the German politician most centrally involved in plans for introducing a new currency, "the only ration card from here on in is the German mark."[107] Gerda Germann, a secretary who had joined the NSDAP in the last years of the war, remembers that "We all got our DM 40 pressed in our hands. The next day, the shop windows were full, everything was available. I don't know where the goods came from, from one day to the next. Inexplicable." In Anna Peters's account: "Whatever you could dream of was there . . . a rug . . . these synthetic rugs. Yes, the day after the currency reform, you saw people schlepping around these rugs. They'd disappeared completely from memory, and suddenly they were available. All at once they were there. All at once everything was there." Unlike Germann, Peters did not find this "inexplicable." She speculated, "I guess the merchants were keeping everything off the market,"[108] and she was right. In anticipation of the new currency merchants had hoarded goods until they could get prices dictated by the market and could exchange their wares for money that had value. The surfeit of goods was also a clear indication that production had already begun to rebound before the Deutschmark was available.[109]

The belief that the beginning of the West German economic miracle could be found in the summer of 1948 was an origins myth created in the fifties. Nonetheless, for those women for whom the war and postwar years had meant hardship and suffering, first from bomb attacks and then from severe scarcities of all necessities, it is not surprising that the new currency registered as a decisive turning point. For prisoners of war and combat forces, the break between war and postwar came when they returned home. For those whose war was the home front, the break came with the new beginning marked by a new currency in June 1948.[110]

Historians of the postwar period remain divided over whether the western Allies intentionally impeded West German initiatives, either homegrown in the underground resistance or developed in exile, for a radical economic and political restructuring, including in particular the socialization of heavy industry. Formulations such as "blocked new order" and "enforced capitalism" oversimplify the complex motives of the occupation powers and domestic resistance to radical experiments.[111] However, there is no disagreement that the forces of occupation were directly involved in economic and political restructuring in the West.

The same cannot be said of Allied concern about the status of women and the family. Administrative structures to analyze these problems remained poorly staffed and underfunded; they appeared as relative latecomers in the occupation bureaucracy. Some assessments of the relationship between an authoritarian family form and authoritarian political attitudes existed, but they played no palpable role in defining Allied policy and ventured little beyond diluted versions of theories of the Frankfurt School.[112] By contributing to the division of Germany, the Allies had ensured that the shape of West Germany—including discussion of women's status and the family's future—would take place against the background of the Cold War. But this was an indirect influence. Perhaps more than with any other aspect of social and political recovery, West Germans were left on their own when it came to defining policies to reshape gender relations in the aftermath of fascism and defeat.

The concerns with women and the family that permeated sociological investigations of the postwar era and lived on in the memories of Germans interviewed years later indicate how ubiquitous these issues were as Germans in the western zones of occupation moved toward becoming citizens of a Federal German Republic in the summer and fall of 1948. Wives of Ruhr miners found common ground with academic sociologists in their view that the war and postwar periods had brought about dramatic shifts in gender relations and that the reconstruction of postwar West Germany would include the reconstruction of the family and "woman's place."

CHAPTER TWO

Constituting Political Bodies

Gender and the Basic Law

In the fall of 1948, Elisabeth Selbert was among the sixty-five representatives delegated by state legislatures in the British, French, and American zones of occupation to meet in Bonn for the purpose of formulating the Basic Law (Grundgesetz), a constitution for a new Germany. Like many of her colleagues in Bonn, Selbert was a lawyer, an expert in constitutional affairs in the Social Democratic party. She was a truly exceptional individual, and her path to Bonn was anything but direct; when she was born in Kassel in 1896, the daughter of a low-level prison official, there was little reason to predict that a half century later she would be taking part in defining the shape of the German state. Selbert had overcome the odds against pursuing higher education, completing secondary school and a further year in a commercial vocational school, where she had learned French and the skills that qualified her for white-collar work in a large export firm. She was politicized by the revolution of 1918 and became active in Social Democratic politics in Kassel, where she met her future husband, a printer who was a leader of the "Workers' and Soldiers' Council." An active advocate of women's equality within the SPD, she served in local government in Kassel. Two small sons and political work did not stop her from continuing her education; at the age of thirty, she completed the *Abitur,* the secondary-school prerequisite for admission to university study, and in 1929 she fulfilled the requirements for a law degree. The following year, she finished a dissertation that explored the arguments for reforming divorce law.

After a legal apprenticeship, Selbert passed all exams required for admission to full practice in the fall of 1934, a year after her husband, also active in local politics in Weimar, had been labeled an "enemy of the state" and shortly before a decree of January 1935 that blocked women from entering the legal profession from that date on. While her husband remained unemployed, sat in "protective custody," and then survived only under the watchful eye of the Gestapo, she continued to practice both criminal and civil law, living a contradictory existence as a lawyer within a political system that suppressed her political beliefs and discriminated against her sex.

Throughout the Nazi years, Selbert maintained illegal connections to former Social Democratic comrades, and she joined them in rebuilding the party in Kassel immediately after the war's end. She was elected as a Social Democratic representative to the Hessen parliament in late 1946, and it was this body that sent her to the Parliamentary Council.[1]

The task confronting Selbert and her colleagues in Bonn was formidable. The first steps toward postwar self-government in Germany had already been taken at the state and local levels and in the German administration of the British-American Bi-Zonal economy and government. In these contexts, postwar West Germans eagerly sought to document their move from dictatorship to democracy and their ability to manage their own affairs. It was up to the Parliamentary Council, however, to determine how these local, state, and regional initiatives would fit together in a national whole greater than the sum of its parts.

Immediately after the war, it was not even certain where the borders of a new German nation would lie, whether there would be one Germany or two. By late 1947, this question had been answered. There was little doubt that any constitutional solution drafted by Germans in the western zones of occupation would not incorporate those Germans across the border to the east. Within the larger context of the Cold War, economic division was tantamount to political division. While the future of a unified Germany would remain an open question in theory, West Germans conceded that in practice the de facto union of the French, British, and United States zones of occupation required a de jure foundation.

At first, the Parliamentary Council had claimed that its task was to outline only a provisional framework, lest any appearance of permanence close off the possibilities of a unified Germany in the future. But by the time it completed its work, most participants accepted that the

Basic Law was anything but temporary. Four years after Germany's final military surrender and the end of the war in Europe, the constitutional basis for a new West Germany was in place.

The Basic Law drafted by Selbert and her colleagues articulated an explicit response to the past of National Socialism, to the social dislocation of the immediate postwar period, and to the present of global conflict between east and west. It defined those fundamental civil rights destroyed by the Nazis and, from the perspective of West Germans, still denied the population in the Soviet-occupied zone. The Grundgesetz also sought to invoke the democratic tradition embodied in the Weimar Republic while avoiding the structural weaknesses of the Weimar constitution, which had made it possible for the Nazis to seize power by legal, electoral means.

These forces profoundly shaped the debates of the Parliamentary Council: they influenced discussions of the catalog of civil rights, the structure of political decision-making at the national level, the relationship of West Germans to the western alliance, and the division of fiscal responsibility and administrative authority between state governments and the central administration. An examination of the Basic Law can illuminate the exercise in political introspection through which West Germans confronted their past by assessing their present and defining their future; behind the sometimes abstract and legalistic debates over the Grundgesetz was a process of painful self-evaluation.[2] Included in this process were lengthy discussions of the status of women and the family. These topics were addressed directly in debates over women's equal rights with men (Article 3, Paragraph 2) and the guarantee of the state's protection of marriage, motherhood, and the family (Article 6).

Anchoring women's equality in the constitution was extremely important to Selbert, though she had come to Bonn not as a spokesperson for women's rights but as an expert on the problem of reconstituting the court system and establishing a national framework for judicial review. She assumed that a new West German state would confront no impediments to reaffirming the equality of women and men prescribed by the Weimar constitution. Reflecting on her experience almost thirty years later, she recalled, "I took it for granted that after two world wars and the experiences that we women had in those decades, equal rights for women would make it through the political process without struggle and with no further ado."[3] These expectations proved unfounded, and before the Parliamentary Council concluded its deliberations, Selbert would emerge as a forceful, articulate advocate for women's equality.

Her goal would be achieved only after the mobilization of public opinion, political struggle, and lengthy debates that allowed her colleagues
to describe in detail their views of women's natural capacities, rights,
and obligations.

No less important for revealing postwar Germans' conceptions of
where women belonged in a new democratic order were the Parliamentary Council's debates over Article 6, which placed marriage, motherhood, and the family under the "particular protection" of the state.
Here the initiative came not from Selbert and Social Democrats but from
the Catholic Church and the Christian Democratic Union. Although the
CDU and its coalition partner, the Bavarian Christian Social Union,
were ultimately willing to accept Selbert's arguments for women's
equality, they insisted on specific language guaranteeing the protection
of a social institution—the family—where women's rights were also
clearly at stake. Women's status in postwar West Germany was defined
explicitly along both axes—the axis of women's individual rights and
equality with men and the axis of women's role as wife and mother.

Public opinion polls in the late forties reflected the profound ignorance of many Germans about the deliberations of the Parliamentary
Council and the form of the Basic Law. West Germans, concluded the
Allies and German poll-takers alike, were at best apathetic about politics after the experience of the Thousand Year Reich. For women, who
had won the franchise only in 1918, their virtual exclusion from political
decision-making under the Nazis compounded the problem. Of West
Germans interviewed in March 1949, forty percent claimed that they
were "indifferent" to the constitution; among women, the figure was
forty-eight percent. Only forty-four percent of women admitted to being
"fairly" or "very interested."[4] A survey conducted by the United States
Office of Military Government after the Parliamentary Council concluded its deliberations revealed that "large numbers of Germans were
not aware that a Basic Law had been framed for a West German Federal
Republic."[5]

The Parliamentary Council's debates over the status of women and
the family's future proved that there were exceptions to this general
apathy, ignorance, and nonparticipation. Many Germans may have
claimed to care little about politics in the late forties, but they revealed
a lively interest in such ostensibly apolitical issues as women's status and
the family's relationship to the state. In their final form, both Article 3
and Article 6 were shaped not only by the politicians meeting in Bonn
but also by the mobilization of public opinion. Women and the family

attracted widespread attention in ways that questions of federalism did not; here everyone could claim firsthand knowledge, here everyone was involved.

The composition of the Parliamentary Council, selected by state governments, not by popular national elections, reflected the balance of political power in West Germany after the war. The SPD and the CDU/CSU coalition had emerged as the most important postwar political groupings, and each sent twenty-seven voting representatives to Bonn.

At the war's end, Social Democrats unearthed the SPD's Weimar foundations from the rubble, and on this solid institutional and organizational basis quickly built a major political force. The SPD offered itself as the political representative of the working class, but such claims did not deter some workers, particularly Catholics, from aligning themselves more closely with Christian than Social Democracy, nor others from remaining to the left of political socialism in the German Communist party (KPD). In the late forties as in the twenties, German workers spoke with more than one public political voice.

The postwar German working class was split not only along ideological lines; it was also divided between East and West. In the Soviet zone of occupation the fusion of Socialists and Communists into the Socialist Unity Party (Sozialistische Einheitspartei Deutschlands, SED), forced through by the Soviets in 1947, was another indication of the split between the two Germanys. "Unity" was a euphemistic description of the end to any attempt at multiparty democratic rule in the East; the creation of the SED tied German Communism even more closely to Moscow and Stalin. In the western zones of occupation, the Communists remained on the margins, winning a high of 15 percent in the first state elections in North Rhine–Westphalia and more often hovering at or below the 10-percent electoral level. Initiatives aimed at reconciling differences between the KPD and SPD and creating a united front were isolated and largely ineffective.

Postwar developments greatly diminished the challenge of the SPD's principal competitor in Weimar's last years, but they also cut the party off from some of its most important proletarian strongholds; Saxony and Thuringia, bastions of working-class political strength since the late nineteenth century, were now "behind the Iron Curtain." Still, the party's aggressive recruitment of a mass membership through the rapid rejuvenation of pre-1933 structures allowed it to do extremely well, vying on roughly equal footing with the CDU/CSU in the earliest elections at the state and local level.[6]

In contrast to the SPD, the Weimar lineages of the CDU/CSU coalition were far less self-evident. Indeed, the emergence of *Christian* Democratic and *Christian* Social political parties represented a deliberate attempt to overcome the deep political divide between Catholics and Protestants, a rift that dated back to Bismarck's attempts in the 1870s to win favor with political liberalism by attacking political Catholicism. Self-identification as Christian and Democratic also allowed a clear self-distancing from *anti*-Christian Nazism on the one hand and allegedly atheistic socialism and communism on the other. In theory, this permitted the CDU/CSU to appeal to a cross-class constituency, and it continued to draw not only on middle- and upper-class voters but also on some Catholic workers.

The CDU/CSU sought to define a position distinct from the anti-democratic German National politics of Weimar, though the Allied refusal to license right-wing parties ensured that conservative voters had little choice but to come to the coalition. Although the CDU/CSU drew on constituencies that had been organized on the anti-democratic right in the twenties, *Christian* and *Democratic* were political labels far easier to wear than *German* and *National* in the aftermath of the National Socialist regime. Names were important. A Christian party was feasible in the postwar period; a national party was not.[7]

Although the CDU/CSU took great pains to establish its identity as the interconfessional representative of *all* German Christians and could claim a strong north German Protestant following, the coalition's close ties to the Catholic church were unmistakable. By absorbing large parts of the Weimar Center party, it became the unquestioned heir apparent to political Catholicism in a new Germany. A revived network of Catholic lay organizations became an important part of the political infrastructure of the conservative coalition. Even more than the Protestant Church, organized Catholicism maintained that it had survived unscathed under National Socialism and thus could claim moral high ground from which it was entitled to shape a postwar political ideology, filling the vacuum left by the destruction of National Socialism. This self-estimation was also accepted by the Allies, who identified the Catholic church as a representative of a Germany that had not succumbed to the National Socialist dictatorship and could more readily be rehabilitated for democracy.

The division of Germany had further strengthened the position of political Catholicism. The eastern regions that made up the Soviet zone were historically strongholds of Protestantism. In the western zones of occupation, Catholics and Protestants were roughly equal in number, ending the minority status of German Catholics that had defined confessional politics since Bismarck's *Kulturkampf* in the 1870s. Thus, the Catholic bishops believed that they should enjoy a privileged position in defining the bases for a Christian reconstruction within the political ranks of the CDU/CSU coalition.[8]

In its early history, Christian Democracy espoused no single programmatic vision and still encompassed conceptions of a Christian socialism, first proposed by left-wing intellectuals and some workers in the Weimar years. By the time the Parliamentary Council convened, however, the coalition had backed away from such initiatives; instead it unified behind Konrad Adenauer, the former mayor of Cologne, who had won favor with the Allies by supporting West German integration into a western alliance and unequivocally endorsing the economic vision of Ludwig Erhard. Erhard, a Bavarian who had risen to prominence as a leader in the Bi-Zonal administration and played a key role in defining the basis for currency reform, argued that German recovery should take place on the basis of a "social market economy" (*soziale Marktwirtschaft*). The emphasis on *social* indicated the CDU/CSU's determination not to emulate a heartless brand of competitive capitalism; but of far greater significance, the emphasis on *market economy* reflected the commitment to an economic order in which state intervention would be kept to a minimum and free markets would reign. Under Adenauer, the CDU/CSU increasingly came to equate socialization with the bureaucratically run, planned economy that Germans had experienced under National Socialism and that Germans to the east experienced under Soviet occupation.[9]

With its five delegates, the Free Democratic Party could potentially tip the balance between Christian and Social Democrats in the Parliamentary Council. New in name, the FDP was tied by its history, program, and personnel to pre-1914 National Liberalism and the German Democratic party of the Weimar years. Its strong commitment to economic liberalism and its opposition to all proposals for a planned economy made it a logical ally for the CDU/CSU on a broad range of issues; its demand for formal separation of church and state and its aversion to state support for religiously oriented schools ensured that it would sometimes break with the conservative coalition.[10]

Six other voting seats were divided among the relatively insignificant German Communist party; the Center, a handful of Catholics who remained outside the CDU/CSU after 1945 until their merger into the coalition eight years later; and the German party, a conservative, avowedly Protestant political grouping, regionally concentrated in Lower Saxony. Like the Center, it presented symbolic resistance to CDU/CSU claims to represent *all* German Christians.[11]

Whatever the ideological divisions among postwar political parties, they shared one thing in common: their representatives to the Parliamentary Council were almost all men. State legislatures sent only four women to Bonn, slightly more than six percent of all delegates (fig. 11). In contrast, thirty years earlier women had made up ten percent of the delegates to the Weimar National Assembly.[12] The *Frauenüberschuss* did not register in an oversupply of women in the corridors of political decision-making. Despite the organizational initiatives among some women at the local level immediately following the war, the creation of a national nonpartisan women's organization by the late forties, and pressure from women for an expanded role in all political parties, when it came to political decision-making at the national level in postwar West Germany, there was apparently no "scarcity of men."[13] The composition of the Parliamentary Council clearly reflected the sentiments of Germans, recorded by postwar public opinion polls, that women need not concern themselves with the business of politics.[14] The state legislatures that sent delegates to the Parliamentary Council agreed that the representation of women's concerns did not require the presence of large numbers of women representatives.

Initial guidelines for the Grundgesetz, which emerged from discussions among the heads of state governments in all the Allied-occupied zones in the summer 1948, did not include any direct treatment of women's status. Some postwar state constitutions had guaranteed women civil equality, and in some cases this was extended to equal rights and wages in the workplace as well. But in the drafts handed on to the delegates sent to Bonn, it was thought that women were adequately covered by general language that ensured all citizens equality before the law and banned discrimination of all sorts.[15]

By the time the Parliamentary Council concluded its deliberations, however, the Basic Law explicitly promised that "men and women have the same rights." This marked a giant step beyond the equal-rights clause of the Weimar constitution and a victory for the SPD, which had mobilized public opinion in what the SPD's Frieda Nadig called the "battle for equal rights" (fig. 12).[16]

The first salvos in this battle had been fired in early discussions of the equal rights provisions of the Basic Law. The promise that all Germans were equal before the law applied to women as well as men, but, as the SPD's Ludwig Bergsträsser emphasized, "After the experiences of the Hitler years, it seems necessary to articulate explicitly the fundamental principle of equality." Twelve years of women's exclusion from politics had made essential a clear commitment to women's rights.[17] Bergsträsser, who along with Selbert was among the principal advocates of women's equality in the Parliamentary Council, expressed a widely shared desire to make a clean break with Nazi misogyny. The Nazis' emphasis on women's role as mothers had relegated them to hearth and home while erasing the distinction between public and private as all mothers became mothers of the nation.[18] In a new, democratic Germany, it would be essential to guarantee women's complete political rights and full access to all occupations.

Although no delegate to the Parliamentary Council disagreed, consensus extended little beyond this general prescription. Did women's equality with men imply equality in all respects and the denial of the significance of sexual difference as the basis for women's special treatment in some areas? Did the equality of male and female workers follow logically from the equal rights of male and female citizens? Was the private sphere of the home subject to a different set of laws, or did the equality of women and men necessitate legislating the equality of wives and husbands, mothers and fathers? Debates in subcommittee and in the plenary sessions of the Parliamentary Council focused directly on these questions and revealed that there were many possible answers.

The SPD was committed to guaranteeing women full equality in all areas; the equality of citizens must extend to the workplace, to the political order, and to the home. These demands were by no means new for Social Democrats. More than any other political party, they could invoke a long tradition of professed commitment to women's rights, dating back to the 1890s. In practice, the party's support for women's equality had often clashed with working-class men's fears of women as competitors in the labor force and Social Democratic and trade-union support for family wages to be paid to *male* heads of households. But at least in theory, socialism's answer to the "woman question" was that women and men should be equal in every respect.[19]

No less committed to women's equality in the late 1940s were organized middle-class women activists. Although absent from the meetings of the Parliamentary Council, their voices could be heard lobbying on the periphery, and on the question of equal rights for women they pushed in the same direction as Social Democrats. Along with the SPD, they also linked demands for women's rights with demands for a complete overhaul of those provisions of the Civil Code (Bürgerliches Gesetzbuch) that regulated marriage and family relations. It is worth reviewing the historical background to this reform agenda, because it was a past in which many of the legal experts delegated to the Parliamentary Council had participated. In discussing the legal status of women and the family, they were picking up where they had left off after the violent disruption of the Nazi seizure of power fifteen years earlier.

Drafted in the 1870s and 1880s, passed in 1896, in effect since 1900, the Civil Code had created legal uniformity in a unified German Empire.[20] According to its provisions governing marital relations, husbands had extensive and explicitly patriarchal rights over their wives. The code's references to *parental* authority in fact articulated *paternal* rights—fathers had the final determination of what was in their children's best interest, just as husbands had the final say over their wives and what was in the best interests of their marriage. A married woman could enter into a wage contract as an individual only with her husband's permission, and a husband could go to court to terminate a contract for his wife's employment outside the home, should he deem it an impediment to the performance of her domestic responsibilities. The Bürgerliches Gesetzbuch also severely limited a married woman's control of property. In theory, once a marriage ended a wife could take from it all property she had brought into it. She also had rights over whatever she earned while married, either from her wages or from any business she controlled. But while the marriage lasted, her husband could administer her resources as he saw fit, and unless otherwise regulated by a prenuptial agreement, he could invest returns without consulting her and claim as his property any profits.[21]

According to the explicit justification for the Bürgerliches Gesetzbuch, these provisions originated in the "natural order of relationships"; they ensured the state's interest in stable marriages as the "foundation of morality and education." This conceptual framework marked a shift from the legal formulations of the late eighteenth century, according to which the family appeared as a collection of individuals with rights. In contrast, the family described by the Bürgerliches Gesetzbuch had assumed the status of a "moral institution," the "organic basis [*Keimzelle*] of state and society." These categories justified the subordination of women's rights as individuals to the good of a larger whole.[22]

In its regulation of marriage and the family, the Bürgerliches Gesetzbuch made explicit the conflict between the ideal liberal conception of the rights of free individuals operating within a bourgeois "public sphere" and the relations of hierarchy and dependence underlying a patriarchal order that defined married women not as individuals but in terms of their relationships to husbands and children. In her 1907 critical commentary on the Civil Code, the middle-class feminist legal expert Marianne Weber charged that in this sense, the drafters of the Bürgerliches Gesetzbuch had been forced to "throw together fundamental principles that basically must destroy each other, like fire and water."[23]

Following the German Revolution of 1918, women had been granted the franchise, and in the spring of 1919 the constitutional assembly meeting in Weimar had added that women and men should "in principle" (*grundsätzlich*) have the same "rights as citizens" (*staatsbürgerliche Rechte*). Some Social Democrats argued forcefully that rights granted "in principle" must in reality extend to all arenas, including the private sphere of the family. Invoking the experience of the French revolutionaries in August 1789, one SPD delegate recalled "that famous evening when the upper estates gave up their privileges."[24] In a democratic state, German men must likewise be prepared to give up the privileges of an estate defined by gender and grant women full equality. The fall of the authoritarian Imperial German state necessitated the fall of men's authoritarian control over women. But in its final form the Weimar constitution extended equality to women only in the public sphere. The Civil Code remained intact; the privileged position of husbands within their families remained inviolable. Private wives were not assured the same equality and individual rights as women in public.

Socialists, middle-class feminists, and liberal legal experts continued to demand a reform of the Civil Code throughout the twenties and early thirties, tying their claims to a half-century of protest by the middle-class women's movement, the discrepancy between a patriarchal family law and women's growing importance as wage earners in an industrial economy, and the irreconcilability of the constitution's promise of equality and the legal authority of husbands over wives. Feminist reformers also argued that it was essential to ensure that married women who did not go out to work, who were "just housewives" (*nur Hausfrauen*), also were granted equal rights. This was vital because only marriages between equals would be stable, and, as liberal politician and feminist activist Marie-Elisabeth Lüders argued, because "the work that the wife does in the home is comparable [in value] with work for wages." The woman who did not work a double shift still deserved full recognition for the endless day that she did put in at her workplace in the home.[25] Sustaining the "Herr im Hause" ideology of the Civil Code was at odds with the ideal of marriage as a union "of two comrades, equal in worth and individual responsibility."[26] At the annual meeting of the professional association of German lawyers (Juristentag) in 1931, where reform proposals took center stage, a male lawyer from Munich condemned a Civil Code that granted husbands not only rights of "rule by emergency decree but also dictatorial powers."[27]

Throughout the Weimar years, the Center party resolutely rejected all reform initiatives introduced in the parliament by liberal and socialist representatives. Despite its attempts to become a broad-based interconfessional party, the Center remained largely dependent on a Catholic electorate and the support of church and clergy; political Catholicism opposed any progressive reform of the Civil Code. Allied with the right-wing German National People's party on many issues affecting the "cultural order" (Kulturordnung), the Center condemned all measures that would ease restrictions on divorce or undermine a hierarchical marriage relationship justified by scripture and grounded in a "natural order" deemed "prepolitical."[28]

Critics also invoked the alleged excesses of the Russian Revolution to justify forceful defense of the status quo. As one German National representative warned, even easing restrictions on divorce, far short of overturning the entire Civil Code, would reduce marriage to "legally recognized concubinage." It followed logically that "if marriage is bolshevized and reduced to concubinage, the family will be destroyed."[29] The alliance of political Catholicism and the conservative right ensured that in Weimar specific proposals for altering the Civil Code never moved beyond the level of debates among lawyers, feminists, and a handful of parliamentarians.

With the Nazi seizure of power in 1933, emergency decrees were exploited to justify the dictatorial powers of the National Socialist regime; the "rule by emergency decree" and the "dictatorial powers" of private patriarchs also remained in place. Indeed, patriarchy received a fresh coat of ideological justification, because a wife's obedience to her husband was deemed analogous to the nation's obedience to its Führer.[30]

Ironically, the Nazis introduced some measures to make divorce easier, which had been proposed by liberal and Social Democratic reformers in Weimar. But these were not justified by the desire to increase a wife's rights within marriage. Rather, Nazi initiatives were part of a larger vision in which marriage served a specific function for the racially defined "national community" (*Volksgemeinschaft*). As with laws that introduced racial and eugenic criteria for marriage, the good of the state was also primary in the criteria for divorce. In Hitler's formulation, marriage was "no end in itself; rather it must serve a greater goal, that of expanding and sustaining the nation."[31] The Nazis' racialist, biologistic, pronatalist intention could hardly be stated more clearly; women's bodies, subordinated to men by the Civil Code, were also subordinated to the expansionist needs of the *Volk*.

Husbands and wives who confronted irreconcilable differences in their relationships or who had lived apart for three years or more should be permitted to divorce; such marriages were not the unions that would provide the Third Reich with its next generation. The Nazi marriage law of 1938 thus aimed not at recognizing the rights of individuals to shape their own lives but rather at the subordination of a married couple's interests to the state and the designation of reproducing the race as a wife's primary responsibility.[32]

This long prehistory of debates over women's equality and family-law reform before 1933 and the abrupt termination of this discussion in the Thousand Year Reich framed the Parliamentary Council's treatment of women's status in postwar Germany. For Selbert, the stages of the debate also marked important milestones in her biography, and it was perhaps this intersection of personal history with political principle that led her to believe that no one would object to guaranteeing women's complete equality in the Basic Law. She was in for a surprise. Even Frieda Nadig, Selbert's only female comrade in the SPD delegation, at first joined many other Social Democrats in fearing that an unequivocal commitment to equal rights would have drastic, unforeseeable consequences because it would necessitate the immediate reform of the outdated family law; such reforms were ultimately essential, but she feared that moving too fast might create a "legal chaos" of enormous dimensions. Nadig counseled patience; the Parliamentary Council could not expect to do everything at once.[33]

Selbert ultimately overcame these reservations within her own party and forcefully demanded the unconditional constitutional guarantee of equal rights for women; the Basic Law's guarantee of equality was essential and should provide the foundation for the thoroughgoing reform of the Civil Code. She sought to complete Weimar's unfinished business, but she also focused on the immediate context of the "woman, who during the war years stood atop the rubble and replaced men at the workplace, [and] has a moral right to be valued like a man." All "ifs, ands, and buts" must be eliminated, Selbert emphasized, particularly given the *Frauenüberschuss,* which, she calculated, left "170 women voters for every 100 men . . . and made the voice of women as voters . . . decisive for the acceptance of the constitution."[34]

The explicit guarantee of women's equality was also essential because of other lessons from the Thousand Year Reich. Selbert's colleague Bergsträsser explained his "insistence about [mentioning] women, because whenever the bureaucracy confronts a so-called emergency, it always thrusts women into the corner. If there are firings, it is women who get fired. If the universities restrict admissions, it's women who get shut out."[35] The Basic Law must provide a clear mandate for the elimination of all forms of institutionalized discrimination against women; discriminatory measures had found their clearest expression in the misogynistic policies of the Nazis, but they were also apparent in renewed discussions of "double-earners" in the wake of currency stabilization and a much tighter labor market.[36]

The SPD's arguments faced opposition from both the CDU/CSU and the FDP. Most troubling to critics of the SPD's demands for explicit guarantees of women's equality were the implications of such guarantees for the reform of the Bürgerliches Gesetzbuch; on this score, Free and Christian Democrats were united. Although within the ranks of the postwar FDP were Marie-Elisabeth Lüders and others who had led the campaign for a reform of the Civil Code during the Weimar years, they were not included in the FDP's small delegation to the Parliamentary Council.[37] Rather, Thomas Dehler, the leader of the Bavarian FDP and the party's chief legal expert, who would become justice minister after the first national elections in 1949, expressed concern that grounding women's equality in the Basic Law would imply that the Bürgerliches Gesetzbuch was unconstitutional. The FDP did not deny the need for a reformed family law, but Dehler argued that it would be precipitous to endorse constitutional measures that made reform mandatory before all implications of such action had been carefully assessed.[38]

The CDU/CSU shared Dehler's fears about the legal vacuum potentially created by declaring key parts of the Civil Code unconstitutional and argued for limiting equality to the "rights of citizens," which did not automatically extend to private affairs. The Parliamentary Council's authority did not include the authority to "jettison and declare null and void regulations affecting marriage and the family" that had been in effect for nearly fifty years.[39]

The conservative coalition also stressed that a language of unqualified equality would violate the natural boundaries of male-female difference. Complete equality would necessitate such unconscionable acts as conscripting women into the military or labor service in time of war. Behind such visions was an implicit reference to Nazi policies and a rejection of the forced mobilization of women into exclusively male occupations in the Soviet-occupied zone. Legislating guarantees of women's equal rights created the possibility of such abominations.

Equality, according to the CDU/CSU, should not erase "those nuances created by nature, which require a different treatment." Although the coalition never offered any single view of what constituted nature or how these nuances were defined, Hermann von Mangoldt, a Christian Democratic representative from Schleswig-Holstein and an eminent legal theorist, offered one alternative. The examples he chose to illustrate this abstract principle indicated that certain ideological persuasions that had flourished in the Third Reich had survived Allied bomb attacks. "Mentally less well-endowed children" and the "mentally ill," argued Mangoldt, were groups that required special schools and treatment. Other examples included "the gypsy, who wanders around [and] can be subjected to certain, special legal regulations." Or in the case of the United States, Mangoldt uncritically observed, the dominance of the intellectual legacy of the French Revolution prompted public declarations of full equality. "But essentially," he maintained, "suspended above all laws in the United States is the idea that we cannot and will not ever permit ourselves to be flooded by a foreign race [*von einer fremden Rasse überfremdet werden*]." Such laws sought not only to block the threat of the "black race," but also to achieve a positive agenda; their purpose was to "preserve the dominance of the nordic race in the USA." Putting such regulations in place confronted lawmakers with practical problems; such objectives could not be admitted openly. Still, Mangoldt maintained, pursuing them was essential.[40]

Coming little more than three years after the destruction of the outspokenly racialist regime that had subordinated gypsies to very special regulation indeed and that had broadly defined mental illness to include many whose insanity was to oppose National Socialism, Mangoldt's analogies are jarring.[41] In the context of the debate over equal rights for women, moreover, they indicated that for him the natural differences between women and men were to be equated with immutable racial characteristics that required and justified special legal treatment. Sexual difference—like race and ethnicity for Mangoldt—was natural, immutable, and the cause for special legal provisions. The proclamation of complete equality for women would make this impossible and would present an immediate challenge to the special treatment of pregnant women or the necessary prohibition of women from certain jobs not suited to their constitution.

Problematic as well was the question of how far the Basic Law should go in stipulating equality's dimensions in the workplace. This issue created some unexpected alliances. If they could agree on little else, the CDU's Helene Weber and Heinz Renner of the KPD were united in their insistence that equal rights must include equal wages for the same work.[42] Weber was a veteran of Weimar politics, a former member of the Center party with a history of activism in Catholic social-work organizations. It was perhaps her experience with working-class families in which women sought employment to support themselves or to supplement inadequate male wages that had convinced her that women should be guaranteed equal wages for performing the same tasks as men.

The SPD also advocated securing wage equality in the constitution, arguing that women's increased labor-force participation in the postwar world made this a high priority. Nadig pointed out that such explicit assurances would represent a "fundamental change . . . for the vast majority of women, who do not get their rights within the economic arena." Women's demands for such an explicit commitment to wage equality also represented a response to similar measures proposed by the Socialist Unity party for the East German constitution, where they built on legal prescriptions introduced by the Soviet occupying forces after the war. Although Nadig conceded that assurances of wage equality in the East might well remain paper promises, she emphasized that discussions of women's status in the Soviet zone inevitably stimulated interest in similar questions in the West and intensified demands that the "Basic Law accommodate the present."[43]

Most of Weber's colleagues in the conservative coalition did not share her enthusiasm for instituting constitutional guarantees of equal wages. Mangoldt feared that such measures would open the door to special pleading "from every corporate estate [*Stand*] and every group of people who will ask the same question: Where are [our interests] considered?"[44] For him, biology constituted well over half of the German population as an interest group with parochial concerns. Moreover, the extension of the Basic Law to contractual relations in the workplace would mean the Parliamentary Council's intervention into the "social order" (*Sozialordnung*), that nebulous arena that all agreed could not be adequately regulated in the Basic Law's language of abstract fundamental rights. Ultimately, the SPD accepted this logic and agreed that an unequivocal language of equal rights would *implicitly* extend to all facets of women's lives, including their work outside the home.[45]

Despite agreement on this question, major areas of conflict remained as draft proposals made their way through subcommittee debates. The implications for the Civil Code of prescribing women's equal rights continued to spark particularly intense opposition to the SPD's stance. In the committee assigned to make specific recommendations, the conservative coalition together with the FDP commanded the two-vote margin sufficient to defeat proposals for a language of unqualified equal rights.

The majority rejection of the SPD alternative in early December 1948 prompted a wave of petitions, which dramatically amplified Selbert's voice. Public opinion, which registered relatively little elsewhere in the debates of the Parliamentary Council, weighed in decisively against the CDU/CSU's and FDP's unwillingness to accept the SPD's straightforward formulation that "men and women have the same rights." From bourgeois and socialist women's organizations alike, the message was the same: the constitution should include a specific acknowledgment of women's equality with men in every respect.

While they emphasized that "no paragraph in a constitution alone could guarantee women the equality—economic and political—for which we must struggle in practice," women trade unionists in Hessen responded with anger and disbelief that parliamentarians in Bonn had not endorsed full equal rights for women.[46] In the name of "40,000 organized female metalworkers" in the British zone of occupation, Margarete Traeder exhorted the Parliamentary Council to create a meaningful basis for the economic and political equality of women.[47] The women's committee of the German Dunlop Rubber Corporation in Hanau insisted that "it is impossible to conceive of a reconstruction of Germany that will not include a role for women's assistance." They rejected the continuation of the "unworthy status that women have had for centuries" and demanded "that the Parliamentary Council in Bonn give us women the status to which we are entitled on the basis of economic conditions."[48] Equally unambiguous was the message from a range of bourgeois women's organizations that had emerged after the war. Their petitions also underscored the need for the thoroughgoing reform of the Civil Code, which would follow necessarily from the constitutional guarantee of equality.[49]

Even more forcefully than SPD representatives, Dorothea Groener-Geyer, head of an alliance of women's organizations in Stuttgart, linked women's experience in the war and postwar years with demands for equal rights:

> After Stalingrad, there is no aspect of life in which the actions of German men have protected German women from want, misery and poverty. After our men fell victim to the obsession of a man and followed him from Berlin via Paris to Stalingrad and then back again, and did not have the energy to contain the delusion of power of that obsessed individual, thus gambling away the sovereignty of our state, leaving our cities in ruins, destroying our homes, and leaving millions homeless and with no basis for their existence, the equality of women has been accomplished de facto. Nothing human or inhuman is foreign to her any longer; she has been spared no terror. This reality places demands on the physical and spiritual power of women, which far exceed anything that women of earlier generations ever experienced, suffered through or accomplished.

The consequence, concluded Groener-Geyer, was obvious: women must be ensured equal rights with men. Arguments that women would have to pay for equality by sacrificing essential protective legislation showed only that the "bourgeois parties" were grasping at straws to deny women their due. Women need not fear this potential loss, argued Groener-Geyer: "Through our legally guaranteed equal participation in the legislature [and] the government . . . we would prefer to learn how to protect ourselves."[50]

The massive negative response to the Parliamentary Council's preliminary recommendation prompted the CDU/CSU and FDP to retreat hastily when debate over women's equality with men resumed in January 1949. Those speaking for the conservative coalition declared that they had never meant to challenge the principle of equal rights for women and scrambled to clarify their position. Some continued to maintain that those who questioned legislating complete equality were those who "most zealously protect woman's honor . . . [and] seek a Christian foundation for our politics, because in our Christian religion, woman's honor is legitimized in a unique fashion," but the coalition acknowledged that its failure to move in the SPD's direction would leave it vulnerable to attack from the left in upcoming national elections.[51]

Walter Strauss, a CDU representative from Hessen, now insisted that there could be no doubt that his party supported full equality for women. He conceded that the CDU "committed an error and then we repeated it—and not just the lawyers among us: we saw things too legalistically and not politically enough." With this myopia corrected, Strauss, echoing categories first introduced by Selbert, emphasized that when women had replaced men at the workplace during the war and in the postwar years they had also continued to carry responsibility for children and for the management of the household; after this experience, they had proven their complete equality with men. However, the CDU still proposed appending the prescription of women's "equal responsibility" to unrestricted "equal rights." *Rechte*—rights—and *Pflichten*—obligations—went hand in hand; if women were granted one, they must assume the other.[52]

The FDP's Theodor Heuss, soon to become the new Federal Republic's first president, was no less eager than Strauss to deny that his party had ever opposed equality for women. Free Democrats' hesitancy to endorse complete equality, he insisted, reflected only their fears that an undifferentiated language could be employed to women's disadvantage, by denying women spousal support in cases of divorce, for example. While Heuss still expressed concerns about such matters, his remarks made clear that the FDP understood the public outcry and acknowledged similar protests from women within the party's own ranks, who forcefully reminded the delegation to the Parliamentary Council that "for us women the question of equal rights, one might almost say, is a vital existential question."[53]

Disclaiming any responsibility for orchestrating extraparliamentary support, an exuberant Selbert credited the "storm outside in the realm of public opinion" with forcing the CDU to revise its position from a "yes, but" to an "unqualified yes." Still, while welcoming this change of heart, Selbert rejected the CDU's proposed alternative of coupling equal rights with responsibilities, because the overwhelming majority of petitions had favored the SPD's unconditional formulation. In addition, the war had provided painful evidence that an insistence on "equal responsibilities" could justify women's mobilization in ways that exceeded her "physical constitution"—"behind the searchlights for anti-aircraft guns, behind the guns, or in the hail of bombs." It could also be used to deny spousal support to divorced women who had not worked outside the home during their marriages and whose ex-husbands might claim that equal responsibility included immediate economic self-sufficiency.

Selbert vehemently dismissed CDU/CSU charges that her party's conception of equality excluded a recognition of sexual difference and the need for special treatment of women in some situations. Women could be different from men and still be their equals, she explained, because "equality of rights is founded on an equality of worth, which acknowledges difference."[54] Her position articulated crucial aspects of the postwar SPD's view of the relationship between women's "nature" and women's rights; behind this careful formulation was the intention of Selbert and the party to distance themselves decisively from any association with the theory or practice of the SED. It marked off important ideological ground for the SPD in its response to the "woman question," and it defined a position that would be invoked repeatedly in the political discussion of women's status in the fifties. Properly understood and enforced, equality would not lead to *Gleichmacherei,* the bogey of an arbitrary leveling of difference conjured up by CDU/CSU critics, who argued that it was this sort of equality that existed in the Soviet zone. There, they charged, the "mechanistic" implementation of equal rights served only to emancipate women to work alongside men in all jobs. As the example of the Soviet Union made clear, this false conception of equality left no room for "the biological basis and the spiritual posture of women."[55] *Gleichmacherei* would lead to the destruction of the family, as women were compelled to work in occupations for which they were unsuited, and would deny women the possibility of fulfilling their obligations as wives and mothers. But such fears were totally unfounded, Selbert countered, because the SPD's conception of equality shared nothing in common with communistic leveling.

Rather, in terms of the line consistently advanced by Selbert and other Social Democrats in the late forties and fifties, equality did not mean that women and men should be alike in all respects. For example, women should have the right to pursue wage work, but the many married women who might choose not to work outside the home must not be considered inferior to their husbands, explained Selbert, because "the husband's obligation to support [the family] is the equivalent of the wife's obligation to educate the children and run the household, in short to perform sociologically valuable labor. . . . [T]he work of the housewife is sociologically of the same worth as the work of the woman employed [outside the home]."[56] To be sure, sociological function did not

draw the same line between women and men as the difference in the
blood described by Mangoldt. But for Social Democrats, separate could
be equal.

By emphasizing the importance of female difference, Selbert also
claimed to distance herself and her party from "women's righters,"
bourgeois feminists often dismissed with the term of opprobrium,
Frauenrechtlerinnen. According to Selbert, the women's righters, unlike
the SPD, claimed that women and men should be equal because in no
crucial respects were they different.

On this score, Selbert protested far too much; she resolutely rejected
a position that was represented by no one at the Bonn deliberations, nor,
for that matter, by any part of the German bourgeois women's movement. The brand of Anglo-American feminism that advocated that sexual differences between women and men were of no social or political
consequence and that equality should be based on the common *humanity* of women and men had never found a substantial audience in Germany. In the categories of the German bourgeois women's movement,
emancipation had consistently meant emancipation of a particular
womanly nature. By allowing women to employ their uniquely feminine
capacities, their "spiritual motherhood," equality would permit them to
participate in a general process of progressive social transformation.
Male virtue and behavior should not become the standard for measuring female worth.[57]

However, Selbert's misrepresentation of the ideology of the bourgeois
women's movement served an important purpose for her party. If the
SPD was at pains to distinguish itself from "communist levelers," it also
sought to keep the middle-class women's movement at arm's length. Selbert clearly echoed directives from the national Social Democratic leadership that women in the party had no business pursuing cooperation
with bourgeois women's righters. This forceful reminder took on particular significance precisely because postwar initiatives for the creation
of a broad-based women's coalition "above the political parties" had
found some recruits within the SPD. Supporters of these "women's caucuses above parties" argued that "women's will" and "women's opinion" could emerge only in an autonomous women's organization, af-
filiated with no single party.[58]

Although it stopped short of forbidding its members from endorsing
such steps, the postwar SPD leadership left no doubt that it disapproved
of any deviation that resulted in cooperation with a cross-class, nonpartisan women's movement. Memories of the deep division between so-

cialist women and the League of German Women's Associations in Weimar remained vivid. According to the SPD's own figures, more than seventy percent of participants in the party's first postwar women's congress had been politically active before 1933;[59] many of them had experienced direct or indirect persecution by the Nazis because of their political beliefs, lending a particularly charged emotional import to accusations that bourgeois women's organizations had all too readily and enthusiastically found a common ground with National Socialism. The long-standing conviction that for women in the SPD, bonds of class identity were far stronger than those defined by gender combined to maintain the distance between bourgeois and socialist women's groups after 1945.

In a characteristic attack, Herta Gotthelf, the highest-ranking woman in the SPD's postwar leadership, dismissed those "ambitious people who are afraid of doing the tedious work" within the party and found their "element in these little clubs." Things were no different than before 1933; any appearances to the contrary, explained Gotthelf, reflected only the "lack of clarity and confusion of our times, and it is our task to make sure that clarity comes into [women's] heads, not more confusion."[60] Clarity was certainly not to be found at the meetings of the "women's caucuses above parties," where, according to one disdainful eyewitness, "the soft voices, the soft satin curtains, and the warmth of the preceding May days that still hung in the air left more and more listeners with their heads nodding. . . . Patience and tolerance, responsibility for life." These were the anodyne messages conveyed by bourgeois feminism, hardly the Social Democratic vision of women shoulder-to-shoulder with working-class men in a common struggle to build a new Germany.[61]

For women who were socialists, insisted the SPD's female leadership, the struggle for women's rights was a struggle to be waged "together with our comrades." The first postwar issue of the party's newspaper for women made clear that "we are no 'women's righters,' either of the old or new sort." For loyal socialists, there could be no "woman question" distinct from the larger social and political questions confronting the party. Answers lay not in organizations "above the parties" but exclusively in a "democratic, socialist Germany in a democratic, socialist Europe."[62] Lest there be any doubt where she stood, Selbert reassured her comrades in the Parliamentary Council that "in the thirty years that I have been politically active, I have never been a women's righter, and I will never be one."[63]

Still, though Selbert and other leading women in the SPD warned of the limits of postwar political initiatives of middle-class feminists in practice, their emphasis on the compatibility of sexual difference with equality left them quite close to bourgeois feminism in theory. In crucial respects, Selbert's insistence that a woman's political participation should be in accord with her "particular nature" and that only the "synthesis of male and female qualities" would bring political progress represented nothing new in the SPD's response to the "woman question"; from the 1880s on, socialist feminists had insisted that a woman's emancipation would not be achieved by forcing her to become like a man or by denying the significance of sexual difference. But missing from the SPD's postwar analysis of gender relations were other mainstays of Social Democratic theory, notably a belief in the relationship between women's status and stages of economic development; the SPD's critique of women's subordination was no longer firmly grounded in historical materialism. Absent as well was any trace of socialist theories that "socially productive labor" outside the home was the key to female emancipation and the basis for establishing working-class marriages between equals.[64]

Rather, reflecting the position of the postwar party leadership, Selbert maintained that although equality must include a woman's right to work, by no means should the achievement of emancipation and equality be contingent on women's employment. This lay behind her insistence that socially productive work for wages was not superior to women's socially *reproductive* labor in the home. Neither communist nor women's righter, Selbert articulated the party's position when she staked out a terrain where difference—defined by "sociological" function and the "natural obligation [of women] as mothers"—was completely compatible with women's equality. This shift in emphasis was significant; in its view of women's rights, it left the SPD far closer to Marie-Elisabeth Lüders and many other bourgeois feminists than to August Bebel, Friedrich Engels, and Clara Zetkin. Herta Gotthelf might remind women organized in the SPD that "the best woman's book is still Bebel's *Woman and Socialism*," and welcome a new postwar edition of the *Communist Manifesto*, but in the party's official answer to the "woman question," these classics were being deployed selectively if at all.[65]

An equality in which separate spheres were equal, Selbert argued, still necessitated a thoroughgoing revision of the existing family law. Revision was the unavoidable consequence of Article 3, as feared by Dehler and Mangoldt, but Selbert assured her colleagues that it should not be a cause for dismay or anxiety. The patriarchal order underwritten by the Bürgerliches Gesetzbuch was inconsistent with a new Germany's commitment to the equality of all its citizens; the Civil Code was long overdue for a complete overhaul. The constitutional guarantee of women's rights provided the legal basis for the claims of unmarried women to equality. However, the existing family law still left married women subordinate to their husbands.

Marriage was, Selbert affirmed, "an association for life that is of a particular nature [in which] . . . [t]he egos [of both partners] have to be subordinated to higher objectives."[66] Nonetheless, marriage must be based on the equality of husband and wife, and laying the proper foundation required a reform of family law. Completing that project would take time, and the Parliamentary Council stipulated that the Bundestag would have until 1 April 1953 to do the job; this was laid out in the Basic Law's Article 117. Should it fail to meet the deadline, the Basic Law's provisions would automatically go into effect as the law of the land; women and men would have equal rights in all parts of their lives, and existing laws that violated these constitutional provisions would be null and void. While some CDU representatives shared Adolf Süsterhenn's view that falling behind this schedule would lead to "circumstances of complete lawlessness,"[67] the Parliamentary Council in Bonn accepted Social Democratic arguments that setting a deadline was the only way to ensure that equality in principle would become equality in practice; four years seemed adequate to the task.

In mid-January 1949, the Parliamentary Council adopted a prescriptive formulation of the equality of women and men, which had been totally absent in the initial draft; delegates voted unanimously to incorporate into the Basic Law a pledge that "men and women have the same rights." All could agree that equality would not erase difference; all accepted that a conception of equality "which acknowledges difference" should be law.

As the debates over Article 3 made clear, any discussion of women's rights immediately raised questions about the family. The discussions of the Basic Law's Article 6, specifying parental rights and obligations and the constitutional protection of marriage and motherhood, showed that any discussion of the family automatically raised questions about women's rights. It was not subject matter alone that linked these two issues in the minds of representatives to the Parliamentary Council. Debates over both provisions involved largely the same party political personnel, and the most extensive discussions of both took place during early December 1948.

Before setting out to define the particulars of the Grundgesetz, the political leaders in the Parliamentary Council agreed that the catalog of basic rights should not touch upon specific social and economic policies or the structure of the "cultural order" (*Kulturordnung*). Cultural policy was to remain the preserve of individual state governments. Tabling social and economic concerns until a later date was justified because of the provisional nature of the Basic Law, and it was this agreement that in part had been used to exclude any explicit language on wage equality from Article 3. It also made it easier for the political parties to skirt the particular interests of their organized constituents—in the case of the SPD, of the trade unions, and for the CDU/CSU and Center, of a range of Catholic lay organizations. Finally, it allowed both SPD and CDU/CSU to postpone choosing among competing conceptions of the social order until some future date, by which time each anticipated an electoral advantage over the other.[68]

When it came to discussions of the family and parental rights, this agreement collapsed under heavy pressure from many church-related associations and the direct intervention of Cardinal Josef Frings, Archbishop of Cologne and spokesman for the Fulda Conference of Bishops, which had successfully mobilized lay organizations within the Catholic Church around this issue. As in debates over Article 3, when women's organizations had become involved, public opinion intervened forcefully in the Article 6 deliberations in Bonn. This time, however, the public opinion of church-based organizations demanded not an expanded notion of women's equality but rather incorporation into the Basic Law of specific guarantees of parental authority and the integrity of the family (see figure 13).[69]

Championing the Cologne archbishop's position in the Parliamentary Council were Helene Wessel, one of the two Center party delegates, and Adolf Süsterhenn and Helene Weber from the CDU. Wessel, trained as a social worker, had served as a Center delegate to the Prussian state legislature from 1928 to 1933, when she was in her early thirties. Active in the reestablishment of the Center after 1945, she came to Bonn with the singular intent of ensuring that the rights of parents, grounded in a prepolitical religious order, be built into the constitution as basic rights and thereby be removed once and for all from the wrangling of political parties. Although the Center party had only a nominal political pres-

ence in the Parliamentary Council, it is hardly surprising that on this issue—a mainstay of Center politics since the party's origins in the
1860s—Wessel would claim an authoritative position.[70]

Süsterhenn, like Selbert, had studied law in the twenties, though his
academic path had not been circuitous. One of the youngest representatives in Bonn, born in 1905, he was politically initiated in Weimar in
a circle of students and intellectuals who advocated a political activism
informed by Christian scripture and social theory. His legal career under
the Nazis included the defense of some clerics and other religious leaders
charged under National Socialist law. With the war's end, he became
active in Christian Democratic politics in Rheinland-Pfalz, serving as
both justice minister and cultural minister in that state's early governments. He was recognized as one of the leading constitutional experts
in the CDU/CSU delegation to Bonn.[71]

Weber, a former schoolteacher, had received political Catholicism in
the cradle; her father, also a teacher, had led the local branch of the Center party in the Ruhr city of Elberfeld in the late nineteenth century. A
key figure in the Catholic Women's League before and during the First
World War, Weber took over leadership of a church-run school for the
instruction of social workers. She entered national politics in Weimar as
a member of the Weimar National Assembly, the Prussian state parliament, and beginning in 1924, the Reichstag. Head of the women's caucus within the Center and after 1925 a member of the party's national
steering committee, she was among the handful of women who played
a direct role in Center politics at the national level in the twenties. She
was also a Prussian civil servant, and in 1920 she became the first
woman employed at a senior level (*Ministerialrat*) in the state's history,
serving in the Ministry of Welfare.

Weber had been outspoken in her opposition to the Nazis, whom she
perceived to be no less a threat to Christianity than the communists. In
the last years of Weimar, she had counseled Catholic women voters to
avoid extremes of right and left and to support the Weimar state. In the
summer of 1933, the National Socialist regime retaliated, labeling her
"politically unreliable" and dismissing her from her position in the Prussian state government. She continued to work as head of a professional
association of Catholic women social workers, a position she occupied
throughout the Thousand Year Reich. Bombed out of her Berlin apartment in 1944, she spent the last war years in Marburg with her sister.
After resurfacing in the Rhineland at war's end, Weber worked to rebuild the organization of Catholic social work agencies and to found the

CDU. Although not a member of the first state parliament in North Rhine–Westphalia, she was chosen by the CDU faction in that state to serve in the Parliamentary Council, probably at the behest of the faction's leader, Konrad Adenauer. Her close personal ties to Adenauer also extended to his wife, who was among Weber's students before the First World War. Sixty-seven when she came to Bonn and never married, Weber would later earn dubious distinction as "Mother of the CDU Faction" during the Adenauer era.[72]

Both Weber and Süsterhenn had close ties to Frings and his representative in Bonn, Wilhelm Böhler, who had been active in Catholic school politics in the 1920s. With vocal support from Wessel, Weber and Süsterhenn represented that part of the CDU/CSU that was committed to a vision of Christian politics as the basis for postwar reconstruction. According to their view, any political system must be founded on a "natural law" (Naturrecht) that stemmed not from the rationalism of the Enlightenment but from a prepolitical order ordained by God and prescribed by scripture. The catastrophe of National Socialism was the consequence of a deviation from these principles, which could be traced back to a process of secularization that began with the French Revolution. In categories that had shaped conservative thought since the nineteenth century, Süsterhenn depicted socialism as the product of the political individualism unleashed by 1789 and the economic liberalism that had spawned an industrial society. Industry created an industrial working class and a materialist socialist political movement. By destroying individualism and glorifying the collective, socialism, in turn, had helped to clear the ground for National Socialism. Both Socialism and National Socialism shared a commitment to a "naturalist-biologistic materialism" that had reached its epitome under the disastrous Nazi dictatorship; both denied the significance of religious belief and suppressed the church; both elevated the interests of the collective above the interests of families.

In the formulation of the CDU's statement of principles adopted in Cologne in 1945, a return to "Christian and occidental human values that once ruled the German people and made it great and respected among the people of Europe" was central to this vision of Christian politics.[73] The destruction of the Third Reich cleared the ground for rebuilding Germany on a Christian basis and reversing the lengthy secularization process. The other alternative, represented by developments in the Soviet-occupied East, was just as deplorable as National Socialism. The CDU/CSU called for rejecting "dictatorship and collectivism in all shapes and forms"[74] and guaranteeing survival of the community of be-

lievers, the Church, and, most importantly, the family, society's fundamental building block. These prepolitical institutions were worlds apart
from the communities embodied in communist or National Socialist
collectives.

"The family," explained one of the CDU's earliest declarations of
political principles, "is the fundament of the social organization of life.
Its living space (*Lebensraum*) is holy." Restoring the sanctity of this
Lebensraum after Nazi attempts to invade it was an essential task for the
state in a postwar German political order. "A nation is worth only as
much as the value it places on the family. . . . National Socialism had
much to say about the German family, but in reality, it did everything
possible to tear it apart." The Nazis had inverted the natural order;
instead of putting the state in the service of families, they had attempted
to force families into the service of the state. In a new Germany, everything possible must be done to reverse this deplorable development, to
support and promote the family.[75] Such demands echoed Center party
platforms from the Kaiserreich and Weimar, but against the background
of the intense debate over "mother-families," "incomplete families,"
"family ruins," and high rates of divorce and unmarried motherhood,
after 1945 they took on an immediate relevance. It was the task of postwar politics to counter these unnatural trends and to restore the proper
"order of life" (*Lebensordnung*).

These priorities were behind the insistence of Süsterhenn, Weber, and
Wessel that the family be explicitly acknowledged in the Basic Law. In
Weber's formulation, "The family belongs to the natural forms of association . . . [and] it cannot be compared to economic or social associations. The family is the basis of all associations, of the existence of the
nation and the state."[76] For Wessel, marriage and family constituted the
starting point for an ordered society, the foundation on which the "construction of our state and social community can begin."[77]

The nature invoked by Weber was defined not by biology or social
function but by a divinely endowed order, which predated all political
institutions and to which the state must accommodate itself. The rights
of the family set limits to the authority of the state; it was the responsibility of the state to guarantee the survival of this natural institution,
to afford it "particular protection." Like other fundamental rights incorporated into the Basic Law, the family was a product of nature, not
society.

For the Center, the German party, and the CDU/CSU, there was no
question of what constituted a family. It was in discussion of Article 3,
not Article 6, that Weber explicitly identified a natural family as one in

which "the wife is free for the life of the family." Weber feared that an
increase in women's labor-force participation in the postwar world
threatened to chain mothers to other tasks. While conceding that in the
unsettled circumstances of the late forties there might be instances
where wives earned more than husbands, she labeled such a situation
"an unfortunate [case], if the mother leaves the family and the husband
stays home and takes care of the children and the wife as well." This was
a "development good neither for the wife nor for the husband nor for
the children. These are exceptional circumstances that we would gladly
change."[78] For Weber's colleague, Mangoldt, such a scenario was un-
imaginable, and he expressed utter astonishment at the prospect of men
caring for children.[79]

Protecting families in the postwar world implied eliminating social
threats to nature and reestablishing families on the basis of a male wage
sufficient to support a dependent wife and children. As one of the CDU's
earliest postwar programmatic statements put it, "The husband must be
the head of the family in a complete fashion." In order to achieve this,
it was the state's responsibility to ensure him the opportunity "to provide for his family with honor. . . . Only then will the wife as the heart
of the family be able with inner freedom to carry responsibility along
with the man and to become the responsible wife for his children."[80] In
postwar Germany, the conditions that prevailed did not allow this; it
was the Parliamentary Council's responsibility to restore an order in
which this was possible.

In the categories proposed by the conservative coalition, "Marriage
is the legal form of the lasting association for life between husband and
wife and the family that comes out of [that union]." *Marriage,* not co-
habitation (*Konkubinat*), should be protected by the law. Although the
CDU/CSU was ultimately willing to accept that parents with adopted
children might also constitute a family and that some married couples
might be a family while choosing to have no children at all, it was self-
evident that for Christian Democrats, nature intended other things. Because a specific family form was preordained, children born outside such
a union could not be on the same legal footing as those who benefited
from it. The differentiation between legitimate and illegitimate children
implied a differentiation between the legal status of those children's
mothers, and between legal marriages and the unnatural unions that
produced illegitimate children. All children and all mothers deserved the
state's protection, but only the "family association" conformed to the
natural order. "Even if we wanted to," explained Wessel, "we could not

place the illegitimate child on the same footing because we . . . start from a different concept of order." Because illegitimate children "are not born into families," Weber added, they could not claim equal status.[81]

The SPD's Frieda Nadig, a regional secretary of *Arbeiterwohlfahrt*, the working-class welfare organization established by the party in 1919, and a member of the North Rhine–Westphalian state parliament, was quick to point out that this view of the family amounted to a denial of social reality in postwar West Germany. Drawing different conclusions than Weber and Wessel from her social-work experience, she emphasized that in many families, children were not growing up in "association[s] for life between husband and wife." Nadig reminded her colleagues that in debates over Article 3, they had acknowledged "the surplus of seven million women, which we now have. If we consider that it is primarily women between 22 and 45 who constitute this surplus of women, then we know that an extraordinarily altered form of living together (*Lebensgemeinschaft*) will emerge. We must take into account that in the future we will have a mother-family." The consequences included a far broader definition of what constituted families, the need to ensure the legal equality of legitimate and illegitimate children, and a condemnation of the "theological preconception [and] Christian worldview" that relegated unmarried motherhood to a second-class status. The existence of large numbers of single women who would pursue their "natural calling as mothers" outside of marriage made clearer than ever that traditional views of the family belonged to the past.[82]

Selbert asked rhetorically, "Is bourgeois [*bürgerliche*] marriage the only form of living together toward which we should aspire?" Like Nadig, she insisted on recognizing "the new forms of organizing existence demanded by . . . the consequences of the war and economic necessity." While Selbert called for the "protection and maintenance of the bourgeois family," she argued that the " 'mother-family' take its place next to bourgeois marriage." Along with married women, mothers who did not marry deserved full legal rights over their children and the "full protection of the state." In fact, it was precisely unmarried motherhood that was founded on a "high sense of responsibility and qualities of moral character."[83]

This critique was given a theoretical framework by Carlo Schmid, one of the SPD's leading constitutional experts. Schmid contended that the family was a product not of nature but rather of the legal order. Responding to CDU/CSU conceptions of natural law, he maintained "that generally, everyone typically proclaims that [to be] natural law which

appears best to suit his hopes for life."[84] As for the definition of a family,
Schmid argued that depending on the legal order, "the family is something totally different in each epoch and in every region; different legal
consequences can be associated with the same biological and sociological facts."[85] The law created families, and laws were historical, not natural, constructions. The structure and objectives of the state ultimately
determined the structure and function of the family.

Evidence for Schmid's position, argued his colleague, Walter Menzel,
could be found in the Soviet Union, an "imperialist nation," which
"probably views marriage from the perspective of population policy,
military preparedness and imperialism."[86] Of course, another imperialist nation that had viewed marriage as a breeding ground was Nazi Germany; implicitly, Menzel's example invoked both a communist threat in
the present and the National Socialist example in the past. Both represented the horrifying inversion of a proper family policy, and both made
clear that families were not natural but rather were the creations of a
particular social order.

The CDU/CSU coalition rejected these criticisms. While admitting
that postwar Germany was a society in which many legitimate children
also might be denied a father, Süsterhenn maintained that "this is not
the normal state of affairs."[87] Putting legitimate and illegitimate children on the same legal footing threatened to do nothing less than "rev-
olutionize completely the existing social and bourgeois law and introduce absolute legal uncertainty in all these questions."[88] It was not the
job of lawmakers to determine "what the natural legal order should be
in the foreseeable future. . . . As lawmakers, we do not determine the
natural legal order; rather the order, naturally given to us and growing
out of nature, is prescribed for us lawmakers as well." Süsterhenn conceded that "in human history and in this and that cultural order, it is
possible to identify different conceptions of family," but the natural family invoked by Center, CDU, and CSU was that which existed "within
the framework of a Christian-occidental [*christlich-abendländische*] or
western cultural order [*Kulturordnung*], and in this order the family is
always conceived of as a self-contained unit."[89]

As Süsterhenn indicated, for the CDU/CSU the natural family, this
"self-contained unit," was a crucial part of a social order that was structuring itself in terms of a larger strategy of containment. Defining the
proper sort of family was essential to West Germany's identification
with a western order on political and economic as well as cultural
levels.[90] Demarcating the border around the "Christian-occidental"

family was part of the task of fixing boundaries between west and east. According to the conservative coalition, the SPD's proposals for recognizing the rights of illegitimate children came dangerously close to legal provisions in the Soviet zone, and it was absolutely essential that lawmakers in Bonn "consciously distance themselves from the east."[91]

Behind the CDU/CSU and Center pressure to ground a particular conception of the family in the Basic Law was yet another agenda—the extension of parental rights to include the determination of the religious orientation of schools and the appropriate training for public-school teachers. Like the emphasis on the fundamental natural rights of parents over their children, these demands had been set pieces of Center-party politics since the emergence of political Catholicism in the nineteenth century. However, the necessity of guaranteeing parental rights, explained Weber, was more self-evident than ever after the experience of the Third Reich, "which has increased our sense of responsibility in all such questions."[92] It was, Wessel reminded her colleagues, "National Socialism that, according to the words of Hitler, wanted to steal children from their parents for the good of the state."[93] Returning children to their proper place and preventing any similar state intervention in the future meant allowing parents to determine the denominational nature of the schools their children attended. On this issue, moreover, the conservative coalition claimed to bow to overwhelming pressure from church-based lay organizations.

The deadlock between the SPD and CDU/CSU over questions of how best to protect the family and ensure parental rights was ultimately broken by the FDP. Avoiding the question of what exactly constituted a family, Heuss agreed that this form of social organization deserved the state's guarantee of its integrity and inviolability. He also seconded SPD arguments that the *Frauenüberschuss* would create a situation in which women without husbands might nonetheless want to have children, and that those illegitimate children deserved the full protection of the law. The Basic Law must "realistically acknowledge this." Although initially concerned that a discussion of the family would involve the state in questions of "morality or tradition and biology," Heuss ultimately accepted bolstering the family as part of the "psychological" response of a generation that had experienced the "violation of family life under National Socialism."[94] Beyond this, guaranteeing the constitutional protection of the family was for Heuss a declaration with no specific content; it was a principle the FDP could support, but its significance was largely symbolic.

Heuss was outspoken, however, in his rejection of extending parental rights to the determination of a school's religious character; here, more than symbols were at stake. While he sympathized with the defensive reaction against the Nazi past "when children were forced into organizations," confessional schools violated the authority of individual state governments to set educational policy. Extending parental rights over schooling had origins not in nature but in the nineteenth-century struggle of political Catholicism to establish state-funded Catholic schools.[95] To no avail was Wessel's eleventh-hour plea that "no believing Christian, nor a true democrat" would understand rejection of this measure.[96]

Combined, the forces of the FDP and SPD could defeat the attempt to create the national basis for the introduction of confessional schools. Adenauer, president of the Parliamentary Council and head of the CDU/CSU delegation, counseled abandoning this lost cause lest the conservative coalition create an unbridgeable gap between itself and political liberals in other issues of "cultural politics" (*Kulturpolitik*).[97] Still, a handful of "believing Christians" and "true Democrats" of the CSU and the German party withheld their support from the ultimate ratification of the Basic Law on grounds that it failed adequately to underscore parental rights.[98]

Heuss and the FDP also favored strengthening the rights of illegitimate children. The forceful opposition of the CDU/CSU to such proposals led to a compromise, which promised *all* children the "same conditions for their bodily and spiritual development and their status in society" but left it to future lawmakers to determine precisely how this should be realized. While no one disputed that "every mother has a claim to the protection and care of the community," the Basic Law did not specify whether, together with their children, mothers who were not legally married were included among those families guaranteed the state's protection. The Parliamentary Council's venture into the definition of the cultural and social order thus set clear limits to attempts by political Catholicism to reopen the issue of confessional schools, but it also blocked Social Democratic attempts to expand definitions of the family.[99]

In its final form, the Basic Law prescribed where women belonged in a new Germany. On the one hand, they should be guaranteed full equal rights with men; on the other, they should be parts of families that would constitute the *Lebensraum* where a new political order would have its foundations. Much of the Parliamentary Council's discussion of women's status was rooted in Germany's past. Paragraph 2 of Article 3 represented a victory in a historical struggle of the bourgeois and Social Democratic women's movements dating back to the late nineteenth century, carried into the Weimar Republic, and derailed by the Nazis. Article 6 incorporated the Center party's long-standing emphasis on the family as society's most important building block, an ideological theme that also was not new in the postwar period.

However, discussions of equal rights and the protection of families did not simply represent the attempt to pick up where Germans had left off in 1933; in both instances the formulations of the Basic Law also represented reactions to Germany's most recent past, the legacy of war and National Socialism. The promise of equality marked an explicit acknowledgment of women's contribution to sustaining Germany during the war and postwar years. And Article 6 represented a response to the perceived threats to the family's stability presented by the Nazis, the *Frauenüberschuss,* and the uncertainty of the postwar world.

The family and women's status also clearly emerged as symbols of the distance between the two Germanys. Equality was not to be equated with a "mechanistic" leveling of difference, any more than the community of the family was to be confused with the collective of the East. Equality, properly understood, and families, properly constituted, explicitly set off some Germans from others. To be sure, West German perceptions had little to do with East German realities. The constitution of the German Democratic Republic, adopted in the same year as the Basic Law, emphasized women's full equality with men, and the Law for the Protection of Mothers and Children, passed a year later, cleared the ground for establishing a range of social services for working mothers, dramatically expanded the opportunities for married women's employment outside the home, mandated equal wages for women and men in the same jobs, and outlined affirmative-action programs to increase women's employment in jobs traditionally restricted to men. The policy of the Socialist Unity party, the ruling party in the East, was motivated by labor scarcities that necessitated mobilizing all available workers, but the party was also ideologically committed to the belief that women's entry into productive labor was essential for female emancipation. High rates of women's labor-force participation in the East, however, did not eliminate nuclear families or level sexual difference.[100] Families were still proclaimed as the fundamental building block of socialist society, and as long as there was no political pressure or explicit legal initiative to alter the sexual division of labor within the home, it was clear that raising the next generation would remain primarily women's work. Indeed, rather than attempting to reformulate the family, the earliest legislative initiatives in East Germany aimed at stabilizing it and underscored the state's responsibility to achieve this objective. No less than in the west, the family was to constitute a vital *Lebensraum*, though of a socialist, not a "Christian-occidental," variety.[101] But for West German politicians, glimpses of East German practice were filtered through the gathering clouds of the Cold War; in this context, it was impossible to see anything in the Soviet zone but the horrifying excesses of totalitarianism.

The debates over the Basic Law reflected that beyond this anticommunist consensus there was agreement across a broad political spectrum that restoring families would create the essential basis for establishing a stable social order. However, there was more than one vision of the form that families might take. The Parliamentary Council stopped short of establishing the Christian natural law foundation for a new Germany sought by Weber, Süsterhenn, Wessel and other representatives in the CDU/CSU and Center party. Early in 1950 the German bishops registered their displeasure that even within the CDU, "a true return to God has not taken place." No less than in the East, postwar West Germans indulged in a "practical materialism" that established economic progress as the only goal and that "seduced the contemporary mass of humanity simply to live it up and enjoy life to the limit."[102] Erhard's "social market economy" was in this world *and* of it. Reflecting more specifically on the work of the Parliamentary Council, Hermann von Mangoldt also regretted that the CDU/CSU had failed to establish marriage as the only "legally recognized form in which women and men live together," and he was troubled by a "certain reluctance to decisively reject extramarital [forms]."[103]

Both Mangoldt and the bishops could take heart, however, in the fact that by elevating marriage and the family to the status of prepolitical institutions the Parliamentary Council had resisted pressures to "get rid of monogamous marriage" and had ensured the moral alignment of West Germany with the "occidental [*abendländische*] world."[104] This was a clear victory for advocates of one view of a natural order, where families stood beyond history and politics, where women and men had unambiguous roles.

This Christian conception of the family prevailed over the alternative vision of the SPD, according to which nature changed over time, and laws and politics shaped families, not families the law and the political system. In the debates of the Parliamentary Council, Nadig, Selbert, Schmid, and others within the SPD had maintained that there was no timeless family nor prepolitical natural law. But demands from within the SPD for recognizing "mother-families," "an extraordinarily altered form of living together," and the rights of women to bear and raise children outside of marriage did not register in the Basic Law. For the majority, these aspects of social reality were symbols of disorder and disruption; they violated the natural order rather than restoring it.

In this losing battle, the SPD did not invoke those within its own tradition who had contributed significantly to the theoretical discussion of the family. When August Bebel's *Woman and Socialism* was cited in the debates of the Parliamentary Council, it was by one of the two KPD delegates, Heinz Renner, not by Social Democrats.[105] The SPD's general retreat from an analysis of the "woman question" grounded in Marxist classics and historical materialism had commenced during Weimar,[106] but the division of East and West accelerated the process. Marx, Engels, and Bebel were now *East* Germans; Social Democrats offered little challenge to SED claims to direct and exclusive lineage from the founders of German socialism.

Distanced from any variant of a Marxist alternative by Marxism's immediate association with the east, Social Democrats had difficulty answering the "woman question" in terms substantially different from those employed by bourgeois feminists. For Selbert, it was not wage work alone that would end women's subordinate status and dependence within families. Equality could also be achieved by recognizing that the unpaid labor of wives and mothers in the home was equivalent in value to the wage work of fathers and husbands. Women and men were different, difference was defined by social function, and acknowledging this difference need not impede the achievement of women's rights.

To be sure, the tension between notions of female equality and female difference, defined in terms of women's relationships to husbands, children, home, and hearth, was not new in postwar West Germany; at least since the late eighteenth century, it has fundamentally shaped all discussions of women's social and political status in Europe and North America.[107] However, the extensive treatment of women and the family in the debates over the Basic Law made explicit how much these themes were on the minds of postwar West Germans. In its final form, the Grundgesetz captured the conflicting images of women in the postwar period—of women's strength and achievements, on the one hand, and their vulnerability and need for protection within families, on the other. The Basic Law did not reconcile these visions; rather, it locked them into place. In 1949, it was not immediately apparent how these general prescriptions would translate into specific policies, but debates over the Basic Law indicated that descriptions of women's equality were inextricably tied to concerns about a mother's responsibilities and the family's future.

A comparison with the debate over equal rights for women in the post–World War II United States effectively illuminates the framework within which postwar West Germans attempted to reconcile the concept of equality with the concept of a distinct female nature. Immediately after the war, the United States Congress took up a proposed constitutional amendment that stated: "Equality of rights under the law shall not be denied or abridged by the United States, or by any State, on account of sex." In this context, feminist proponents of the amendment confronted a strong feminist opposition led by the Women's Bureau, a federal agency housed in the Department of Labor, which was solidly backed by trade unionists, the League of Women Voters, church groups, and the American Association of University Women. These opponents feared that equal rights would eliminate the protective legislation for women workers won by trade unionists. Demands for special treatment were linked to the acknowledgment that women were different because of their role as mothers; protection for women was linked to a commitment to protection for families.

Composed largely of well-educated middle- and upper-class women, the National Women's party had argued since the 1920s that all labor laws should apply equally to women and men or should be eliminated altogether. Every public activity open to men should also be open to women. Legislating special treatment created an image of women not only as different but also as vulnerable, needy, and dependent. After the war, advocates of equal rights could add that women's contribution to defeating fascism revealed how able women were to take on any task.

Although yeas outnumbered nays when the measure came to a vote, the Equal Rights Amendment did not win the two-thirds majority required for the Senate to approve a potential amendment to the United States constitution. In an uncomfortable alliance with probusiness Republicans and antilabor southern Democrats, some well-organized feminist activists succeeded in defeating a language of equal rights for women proposed by other well-organized feminist activists. The United States Congress was not ready to "amend motherhood," to repudiate a definition of sexual difference according to which women's equality with men would always be modified by their reproductive capacity.[108]

Three years later, an even stronger language of equal rights became part of the West German Basic Law, but not at the cost of amending motherhood. The feminist position that downplayed gender difference and emphasized the common humanity of women and men as the basis for women's equal rights did not exist in German feminism and did not emerge in the debates over the Basic Law. Transplanted into the politics of the postwar United States, Elisabeth Selbert doubtless would have joined the Women's Bureau and opponents of the ERA; the National Women's party represented precisely that brand of Anglo-American feminism from which Selbert relentlessly distanced herself. In a German context, she could champion an unequivocal language of women's rights while insisting that equality "acknowledge difference."

The Basic Law proclaimed that "men and women have the same rights," but it did not question that a woman's principal identity was as wife and mother. Rather, the Parliamentary Council's debates indicated that in the categories of West German politics, it was entirely possible, indeed essential, to protect motherhood while recognizing women's equality. The constitutional basis for a new political order identified the family and women's status as central concerns of the postwar era and structured the framework for the political discussion of those issues in the Federal Republic's first decade.

CHAPTER THREE

Legislating Women's Place

Dr. Dorothea Klaje, a secondary school teacher, had achieved a modest renown in the late forties with her proposal to the Parliamentary Council that it consider introducing a legally sanctioned matriarchal order, a "Mother-Family." Marriages, but not families, required adult men. By sanctioning female-headed households as a new form of family, the Parliamentary Council could bring legal prescription in line with social reality and offer a creative response to the postwar "surplus of women." "Every mother together with her children," argued Klaje, "constitutes a family." Such families should be supported by transfer payments from the state, financed out of additional taxes on single men and women and couples without children. The multiple burdens of wage work, child care, and domestic responsibilities might be managed more readily by two women living together, an arrangement that Klaje maintained was already a fact of life for many women and children. "In order to save our culture," Klaje reasoned, "it is necessary to change the laws of morality and to place motherhood firmly at the center." In a new Germany, "men must be ready to make sacrifices by giving up their role as head of the family." " 'Marriage' and 'family,' " Klaje argued, "must be completely redefined."[1]

Klaje's proposal—which combined reflections on postwar conditions and mystical visions of motherhood with feminist rhetoric that harked back more clearly to the pre–World War I ideas of Helene Stöcker's League for the Protection of Mothers (Bund für Mutterschutz) than to the Nazis, as some critics charged—received no hearing at deliberations

over the Basic Law. But her redefined family and her reflections on relations between women and men in the first postwar years did echo a
much broader debate that registered in the calls by Elisabeth Selbert and
Frieda Nadig to take seriously the new forms of social organization, including "mother-families," that had emerged in the postwar years and
in Carlo Schmid's insistence that families were defined by history and
politics, not natural law or divine order. The themes addressed by Klaje
also ran through the pages of women's magazines and were taken up in
the work of contemporary sociologists who pondered the future of marriage and the family in a Germany ravaged by the crises of the war, destruction, and defeat. The magazine *Women's World* announced with
"surprise and pleasure" its readers' response to the question, "Can marriage be saved?" The answer was a resounding yes, and unlike Klaje, neither the readers nor the magazine proposed that it was time for dramatic
alternatives to conventional forms. Still, the fact that the question was
so frequently posed belied the apparent conviction behind such responses and reflected the continued uncertainty over relations between
the genders in the years immediately following the end of the war.[2]

Unperturbed by her lack of influence on the final form of the Basic
Law, two years after its passage Klaje was once again ready to offer un-
solicited advice to the Ministry of Justice as it confronted the problems
of reforming family law to bring it into line with the new constitutional
guarantee of equal rights. Dramatically altered circumstances demanded bold new legal thinking, Klaje argued. "The immeasurably
great catastrophe of the Second World War completely destroyed the
German social order. . . . This offers us the unique opportunity to erect
the social order anew, and on a healthy foundation, not on the perver-
sions tied to tradition, which were part of historical development. For
tradition . . . has often become a curse for the Germans." Returning to
her favorite theme, Klaje applauded the collapse of the "father-family,"
an "outmoded and insupportable form" that had revealed its true nature in the "authoritarian male state," irrefutable evidence of what the
"patriarchy" could achieve. Private patriarchs were little better, and
Klaje maintained that the male sex drive, "a powerful, primeval force,"
did not translate into any natural inclination toward proper paternal
sentiments. Rather, only social pressure intervened to make a man into
a father; the move from "procreator" (*Erzeuger*) to father was a "creation" (*Erzeugnis*) of society. Klaje's recommendation remained the
same: radical reform of the Civil Code to include a legally sanctioned
"mother-family."[3]

Klaje influenced the Bundestag no more than she had the Parliamentary Council. More remarkable, however, is that by the early fifties not even muted variations on these themes resounded in women's magazines, sociological literature, or the halls of parliament.[4] The early years of the Federal Republic witnessed the emergence of a far-reaching consensus about what constituted families and what defined the relations of women and men, wives and husbands, mothers and fathers. Policymakers showed little of Klaje's optimistic enthusiasm to "erect the social order anew" and no longer were interested in even considering the alternative forms of "living together" advocated by Selbert and Nadig in the debates of the Parliamentary Council.

Defending the ideal of the stable nuclear family emerged as a particularly important political focus of the CDU/CSU coalition. As West German women and men neared the polls in the summer of 1949, Konrad Adenauer sought to confront voters with a single question: "Will Germany be governed in a Christian or a socialist fashion?"[5] For the CDU/CSU the choice between Christianity and socialism implied a choice between economic and social systems. It also implied a choice among alternative conceptions of the family. Trumpeting Christian values included advocating both a capitalist economic order and a reproductive order that predated politics and was dependent on no particular economic structure.

For the conservative coalition, the most readily available negative point of reference remained East Germany, where centralized planning was destroying the economy and where the rejection of Christian values and the unrestricted mobilization of women into wage labor was destroying families. Defining a postwar politics of the family took place against the backdrop of an intensifying Cold War that threatened to turn hot when United States forces confronted Communist Chinese and North Koreans in armed conflict in the early fifties. Discussions of the family continued to be an important arena for West German self-identification with the west in a world where the east-west gap appeared unbridgeable.

By claiming responsibility for advancing an economic agenda capable of bringing growth and prosperity, the CDU/CSU also presented itself as the political vehicle that would carry West Germans most rapidly away from the hard times and painful memories of the war and postwar crises. Returning to normalcy included forging the social order that would allow normal families to thrive and identifying "incomplete families" and "mother-families" as products of abnormal times, peculiar legacies of a past that would soon be left behind.

Social Democrats, the principal political opposition to the CDU/CSU, were hard-pressed to provide alternatives. While they continued to stress that democracy meant allowing women complete equality, they too held that given a choice of places to work, women would prefer the home. The SPD's continued defense of the interests of women whose wartime losses and postwar sufferings deserved particular recognition did not mean advocating alternative conceptions of the family. Increasingly in the rhetoric of Social Democrats, the adult woman who lived without an adult man was a "woman standing alone" (*alleinstehende Frau*), part of the *Frauenüberschuss:* a woman denied the chance to find a mate or a widowed mother in an "incomplete family," not a woman who might freely choose to live as part of a "mother-family."

The powerful ideological themes of Christian values, anticommunism, and the immutable and fundamental difference between women and men that made motherhood and housewifery women's natural obligations profoundly shaped the West German discussion of "woman's place" in the fifties, pushing to the margins visions like those outlined by Klaje and labeling as anomalous the millions of adult women who were not married. Such themes reinforced limits to visions of women's equality and underscored an agenda for reestablishing the "normal family"—always understood to be two married adults with at least two children—threatened by the crises of the war and postwar period.

How these forces combined was elaborately illustrated in the parliament's efforts to legislate women's rights, responsibilities, and obligations in those parts of the Civil Code regulating relations between husbands and wives, and parents and children. The constitution had allowed lawmakers three-and-one-half years to carry out those legal reforms needed to realize Paragraph 2 of Article 3, the promise of women's equal rights; it specified that if the job was not done by 31 March 1953, then all laws that were inconsistent with the promise of equality would lose their power overnight, leaving to the determination of the courts whatever parliament might have failed to lay out in black and white. The drafters of the Basic Law were aware that an unrestricted language of equal rights would necessitate far-reaching reforms. Indeed, the enormity of this task was a principal argument against incorporating this language into the constitution. However, the victory of Selbert and the SPD ensured that many laws, particularly those regulating marriage in the Bürgerliches Gesetzbuch, would not survive unchanged. Democracy and equality could not end on the front stoop, though exactly how they would be brought into the home was a question left open by the Parliamentary Council.

In Germany's codified legal tradition, the executive and legislature, not judges, bore responsibility for defining the law to the fullest extent possible. For the first time in the history of German jurisprudence, the Basic Law instituted a Constitutional Court (Bundesverfassungsgericht), an agent of judicial review empowered to determine whether laws violated the Grundgesetz. This marked a definitive break with a legal tradition in which judges theoretically enforced but did not make or interpret the law, though the authority of the new national court extended only to determining the constitutionality of laws. After 1949 as before, it was primarily up to lawmakers to specify the law and up to judges to apply it, in sharp contrast with the Anglo-American case-law tradition, in which courts and judges joined, indeed sometimes led, legislators in defining normative practice and determining how laws limited the state.[6]

Contrasting German legal practice with the common-law tradition in England is revealing. Feminist legal historians have analyzed the *unwritten* marriage contract in English law of the fifties, which defined the home as a wife's most important workplace.[7] This was never made explicit in the law, but reading between the lines reveals that this was the intention of the courts and the legislature. In the debates over reforming German family law, it is possible to read the lines themselves to determine where legislators and legal experts believed that wives should be employed. It was the responsibility of the legislative and executive branches to leave as little as possible to the imagination of lawyers and judges and, for that matter, of West German citizens.

On Sunday, 14 August 1949, West Germans freely chose their national political representatives for the first time in more than sixteen years. For 402 seats in the Bundestag, voters chose candidates from among sixteen parties. The campaign did not want for dirty tricks; from both of the leading parties, the CDU/CSU and SPD, politicians hurled mud at each other. In Adenauer's speeches, Social Democrats appeared as "fanatics," virtual agents of the forces of occupation, while Kurt Schumacher, head of the SPD, charged that Adenauer's strong ties to the Catholic clergy would leave West Germany under the control of a "fifth occupation force," the papacy. Schumacher's anticlerical excesses only made it easier for Adenauer to claim that the CDU/CSU was the protector of Christian interests and institutions, including the family.[8]

Because the ballots were counted by hand, it took more than a day for voters to learn the collective consequences of their individual decisions. Slightly less than 80 percent of eligible voters went to the polls, lower than the average of the last Weimar elections but impressive given the claims of widespread political apathy among West Germans only a little over four years after the end of the war. With 31 percent of the popular vote, the CDU/CSU enjoyed a slim margin over the SPD, winning 139 of the seats in the Bundestag compared with the SPD's 131. Communists controlled only 15 seats, the conservative German party, 17. The FDP continued to tip the balance, as it had in the Parliamentary Council; its 11.9 percent of the vote gave it 52 votes in the Bundestag. What seats remained were distributed among a handful of special interest and regional political groupings.[9]

The electoral propaganda of all political parties directly addressed women, the *Frauenüberschuss,* and the "incomplete family"; all promised a better future, whether through "peace, freedom, and justice" or through protection from menacing forces coming from the east (figs. 14–21). As they had in the Weimar Republic, women gave their votes to conservative parties in numbers greater than men. The CDU/CSU also benefited from its status as heir to large parts of the Center party constituency; in Weimar, the Center had always relied heavily on a female electorate, and the correlation between practicing Catholics and voters for the CDU/CSU was particularly high for women. In the predominantly Catholic parts of Rheinland-Pfalz, for example, as many as 30 to 50 percent more women than men voted for Christian Democrats. Even in Protestant areas like Schleswig-Holstein, the differences were significant. This gender gap, exaggerated by the *Frauenüberschuss,* which had resulted in more eligible female than male voters, meant that the CDU/CSU's political margin depended on women's votes despite a rate of electoral participation slightly lower for women than for men.[10]

Reflecting on this gender-specific behavior at the SPD's annual party congress in 1950, Herta Gotthelf blamed the German cardinals for abusing their privileged position in the pulpit. They had created an "eleventh commandment that says: Thou shalt vote CDU." This clerical partisanship represented "one of the saddest chapters of postwar German politics," the "misuse of Christianity by a reactionary, backward party."[11] Gotthelf condemned a new variety of *Kulturkampf*—not a Protestant Prussian state's attack on Catholicism, but the CDU's dire prognosis on the eve of the election that unless the coalition emerged triumphant, "Christianity is in danger."[12] Her frustration over the results notwithstanding, Germans' electoral behavior in 1949 revealed remarkable continuities with how they had voted in the interwar period. Women and men alike selected their political representatives following lines that stretched well back into the twenties and remained largely unaltered.[13]

Despite their direct appeals to women voters, no major political party included large numbers of women in its Bundestag delegation. Over the protestations of their female membership, male-dominated party structures apparently remained convinced that they were able to be effective advocates for both genders. A total of twenty-nine women, proportionately only a small increase over the representation of women in the Parliamentary Council, entered the first Bundestag, including thirteen Social Democrats, eleven representatives from the conservative coalition, and two from the FDP.[14]

At least in part because of the SPD's stance on "cultural questions," Adenauer rejected the counsel of those within his own party who argued for a broad-based coalition government extending leftward. "One need only consider their position on questions of the family, marriage, and the school in the Parliamentary Council," Adenauer elaborated, in order to realize that on these issues, Social Democrats were "our deadly enemy."[15] In response to a political ally who advocated bringing Social Democrats into the government, Adenauer fumed that their position on the Basic Law revealed that the party was "completely [and] officially against marriage and the family, which they labeled as 'outdated institutions.'"[16] Ultimately, Adenauer forced through his own conception of a union that included the FDP and looked to the right toward the German party to ensure a narrow parliamentary majority. It was this coalition that elected the seventy-three-year-old former mayor of Cologne as the Federal Republic's first chancellor and that took up the Basic Law's mandate to realize women's equality.

Addressing the national professional association of German lawyers (Juristentag) in 1950, Theanolte Bähnisch pointed to the "huge gap between law and reality that has developed concerning the differential treatment of man and woman." It was the job of the Bundestag to close this gap: "The law should not precede reality; rather, the reality that has emerged should make its mark in the law."[17] Bähnisch's postwar reality was at odds with the law because in her view German society had been totally restructured by the social and economic impact of two world wars; nowhere was this more apparent than in relations between the sexes. The war had also meant the loss of her husband, a Social Democrat who, relieved of his post as a district administrator (*Landrat*) in 1933 for political reasons and drafted into Hitler's army, had been missing in action in the east since 1943. The mother of two children, Bähnisch could speak from firsthand experience about the consequences of the war for women.[18]

At the war's end, Bähnisch had decided that women's equality should be pursued in organizations outside the SPD. A high-ranking government official in the state of Lower Saxony, she won the ire, disbelief, and disdain of her political comrades because of her key role in creating "women's councils above the parties" and a national umbrella group for all West German women's organizations after the war.[19] Her willingness to cross class and political boundaries in pursuit of women's rights was no less apparent in 1950 as she stood before a decidedly nonsocialist gathering, the Juristentag.

Bähnisch's theme, the need for thoroughgoing reform of German family law, took center stage in the first postwar meeting of this national organization. Not surprisingly, those whose primary business was the law claimed particular authority as to the best way to proceed. Their opinion was especially weighty, because in Germany lawyers had historically played an important role in politics. Lawyers also enjoyed high social status and influence because of the number of upper-level civil service positions for which a law degree was a prerequisite.[20]

Bähnisch described how in and after the war women had been called upon to shoulder responsibilities at the workplace and in public life with the consequence that women now stood in a totally altered relationship to men. "She cannot take off this newly won independence like a work coat (*Arbeitskittel*); it is impossible to undo a development once it has taken place." This, concluded Bähnisch, was the unequivocal message of the Grundgesetz; it established a clear agenda for the executive and legislature as they approached the task of establishing the bases for women's equality and for bringing the law into line with reality.[21]

Those West Germans engaged in discussions of how to meet this agenda in the fifties could all accept Bähnisch's assessment of the necessity for change. However, prescriptions of what reforms were essential varied according to different experiences of the gap between reality and the law and different conceptions of how to balance the needs of families, the rights of women, and the responsibilities of wives and mothers. Even before the Civil Code appeared on the Bundestag's agenda, it became apparent that certain visions of what was essential for guaranteeing women's equality with men would not appear in the final version of the law.

For example, some feminist lawyers and judges argued that equality for women should include the right for a married couple to choose the wife's name or to attach their names with a hyphen, rather than automatically taking on the husband's name. Erna Scheffler, who in 1951 became the first female justice on the Federal Constitutional Court, objected to a legal order that led to privileging the birth of a newborn male heir (*Stammhalter*) over that of a daughter. Airing these views to the same audience of legal practitioners addressed by Bähnisch, she ridiculed men's resistance to any changes that would threaten their "honest, good name." Years later, Scheffler still had vivid memories of her male colleagues' emotional, negative reaction to this idea, which she attributed to the "patriarchal attitudes, not to mention male vanity," that had yet to be overcome in the postwar world.[22]

Denying charges of any patriarchal prejudice, one opponent of Scheffler's proposal claimed it would create enormous confusion when the "grandfather is called 'Krause,' the son, 'Müller,' and the grandson, 'Schulze.' " This "zig-zag possibility" undermined family tradition and threatened the very concept of the family.[23] The national Council of the Protestant Church warned that experience with this practice in "Soviet-Russian law" indicated that it made families "anonymous," "leveling and ultimately dissolving human existence."[24] The proposal of a hyphenated last name was ultimately rejected by the Ministry of Justice and Adenauer's cabinet, with the argument that a single name testified to the union of husband and wife and conformed to the need for order. With no irony intended, they maintained that this did not represent patriarchal privilege, only conformity with German tradition. At most, wives, not husbands, could use hyphenated last names, and children would all carry the name of the father.[25]

Attempts to expand discussions of women's equal rights to include women's job opportunities were also met with little enthusiasm. In the earliest parliamentary discussions over the meaning of women's equality, Helene Weber and Margot Kalinke, a German party representative and cofounder of the Association of Female Salaried Employees, joined Social Democrats in calling for measures to expand women's participation in all civil-service positions and at the highest levels of the state. However, Weber's insistence that this was essential because "we experienced what constitutes the male state in the Third Reich" brought only derision from her colleagues. CDU Interior Minister Robert Lehr countered that "not only men have bellicose qualities, rather there are many representatives of a temperamental and aggressive [nature] among the female sex as well." Kalinke's call for using discussions of women's equality to move beyond the reform of marriage law to include a thorough consideration of the needs of working women in the areas of social insurance, housing, and occupational training also received no serious hearing and remained at the level of rhetorical exhortation.[26]

KPD proposals for guaranteeing equal wages for equal work as the essential economic basis for true equality were also brushed aside. Communists, a marginal presence in the Bundestag, were alone in arguing that reforming family law could not be isolated from regulating the paid workplace where "hundreds of thousands of women engaged in wage work provide for a family and work under decidedly worse conditions than men." Social Democrats accepted the KPD's assessment that because of the "structural change in the population after two world wars . . . and the entire state of economic development, women's work cannot be eliminated from society,"[27] but they refused to support the KPD in linking parliamentary discussions of the marriage contract to the wage contract. Rather, the SPD maintained that women's rights in the workplace were already guaranteed by the Basic Law's prohibition of all forms of discrimination. Determining the particulars was the task of organized capital and labor, the "social partners," not the legislature.

With no greater success, some Catholic lay organizations attempted to expand the dimensions of family law debates, though in very different directions. In particular, they proposed elimination of obligatory civil marriage for those also married in the church, a measure first introduced by Bismarck in 1873 as part of his attempt to win support among political liberals for the newly unified German Empire. In terms that were as old as the measure itself, some Catholics opposed civil marriage as an "intervention into the freedom of conscience of Christians, an involvement by the state in the realm of conscience and the Church."[28] They also sought a revision of the Nazi reform of the divorce law that allowed "marital disintegration" (*Ehezerrüttung*)—a designation open to elastic interpretation by the courts—as legitimate grounds for divorce. This law had been left in place by the Allies, and some Catholic organizations charged that it amplified the wave of postwar divorce. But conservative Catholics did not find support in the Bundestag for their particular concerns. Even those within the CDU/CSU who lobbied hardest for

Catholic interests conceded that insisting on such controversial measures would hopelessly complicate reform discussions; all issues not immediately affected by the equal-rights language of the Basic Law should
be postponed to a later date.[29]

Leaving aside the demands of those who sought to expand the boundaries of legal action to achieve women's equality and the proposals of
conservatives who sought to turn back the clock to the 1870s, the Bundestag restricted its discussion of how best to realize Article 3 to a discussion of the provisions of the Civil Code governing marriage and the
family. Addressing the lawyers' congress in 1950, Erna Scheffler expressed the consensus view that "with regard to the unmarried woman,
no changes in the law are necessary in order to realize the fundamental
principle of equal rights. Only the married woman is still in many decisive ways disadvantaged by the law."[30] The single woman was free to
defend her own rights in the "social market economy"; married women
were part of a different social organization, regulated by different laws,
and those laws were in need of reform. Ultimately, it was on this single
dimension of postwar reality that debates over women's equality
focused.[31]

There was general agreement that any reform of marriage law would
necessitate a revision of provisions regulating the control of property
within marriage and the division of property should a marriage end in
divorce. No one questioned that the Bürgerliches Gesetzbuch had discriminated against wives. A wife's equality within marriage made it essential that she have equal claims to property should the marriage end,
whether she had worked for wages outside the home or had toiled only
in an unpaid domestic workplace. Women who were "only housewives"
(*nur Hausfrauen*) deserved particular consideration and compensation
for their unpaid household labor.[32]

With few exceptions, those involved in discussions of family-law reform accepted that other provisions of the Civil Code were also patently
at odds with the Basic Law's mandate. Allowing a husband to invoke
court intervention to terminate his wife's contractual agreements, including employment outside the home, was one such undeniably patriarchal principle that violated any notion of a wife's equality in marriage.
Consensus also extended to the reformulation of wives' and husbands'
responsibilities for the economic maintenance of the family. The Civil
Code specified that under normal circumstances a husband was responsible for providing financially for his wife and family. Advocates of reform argued that if women and men were equal, then a wife and husband should both be liable for the financial security of the family.

However, in most cases it was taken for granted that a wife's principal contribution to the family would be her non-wage work in the household. Indeed, this conception was underscored by equating the economic value of unpaid household labor with income earned from work done for wages outside the home.

Social Democrats, the FDP, and the conservative CDU/CSU coalition all accepted this conception of the normal sexual division of labor within the family, though for different reasons. Echoing Selbert's position in debates over the Basic Law, Herta Gotthelf stressed that socialists' demands for equality for women should not be confused with the demands of "the old women's righters, who believed that it would suffice to be taken seriously if one behaved like a man." Gotthelf emphasized that her position was not an admission that women were "less bright or less capable of dealing with life"; the postwar years testified amply to women's capacities to preserve and sustain society.[33] But recognizing difference justified gender-specific rights and responsibilities in marriage.

A Social Democratic legal expert, Nora Platiel, explained that socialists subscribed to "the functional division [of labor] in the family, for which the image is often used of the husband as the 'head' and the wife as the 'heart' of the organism."[34] At least in principle, the "head" might stay at home while the "heart" went out to work; in theory, housework was the equivalent of wage work regardless of which spouse did which. But even women within the SPD saw this as an extraordinary situation. Married women might be compelled to work for wages out of economic necessity, but if they were mothers, they should avoid employment outside the home if at all possible.

Social Democrats along with some bourgeois feminists did question how far the law should go in detailing the specifics of wifely responsibility and questioned the double standard that explicitly defined a wife's job but not a husband's. Each couple should be allowed to divide up tasks in its marriage as it saw fit, without reference to any legal prescription. Such flexibility was even more essential in a postwar world where increasing numbers of women—often married to men disabled by the war—were entering the labor force, and husbands might well be expected to shoulder at least some responsibilities in the home.[35] The SPD's Jeanette Wolff stressed that the romantic vision of "secure family circumstances" must give way to the "reality of the division of labor between husband and wife," and the fact that "in 85 to 90 percent of the cases, women were forced out to work, because there is simply no alternative."[36]

Adolf Arndt, a lawyer and SPD representative to the Bundestag from Hessen, questioned the "preconception—regrettably widespread in Germany—that it's the obligation of the wife to make the beds, clean the boots, go shopping, take the children out for walks and similar things, and that these are of no concern to the husband." In a society of equals, argued Arndt, the "husband should make his own bed too, clean shoes and push the baby buggy, carry the shopping bag when his wife goes to market and see to it that the potatoes get washed and peeled."[37]

However, there was no disagreement among Social Democrats that even if husbands might carry the shopping bag, wives were the ones who should plan the menus, do the marketing, cook, and look after children. It was increasingly apparent that for Social Democrats, the wage-earning woman should be childless; ideally, the "working mother" (*erwerbstätige Mutter*) would not exist. "If society will provide the material security for the family," argued Emmy Meyer-Laule, who identified herself as a "housewife"—whose house had been searched by the Gestapo in the thirties—"then many women would gladly return to the occupation of motherhood as their essential, though not their only, social task."[38] Although the SPD conceded that in the postwar world, choices might not exist for those mothers forced out to work by economic necessity, it subscribed to a vision of motherhood and housewifery as a woman's highest calling, thereby distancing Social Democrats from Communist recommendations that working mothers—supported by a network of social services—should become the rule, not the exception. In its official party platform, the SPD specified that its goal was "an economic order in which no mother of preschool- or school-aged children should be forced out to work because of economic need."[39] This theme was emphasized repeatedly in the official pronouncements of the party and its women's organizations: Stable families and children's welfare were best secured by adequate male wages, not by more work for mother. Social Democrats accepted that the most effective way to acknowledge a mother's work was not to urge men to clean shoes, push prams, and peel potatoes but to recognize that these wifely tasks were the equivalent of the work that fathers did outside the home for wages, different but in no way worth less.

The CDU/CSU did not question this definition of women's and men's work. The valuation of women's unpaid labor as housewives and mothers was acknowledged as the essential basis for women's claims to property within marriage. But particularly for those in the Catholic conservative camp who were outspoken in debates over family-law reform, the difference between women and men within marriage lay not in a socially defined functional division of labor, but in an immutable natural order that was solidly grounded in religious doctrine.

As they had in debates over the Basic Law, Catholic bishops weighed in with particular authority on this point and claimed direct access to the proper scriptural understanding of female-male relations. They also insisted that the constitution's guarantee of the family's protection necessitated limiting demands for equality when they threatened the stability of marriage. From this perspective, marriage was not a legal institution but a Christian sacrament. Rights within marriage were subject to an order outside the state's control; measures deemed essential to preserve this institution included defining distinct tasks for husbands and wives and specifying women's responsibilities in the Civil Code.

From the highest ranks of the Catholic church came warnings that an "individualist or liberal perspective" on marriage reform might bring West Germans dangerously close to the "radical changes that certain states with materialistically oriented governments have undertaken in the area of family law." To the Federal Republic's east, economic expansion was achieved by robbing the family of its spiritual essence. A failure to designate the home as women's primary workplace would "prepare the way to the collective."[40] Helene Weber underscored the intersection of "individualism," "materialism," and the "collective," and condemned those "intellectual circles" calling for a woman's rights as an individual while forgetting that similar tendencies "in the Russian Revolution had led to a complete dissolution of marriage and family."[41] Even though laws must be adjusted to accommodate changes in social conditions, some realities were unchanging and of a higher order.

Those within the CDU/CSU who relied less exclusively on the primacy of scriptural mandates still unquestioningly accepted the principle of strengthening the family by emphasizing a woman's role as wife and mother. Luise Rehling, a middle-class activist for women's rights within the CDU, endorsed her party's position that "according to a Christian view, the family is a preordained institution, a community into which man and woman enter but which they cannot control." More than a spiritual order was at stake, however, and Rehling also pointed to the more worldly context of postwar reconstruction. The mother of three children, she came to Bonn from Bochum, and her own experience made her aware of the difficulties of juggling professional and familial responsibilities.[42] Doubtless this informed her opinion that the postwar "crisis of the family was simultaneously a crisis of the entire community that had the greatest effect on young people." Surely it was no coincidence, Rehling maintained, that "criminologists are always confirming that 90 percent of criminal youths come out of destroyed homes."[43]

Rehling admitted that times had changed; women's wage work was a twentieth-century reality that could not be legislated out of existence. In addition, women's work in two world wars provided ample evidence that they were "in no respect the inferior of men in the material and spiritual maintenance of the existence of the family and nation [*Volk*]." But she also warned that the lesson to be drawn from this experience was not that implemented in the East, where freeing women from obligations to marriage and family was motivated by the completely instrumental objective of pushing married women into wage labor. Rather, it was essential that women's wage work be "limited by her obligation to work for the family, because we do not wish to see the double burden as the norm and in addition because we are aware of the significance for *Volk* and state of those tasks that a mother fulfills at home through the education of her children."[44]

Rehling's CDU colleague in the Bundestag, Eduard Wahl, a professor of law, also explicitly placed the discussion of women's work in the categories of the Cold War. Perhaps it was his area of specialization, comparative civil law, that led him to locate Germany at the "ideological intersection" of forces coming from west and east; he left no doubt that he opted for the "western solution" in questions of marriage and the family. Wahl claimed to defend a married woman's right to choose, a right robbed from women in East Germany in the name of equality. By pointing to an "obligation to work" (*Arbeitsdienstpflicht*) in the East, Wahl also implicitly invoked the measures introduced under the National Socialists in their attempt to mobilize women and men for total war. The consequence for women was that "they must enter the mines or the military," a "Russian conception" that violated German traditions.[45]

The majority of the conservative coalition conceded that it would be unconstitutional to bar mothers from working outside the home. This was one message learned from the overwhelming Free and Social Democratic rejection of die-hard attempts by Helene Weber and others to incorporate into the final version of a reformed civil-service law provisions forbidding the employment by the state of married women who were adequately supported by a male wage. By a wide margin, the Bundestag judged calls for such provisions, reminiscent of Nazi laws against so-called *Doppelverdiener* and the Nazi exclusion of women from many areas of state employment, to be at odds with constitutional guarantees of women's equal rights.[46] However, the CDU/CSU left little doubt about which obligations for mothers and which rights for fathers should be grounded in a new family law. It was the state's responsibility, explained Wilhelm Poetter, a Rhenish member of the CDU and a government adviser, "morally and with its legal initiatives, to provide a foundation for the normal case [where] the husband is in a position to guarantee his family with a dignified existence. That is a problem for the long term. War and postwar conditions have all but destroyed this normal picture making it nearly unrecognizable." Acknowledging this changed postwar reality was the first step toward bringing the "normal picture" back into view.[47]

To these strains, the FDP added the voices of a forceful feminist caucus that seconded many positions put forward by Social Democrats and pushed for a broad definition of women's equality within marriage. Often representing the views of middle-class women's professional organizations and feminist legal experts, women within the FDP lobbied for a wife's unrestricted right to pursue all occupations and warned against explicitly defining women's obligations in the home without also prescribing in detail the familial roles of fathers and husbands.[48] But the FDP also encompassed viewpoints such as that expressed by August-Martin Euler, a lawyer and head of the regional party in Hessen, who argued that equality must be narrowly circumscribed because a "formal equality of rights between man and woman would lead to permitting women to be pistol-packing mamas (*Pistolenweiber*), to work in the mines, and to carry out the most difficult tasks in the steel mills."[49]

On questions of family-law reform, the Free Democrats' most influential spokesman was Thomas Dehler, the Bavarian who entered Adenauer's coalition cabinet as justice minister and who had counseled caution and patience when the Parliamentary Council had debated equal rights for women. Now responsible for overseeing the government's draft of family-law reform proposals, Dehler was sensitive to his party's allergic response to all signs of clerical influence on the CDU/CSU and could not easily deny feminist pressures within Free Democratic ranks.

Via these different ideological and rhetorical paths, the conservative coalition, Social Democrats, the FDP, and Adenauer's cabinet converged on definitions of women's non-wage work and the limitations to women's work outside the home imposed by the responsibilities of housewifery and motherhood. In the language of the draft law, a wife should be "entitled to work for wages insofar as this work can be reconciled with her obligations to marriage and family." As the government's justification elaborated: "She must run the household and devote herself to the children's education. No employment outside the home should endanger the fulfillment of this primary task."[50]

Presenting this position in the Bundestag, Dehler explained that though a wife might be forced to go out to work in exceptional cases, it was through her unpaid labor that she would typically fulfill her familial responsibilities.[51] This work was of vital economic importance, but it also embodied a specifically female set of priorities and values that could not be measured in strictly economic terms. No one in the Bundestag disagreed. Whether defined by society or scripture, mandated by the "crisis of the family," or part of a West German defense against "Russian conceptions," in debates over a revised family law the political discussion of women's work remained firmly tied to conceptions of difference grounded in a specific sexual division of labor.

Parliamentary consensus disintegrated not over definitions of mothers' responsibilities and obligations to the family but over how best to resolve disputes between husbands and wives. Who should settle irreconcilable arguments between marriage partners and between parents over children's welfare? Who had the final say when compromise was impossible? The Civil Code had an easy answer: In the case of conflict, husbands and fathers had the last word. Although this provision was rarely invoked in divorce cases,[52] it took on enormous symbolic significance because it so stunningly communicated the patriarchal foundations of the Civil Code.

From the earliest discussions of family law reform, the SPD, KPD, non-aligned middle-class women's groups, and most female representatives of the CDU/CSU, FDP, and the German party left no doubt that they believed such remnants of explicit, patriarchal authority were unconstitutional. Equality and individual rights could not be subordinated to the needs of any institution, not the state, not the family. Indeed, the only families that deserved the state's protection were those constructed on the solid basis of the equality of husband and wife. Arrayed against these forces were the Catholic Church, the overwhelming majority of delegates from the CDU/CSU, and most of Adenauer's cabinet. Invoking biblical authority, beginning with Eve's subordination to Adam, reiterating papal pronouncements about the sacramental nature of the family, and underscoring that order ensured stable marriages, they argued in favor of a necessary natural hierarchy that no mandated equality could alter.

The draft law pushed forward to Adenauer's cabinet by the Justice Ministry attempted to steer a middle course between these sharply opposing camps. Dehler insisted that a husband's authority to override his wife's opinion in issues concerning their relationship clearly undermined the principle of equal rights. Not even scriptural authority justified violating the constitution. But he still supported a father's final authority in matters involving children, a measure he deemed necessary to realize the Basic Law's Article 6, the constitutional guarantee of the family's protection. Families without the means to resolve potentially irreconcilable differences between parents left children at risk.[53]

Dehler's attempt at compromise satisfied no one. In its official response to the government's proposals, the national umbrella organization for the middle-class women's movement, the German Women's Ring, headed by Bähnisch, rejected all restrictions of married women's authority as unconstitutional and countered clerical arguments by contending that "patriarchy as such is not Christian." Indeed, its origins lay not in the Christian tradition but rather "with non-Christian nations (Japan, India, in the Orient)." Christianity had failed to conquer the "raw patriarchy" of these older nations, but surely the Bundestag need not repeat the error by "neglecting a wife's personality and sphere of natural rights." Wasting no rhetorical fury, the position paper concluded that the "government's draft contradicts the legal conception of the entire civilized world." It would permit every husband to prevent his wife from participating in political life. Opposing the draft statement was essential to guarantee that "the struggle for democracy in Germany will not be lost a second time."[54]

The national women's caucus of the CDU unanimously called for the equal rights of mothers and wives with husbands and fathers and was no more sympathetic to the government's position. Precisely because fathers were more likely to go off to work, mothers who stayed at home were in the best position to judge a child's needs; their competence and expertise should be unrestricted in all matters affecting children's welfare.[55]

Protestant women's organizations joined in this chorus of outrage and criticism. Dismissing the scriptural arguments cited by the CDU/CSU, the umbrella organization for women's associations within the

Protestant Church, Protestant Women's Work in Germany, countered
that Eve's lesson in Eden was that sin had consequences, not that she
must submit to Adam's will. Confronting exegesis with exegesis, this
group of women argued that the Ten Commandments ordered children
to honor their parents, not just their fathers. Nor was Paul's exhortation
to the Ephesians that wives obey their husbands necessarily the best advice for West Germans in the fifties.[56]

As during the Parliamentary Council's debates over women's rights,
outraged individuals added their opinions. One woman took the time to
inform the justice minister that "it is of course understandable that the
old men [in the government] are unwilling to divorce themselves from
the male privilege that has been entrusted to them since infancy. But it
is nonetheless embarrassing when the government of an otherwise
highly developed, if politically inept, nation doesn't have the courage to
say openly, 'we don't want any equality.' " For her, the government's
draft represented nothing less than a breach of the constitution, a precedent with ominous implications.[57] Melitta Schöpf, a member of the
FDP, angrily lectured Dehler that offering women rights to run the
household while allowing husbands ultimate authority was a pathetic
attempt to "hang a little coat around the naked fact of clubbing wom-
en's will, so that it needn't look so ugly." What did such an acknowledgment of women's rights amount to, she asked? "Perhaps in the
wife's independent judgment of whether to cook cabbage or turnips for
lunch, whether to wash the floor or paint it, whether the child should
wear a blue or a red sweater? Do you honestly hope that for such things
a woman of normal intelligence will give the man the last word?"[58]

For defenders of a legally grounded patriarchal order, this question
was not rhetorical. Leading the charge from within the CDU was Helene
Weber, who maintained that "only a few lawyers" from the "circles of
outspoken women's righters" confronted "millions of Catholic women"
who wanted no abrogation of the rights of fathers and husbands. Weber
picked up where she had left off in the debates over the Basic Law, insisting that "simple, uneducated women do not demand equality in marriage, rather this was exclusively the concern of intellectual, professional
women, some of whom demanded an equality of the sexes, which allowed for no exceptions."[59]

Catholic jurists also provided detailed analyses of the scriptural and
legal bases for patriarchal authority within marriage. Among the most
prolific and influential was F. W. Bosch, who was well known in the Justice Ministry as an advocate for the abolition of obligatory civil mar-

riage and a "representative of the Catholic-theological standpoint that the husband is the head of the family."[60] Bosch categorically rejected the "cry for absolute equality," calling instead for "an organic solution, no revolution, but a new order—a legal order that corresponds to the age-old natural law that Christ confirmed, and that Paul . . . and the teachings of the church have repeatedly expressed." For Bosch, demands for complete equality were "nothing other than heresy."[61] Realizing equality was not simply a legal problem, it was also a theological problem. The Grundgesetz could not justify violating another "Grundgesetz," that of Pius XI and his 1930 encyclical on the family, in which "marriage and the family were designated as granted and invested with authority by God himself." Potentially more important than the government's negotiations to reintegrate West Germany politically and militarily into the western alliance, Bosch argued, were measures to reintegrate the German family into the "occidental Christian" community; this project had the full support of the silent majority of "women and men in Germany who deny that the endangerment or even the destruction of marriage and the family could be accomplished with legal norms."[62]

Protestant and Catholic leaders, including Bosch and Wilhelm Böhler, who represented the Fulda Conference of Bishops and the archbishop of Cologne, Josef Frings, summarized their opposition to Dehler's draft at a meeting with him and other Justice Ministry officials in April 1952. Although national Protestant leaders accepted that a husband's final say over a wife was inconsistent with women's equality, they agreed with their Catholic counterparts that when children's welfare was at stake, the Basic Law's Article 6 took precedence. Catholic leaders went even further to question explicit language that acknowledged a woman's right to work outside the home, insisting that marriage should be subject to higher laws. A husband was entitled to be the enforcer, to assess whether a wife was adequately performing her household responsibilities, restricting her work for wages when necessary. Eliminating such safeguards only "supported efforts to draw the wife and mother out of the home" and threatened to reproduce tendencies that they observed in America, where "the family is severely endangered because of women's occupational activity."[63]

If the church fathers were disappointed by Adenauer's willingness to compromise on questions of parental authority in the Basic Law, they could applaud his support for maintaining patriarchal authority in a revised Civil Code. In responding to Dehler's draft, the chancellor accepted arguments that husbands and wives must subordinate individual

interests for the good of the relationship formed out of their union. This
in turn required establishing a court of last resort in cases of serious disagreement. The husband should be judge and jury. In the words of
Adenauer's chief adviser on reform proposals, Hermann Spieler, it
was essential that "the man, as it were, should have the last word. If
in these sorts of cases [of conflict], the binding nature of the husband's
decision can be called into question by a hard-nosed wife . . . then, in
my opinion, that would achieve the opposite of what should be
accomplished."[64] Adopting this formulation virtually unaltered, a hard-
nosed chancellor added, "Just as the mother fundamentally has to subordinate herself to the father, so should the wife also be expected to do
the same in relation to the husband."[65]

Echoing the language of church leaders, Adenauer emphasized that to
violate the principle of patriarchal authority was to threaten the stability
of the family; protecting the family took precedence over women's
claims to equal rights. Adenauer's agreement with the bishops went even
further, and he questioned proposals for the elimination of a husband's
prerogative to end his wife's contractual wage relationship; surely, "the
household and the education of the children would suffer" from such
innovations.[66] Over protest from Dehler, other cabinet officials, and a
majority of the members of the Federal Council (Bundesrat), the body
that represented the interests of individual state governments at the national level, this "patriarch at the head of the state"[67] exercised his own
brand of paternal authority, rejecting the Justice Ministry's draft and insisting on a version that maintained the ultimate rights of husbands over
wives.[68]

By taking a giant step backward from the point reached in two years
of preliminary discussion of laws regulating family relations, Adenauer
provoked the protest of his own justice minister, women's organizations
across the political spectrum, and Social Democrats, precipitating the
collapse of parliamentary discussions around reform. The four months
granted the Bundestag to debate the government's final proposals before
the April 1953 deadline shed little additional light on key reform proposals, but the rhetorical heat generated by parliamentary discussions
was substantial. Presenting the government's case to the Bundestag,
Dehler defended a position he did not share, conjuring up visions of the
"legal chaos" that would result were lawmakers not to act swiftly on the
government's draft. But such dire predictions did nothing to define a basis for compromise.[69]

How, asked the SPD's Frieda Nadig, could "lawgivers fail to acknowledge the great contribution of the present generation of mothers?"

Were not women's accomplishments during the war and the postwar crisis adequate proof that they were the equals of men? How could parliament give fathers the rights, "which so many mothers had exercised for so many years and with such great sacrifice, as they were forced to exercise parental authority by themselves?" What the government proposed was "no parental, but rather a paternal power," Nadig insisted.[70] The SPD, joined by many women representatives from within the FDP and Christian Democratic advocates of women's rights, repeated their contention that the recognition of a mother's work must register in the acknowledgment of a mother's rights, both over her children and in relation to her husband.[71]

Social Democrats also categorically rejected any notion that protecting families could justify limiting individual rights. The CDU/CSU warned of the dangers of a communist order that obliterated the differences between women and men, but Social Democrats did not hesitate to invoke a different image of the east to advance their arguments. They emphasized that "in a democratic political order, the state does not fulfill the task of prescribing to its citizens how they should regulate their personal relations. That happens in totalitarian states." The equality of mothers and fathers was essential precisely because mothers had primary responsibility for children, and because "it's in the children's room that the democrat, the citizen, is initially shaped." Mothers, robbed of authority, would poorly educate their children; the next generation would remain ignorant of the true meaning of equality. Scriptural arguments in no way altered this conception. "God," Frieda Nadig insisted, "gave man a partner, not a slave."[72]

Speaking for the FDP, Herta Ilk expressed her disgust "that a woman can use her voice to decide the fate of an entire nation in the Bundestag, while at home, she has to accommodate herself to her husband's vote, if she's not getting along with him." If the government had its way, there would be nothing to "stop him from telling her, 'You must not go to the Bundestag.' "[73] Hildegard Krüger, a Catholic jurist who wrote prolifically on family law in the fifties and articulately took on the challenge of her conservative coreligionists, similarly decried legal structures that allowed a woman to determine educational policy as a state minister of culture but did not allow her to determine where her daughter would attend school, to serve as the director of a bank but not to open her own account without her husband's consent.[74] The Catholic church's massive intervention also sparked intense opposition from political liberals, and an outraged Marie-Elisabeth Lüders sarcastically observed of the bishops, "It is difficult to talk about the problems of patriarchy with the representatives of an institution that in the last analysis is itself of a purely patriarchal and authoritarian nature."[75]

The overwhelming majority of the conservative coalition remained no less intransigent. They insisted that troubled times threatened marriages, stable marriages required a hierarchical order, and a proper hierarchical order need not be invented, because it was preordained by God.[76] Leaving absolutely no doubt where they stood, the Catholic bishops fired off another rhetorical round in January 1953, exhorting the state to join the church in countering "the growing endangerment of Christian marriage and family." Completely unacceptable were those "radical changes in family law taken by certain states with materialistically oriented governments. We are no less alarmed by demands that stem from outmoded individualist or liberal viewpoints." Unabashedly underscoring the intersection of politics and theology, the bishops warned that those who rejected Adenauer's demands for patriarchal authority opposed not only the government but also the scripture and the teaching of the church. When Basic Law challenged higher law, there was no doubt where Catholic sympathies should lie.[77]

As the April 1953 deadline for specifying the dimensions of a reformed Civil Code approached, it became increasingly apparent that the Bundestag would not complete the task. Parliamentary debate shifted from the particulars of reform proposals to the growing recognition that the government's draft could win no majority. Arguing that any attempt to alter the deadline specified in the Basic Law would amount to an unjustifiable revision of its terms, Social Democrats resolutely rejected the two-year extension proposed by the conservative coalition. Unconvinced by predictions that a "lawless condition" was imminent, the SPD's Otto Heinrich Greve, a lawyer, likened the inflammatory rhetoric of the debates over family-law reform to the conservative coalition's tactics in the debates then under way over German rearmament: " 'Whoever opposes [it] is for Moscow'. . . . 'Whoever opposes the extension is against marriage.' " Neither for Moscow nor against marriage, Greve insisted on his party's well-founded reasons for opposing the government on both issues.[78]

In the balance, maintained his colleague Adolf Arndt, were fundamental ideological differences over the meaning of equality, which would not be easily resolved. Completely rejecting Helene Weber's arguments that biological difference justified differences in legal treatment, Arndt reminded her and the other members of the conservative coalition that under the Nazis, a leading legal authority, now a high-ranking adviser to Adenauer's government, had contended that the "biological difference between Aryan and non-Aryan individuals was so great that the equality before the law proclaimed by the Weimar constitution" was consistent with the discriminatory practice of National Socialism. Arndt concluded that the CDU, "at present the strongest party in government," simply did not support the Grundgesetz and had offered a "clear declaration of war against [women's] equal rights."[79]

In waves of mutual recrimination, Social Democrats and Communists charged the government with intentionally delaying discussion of the law, Justice Ministry officials blamed Adenauer and his chief advisers for their intransigence,[80] and Christian Democrats condemned the opposition as unable to summon the patience essential for considering such complex legislation, to take "the deep breath that we ceased to be accustomed to in the time of the Third Reich, with its hasty law-making." The consequence of not agreeing to extend the deadline, conservatives maintained, would be the "splintering of law" (*Rechtszersplitterung*), "a door wide open to legal uncertainty," "catastrophe and chaos," "a vacuum, a space with no air, a space with no law."[81]

Within the FDP, some shared Herta Ilk's fears that indefinitely postponing reform to an unspecified future would allow room "for the agitation of church circles in a form that will be grotesque." Ilk also warned that delays further separated West Germans from 1945; that period "in which woman so notably and visibly proved herself" would become less and less compelling as a justification for women's equal rights.[82] Still, these arguments confronted the principled objections of those Free Democrats who opposed setting the precedent of revising the constitution, along with the arguments of others, particularly women, that the principle of women's equal rights would fare just as well in the courts as in the Bundestag.

SPD opposition to any extension of the 1 April deadline and divided opinion within the FDP guaranteed that it would be impossible to obtain the two-thirds parliamentary majority necessary to alter the constitution. An exasperated Arndt conjectured that "if we'd devoted the time we've spent on discussions about altering the Basic Law to continuing with our substantive work, we could almost have finished."[83] The parliamentary deadlock guaranteed that substantive work would continue, but following no specific timetable.

The "vacuum" created by the Bundestag's failure to take action was filled not by "catastrophe and chaos" but by the courts, as will be detailed in Chapter 6. In the meantime, the parliament that continued talking while the courts moved into the "space with no law" was not the same one chosen by West German voters in 1949. National elections in September 1953 decisively changed the face of the legislature, delivering Adenauer and the CDU/CSU an overwhelming mandate, increasing their share of the popular vote by more than 14 percent, augmenting their seats in the Bundestag by more than one hundred, and taking even the most committed adherents of the coalition by surprise. Both the SPD and FDP registered slight declines in their share of the popular vote, and the KPD fell to 2.2 percent, below the 5 percent minimum required by the electoral law for representation in the Bundestag.

Sorely disappointed were those within the SPD who hoped that their party could win votes from disgruntled women by capitalizing on charges that the conservative coalition had intentionally delayed reform of the family law. No more realistic was the prediction of many women in the FDP that their party's failure to push forcefully for mother's rights would drive female voters to elect Social Democrats.[84] An overwhelming majority of West German women chose Christian, not Free or Social, Democrats at the polls, and in heavily Catholic regions, as many as 75 percent of all women gave their votes to Adenauer's coalition. Furthermore, voter participation rates among Catholic women were nearly 5 percent above the national average for all women, and in the 10.6 percent of the cases where wives and husbands chose different political parties, women married to SPD voters cast their ballots for the CDU.[85]

At least in part because of this undiminished gender gap, Adenauer's second cabinet took office with tremendously increased political leverage. Women activists within the FDP and SPD were left to conclude that first-time voters no longer thought it necessary to fight for equality, while the female electorate—young and old—was more likely to respond to the dictates of the church and to CDU/CSU claims of responsibility for clear signs of postwar economic recovery than to the government's forceful stand against women's equality within marriage (figs. 22–25).[86]

In what remains the most comprehensive analysis of West German women's voting patterns in this election, political sociologist Gabriele Bremme, writing in 1956, concluded that at the polls West German women demonstrated a continuity in basic political orientations that stretched back to the twenties, not a response to specific electoral appeals. For Catholic women, religion solidified these loyalties, and Bremme noted a strong direct relationship between women's over-representation both among churchgoers and among CDU/CSU voters. The church also controlled an extensive network of women's associations, more than half of all such groups in the Federal Republic in the fifties. Most of these in turn were Catholic, and the Central League of Catholic Women's and Mothers' Associations alone counted a membership of about 800,000, only 239,000 fewer than the female membership of the German Trade Union League (Deutscher Gewerkschaftsbund) in the same period.

Through this extensive network and directly from the pulpit, Bremme observed, the Catholic faithful were reminded that the pope himself believed that "today in women's hands the ballot is an important means for fulfilling the religious obligations of conscience." Christian politics was politics that sought to "guarantee for families of all strata the essential conditions of life, so that the family as economic, legal, and moral union exists and develops. Then the family will truly become the core of life (*Lebenszelle*) for humanity. . . . The true woman of today understands all of this."[87] There was no question how the true Catholic woman should cast her ballot. Nothing the SPD or FDP had to offer could challenge this vision or rupture well-established patterns of voting behavior.

The shift in the political climate after the election of the second parliament registered in the creation of a new cabinet Ministry of Family Affairs, with Franz-Josef Wuermeling, the self-proclaimed "protective master" and "patron" of the family (fig. 26), at its head. Son of a long-time veteran of Center party politics and active in the Catholic student movement, he had worked in the Prussian civil service in the Ministry of the Interior in Weimar and, in the thirties, had been a financial adviser to the regional government in Kassel, a post he left in 1939 to work in the basalt-mining industry. Although these credentials, combined with his claims to have opposed National Socialism, served as a springboard for Wuermeling's entry into the CDU at the war's end, it was his close ties to Catholic lay associations and his outspoken defense of marriage relations based on the "Christian-occidental tradition" that were doubtless more important qualifications for his entry into the Family Ministry.[88]

Wuermeling had also distinguished himself in the late forties as a zealous proponent of parental rights and had argued for lodging them firmly in the Basic Law. Lumping together socialism and liberalism, both of which he considered similar to National Socialism in their unwillingness to recognize "the divinely ordained natural order," Wuermeling proposed to Frings an all-out "war" against any constitution that did not guarantee patriarchal authority, claiming that "the believing Christian people of the future West German state are strong enough" to take on the "socialist-liberal united front." He predicted that "in that moment when the CDU/CSU proves that it is prepared, no matter what, uncompromisingly with all its reserves to take up the Christian cause, the masses of both faiths who are true to the church will rally behind the party." In 1949, his ultimata drew criticism even from Süsterhenn, among the staunchest defenders of Catholic interests in the Parliamentary Council, but his actions did offer convincing evidence that he would be a committed advocate of a Christian political vision.[89]

With his appointment of Wuermeling, Adenauer provided no comfort for those who feared that the outcome of debates over family-law reform would be determined by a "worldview [*Weltanschauung*] rather than a vision of reality [*Wirklichkeitsanschauung*]."[90] No one else so fully elaborated the larger ideological framework that surrounded the CDU/CSU's pronouncements on reforming the Civil Code. From the start, Wuermeling explicitly denounced any conception of women's equality that might shake "the Christian foundations of the family authority exercised by the father" and pronounced his post to be a "defensive position" against any misunderstanding of equality. The "protective patron of the family" was no advocate of women's rights.[91]

Adding an important dimension to debates over the family, Wuermeling also insisted that ensuring the "inviolability of the *Lebensraum* of the family" was essential to prevent "a people [from] dying out," particularly when the "communist-ruled eastern nations" showed signs of being remarkably prolific. The family minister was concerned that a weak German national spirit would not be fruitful and multiply and could be overrun by the populous communist nations of the east. Thus, concerns about stable families were concerns about population growth and West Germany's ability to stem the spread of communism.[92]

With the June 1953 workers' uprising against the communist regime in East Germany and the Korean War exploding in the background, setting the stage for the initial debates over West German military rearmament, Adenauer's east was vast. Korea might be geographically removed, but from the chancellor's perspective it was "just one more place along the same front" that began in East Germany.[93] In Adenauer's formulation, Moscow was not part of Europe but was rooted in the "culture of the most backward part of Asia"; the Soviet Union repre-

sented the "monstrous power of Asia," and "Asia stands on the Elbe."
Only an "economically and spiritually healthy western Europe . . . that
includes as a vital part that portion of Germany not occupied by the
Russians can stop the further forward pressure of Asia, both as force
and spirit." The fight against Soviet communism was the fight for everything "that seems of value in life."[94]

Wuermeling made explicit the connections between his chancellor's
geopolitical visions and CDU/CSU proposals for reforming family law:
marriage and the family were among those cherished goods threatened
by communism. A secure home front was essential in the war against the
east—whether embodied in East Germany, Moscow, or North Korea—
and in the front line of defense, a secure family was the most basic unit.
When Wuermeling railed against threats to the "Christian basis of the
authority within the family exercised by the father," he was describing
only one piece in a larger mosaic. His entry into Adenauer's second cabinet ensured that these themes would be broadcast with full force at every opportunity when the family was on the agenda of the Bundestag.

It took West German lawmakers four more years to fulfill the charge
given them by the Parliamentary Council; a new family law went into
effect at the beginning of 1958. By the end of 1953, however, key lines
of dispute and modes of argumentation were firmly established. Adenauer and the CDU/CSU coalition had run their 1949 parliamentary
campaign on a platform that stressed the necessity for West Germany to
look to its "occidental Christian roots." Behind this religio-political
worldview was a commitment to unambiguous and enthusiastic integration into a western European security system, strongly influenced by the
United States. The "Chancellor of the Allies," as his critics dubbed Adenauer, showed no inclination to diverge from the course set in the immediate postwar years.[95]

At home, West Germany's "occidental Christian roots" sank deep
into the soil of competitive capitalism. Erhard's "social market economy" went hand in hand with the condemnation of anything vaguely
hinting of socialization or centralized planning. The "occidental
Christian" tradition advocated by Adenauer also meant no "farewell
to legal patriarchy" championed by middle-class feminists and Social
Democrats,[96] but rather the unequivocal "rejection of the socialization
of the family."[97] In this domestic realm, socialization included any
moves toward a misguided implementation of equal rights for women

and men. Leveling of difference—whether in the economy or the
home—was the consequence of socialism. For the ruling coalition,
hierarchy within the family was no more unnatural than hierarchy
within the "social market economy."

While the Bundestag debated reform of the Civil Code, it also addressed proposals for reestablishing a West German army. In 1949, Adenauer had applauded the Allied decision in the Petersberg Agreement to
end the dismantling of German industry, which he heralded as representing not only the first postwar recognition of the new West German government as a rehabilitated, legitimate, independent, international actor
but also an important step toward the recognition of Germany's return
to "equal rights" (Gleichberechtigung) in the world community.[98] From
here, he moved forcefully toward West German rearmament, overcoming substantial internal opposition both from Social Democrats and
from those within his own party who feared it would present insur-
mountable barriers to the reunification of the two Germanys. For Adenauer, rearmament became the prerequisite for becoming a "partner as
a free state with equal rights in a European and thus in a North Atlantic
defense system against every aggression of Soviet Russia." Equal rights
were the reward for West Germany's willingness to bear its share of the
burdens in defense of "a common occidental heritage" and the "ethical
and spiritual bases of Christianity" against the menace of the "greatest
Asiatic power, Russia." The choices were simple—between "freedom,
human dignity, [and] Christian-occidental thinking of mankind," and
the "spirit of darkness and slavery," the "anti-Christian spirit"; "between good and evil, between life and destruction."[99]

Marriage and the family became additional armaments in the Cold
War campaigns of Adenauer and other postwar West Germans. For a
majority of the ruling coalition, West Germany's equal rights and national sovereignty in the world community were completely consistent
with a very restricted notion of equal rights for West German women
and the sovereignty of West German men in the family. The "spirit of
darkness and slavery" was present not only in communist military
might but in "Russian conceptions" of women's equality that pointed
toward the collective, destroying families, tearing children from their
mothers, and sending all women to work in the mines. Rearming the
West German military and rearming West German patriarchs were both
defenses against the same menace.

In the form of the Catholic bishops, God was on the side of Adenauer
and the CDU/CSU in both campaigns. Frings denounced the pacifist sen-

timents of left-wing Catholics protesting German rearmament in the early fifties just as he denounced the subversive sentiments of those attacking the patriarchal family. Invoking the theory of "just war," Frings argued that ensuring order necessitated alliances of states.[100] Order was important in the family as well; it would best be ensured by defending the authority of husbands and fathers.

To be sure, even Adenauer, Wuermeling, and the bishops could not completely dismiss the fact that within the conservative coalition not everyone agreed that hierarchy and freedom were so easily reconciled. The women's caucus within the CDU forcefully stated its opposition to patriarchal authority, and even the leaders of the Protestant clergy were not ready to sanction a husband's authority over his wife. Still, in the summer of 1952 it was the church's massive, direct intervention with Adenauer that significantly influenced the chancellor's response to the question of women's equal rights.

Naming Wuermeling to a newly created Ministry for Family Affairs in his second cabinet was another indication that Adenauer took seriously the influence of conservative political Catholicism. The chancellor's own Catholic background and his close ties to church leaders also meant that his decision to defend a religious agenda on the issue of family reform was not dictated exclusively by political expediency. On questions of economic policy or foreign relations, Adenauer turned elsewhere for advice. But on questions of the family and women's status, Christian Democracy was particularly susceptible to conservative Catholic influence.

The ubiquity of anticommunist metaphors in the debate over family-law reform is striking. They were by no means the exclusive preserve of the CDU/CSU. Social Democrats opposed patriarchal authority by arguing that totalitarian systems, not democracies, dictated the sexual division of labor in the home, just as Christian Democrats rejected an end to patriarchal authority as paving the way to the collective. What united these divergent views was their insistence on distancing themselves from the east.

In the intersection of anticommunist and anti-Asian sentiments, moreover, the east became a highly elastic designation, extending from the border separating the two Germanys to the Sea of Japan. The east not only embodied the threat of Soviet and Chinese communism, but as middle-class feminists emphasized in opposing patriarchal provisions in the family law, it also represented the "culture of the most backward part of Asia." What produced raw communism for Adenauer produced "raw patriarchy" for middle-class feminists. Deployed on opposing sides of West German debates over family-law reform, what these images shared was a common basis in anti-Asian prejudice.

No less frequent than implicit or explicit references to the negative example of the east and common to all participants in debates over family-law reform were attempts to tar opponents with the brush of Nazi legacies. The CDU/CSU associated Social Democratic and communist insistence on female equality with Nazi attempts to drive women into the wage-labor force during the war. Social Democrats compared the contorted arguments of the conservative coalition that hierarchy was consistent with equality with the casuistic arguments of Nazi legal scholars that discrimination on the basis of race was consistent with the Weimar constitution.

What separated Adenauer and his party from their opponents was significant. Whether the law would continue to sanction the real and symbolic authority of husbands and fathers, whether such measures were consistent with the constitutional guarantee of equality, whether state policy would borrow from a language of scripture—these questions defined a great divide. However, the first round of debates over family-law reform was also remarkable for the substantial areas of agreement that it revealed among parties across the political spectrum. Continuing their determined march away from any theoretical conception of work according to which women were as likely as men to be engaged in wage labor, postwar Social Democrats never tired of reiterating that when it came to the "woman question," they were neither women's righters nor communist levelers. Without hesitation, they concurred with the CDU/CSU that married women should be wives, wives should be mothers, and mothers should not work outside the home. To be sure, their insistence that women were forced out to work by economic necessity led them to place greater emphasis than the ruling coalition on the need for a social order that would grant male providers the jobs that could allow their wives to stay at home where they belonged. But what was apparent to Wuermeling and anyone else following parliamentary discussions was that not even "emancipated women's righters" or "the most radical defenders of equality in the western zones" were ready to deny that biological difference translated into distinct occupations for women and men.[101] When the problems of the working mother were addressed as anything more than an unfortunate consequence of the *Frauenüberschuss* and the high costs of rebuilding after the war, it was not usually by Social Democrats but by professional women in bourgeois feminist organizations or from within the FDP.

Although the SPD insisted on eliminating inequalities *within* families, the party did not use debates over family-law reform as a forum for addressing inequalities *among* families. The contrast with parliamentary debates around the family law in the original Civil Code is revealing. In the 1890s, socialists argued against the dominant tendency to elevate the bourgeois family to a normative level. August Bebel, whose theoretical writings provided an important basis for socialist analyses of the family and women's oppression, reminded his parliamentary colleagues that they were describing not all marriages but rather "the bourgeois marriage, that is, that marriage that is the only one that can be normative and recognized in today's bourgeois society, in a constitution that is linked intimately to the essence of bourgeois society." Bourgeois marriage, Bebel maintained, "is based on bourgeois property, private property; but the owner wants to will his property after his death. Thus it is logical that the need for legitimate heirs appears," and it was this need that was at the basis of marriage.[102]

In the 1890s Bebel looked confidently to a brighter future that he claimed was already outlined in the present. Relationships were on a different basis for the "millions of women who contributed materially to the maintenance and preservation of the marriage-community in the same measure as men," who had "stepped away from their former relegation to and isolation in the home," ineluctably drawn into wage work by the development of the capitalist economy. With nothing of value but their labor, proletarian families were already founded on the equality of women and men. Thus, the Civil Code might accurately describe bourgeois social relations under capitalism, but it would not be long before the bourgeoisie and capitalism were abolished.[103]

Bebel's critical perspective was absent from discussions of family law reform in the early fifties; in these debates, the family appeared as a universal, classless institution. All wives were workers—workers in the home—but no wife was identified as a member of the working class. Inevitable proletarianization, that dominant strain of pre-1914 German Social Democratic theory, meant a leveling of difference—difference not only between classes but between women and men—and any such leveling was something that the post–World War II SPD was willing neither to advocate nor to predict. Rather, Social Democrats were at great pains to distance themselves from charges that they proposed a "socialist ideal of equality" which eliminated "pre-given differences."[104] They hurried to assure those making such allegations that "whoever conceived of socialism as if it promoted an absolute leveling has a primitive conception of socialism's true intention."[105]

With this door left open, what distinguished Social from Christian Democrats on many key points of family-law reform became questions of form, not substance. Lambasting the CDU/CSU for supporting the final say of husbands and fathers allowed Social Democrats to charge that the ruling coalition did not support equality as defined by the Basic Law. However, while Social Democrats became expert at identifying what they did not like—in particular, the theological overtones of the CDU/CSU's argumentation and the explicit influence of the Catholic church on the conservative coalition—what they were willing to endorse looked in many respects little different from what was proposed by Adenauer's party.[106]

Alternative conceptions of "woman's place" were increasingly rare as West Germans moved into the Adenauer era. In 1953, final reform of the Civil Code's regulation of marriage and family life still lay in an unspecified future. But in these initial discussions of how best to achieve women's equality with men within marriage, there was no indication that West Germans could envision more than one type of family, and little reluctance to legislate women's labors and to define the home and family as her primary workplace.

Figure 1. "Security for the family" under the Nazis. The caption reads "The NSDAP secures the national community: Fellow Germans, if you need advice or help, turn to the local [party] organization." Courtesy of the Hoover Institution Archives, Poster Collection.

Figure 2.   Attempts to mobilize women workers intensified under conditions of "total war." The caption reads "You should help, too!" Courtesy of the Hoover Institution Archives, Poster Collection.

Figure 3. This Nazi poster was intended to evoke racist memories of black troops, who were among the Allied forces of occupation in the Rhineland after Germany's defeat in the First World War. In the background looms a caricature of a Jew, clearly associated in Nazi ideology with the Allied attack on Germany. The caption, addressed to a male audience, reads "German! Should this once again become a reality?" Courtesy of the Hoover Institution Archives, Poster Collection.

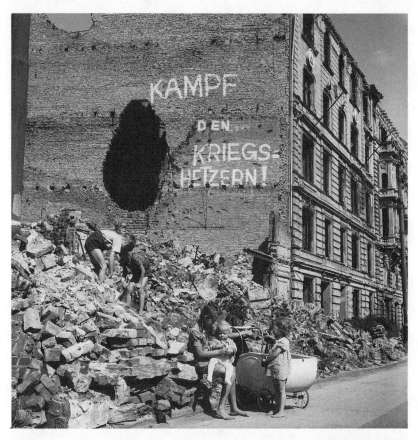

Figure 4. Children playing in the rubble, ca. 1948. The graffiti on the wall
reads "War against the war mongers." Courtesy of Landesbildstelle Berlin.

Figure 5. "Women of the rubble" cleaning off the bricks, October 1946. Courtesy of Landesbildstelle Berlin.

Figure 6. "Women of the rubble" taking a break from their work, 1945. Courtesy of Bildarchiv Preussischer Kulturbesitz.

Figure 7. In the immediate postwar years, women's unpaid labor extended well beyond the walls of their "private" homes. These women are collecting firewood near the Tiergarten district of Berlin, ca. 1949. Courtesy of Landesbildstelle, Berlin.

Figure 8. City women riding trains to the countryside to try to barter directly with peasants, 1946. These *Hamsterfahrten* were also "women's work" in the postwar period. Photo by Friedrich Seidenstücker. Courtesy of Bildarchiv Preussischer Kulturbesitz.

Figure 9. A basement apartment, serving as emergency housing after the war, ca. 1946–1947. Courtesy of Nordrhein-Westfälisches Hauptstaatsarchiv.

Figure 10. Soldiers' grave and the *Frauenüberschuss*, ca. 1946. Courtesy of Landesbildstelle Berlin.

Figure 11. The four women sent by state legislatures to serve in the Parliamentary Council. Left to right: Frieda Nadig, Elisabeth Selbert, Helene Weber, and Helene Wessel. Courtesy of Friedrich Ebert Stiftung.

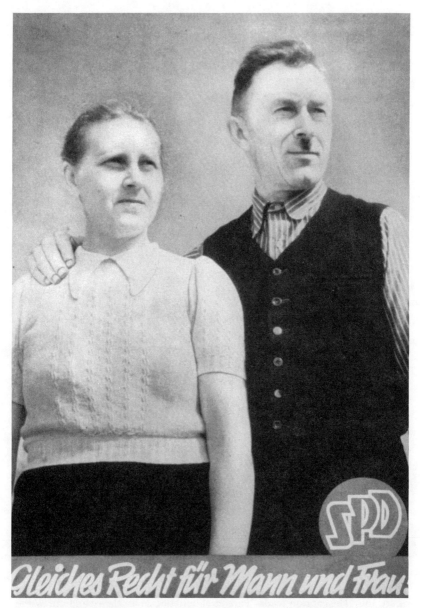

Gleiches Recht für Mann und Frau!

Figure 12.   The caption reads "Equal rights for man and woman, SPD." The SPD championed this cause, anchored in Paragraph 2 of Article 3 of the Grundgesetz. Courtesy of Bundesarchiv, Koblenz.

Figure 13. The caption reads "Parents should decide for their children! We're fighting for the rights of parents—you too should vote for the CSU." The fight for parental rights was central in debates over Article 6 of the Grundgesetz. Courtesy of Stadtmuseum Munich.

Figure 14.   In this SPD electoral poster, children announce "Mother, we want a peaceful and happy future." Courtesy of Bundesarchiv, Koblenz.

Figure 15.   Visions of a better future for mothers and their children were com-
mon to the electoral appeals of all political parties in the first postwar elections.
The caption reads "With the SPD for a free and better future." Courtesy of
Bundesarchiv, Koblenz.

Figure 16.   A "mother-family"? By "giving your vote to the SPD," this poster encourages the postwar woman to vote "for a better future, for a better Germany, for a Germany of peace, freedom and justice." Courtesy of Bundesarchiv, Koblenz.

Figure 17.   Particularly in the late forties and early fifties, the SPD was far more likely than the CDU to champion the cause of the woman who worked outside the home. The caption of this electoral appeal reads "The working woman votes for the SPD." Courtesy of Bundesarchiv, Koblenz.

Figure 18.   The caption reads "Protect Us, Be Ready for Defense, Vote for the CDU." In the original, the menacing hand is red, symbolizing the threat posed to mother and child by communism. Courtesy of Nordrhein-Westfälisches Hauptstaatsarchiv.

Figure 19.   For the FDP as well, the future was represented by a mother and child. The caption reads "And the Future? Free Democratic Party." Courtesy of Archiv des deutschen Liberalismus.

Figure 20.   Like all the other political parties, the FDP encouraged "women standing alone" (*alleinstehende Frauen*) to believe that its candidates were "Your Choice." Courtesy of Archiv des deutschen Liberalismus.

Glückliches Deutschland
der Kommunisten Ziel

Figure 21.   The KPD was never more than a marginal presence in postwar West German politics, and the party was officially outlawed in 1956. In the early fifties, however, it too claimed that a happy mother and child represented "The communists' goal [of a] happy Germany." Courtesy of the Hoover Institution Archives, Poster Collection.

Figure 22.   In its appeals to women, the CDU repeatedly depicted itself as the only true representative of "Christian" interests. The caption reads "Christian woman, where do you stand? Vote CDU." Courtesy of the Hoover Institution Archives, Poster Collection.

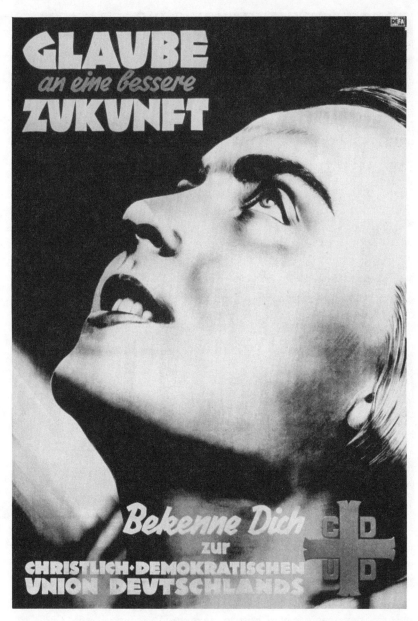

Figure 23. The equation of religious and political commitments was implicit in this CDU electoral poster exhorting women to "Believe in a better future: embrace the Christian Democratic Union of Germany." Courtesy of the Hoover Institution Archives, Poster Collection.

Figure 24. Adenauer's CDU/CSU coalition claimed responsibility for the success of the "social market economy" and improved economic circumstances. A fuller shopping basket and a shrinking ration card were symbols of postwar recovery addressed to a female electorate. The caption reads "And again CDU. Because things should get even better." Courtesy of Nordrhein-Westfälisches Hauptstaatsarchiv.

Figure 25.   The caption reads "Finally, we can buy again. Vote for the CDU."
Courtesy of Nordrhein-Westfälisches Hauptstaatsarchiv.

Gesunde Familie
Gesundes Volk
F.Josef Wuermeling CDU

Figure 26.   Following the 1953 electoral victory of the CDU/CSU coalition, Franz-Josef Wuermeling was named to head the newly created Ministry for the Family. In this CDU electoral appeal, Wuermeling promises a "Healthy family, healthy nation." Courtesy of Bundesarchiv, Koblenz.

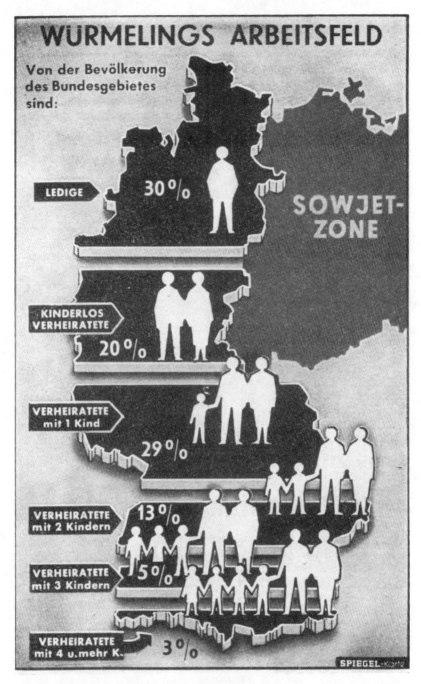

Figure 27.   The map illustrates "Wuermeling's work area." It graphically presents the numbers of West Germans who were, from top to bottom, "single," "married with no children," "married with one child," "married with two children," "married with three children," and "married with four or more children." For Wuermeling, the number of families "poor in children" (*kinderarm*) was alarmingly high. The map appeared as part of a feature article on Wuermeling in *Der Spiegel,* 15 September 1954. Courtesy of *Der Spiegel.*

Figure 28. The caption of this CSU electoral poster counsels West German voters to abide "No experiments." The poster depicts the chancellor, Konrad Adenauer. Courtesy of Stadtarchiv Munich.

Figure 29. "SPD Program—CDU Achievement." The poster compares the barrack-like housing and limited consumer opportunities of the German Democratic Republic with the accomplishments of the "social market economy" in the Federal Republic. Social Democrats are associated with the Apparatchik of the planned economy in the "Soviet-Zone." The caption at bottom reads, "The Planned Economy Makes us Sick / We're all Voting for Adenauer." Courtesy of Bundesarchiv, Koblenz.

Figure 30. "Security for the family, Vote for the SPD." Courtesy of Hoover Institution Archives, Poster Collection.

Reconstructed Families in Reconstruction Germany

Gerhard van Heukelum, head of the Office of Labor and Welfare in Bremen, reflected in 1949 on the problems of economic recovery in a Germany devastated by war. Germans confronted the challenge of finding sources of capital for economic reconstruction, but Heukelum insisted that even an adequate supply of "material capital" was not sufficient to rebuild Germany. All the machines, money, and factories in the world were of no use if economic planners overlooked the significance of human capital and did not consider the "individual as a bearer of labor." When Heukelum expressed his concerns about the "dangerous dismantling" of the postwar years, he was referring not to the tremendously unpopular Allied policy of dismantling entire factories—a direct form of seizing reparations after the war—but to the dismantling of the factory that produced human capital, the family.[1] "It is high time that we once again consider the significance of people as a factor of production. Equipment and plant capacity can more readily be replaced than people."[2]

At present, judged Heukelum, future supplies of human capital were endangered. The introduction of a new West German currency a year earlier had opened a gap between prices and wages, making a bad situation worse for many families. Wage levels for unskilled and some skilled workers were so low that the father of a large family was better off living from welfare than work. Family wages—remuneration pegged to family size—offered no acceptable solution to this dilemma, because they would lead firms to fire fathers who had many children and because any employers willing to pay such rates would be operating at a competitive disadvantage. Wages could only be based on performance, the *Leistungslohn,* not family status.[3] Heukelum's alternative was a base wage sufficient for a male worker to support a dependent wife and two children. Young unmarried workers who did not yet have families could use the higher base wage as a source of savings for a future when they too would establish a family. For larger families, he recommended a system of state-funded supplements to this basic wage. Parents had a moral responsibility to support their children, but society had an equally compelling obligation to create the conditions that would allow parents to do their work. Heukelum insisted that it was imperative to act with speed and determination to meet families' needs. The destruction of the war had left Germany behind in the arena of social policy, and it was essential that West Germans move quickly to catch up.

No casual observer of postwar developments, Heukelum voiced these opinions as the head of a government commission charged by the Federal Council with drafting strategies for devising a scheme of family allowances in the late forties. Composed of representatives from the business community, trade unions, social welfare agencies, and universities, the committee unanimously concluded that the family's needs could not be addressed adequately either by the "performance wage" or by existing social-welfare measures. Present wage levels, explained another commission member, the Social Democrat and trade unionist Clara Döhring, were "adequate neither for the wife nor for the children, so that the wife is also forced to earn."[4] This was an unacceptable turn of events that threatened family stability.

Heukelum and his colleagues summarized sentiments widely held among politicians and policy-makers—in any plan for postwar West German economic recovery, production and reproduction were inextricably linked. Building a new Germany required building new Germans, and this was work that began at home. Families as well as factories were sites of production, severely damaged by the war, and it was essential to restore both to prewar output levels. The Parliamentary Council's prescription that the state protect the family was at best a blueprint; Heukelum and others involved in the discussion of how best to supplement wages through "money-for-children" (*Kindergeld*) sought to provide the bricks and mortar for carrying out the project.

Family allowances were intended to distribute the costs of raising the next generation. The language of "equalizing the burdens of families" (*Familienlastenausgleich*) used to describe the proposed system associated family policy with discussions that had commenced immediately after May 1945 as to how most equitably to "equalize the burdens" (*Lastenausgleich*) of the war. Adopted in 1952, the Law for the Equalization of Burdens represented a mechanism for taking from those who had survived the war relatively unscathed and giving to those who had not—those bombed out or permanently disabled, and in particular those who had fled with nothing to escape the westward movement of the Red Army in the last years of the war. The law specified that individual wealth of more than DM 5,000 on the day of currency reform would be taxed at a level of 50 percent and redistributed to those claiming compensation for their war-related losses. A formula that seriously undervalued fixed assets and distributed payments over thirty years guaranteed that this scheme did not lead to any radical redistribution of wealth, but it did represent a symbolic "reckoning for Hitler's war," which provided nominal material benefits to some.[5]

"Equalizing the burdens of families" was part of this larger project of accounting for the past, but, as advocates of family allowances insisted, it was also aimed at outlining the future. In 1952, in an address to the annual meeting of the Association for Social Policy (Verein für Sozialpolitik), a congress of academic sociologists and policy-makers, Gerhard Mackenroth, a professor of social welfare, maintained that in social-policy discussions of the needs of families it was possible to look away from the "defeatist atmosphere of the postwar period" toward "present performance, whose costs must be evenly balanced—the costs of raising the next generation, without which no nation and no culture can preserve and pass on its values."[6]

The discussions of "equalizing the burdens of families" articulated conceptions of women's essential contribution to rebuilding Germany. It was women who literally bore the "bearers of labor," women who would be forced out to work if male wages were not adequate to support a family, women who would preserve and pass on culture within the context of the domestic sphere. The state must ensure them the opportunity to do their work. While the Bundestag explored how best to specify women's rights and responsibilities in a reformed Civil Code, it approached the same question from another perspective in discussions of family allowances. In this context, women were often not mentioned explicitly, but they were never invisible. Underscoring his party's commitment to supporting the family's work, Richard Hammer, a medical doctor and a Free Democratic representative to the Bundestag, quoted the words of the pre-1914 Christian social reformer Friedrich Naumann that "too few children are a loss for the body of the nation," and thus "politics is made by mothers."[7] Analyzing the broad-ranging

discussion of family allowances in the late forties and fifties allows us
to reverse this formulation, to see not how mothers made politics, but
rather how the politics of the family constructed postwar West German
conceptions of motherhood.

When van Heukelum and his associates finished their work in late 1949,
they anticipated that their recommendations would become the basis for
immediate legislative action. Opinions differed as to whether family allowances should be granted for every child or should commence with
the second or only with the third, and details of appropriate levels and
sources of funding were also left open. But there was general agreement
that assisting the family was vitally important, that the state was the
most appropriate agent for making payments, and that for specifics, lawmakers could look to Nazi precedents, suspended by the Allies because
of their racialist and pronatalist content. There was much to be re-
claimed from the National Socialist past: "The principle of granting a
state subsidy for children, established by the National Socialists, was
correct; [what was] wrong was administering it according to considerations of race and population policies."[8] It was up to West Germans to
define alternatives not similarly flawed.

As the Bundestag took up its charge of translating these general recommendations into policy in 1950, there was a broad political consensus that the war had placed particularly great strains on the family, and
that it was the state's responsibility to identify and meet the family's
needs. Unanimity broke down quickly, however, over very basic questions: What exactly constituted a family, and what system could best
support it?

Once again, as in discussions of the Basic Law, representatives for the
CDU/CSU refused to identify as "families" the large numbers of households headed by single women—whether never married, widowed, or
divorced—who carried responsibility for children or dependent adults.
The "normal family," consisting of a male in regular employment and
a wife who stayed at home with at least two children, was at the core
of CDU/CSU proposals. The coalition emphasized the threats to this
family posed by a mother's decision to enter wage work, implying that
in a family, there was also a father who earned a good wage.

Support for families was essential in order to have a "higher ethical
estimation in particular of the mother and child."[9] Indeed, Article 6 of
the Basic Law dictated that "marriage and the family were under the
particular protection of the state." Family allowances would reduce the

chances that married women with children would be forced out to work to supplement their husbands' income, and it was necessary to respond immediately to the "thousands of children who today are complaining that their mothers have taken a job in the factory in order to bring a supplemental income into the family." Family allowances would "once again give the mother back to many families." At stake was ensurance of the "strongest bulwark of individual freedom in the struggle against collectivism," the "primordial nucleus of society" that had "survived because of its ethical foundation and its spiritual independence from all human, time-bound forms of the state."[10]

"Money-for-children" would also defend German families against potential crises in the future. Supporting the CDU/CSU position, an FDP spokesman explained that "it is completely undesirable for a citizen to be unmarried. There can be no form of existence less resistant to crisis than that of the individual who remains unmarried."[11] He cited as evidence the role of families in the war and postwar period, completely overlooking the fact that the *Frauenüberschuss*, another of the war's legacies, guaranteed that many women would never be able to opt for this form of social insurance.

According to the CDU/CSU's proposal, the state should not fulfill its obligation by instituting a system of across-the-board payments to all children, because a male wage should support at least a wife and two children. In fact, it was a fundamental right of the male provider to found a family and to "procreate" (*erzeugen*); basic wage levels should guarantee that right.[12] It was with the third child that families truly confronted extraordinary expenses. Testifying before the parliamentary committee debating alternative schemes, Joseph Höffner, a professor of "Christian social science" (*christliche Sozialwissenschaften*) in Münster, cited the evidence of statistical surveys that supported this position. With the third child, he explained, "baby clothes have to be replaced; the clothing of the first child can be worn by the second, then it's in tatters; new beds have to be bought, in particular, because of the likely differences in the sex of the children; the apartment has to be expanded, and so forth."[13] Proposals to limit family allowances to families with more than two children were also forcefully seconded by officials within the Finance Ministry and the business community, who were less concerned with threadbare hand-me-downs than with the fragile condition of the fledgling republic's treasury, particularly at a time when the government was confronting the potentially massive costs of rearmament.[14]

According to the CDU/CSU proposals, determination of the *Leistungslohn* was the business of the "social partners"—capital and labor—not the state. Allowing the state any direct role in regulating the system of family allowances represented a return to the institutional forms of National Socialism and mirrored the centralized planned economy in East Germany; it was an intolerable and dangerous expansion of the state's authority over private relations. Rather, self-regulation by the private sector was the only acceptable administrative solution. Proposed was a system of employer contributions that would be redistributed to families with more than two children through the existing framework of occupational-insurance providers. These principles embodied the CDU/CSU commitment to the "social-market economy." Though it must not lose its social conscience, the German economy must be reconstructed according to the competitive laws of the market with as little state intervention as possible; "what we need," insisted Ludwig Erhard, Adenauer's Economics Minister, "is not *more* government, but rather *less.*"[15]

Rejecting suggestions that such a program shared anything in common with a National Socialist, racialist, pronatalist past, Free Democratic spokesmen and their allies in the CDU/CSU warned against associating Nazi *population* policy with a free, democratic *family* policy. Was the "population pyramid," the graphic expression of a society's age and gender distribution, not the "invention of one of our Jewish citizens, who surely can't be suspected of making Nazi policy," was the rhetorical question of one FDP representative. Condemning racialism did not mean denying that "between sucking at the mother's breast, the soup bowl, and the loaf of bread . . . the first decisive unfolding of the human soul occurs and . . . the human ability to love develops." Supporting the "shelter of the family" to produce many children smacked not of pronatalism, but rather reflected the knowledge that the only child was more likely to enter into youth criminality or, once an adult, to get divorced.[16] Declining family size also raised ominous implications about the future of social security. Who would pay in while others withdrew their pension funds? There was no denying that "it makes a big difference whether the elderly, the sick, the crippled are maintained by two able-bodied workers or three."[17]

At the CDU's third party congress in October 1952, Änne Brauksiepe, a member of the Bundestag delegation and a leader of the German Catholic Women's Association (Deutscher Katholischer Frauenverband), elaborated on these themes in her remarks on "The Individual in the Family." Providing families with material support was part of a "task of virtually historic significance, to keep Europe vital and alive and to [prevent it] from being washed away by the east." Families tied individuals to the state, and "the concern of each individual family for peace was the common element that bound together Europe, despite all the political divisions that existed." Securing mothers' place within the family was essential because "next to men's politics, [which is] securing and developing power, is the politics of women, [which is] securing and developing freedom." Echoing her party's familiar litany, Brauksiepe insisted that it was through their treatment of women's status within the family that West Germans would indicate their choice for "freedom or slavery." Mothers and fathers, companions in marriages, companions in establishing a strong defense while fostering peace and freedom, needed the solid support of a systematic family policy.[18]

Doubtful that capitalism and less government would necessarily guarantee just solutions, critics from within the ranks of the opposition SPD, trade unionists, social workers, and some middle-class feminists were skeptical of CDU/CSU proposals. In particular, they argued that though wages *should* support a family of four, they might well not. The discrepancy weighed heavily on mothers "who were in charge of the care and education of children and managed the family's budget."[19] In addition, excluding those with only one or two children from benefits would disadvantage widows and divorced women whose needs were just as great as those of low-income family fathers; family allowances must also be extended to these families, who still bore the scars of the war and postwar crises.[20]

Social Democrats subscribed enthusiastically to the theory that large families were the key to economic prosperity and future social security. They also completely accepted the crucial importance of the "healing power of the motherly sphere of life."[21] Where they differed from the CDU/CSU coalition was in their demand that families of four needed help and that families without fathers were families as well. A policy of equal payments to all children and the elimination of the highly regressive system of tax deductions for dependents—a Nazi legacy that most helped the families who needed it least by granting a higher deduction to those with higher incomes—would permit all mothers to stay at home and would not limit benefits to certain groups.[22]

The SPD countered fears that the costs of this alternative would be prohibitive with claims that family allowances would redistribute wealth to those lower-income families more likely to spend most of their earnings on consumer goods, thus stimulating demand, spurring economic growth, and generating more taxes. The party proposed a system of state administration financed through a tax on the gross income of all wage-earners and argued for the elimination of all other deductions for minor dependents.[23]

This alternative won approval from some middle-class women's organizations, which also echoed the SPD's recommendation that payments should be made directly to mothers, not as a supplement to a male wage. Responding to the objections of German party and CDU representatives, who held that this would violate the rights of fathers ensured by the Civil Code, the SPD's Clara Döhring insisted that mothers, not fathers, managed the household budget; giving family allowances directly to them would ensure that money would be spent most effectively. The CDU/CSU's proposal—family allowances as a supplement to wages—would in almost every instance mean supplements to men, only increasing the economic dependence of wives and mothers whose wages came only from their husbands. Paying mothers directly would guarantee that family allowances were a tangible recognition of the value of their work.[24]

The Center party, only nominally represented in the Bundestag and drawing its support largely from the heavily Catholic areas of North Rhine–Westphalia, used the general discussion of "money-for-children" to present its own conception of how best to protect the family. Proposing a system of payments through local tax offices, the Center argued that the program should be funded by levies on unmarried individuals and those married couples with one or no children. Denying the striking similarities between their suggestions and policies instituted under the Nazis, Center party delegates reminded their colleagues that National Socialist policy had been motivated by the conviction "that the family is there for the state, and the state later claimed the children." In contrast, the Center maintained that at the basis of its redistributional scheme was the conception that "the state is there for the family, and that the state, if it has any desire to build itself up, must first build up a healthy family." Critics who objected to the pronatalist overtones of such proposals and argued "we have enough unemployed or we will just create the conditions for the next war by delivering the cannon fodder" missed the point. Economic development would end unemployment, and prosperity would ensure that population growth would not lead to war. Surely, "the German people is fundamentally cured of the slogan 'Volk ohne Raum.' " For Germans, the lesson of the war was that it was possible to live in a "more confined space. . . . We don't need to fight a war to gain more space."[25] The space that West Germans needed to flourish and prosper was to be found not in the east but in the privacy of the family, properly supported and encouraged by state policy.

By mid-1953 these conflicting views were still unresolved. A leading expert from within the Labor Ministry temporized that "a law that is so complicated and that has implications for so many other established legal measures cannot be rushed; rather it requires the most careful planning."[26] In the interim, the debate around family allowances created an opportunity for academic sociologists and social theorists to leave the ivory tower and tie their analyses of the postwar German family to specific recommendations for policy reform. Their writings were particularly important because their views were incorporated into parliamentary and ministerial discussions and because their theoretical formulations made explicit key elements underlying Bundestag debates over family policy.

In 1948, Helmut Schelsky became the director of the newly founded Academy for Communal Economics in Hamburg. He was a leading proponent of an empirical sociological method that claimed to be more concerned with problem-solving than with grandiose theories.[27] The author of a major study of expellees who fled to West Germany from the east after the war, Schelsky argued forcefully that the family's stability in the face of a general societal collapse justified its elevation to the central focus for social policy in the postwar era.

Differentiating between the short-term effects of the war and longer-term developments, Schelsky located Germany's recent past in a larger framework. Industrial expansion and the growth of the modern state resulted in the shift of some functions from the family to anonymous bureaucratic institutions. Production now took place in factories, not in home workshops or on family farms, and the welfare state, not children, took care of parents' old age. But these changes in no way detracted from the family's importance as a fundamental social institution, as had been demonstrated dramatically by the war. Of far greater significance than short-term consequences of the war such as a rising divorce rate, according to Schelsky, was the ability of large numbers of stable families to survive the years of crisis. The family was "safe from catastrophe"; those who had emerged from the forties into the fifties should "thank the family for the German miracle" of rapid recovery.[28]

In Schelsky's analysis, it was particularly women's work, "motherly care for the life of future generations," that had contributed significantly to holding families together. There could be no more compelling evidence that the family's great "tenacity" (*Beharrlichkeit*) was rooted in "the biological ground of sexual relations and a mother's existential care for the next generation"—in short, in structures independent of any specific time or place. By proving their indispensability in the post-war years, women had won respect and authority within families, and marriages were increasingly based on relations of equality between husbands and wives.[29]

However, women's expanded responsibilities should not be confused with the individualist equality that, in Schelsky's account, had been advocated by the bourgeois women's movement in the Kaiserreich and Weimar. Women's emancipation in the context of the war and postwar years was an "emancipation out of necessity," and complete equality for women was a dubious gain when it provided a basis for mobilizing women for compulsory work during wars.[30] Women's emancipation, defined as women's access to all jobs and educational opportunities on an equal basis with men, was sought only by women of upper-middle-class families, where women's responsibilities were reduced to the duties of representation and giving orders. The lack of accomplishment and dissatisfaction in such women's lives, argued Schelsky, led them to seek other experiences outside the home, and in their private lives to place "inordinate emphasis and extraordinary demands on personal relations, in particular romantic relations between the sexes, in short a heightening of the erotic." Claiming to represent all women, bourgeois feminism in fact articulated the interests of only a handful of professional women in large urban areas, "who in addition often find themselves in certain material and spiritual difficulties." The woman they championed did not exist.[31]

It was essential that social planners consider the needs of housewives, young working women, rural women, and women whose lives had been destroyed by the war. Middle-class feminists did not articulate their demands and did not understand that what most women sought, "in the twenties just as today," was to enter marriage, not to leave it, precisely because marriage and family embodied a retreat from "soullessness and leveling," those characteristics of bourgeois society so harshly criticized by the women's movement. "How many working women," Schelsky asked rhetorically in 1952, "would resign their jobs, if they could pursue their wishes? For them work does not mean acquisition of property and personal economic independence, but rather an uncertain income, competition, monotonous labor in order to ensure the most basic provision for themselves and for those others for whom they must care."[32] According to Schelsky, working-class women saw with clarity what evaded bourgeois feminists altogether.

Just as misguided as bourgeois feminism was the Frankfurt School's attempt to locate authoritarian proclivities in families in which private patriarchs were robbed of real authority, thus predisposing youth to find a surrogate in a strong state. On the contrary, the war and postwar period provided striking evidence that German families were anything but patriarchal; rather, they relied most heavily on mothers, not fathers. Ultimately, self-proclaimed emancipatory movements emancipated individuals only for greater subordination to the "rule of bureaucratic power and abstract authority." For Schelsky, the best negative example could be found in East Germany, where the protection of mothers served the interests not of families but of the state, where children became charges of a faceless bureaucracy, and where personal relationships were ultimately destroyed. Middle-class feminism, the Frankfurt School, communism—all were travelling to the same destination, the denial of women's true needs and the destruction of the family.[33]

Equally critical of National Socialism and Soviet communism, Schelsky was nonetheless ready to learn what he could from both Bolsheviks and Nazis. Although these totalitarian regimes reversed the relationship between family and state by attempting to subordinate the former to the needs of the latter, their policies for the protection of families had been successfully adopted in revised form by democratic governments.[34] The ends of these regimes were horrifying, but the means by which they sought to enhance the family's stability were worth careful study.

Translating his observations about the strength and endurance of families into specific recommendations for the reconstruction of the postwar West German welfare state, Schelsky argued that social policy had been tied to a "strata- or class-bound" perspective for too long. Outdated measures had aimed at increasing chances for social mobility by encouraging the collective advancement of the working class. The upward movement of some, accomplished by these policies before the Second World War, had combined with the downward mobility of others, caused by the bombs and devastation of the war and postwar years, to create a "leveled-out petit bourgeois–*mittelständische* society" (*nivellierte kleinbürgerlich-mittelständische Gesellschaft*). Schelsky's use of the category *Mittelstand*, the nineteenth-century term for describing shopkeepers, independent craftsmen, and small-scale entrepreneurs, as well as the "new *Mittelstand*" of white-collar workers, invoked an image of a society in which class differences were less extreme. According to Schelsky's analysis, class lines in postwar West Germany were blurred or totally dissolved. German society was now "characterized by the loss of class tensions and social hierarchy, neither proletarian nor bourgeois."[35] Social differentiation continued to exist, but social conflict was now defined by organized interests not synonymous with classes. At most, class was a residual analytic category that no longer described social reality.[36]

Under these altered circumstances, the family, not social class, became the agent of upward social mobility and the appropriate object of state social policy. It was not the family that should be forced to adjust to the demands of advanced industrial society; rather, society should capitalize on its most important asset and make every effort to support and maintain the family. This was the lesson of the war and postwar crises, and it was up to policy-makers to see how well they had learned it.[37]

No other postwar West German social scientist addressed more fully the range of issues relevant to the political discussion of women and the family in the early fifties, but others did provide interesting variations on the themes Schelsky outlined. Gerhard Mackenroth's proposals for a "Reform of Social Policy by Means of a German Social Plan" represented an important point of reference in debates over social welfare reform in the fifties. Mackenroth, a professor of national economy in Kiel from 1934 to 1941, took over the chair for sociology, social science, and statistics in Kiel in 1948.[38] With Schelsky, Mackenroth argued that the collapse of Germany after 1945 had cleared the ground for the construction of something new.

Mackenroth also maintained that the family should replace class as the focus of social policy. Although the family no longer constituted a unit of both production and consumption that brought children into the world according to a cost-benefit analysis, as it had in preindustrial society, children were no less important. They were the future labor force of a prosperous economy, and they would pay into the social insurance funds from which pensioners lived. While children's economic contributions were now redistributed through collective institutions, however, the cost of raising children was still borne by individual families. Because families were of different sizes, some benefited unfairly from the work of others. This inequitable situation resulted in social divisions not along the class lines separating rich and poor, but between those with and without responsibility for children. According to Mackenroth, it was essential to "equalize the burdens of families," transferring resources from the rich but "poor in children" (*kinderarm*) to the "rich in children" (*kinderreich*) but poor; redistribution should take place not among income groups but among families, from those without children or with few children to those with many children.[39]

Mackenroth saw family policy as a crucial part of any thoroughgoing reform of the social-insurance system. He expressed concern that providing too much support for some groups—particularly those with claims to damages for losses suffered during the war—would lead to the "sterilization of labor power." Able-bodied individuals would have no incentive to work once they determined that they could live better on social security than wages.[40] On the other hand, social-welfare programs geared only to individual requirements neglected the needs of families. Mackenroth, an expert on demographic theory and methods, claimed to speak with authority about what caused couples to limit family size. A falling birthrate was attributable not to a "biological decline or the lack of vitality" but to the fact that some families "assumed the entire economic burden of raising children (*Kinderaufzucht*)." This was "one of the major reasons for the declining birthrate." Social policies to shore up the site of reproduction were essential "if we are not to be outdone by the east."[41] The sexual division of labor behind Mackenroth's analysis was obvious: social reform must not "sterilize" workers, nor should it leave families infertile; it must ensure that men could be productive while women were reproductive.

Closely paralleling Mackenroth's arguments were the reflections of Hans Achinger, a professor of social policy in Frankfurt and coauthor of an influential academic white paper commissioned by Adenauer to outline a total overhaul of the postwar social welfare system.[42] Achinger praised the "family as the source [*Pflanzstätte*] of life . . . the decisive site of shaping humanity," and when he asked, "Does the wage suffice for children?" (*Reicht der Lohn für Kinder?*) the question was rhetorical.[43] If men's wages were inadequate to support the family, asked Achinger, "should the married woman pursue wage work, even when she has children? Russia answers this question very differently than the tradition in western Europe."[44] The inability of the male wage-earner to support a family deserved serious consideration, "because psychologically and in terms of the principle of the family it is not a matter of indifference whether the family father finds what he needs to cover his own needs and those of his family in his wage packet, or if he allows himself to be given something extra." A system of family allowances could provide assistance without stigma and without endangering the "performance wage," the essential basis for competitive capitalist economic development. Although "the performance wage might not guarantee that the pie will be cut up evenly . . . only the performance wage can guarantee that there will be a pie to cut up."[45] Transfers could be financed by forcing "those without children [to] forgo consumption."[46]

The sociological approach represented by Schelsky, Mackenroth, and Achinger emphasized that the family was society's bedrock, and women were the bedrock of families. This message was also broadcast by those who defended family allowances with the scientific elaboration of fears about the declining birth rate and the dwindling supply of human factors of production. Friedrich Burgdörfer, a demographer whose pronatalist past dated back to the 1920s and whose credentials included loyal service to the National Socialists, found that in postwar West Germany he could still find work as an expert on questions of family allowances. His thoughts on the "aging of the national body [Volkskörper] and the social burdens of the future" were no less relevant in the fifties than they had been in the thirties.[47] Although purged of some overt proposals for racial hygiene and "qualitative negative selection"—the antinatal dimension of Nazi eugenic policy—Burgdörfer's pronouncements continued to repeat his dire predictions of the twenties that Germans "are on the way to a two-child system" that threatened not only "population growth but also . . . the maintenance of the very bases of the population."[48]

In a lengthy analysis commissioned by the Bavarian Free Democratic party, Burgdörfer rejected as outdated the argument popular in FDP circles that the state should in no way interfere in the private sphere of marriage, particularly in the most intimate decisions about reproduction. Unabashedly citing work he had done in the Thousand Year Reich, he advised that it was the state's responsibility to ensure the preconditions for growth and prosperity, which included policies to "surmount the socio-biological climate that was inimical to families and the new generation." With approbation, he pointed to the "renewed increase in the birth rate in the years 1930–40 that delivered irrefutable evidence that our nation [Volk] was biologically healthy and . . . was prepared to respond to population policies."

No believer in Schelsky's classless society, Burgdörfer cautioned that supplementary payments should not be restricted to low-income groups, because this would contribute to a "negative selection" that was already under way. It was precisely "among the economically, politically and culturally leading strata that the restriction of births has found entry and has had the most extensive consequences." Barring these groups from supplementary payments would only intensify this troubling trend. Family allowances should also not be too large, lest the wrong families be encouraged to procreate. Burgdörfer could make no more explicit his continued commitment to some of the same eugenic principles he had championed under the Nazis: Germany needed not just more children but children of the right sort. Misinvestment in social policies affecting the family was "misinvestment of larger dimensions and more ominous consequences than could ever take place in financial or capital markets."[49]

Although Burgdörfer did not mention women explicitly, they were never distant from his analysis. There was no doubt that in the ubiquitous language of "reproduction" (*Fortpflanzung*) and biology, it was women for whom biology was destiny, women who were responsible for maintaining the "national body." Which West Germans should manage investments in finance and capital and which were responsible for the "living human capital" produced by families also required little imagination. Reversing the trend toward family-size limitation required social and economic measures, but the declining birth rate called for a spiritual response. Burgdörfer did not need to specify that this was work best accomplished by mothers. In addition, his criticism of the middle classes for restricting family size evoked familiar attacks on bourgeois feminism, which could be heard in Schelsky's analysis as well. The assumption that it was women, not men, who could control reproduction placed the blame for smaller families firmly on women.[50]

Explicitly acknowledging his intellectual debt to Burgdörfer, Ferdinand Oeter went a step further to locate the debate around family allowances within the context of a general theory of economic growth. Oeter served as an expert witness for the parliamentary committee that debated legislative proposals for *Kindergeld,* and he was particularly influential in one draft plan for thoroughgoing tax reform according to principles of family size.[51] According to Oeter, increased accumulation by those who did not bear the additional expense of raising children skewed consumer demand in favor of luxury goods and away from basic necessities. He predicted long-term consequences for a society with a dwindling labor supply and a debilitated social-security system as couples had fewer children, resulting eventually in an economy capable of producing televisions, motorcycles, and other nonessential luxuries but not a decent loaf of bread.

For Oeter, the problem with conventional economic theory was its inability to conceptualize the family except as the site of consumption; it was the site of production as well, the production of human capital.

The family was the "Cinderella" of a competitive market economy, locked in "indentured servitude to the social collective in a fashion completely irreconcilable with the present-day principles of freedom and equality before the law."[52] Family allowances were essential to make sure that the prince found the scullery maid, and that families were liberated and properly compensated for their labor. This, not strengthening the collective, "the way . . . that leads directly to the east," was the means "to orient the social order toward the family and not—as it presently occurs as an inversion of the Godly world order—according to the opposite principle."[53] Hardly pessimistic about the potential rewards of a properly conceived family policy, Oeter heralded it as making Germany the "birthplace of a new social order, from which a new culture of western humanity can emanate."[54]

Although this brief survey in no way exhausts the academic treatments of family policy in the early fifties, it does identify certain central themes that resounded in other accounts. The discussion acknowledged that the work of reproduction was clearly on a par with the work of production; human capital accumulation was equated with other forms of created value, the "body of the population" was seen as part of the capital stock, and economic planning necessitated paying attention to the costs of production and circulation of this human capital.[55] The emphasis on the family as the vehicle for upward social mobility indicated that women's work in the home had intensified since the war. According to sociological investigations of women's unpaid labor, what time women gained from advances in the rationalization of housework and the transfer of some services from the home to the economy was now spent checking over children's school assignments and caring for their psychological as well as their physical needs.[56] Indeed, the repeated insistence that "mothers be returned to their children" and "mothers belong to children" suggested that the proprietary interests of the next generation came before the interests of those who had brought them into the world. Mothers were also accountable for children's proper moral education and for preparing children to enter society as responsible individuals. The home was no "haven in a heartless world"; it was the site of important work. Family allowances could not compensate women fully for their labors, nor should they; love was work, but at the same time, women's care for their families was motivated by instincts that could not be measured in monetary terms. As commentators from left to right agreed, the home "should not be a hotel in miniature," and the "warmth of the nest," not the furnace's hot blast, was the atmosphere that the mother should achieve in her domestic workshop.[57] Still, supplementary benefits could at least enhance a mother's ability to work at one job, not two. Totalitarian states forced women to carry a heavy double burden. In the west, social policy should aim at making women offers they would not refuse by allowing them to opt for the work of housewifery and motherhood.[58]

"Money-for-children" represented society's recognition of the importance of women's work in the home and the need to elevate the value of this non-wage labor. This recognition was to take the form of a supplement to a male wage. Fattening a man's paycheck was a way to allow the family father to accept assistance without doing him psychological damage. Male egos would be preserved, women's work could be accomplished, companionate marriages where women and men were separate but equal would flourish, and the next generation of German workers would thrive. While occasional critics pointed out that plans to tax those "poor in children" discriminated against women denied the possibility to marry because of the *Frauenüberschuss*,[59] no one questioned that "money-for-children" was a good investment in the future of production and reproduction in a new Germany.

By late 1953, when a newly elected Bundestag resumed discussions of family allowance proposals, the initial emphasis on the "equalization of burdens" from the war's destruction had completely given way to a focus on the reproductive work of the family in an expanding economy. In his opening remarks to a parliament that included a dramatically expanded CDU/CSU delegation with as many votes as all other political parties combined, Adenauer showed how the themes of academic social theorists had become common political currency. The chancellor explained that West Germany was a rapidly aging nation. This threatened the future of economic growth and the stability of the social security system; at present, there was not a one-to-one relationship between those entering the labor force and those leaving it. Adenauer expressed his dismay over the "entire development of our era that is inimical to the foundation of a healthy family." Technological advance might slow down the corrosive effects of a declining birth rate, but it could not completely reverse a process that threatened to "destroy our entire population in the course of a few generations." A constant birth rate, not machines, was the best guarantee of prosperity and social security. "Only one thing can help: strengthening the family and thereby strengthening the will for children [*Stärkung des Willens zum Kind*]."[60]

From his recently created office as minister for family affairs, Franz-Josef Wuermeling enthusiastically championed this cause. The labor minister, Anton Storch, not Wuermeling, bore ultimate responsibility within the cabinet for overseeing proposals for family allowances, but Wuermeling made clear that he and his staff would play an active and vociferous role in debates over "money-for-children" and all other aspects of family policy.[61] Lauding the family's natural sacramental quality and leaving women no identity but as wives and mothers, Wuermeling made it clear that in his opinion there was only one family that fully deserved protection and support from the state. Themes intoned by Wuermeling as part of a larger framework for discussion of reforming the Civil Code were developed extensively in the context of debates over how most effectively to protect the family.

Addressing the CDU's annual congress in April 1953, Wuermeling explained that "both of the totalitarian systems" shared in common their attempt to "make individuals into slaves of the collective." The CDU/CSU must distance itself both from the "temporal background . . . of the desacralization of the state during the inhumane National Socialist reign of terror [and from] the spatial background . . . of the power sphere of Soviet terror with its humiliating reduction of humanity to a soulless machine." A Christian and democratic west must find ways to support families without enslaving them. In return, a protected family would ensure the "protection of our state."[62]

The CDU/CSU wasted no time in charting this route, the path that would lead to the *Wille zum Kind* and away from National Socialism and Soviet communism.[63] The coalition's solution had not changed from the initial discussion of family allowance proposals. The SPD, along with some Free Democratic allies, continued to propose state-administered payments to *all* children, or at least to the second and all others, and contended that the "normal family" of two adults and two children living from a male wage did not fully capture the social reality of postwar Germany, where female-headed households were anything but abnormal.[64] Social Democrats also criticized the conservative coalition's conception of "money-for-children as a work-based entitlement." The consequence was that the widow with three children who survived by piecing together social security payments but did not work for wages would receive no family allowance and might be forced out to work, neglecting the care of her children in order to supplement her inadequate income. By proposing such measures, Wuermeling and his ministry revealed themselves to be the family's enemy, not its friend.[65]

The CDU/CSU coalition continued to place the "normal family" at the core of its proposals.[66] Speaking for her party, the CDU's Elisabeth Pitz was particularly outspoken in rejecting any policies that would sanction unmarried motherhood. Pitz, whose husband had died in a Soviet prisoner-of-war camp, was an adviser on youth affairs to the state government of Hessen. To the Bundestag, she insisted that unmarried motherhood was an "exceptional state" that must be tolerated but should not be legitimized. The mother's sins should not be visited upon the child, and "the child has a right to a protected living space [*Lebensraum*]," but this in no way justified supporting a "flawed sociological development." Unmarried motherhood, like the *Frauenüberschuss*, would disappear as normal times created the conditions for the "normal family." CDU/CSU proposals represented a "morally defensible balance between the responsibility of the individual and social security."[67] The needs of other groups—the unemployed, war widows, unmarried mothers—should not be forgotten, but they were not properly a part of a program aimed at supporting families.

Behind the CDU/CSU's conception was a clear differentiation between those whose circumstances were the short-term consequences of the war and those who had legitimate long-term claims on the postwar state, in short, between those whose existence was rooted in a past to be overcome and those who embodied the future. Single women with minor dependents were in the former category, fathers of more than two children in the latter.

From its powerful position in parliament, the CDU/CSU coalition could ensure that controversy would not lead to stalemate as it had two years earlier. Fearing that further delays would create the space for the more forceful presentation of SPD alternatives, the coalition railroaded through a law in 1954 that provided monthly payments of 25 marks per child to wage earners with three or more children.[68] According to contemporary estimates, the amount did not cover the cost of feeding and clothing an infant and represented less than one-half of what was needed to support a school-aged child.[69] Although in theory single women in wage work were eligible for these payments, few had three or more children, and the normative conception underlying the law was that of a male breadwinner and a non-wage-earning wife. With no sense of irony, Heinrich Krone, head of the CDU parliamentary delegation, explained that this did not represent an attempt to "create any privilege for the married man, but rather was informed by practical concerns [because] by and large only the man worked for wages in households with many children."[70] In cases where both parents worked, payments went to the husband. Excluded were all those not in wage work—the unemployed, those on welfare and pensions—all those with only one or two children, and public employees, who already received family allowances as an automatic supplement to their salaries.[71]

Even after payments were extended to the unemployed and to recipients of welfare assistance in 1955 and increased to 30 marks monthly in 1957, family allowances did not make a significant difference in the lives of many German families.[72] The restriction of payments to those with at least three children guaranteed that the majority of West German families received no benefits at all. The 1957 census recorded that 57.7 percent of all married couples with children living at home had only one or two children. Only 20.3 percent had more than three. Sixty-nine percent of divorced and widowed parents—overwhelmingly women—had too few children to qualify for *Kindergeld,* and only 13 percent could receive more than 30 marks monthly, provided that they were in the wage labor force and not living from public assistance or some form of social security. Single women with dependent children received little "money-for-children." Both before and after the policy was introduced, they remained overrepresented among those living below the poverty level and dependent on public assistance or other forms of limited pensions, those "alms from the state" for which, according to the CDU/CSU, true families should not have to beg. Moreover, contrary to Burgdörfer's eugenic nightmares, there were many indications that family size increased slightly with income; thus, those likely to be entitled to *Kindergeld* were in higher-income groups and received correspondingly high benefits from tax deductions for dependents as well.[73]

There was certainly no evidence that the system of family allowances triggered a baby boom. On the contrary, statistics for the late fifties suggested that within all social groups, the long-term tendency toward smaller family size was in no way altered by "money-for-children." One representative sample of adults married in the decade of the fifties revealed that they had 40 percent fewer children than their parents. Among lower-income groups, the decline was even greater, approaching 50 percent.[74] A rising birth rate after the middle of the decade reflected not the influence of the nominal sums paid to large families but a slight decline in the age of first marriage among women and more generally a catching up, a response to the return of economic stability after the war and postwar crises. By the mid-sixties, the trend had once again reverted to the long-term tendency toward declining family size. While many women did cease full-time work outside the home when children arrived, "money-for-children" in no way compensated them for lost wages. Their decision to quit work was influenced by the adequacy of their husbands' earnings and the absence of alternative child-care arrangements, not financial support granted by the 1954 legislation.[75]

Once the basic outlines of the system were in place, there were few attempts to question its underlying premises. It would be almost another decade before the CDU/CSU would drop its objections to a system financed out of tax revenues and administered by a state agency, finally accepting the logic that *Kindergeld* was the responsibility of the entire society, not just employers and employees. In the meantime, Social Democrats and trade unionists concentrated on increasing benefits within the existing framework, never challenging the assumption that mothers of preschool- and school-aged children should be spared from work outside the home. With intensifying volume, Social Democrats emphasized that "state and society must protect, strengthen, and promote the family," the "nucleus of the state." For women, this meant guaranteeing their right "to be housewife and mother, [which] is not only a woman's natural obligation but of great social significance."[76] Nor were Social Democrats any less critical than the ruling coalition of family policy in East Germany, which, according to the SPD women's weekly, *Gleichheit,* was intended only to "increase the human reserve that can be economically exploited."[77]

The Social Democratic objective of extending payments to all families with more than one child, not the two specified by the law, made the SPD an unlikely ally of the Minister for Family Affairs. Much to the dismay of his own colleagues, Wuermeling called precisely for this course in a white paper, "The Equalization of Family Burdens," issued soon after passage of the initial legislation. Drawing heavily on Oeter, Schelsky, and other members of a "scientific advisory committee" that assisted in the report's formulation, Wuermeling emphasized the troubling decline in the birth rate. In familiar terms, he stressed that this development undermined West Germany's claim to status as an "occidental cultural center." Wuermeling also pointed to alarming signs that ever larger numbers of young mothers—the last available supply of potential workers in an economy approaching full employment—were being drawn into wage work, bringing West Germany perilously close to the pattern "that already reigns in states of an eastern character." While rejecting a system of "state population policy, which reduces the individual to an object," Wuermeling also roundly criticized the alternative that prevailed in West Germany, the "state-sanctioned reduction of the birth rate." Precisely this existed de facto in the West, a policy tantamount to "encouraging the murder of the nation [*Volksmord*]" (fig. 27). The selfishness of those without children would ultimately backfire; their savings would do them little good "if there was no productive generation to make the daily bread to be purchased from those savings."[78]

Social Democrats were careful not to join in this explicitly pronatalist chorus and continued to insist on eliminating tax deductions that most benefited the wealthy. Nonetheless, like Wuermeling they called for the dramatic expansion of the existing system of *Kindergeld*, rejected eastern models, and insisted that a mother's place was in the home. Clara Döhring was just as outspoken as Wuermeling in her insistence that "a substantial number of those mothers who are employed would give up their jobs sooner rather than later, if the economic circumstances of the family were easier and better. We Social Democrats support the family minister fully when he says that the housewife is the soul of the family and that it is decisive whether a housewife and mother can pursue her true occupation or is forced to pursue wage work."[79] To be sure, Döhring and her colleagues were out to illuminate the gap between the government's profamily pronouncements and its willingness to provide families with meaningful assistance; they sought to call the government's bluff and to present themselves as the family's true friend. But just as vigorously as the CDU/CSU, they declared their support for the "normal family," enthusiastically advocating the sexual division of labor and the system of social reproduction at its basis.[80] Champions of the family on the right and left insisted that increased benefits would achieve a vital objective—allowing all mothers to stay at home.

"Money-for-children" was only one part of a much larger social policy agenda set in place in the fifties, including the improvement of unemployment benefits, health care, and disability insurance, and the capstone, a thorough reform of retirement pensions in 1957. Along with the Law for the Equalization of Burdens of 1952, the Pension Reform Act of 1957 was among the most important social-welfare reform measures of the Adenauer era. Public-opinion polls in 1958 justified the conclusion that "up until now there is no known example of any law, institution, or even constitution and symbol of the state, which has received anywhere near such positive response."[81] Heralded as a pathbreaking innovation, this measure indexed pensions, tying them to general changes in wage rates. In addition, it reduced the differentials in pension payments to wage-earners and salaried employees and increased the level of payments by as much as sixty-five to seventy percent. At these higher levels, pensioners might actually live from their retirement income, and the 1957 act attenuated the almost axiomatic connection between old age and poverty that had characterized the lives of the overwhelming majority of Germans. Before this reform, payments out had been directly tied to payments in; retired workers had no hedge against general price increases and drew only on the resources they had accumulated over the course of their working lives. Now the younger generation's contributions financed the older generation's retirement.

As it had been since the founding of the German social insurance system under Bismarck in the 1870s, the basis for claims on the postwar welfare state remained employment status. Those who contributed to pension funds when they were employed were entitled to receive payments from them when they were sick, out of work, or eligible to retire. The labor contract constituted the essential point of entry into the greatly expanded postwar social contract. Social security and social insurance ended wage earners' total dependence on the vagaries of the market; reforms in this area were the most important social components of the "social market economy."

The consequences of this system for women—both those who worked for wages and were insured and those whose unpaid and uninsured workplace was the home—were easily fathomed. Women who interrupted their lives as wage earners to devote themselves exclusively to mothers' work paid less into social insurance funds and were entitled to take less out. In addition, the continued differentials in men's and women's wage levels translated into different levels of benefits, even for women who remained in full-time work. Women in part-time jobs received payments that reflected their reduced working hours and wages. A few figures illustrate the point. Three years after introduction of the "dynamic pension" system, the average pension for wage-earning women was less than half that of male wage-earners (*Arbeiter*), and less than one-third that of male salaried employees (*Angestellten*). Even women who worked in higher-paying white-collar jobs were likely to receive less than blue-collar men and on average only 58 percent of what went to their male counterparts. For most women, not even "dynamic pensions" provided a living wage at retirement; in 1960, 97 percent of all women who had worked as wage earners and 68 percent of those who had been salaried employees received retirement pensions that left them below the poverty line.[82]

Married women who did not work outside the home had claims to social security only through supplements for dependents paid to their husbands; for many adult women, access to the social contract came not through the labor contract but rather through the marriage contract. Despite all the political paeans to the value of women's work in discussions of "money-for-children," when it came to listing occupational categories or establishing the bases for accident and disability insurance and retirement pensions, housewives and mothers had no jobs.

The head of the social-welfare court in Hessen condemned a system that glorified motherhood while failing to guarantee this profession the same benefits as other types of work. Were a woman employed as "domestic servant, cook, secretary, [or] kindergarten teacher," she would be insured. Fulfilling the same functions as an unpaid housewife, she was not. In her daily routine, a housewife "schlepps wood and coal from the cellar, takes preserves into the cellar; she hurries up and down the staircase in wet shoes or with torn soles, perhaps in high heels, she wields electrical machines, works with acids and poisonous materials in containers that are unmarked or are not properly closed. She has to work with glass and porcelain, she sticks herself sewing, crushes herself moving furniture, falls when rummaging around on a ladder, [or] from the windowsill when cleaning windows." The housewife was an uninsured worker, her workplace an accident waiting to happen. It was the absence of any supplements for the housewife to the husband's retirement income that brutally accentuated her "second-place status and undervaluation."[83]

For widows, matters were only worse. Even after the 1957 reform, a widow was entitled to only 60 percent of her husband's pension. Drawing again on figures for 1960, this meant that 95 percent of the widows of workers and 65 percent of the widows of salaried employees received pensions insufficient to keep them out of poverty. For a woman, marriage to a healthy husband who earned well and outlived her was the best form of social security. Critical voices contrasted the development of postwar social security with the "social insecurity of German women,"[84] but in the fifties such perspectives remained exceptions, buried by a politics of the family that idealized women's work while legislating their dependent status.

The relationship between family policy and pension reform was immediately apparent to those who designed the "dynamic pension" system. Wilfrid Schreiber, the economist whose proposals for *Existenzsicherheit in der industriellen Gesellschaft* (security of existence in the industrial society) profoundly influenced Adenauer's thought on social welfare reform in the mid-fifties, was an outspoken advocate of barring all mothers of young children from the wage-labor force. Instead, he argued that they should be supported by a dramatically expanded system of family allowances, "the most profitable of all possible investments." A system of credits for children would make explicit what connected one generation to the next; parents should receive loans from the state for raising children, debts which the children themselves would assume upon reaching adulthood. What adults paid back would be dependent on how many children they raised; six and more children would mean cancellation of the debt, while those who never married would pay the most. Schreiber admitted that this system evoked associations with population policies that currently were rejected as "reactionary or ominous by a pack of self-proclaimed modern critics," but he countered that population policy was an essential part of economic policy.[85]

Schreiber's plans for institutionalizing a system of family credits that would tax those who were *kinderarm* and relieve those who were *kinderreich* found few supporters, but his conception that "the institutions of old-age pensions and money-for-children necessarily go hand in hand and [should] be viewed as a unity" was already familiar from the writings of Mackenroth, Achinger, and others who, like Schreiber, strongly influenced the debate over social reform in the mid-fifties. Drawing clear boundaries, Schreiber declared that it was "irrefutable that a married couple that brings more than 2.4 healthy children into the world has done society a service, while those who remain without children or the married couple with fewer than 2.4 children must render society a service." Those who failed to do their part were "parasitic consumers of the overproduction of those with many children."[86]

The debates over "money-for-children" expressed these themes in elaborate detail; they made explicit where married women fit into the welfare state. To be sure, women were workers; indeed, their work was essential to the welfare state's survival. Without the next generation, the economy would falter; without new workers to pay into insurance and retirement funds, there would be nothing left to take out. Indexing pensions on the basis of wage rates was cast explicitly as a "contract between generations," between one generation of workers paying into social insurance funds and another enjoying retirement, between wage levels of workers in the present and the retirement compensation of those who had worked in the past.[87] As producers of the next generation, women could be part of this contract as well. However, they signed not with their wage work but with their marriage vows and a lifetime of unpaid labor, through their status as wives and mothers, not as individuals. Social security was founded in a productive order and the world of paid employment; it was also founded in a reproductive order and the world of women's work in the home.

The emphasis of West German social policy on women's dependent status within nuclear families reiterated themes already familiar from the public deliberations over the reform of the Civil Code. The constitutional guarantee of the family's protection was frequently invoked by those advocating family allowances. The Basic Law's promise of women's equal rights received no explicit mention, though discussions of "woman's place" in the welfare state made apparent that difference was compatible with equality. Husbands and wives, fathers and mothers, families had their work cut out for them in building a new Germany. Conservatives encouraged families to produce more than two children. Socialists argued that only increases in male wages could make the "normal family" a reality for all. But no one examined families as arenas of conflict and power relations between genders and generations, and no one questioned their fundamental importance.

Alternatives to the West German "normal family" as the conceptual basis for postwar social policy were not entirely lacking in other western European countries. For example, in the French system high rates of women's labor-force participation had long been accepted as crucial to dynamic economic development. State social policy acknowledged employers' reliance on a female labor force, and the French left supported the ideal of women's wage work, because of its continued belief that women's entry into political consciousness would be facilitated by their entry into industrial labor. This political combination led to emphasizing the right to work for all citizens in the postwar French constitution. On this basis, trade unions and the left intensified their demands for equal wages and equal treatment in the social-security system for women and men. The other pillar of postwar French social policy, a system of family allowances, was informed by many of the nationalist and pronatalist sentiments that were ubiquitous in the postwar West German discussion, but the French program was not based on the assumption that only non-wage-earning mothers would raise children, or that only married couples were families; families in which parents were not married and single mothers were entitled to the same financial support.[88]

In postwar Britain, family allowances incorporated the same vision of a "normal family" enshrined in West German measures. However, throughout debates over how best to aid families there also resounded a feminist critique of women's dependency within marriage and wives' subordination to potentially abusive husbands, who might be as likely to spend their wages on drink as on their children. Although family allowances were ultimately much smaller than those proposed by feminists, and policy-makers affirmed beliefs that mothers should stay out of the wage-labor force, the decision to issue payments directly to mothers, not as a supplement to a male wage, represented a clear concession to feminist pressures.[89]

In Sweden, where discussion of family allowances intensified in the 1930s, the needs of children without fathers and of unmarried single mothers had been at the center of policy formulation from the beginning, not treated as anomalous. Not the family but the citizen was the focus of social policy. From this starting point, it was possible to develop programs of income maintenance based on the assumption that all adults would work outside the home and that single women with children needed particular assistance so that their children's standard of living would not fall below that of families with two incomes.[90]

As in Sweden, France, and Britain, fears of population decline had intensified the move toward a comprehensive family policy in Germany in the thirties and forties, but Nazi policies were based on very different conceptions of family and citizenship and left no space for a feminist critique of married women's dependence. Although the National Socialist objective of an expanding birthrate had justified a tolerance for unmarried motherhood, this was still viewed as an exception to the rule. After 1945, the massive loss of adult male life and the consequent "surplus of women" made it possible to define the needs of single women responsible for the care of children and adult dependents as extraordinary, requiring only short-term solutions and vanishing as Germans distanced themselves from the crises of the war and postwar years. In contrast, the needs of "normal families" were there to stay, constants in an advanced industrial society.

The Nazis' war was thus the explanation for the *Frauenüberschuss* and the problems of "incomplete" families. It also shaped the idealized visions of motherhood and "normal families" in the postwar period. Possibilities for any post-1945 critique of these visions were diminished by yet another consequence of National Socialism, the exile of those most accomplished at delivering alternative analyses of the family in the 1920s. The Institute for Social Research, including Max Horkheimer, Herbert Marcuse, and Erich Fromm, left Frankfurt in 1934, first for Geneva, then New York. Its major collective project of the thirties, *Studien über Autorität und Familien* (Studies of authority and the family) was a massive investigation of the political consequences of familial socialization; it appeared in 1936 not in Berlin or Frankfurt, but Paris. Although Horkheimer and Theodor Adorno returned to Frankfurt after the war, it was not their brand of critical theory but the optimistic accounts of Schelsky, Oeter, Mackenroth, and Achinger that most influenced the political analysis of the family in the fifties.[91] When Horkheimer or Adorno was cited by sociologists like Schelsky, it was as a negative point of reference, not as a positive tradition.

As for other critical perspectives from the left, when Engels' *Origins of the Family* was quoted in the discussion of family in the fifties, it was not by Social Democrats but for excoriation by Wuermeling.[92] Although women in the SPD and the trade-union movement placed greater emphasis on the economic needs motivating women to work outside the home, they would not be outdone in their assertion that "socially just wages" for men would allow women to work at raising the next generation, providing an adequate supply of "the new blood essential for economic advance."[93] Women in the SPD also subscribed completely to the belief in the essential bond between mother and child and prescribed the "Vitamin of Mother's Love" for the physical and psychological well-being of children.[94] This was a medication best administered in the home.

Compared with their active engagement in debates over reforming the Civil Code, organized middle-class women's groups were relatively silent in discussions of "money-for-children" and the larger agenda of reforming the social insurance system. There were many women among the lawyers who could claim expertise in the intricacies of the Civil Code and family law but not among the professors of social policy who could claim a privileged voice in discussions of social-security reform and family allowances; women had never gained significant access to employment in state-run social-welfare agencies.[95]

When middle-class feminists did intervene, they too were committed to a politics of difference in which motherhood took center place as the apotheosis of womanhood and in which, in contrast to the perspective of their British counterparts, the problem was not abusive husbands but insufficient male wages. To be sure, from their ranks came the loudest protests against schemes to place greater taxes on the childless and against the "identification of those without children with the cheery consumer, driven by the need to spend." However, they did not emphasize the autonomy and independence of the single woman or the possibility that some women might choose to remain unmarried; rather, they stressed that women who would otherwise happily be wives and mothers were robbed of the opportunity by the war. Were mates available, most women would gladly abandon work outside for work inside the home. "Loneliness was a weighty fate to bear," not voluntarily chosen, "as the millions of soldiers' graves made only too clear." The Nazi state had forced this fate on women; the new West German state should consider carefully whether it would now impose additional burdens on these victims in the form of special taxes for those without children.[96] Schelsky's invective against a bourgeois feminism that denied the crucial significance of sexual difference was aimed at something that did not exist. His emancipatory, individualistic feminist was an imaginary target.

Fears of West Germany's dwindling population in the fifties had no firmer basis in reality. Gains from postwar immigration into West Germany more than canceled out war losses. The populous "peoples of the east," conjured up by Wuermeling, were certainly not in the German Democratic Republic, which experienced a net population loss in the fifties. In contrast, between 1939 and 1950 the population of those areas constituting the Federal Republic grew by 7.6 million, an increase of 18.2 percent. Throughout the fifties, a steady stream from one Germany to the other continued, dammed effectively only in August 1961, with the closing of the East German border.[97] Nonetheless, West German policy-makers remained obsessed by concerns with declining birth rates, and these fears translated unambiguously into pronatalist sentiments. To be sure, it was no longer the *Führer* and the Reich that demanded population growth, but the needs of the economy and the social security system delivered new justifications for familiar rhetoric.

Connecting economic prosperity to population growth raised difficult questions about where to set the boundaries between state social policy and the private sphere. The past of National Socialism made it only more pressing to provide clear definitions; memories of the Nazis' attempt to invade the family made it essential for the state in the fifties to make explicit how its intentions differed from those of the state that had ruled from 1933 until 1945. Denise Riley, writing of postwar British attempts to define a language of pronatalism distinct from that of fascist regimes in the interwar period, emphasizes how British policy-makers were at pains to prove that "*we* were not Germans."[98] In the fifties, West Germans had to prove that they were not *those* Germans either.

In the confused categories of totalitarian theory, it was possible to establish an identity as a new sort of Germany by associating National Socialist family policy with communist family policy and, by rejecting both, to claim to be something completely different. Drawing on the repertoire played out in discussions of family law reform, the ruling CDU/CSU coalition in particular emphasized state support of the family as an intimate, inviolable "nucleus of society" in contrast to Nazi and communist attempts to subordinate the individual to the nation directly by weakening the link—the family—that should hold the two together.[99] Communists and Nazis alike sought to transform private spheres into public places; West Germans claimed to maintain the boundary, precisely by using public policy to strengthen the family against any potential intervention by the state.

Still, the Nazis' misuse of population policy, argued social theorists and politicians of all political stripes, was no reason to exclude concerns over population size from the legitimate agenda of a democratic political order. It was time for Germans to move beyond this "past that had not been overcome" (*unbewältigte Vergangenheit*).[100] The debates over "money-for-children" indicate that many West Germans moved too quickly and without reflection. The shock therapy of defeat in war had done much to kill off the National Socialist virus of eastward expansionism, but in the debates over family policy racialist overtones continued to abound. By 1958 Wuermeling had so comfortably surmounted the recent German past that he could openly articulate his concern about the "overpopulation problems of the colored peoples of Asia," a problem not for them but for western Europeans and in particular West Germans, who continued to practice a "state-directed restriction of births." The family minister was dismayed over a present in which only one in three people in the world was white, and a future in which by the year 2000, the ratio would be one in five.[101] Nor were the National Socialist links between population growth and militarism so cleanly severed when Wuermeling praised the "millions of inwardly healthy families . . . [who] are as important as all military security as a defense against the threatening danger of the families, rich in children, of the east," whether that east was in central Europe or in Asia.[102] Declarations that family policy sought only the "freedom of the living space [*Lebensraum*] of the family, not success in population policy"[103] revealed remarkable continuities with a history that was too easily forgotten. They also indicated that for women in a democratic republic no less than under National Socialism, freedom found its limit in biology.

Women's work as wives and mothers was not romanticized and certainly not made invisible; rather its economic value was reckoned to the last pfennig. In terms that would reappear in a very different political context in the debates among feminists in the early seventies over the value of women's unpaid labor in the home, sociologists, economists, and policy-makers in the fifties painstakingly calculated women's non-wage contributions to economic development. Of course, for them women's unpaid work was in the service of the nation, the family, and the *Volk,* not capitalism or patriarchy.[104] Arnd Jessen, an economist who had already detailed the costs of "raising children" (*Kinderaufzucht*) for a publication series entitled "The National Socialist Bibliography" in 1937,[105] explained to his listeners at the annual meeting of the Society for Social Progress in 1955 that at an imputed hourly wage of 1 mark, housewives contributed labor worth 11.3 billion marks annually to the West German economy. This wage, if actually paid, "would force married men to declare bankruptcy and to fire their wives." Jessen calculated that a housewife's wages were actually about 17 pfennig per hour; a real wage in accord with the rules of market competition was completely out of the question. Should society not devise other means to acknowledge their contribution, housewives might go on strike, not by withholding their labor but by seeking other jobs. The unavoidable result would be more and more latch-key children, who, according to Jessen, already numbered 2.1 million, more than the populations of Munich, Cologne, and Essen combined. Family policy was essential for banishing this nightmarish vision of huge metropolitan areas overrun by children left to their own devices and denied a mother's love, "orphans of [the] technology" that drew women from their workplace in the home.[106]

As the economics minister, Ludwig Erhard, emphasized, in the "economic miracle" women's unpaid labors also included their crucial role as guardians of consumption, spending the money that men earned. In the early fifties, Erhard reassured those anxious about buying on credit that the demand for a "refrigerator in every home" was no expression of unbridled greed; rather it was what would lead to economic growth and prosperity. "Free consumer choice" belonged to the "inalienable freedoms of humanity." This "civilized progress" would in turn free the harried housewife and mother to devote herself more fully to her family. The "will to consume" (*Wille zum Verbrauch*) was the engine that drove uninterrupted output, economic rationalization, efficiency, and gains in productivity; as "economics ministers" of their families, women controlled the throttle.[107] Competitive capitalism—the "social market economy"—could not threaten the family. Only within this economic framework would the "state-free sphere of the family" be possible. The experience of totalitarian and communist state-run economies, their attempts to subordinate families to their needs, was proof positive.[108]

As social commentators warned, however, though women should not be shy about spending they must also avoid the pitfalls of unlimited materialism, particularly when it came to determining family size. The linkage woman-home-consumption was not without its dangers.[109] The temptations of economic prosperity were enormous. When the "craving for pleasure and the striving for exaggerated security" took hold, luring women into wage labor, women would also find themselves driven to contraception and abortions, endangering their own health as well as the existence of future generations.[110] In pursuit of consumer desires, women who worked outside the home—"amazons in the midst of a world of steel and iron"—might even develop a fear and loathing for housework, a pathology dubbed "Oikophobia" in one widely cited study. A society in which new car registrations outnumbered newly registered births, in which too much leisure left idle women subject to the lures of the "pleasure industry" of cinema, dance, radio, television, and sports, was a society in trouble. Men *had* to go out to work; women *chose* to go out to work. For mothers the choice meant turning their backs on their primary responsibilities; their motivations were under particular scrutiny.[111]

Fortunately, not all women had succumbed to a pervasive "democratic demand for luxuries";[112] most mothers knew best that a vital family life was worth far more than the "auto, the television set, the luxury dog, which have become the indirect means of contraception."[113] But social theorists seemed to agree that repeated warnings were essential: women should consume, but they should be careful not to consume too much. The family should remain the "non-commercialized nucleus" in a commercial society.[114]

The debates over family policy also made clear that postwar West German consumer society was to be a society without classes. The "end of ideology" in the west, measured in the fifties by French and American intellectuals in terms of the decline of the political extremes of the interwar period,[115] registered in material calculations in West Germany. To be sure, all the rhetoric in the world did not eliminate the striking differentials in income and access to education that divided West Germans and that guaranteed that women and children constituted the vast majority of those living in poverty. Even those who saw the classless family as the new agent of social mobility often implicitly acknowledged the reality of socioeconomic differentiation by insisting that families with children should be supported in accord with their different standards of living. Muted here, eugenic undertones could be heard more clearly in expressions of concern that the middle classes were most guilty of limiting family size and most in need of expanding their numbers, and in the emphasis on the importance of healthy offspring. Still, in Mackenroth's distinction between *kinderarm* and *kinderreich* and in Schelsky's description of a "leveled-out petit bourgeois–*mittelständische* society"[116] was a vision of a new Germany freed from the class struggles that had torn apart Weimar and from the artificially imposed unity of race proclaimed under the National Socialists.

"We are happy to turn over to the experts discussion of the theory of quantum physics, of cancer research, or of the international balance of payments," observed the journalist Rüdiger Proske, writing in 1951 in the *Frankfurter Hefte*, a leading postwar journal of left-wing political commentary. "In the discussion of the family, or more precisely, the crisis of the family, we all take part. Everyone feels in a certain sense entitled to an opinion on this topic. To be sure, everyone has some experience in this area. Unfortunately, when most people talk about the family, they are talking about what they think should be, not what really is."[117]

The family that should be, as it emerged in debates over "money-for-children" in the early fifties, confronted innumerable vital tasks, all of which translated into more work for mothers. Threatened in the forties by bomb attacks and scarcity, the family now confronted a potential enemy no less lethal—the mother who worked outside the home. No longer between rubble and ration line, in the fifties, women were between family and factory. By locating women in "normal families" with male providers, West Germany social policy sought to remind women of their enormous responsibilities, best serving Germany by best serving German families.

CHAPTER FIVE

Protecting Mothers' Work

"My entire hope is the West German Basic Law," explained Anneliese Teetz to the reporter from the weekly news magazine *Der Spiegel* as she cut up greens for her family's midday soup. It was the spring of 1949, and Teetz was out of work. This alone would not have justified news coverage of Teetz's plight; female unemployment had risen sharply in the wake of currency reform nearly a year earlier. In large numbers, women whose work as housewives and mothers had won them exemption from labor mobilization under the Nazis and whose services as scroungers, black marketeers, and managers of scarcity had kept them out of the wage-labor force in the immediate postwar years now sought paid employment. What set Teetz apart and what caught the reporter's attention was that she wanted a job as a ship's captain. Teetz had practiced this profession since 1943, the only woman in Germany to complete the necessary training. In search of a new position, Teetz complained that she was facing resistance from the Public Transport and Traffic Workers' Union, which threatened to block its membership from working on any ship piloted by Teetz. The union argued that there were plenty of unemployed men available for any open slot and also claimed that Teetz was disqualified because of her past membership in the Nazi party.

For Teetz, more was involved than her "irrepressible desire" for the life of the sea; she also needed to pay the rent for her modest one-room apartment near Hamburg. Not just romance, but the Deutschmark was at stake, the *Spiegel* reporter commented dryly. Teetz, "with her masculine haircut and perfectly round eyes," supported her unemployed husband, a machinist who was also looking for work on a ship, and who testified to his complete confidence in his wife's leadership abilities. The couple's shared love affair with the sea found expression in walls covered with pictures of ships from a recent series in a Hamburg newspaper and a large spyglass with which they could identify who was sailing by on the Elbe. Teetz justified her desire to pursue her passion by identifying herself with a long line of "heroines from folk tales, queens, female sea pirates, and freedom fighters," all of whom had gone to sea. And why not? After all, she added, "in reality the two sexes are really not so different."[1]

If Hans Böckler read the *Spiegel* story, he was not learning of Teetz for the first time. Böckler was head of the postwar German Federation of Trade Unions (Deutscher Gewerkschaftsbund), the single national representative of organized labor. Created to eliminate the splits among socialist, Catholic, and liberal organizations that had divided trade unionists in Weimar, it was the realization of Böckler's vision of mixing "all unions in one pot" (*Eintopfsgewerkschaft*). In July 1948, the would-be female ship's captain sent him a long letter, soliciting his support and describing her circumstances in detail. Teetz's father, a physical education teacher, had opposed his daughter's aspiration to pilot an ocean-going steamship. Despite her love of the sea, in her youth she tried to accept the fact that such employment was out of the question for a woman. After completing her secondary school education (*Abitur*) in 1929, she resigned herself to a profession as a teacher, but in school vacations, she learned more and more about the ocean and ships. Disguised as a boy, she even managed two trips, one on a fishing boat, one on an ocean-going sailing ship. While this experience only heightened her passion, it also reaffirmed that as a woman she had no prospects of making a living at sea, and she fought to repress her "unruly desire." But after completing her training as a schoolteacher in 1932, her common sense and pragmatism were still on a collision course with her dreams. Despite attempts to remain fully occupied with her job, a gymnastics club, and volunteer work with a local civil defense organization and the Red Cross, she ultimately conceded that "the battle against nature was to no avail. . . . With every strong wind [my thoughts] went to sea and returned to beckon me."

In her appeal to Böckler, Teetz made no secret of her National Socialist past. She entered the NSDAP in 1937 as a teacher, she explained, both out of "honest conviction to serve in a good cause and in part because I hoped through practical work to change some things that I did not like." Her frustration with the limits to her success in the classroom, however, only intensified her desire to pursue the career of her choice. Finally, her persistence won out over the opposition of the Nazi organization of workers (Deutsche Arbeitsfront), and the Transportation Ministry approved her application to sign onto a steam-powered vessel. Still, it required years of additional petitions and personal appearances in Berlin before she landed a position as the pilot of an ocean-going fishing boat. Happily for Teetz, personal and professional life coincided; she married a machinist under her command, and until 1948, when they quit to look for better jobs, they remained employed together.

Teetz categorically rejected charges that she was "politically encumbered" (*politisch belastet*); she had been officially "denazified" in 1946. She countered that the real "point of contention is naturally the status of women in a community of men and in an outspokenly difficult male profession." To be sure, for a woman extraordinary responsibilities came with such a job; it was up to her to ensure that "in the close quarters of these primitive surroundings" on board the ship, relations with the crew remained purely professional. But Teetz pointed out that she made this easier by ensuring that crew members "never see me decked out like a woman." Moreover, the demanding work on a ship left little time for sleep, let alone for "flirtatious thoughts."

Even more importantly, Teetz lectured Böckler, "the differences between the sexes are much more subtle than we generally see," and she attributed the blurred vision of male trade unionists to a "thousand-year-long education since the introduction of the law of the father that surely went hand in hand with the discovery of iron and the spread of armed conflict, that led girls . . . to dependence and subordination, while boys and men felt like powerful rulers." Given the opportunity, women could pursue many professions denied them by the "tyrant 'tradition.' " How could Böckler deny that twenty years of difficult struggle against tenacious opposition were evidence that Teetz's commitment to her profession was more than a passing fancy? Crossing the line between dispassionate description and melodrama, Teetz claimed that for her a life without the ocean and fishing would be like a life in prison.[2]

Böckler and the trade union were unmoved by such appeals, and for the next five years Teetz pursued her "paper war," as her case made the rounds of the Federal Transportation Ministry, the Labor Ministry, and even the Bundestag. Throughout, she invoked the Basic Law's promise of women's full equality with men, charging the trade union with em-

ploying "dictatorial measures" to keep her from going to sea. Supporting herself by working as a schoolteacher in Hamburg, she awaited vin-
dication and reentry into her other profession.[3]

The trade union countered that it was "no enemy of women"; indeed,
it was the union's "well-meaning attitude toward women" that prevented it from sanctioning women's employment on deck or as machin-
ists until there was protective legislation in place that would regulate
women's working conditions in the maritime industry. Such laws would
ensure "proper moral conditions" and take into account the "physical
constitution of a woman and the function of motherhood," lest women's
work endanger their "bodily and spiritual health." The constitutional
proclamation of female equality did not eliminate the need for consideration of women's "bodily constitution"; protective legislation was
in no way inconsistent with women's equality, and exceptions were
justifiable only in the face of shortages of male workers—such as had
existed in the war and the immediate postwar years—which no longer
prevailed.

Critical of Teetz's tendency to the romantic, the union disputed her
self-portrayal. Why had she left teaching, which "should offer a woman
myriad possibilities for inner satisfaction" and which promised far
greater economic security, particularly for older women, than a life at
sea? The union also charged that Teetz had initially gained entry into the
profession through her brother's personal connection to Hitler. This was
all the more necessary because in her trips to sea as a sailor before ob-
taining a post as a pilot, she had served more "for the entertainment of
the crew than to fill a position on board," though the union agreed that
she was innocent of any specific moral infractions. Still, past history was
no necessary predictor of future behavior, and there were precedents for
"doubting whether an individual could enter into the close community
of the crew, for example, in the case of homosexuals; women are an alien
body in a close-knit crew, and [they] endanger it." It was precisely for
this reason that wives of seamen had already made known their intention to keep their husbands at home should women be allowed on
board.[4] Wives were not the only ones with problems. When trade-union
representatives asked, "Can a woman stand at the head of a unit that is
organized in an almost military fashion?" the question was rhetorical.[5]

Specialists within the labor and transportation ministries took seriously their charge to break the impasse, even visiting the Hamburg
wharves to inspect firsthand the working conditions on ocean-going
ships. They could find no laws explicitly prohibiting women from

becoming captains, but this was a reflection of the exceptional quality of Teetz's case; were more women in the profession, there would be more laws regulating their work. No one disputed that any *"mechanical equivalence of the rights and associated obligations of women with those of men"* was risky "because such an interpretation would pay no heed to the differences in the sexes given by nature."[6] The Nazis had provided elaborate descriptions of those differences, and labor ministry officials drew on their efforts. Citing a 1941 report, they emphasized that because of their pelvic structures, women could not carry heavy loads. Women had lower average body weights and smaller hearts, less physical strength, higher pulse rates, and in addition, their job performance was jeopardized by menstruation. At least three to four days out of every twenty-eight, women's physical capacity was decisively diminished, while one-third of all women experienced even greater discomfort, approaching illness. Women's bodies and characters were not fully developed before they were twenty-four; by fulfilling the normal requirement of fifty months "before the mast" between the ages of 15 and 20, they ran extraordinarily high risks. Menopause presented still other problems that deserved special consideration.[7] These natural barriers combined with concerns about ethical behavior on board set limits to the Basic Law's promise of women's equality. Some jobs endangered women's bodies; others endangered their morals; in still others, because of their bodies, women presented a threat to workplace morality. The occupation of sailor or ship's captain seemed to present problems on all counts.

Summarizing this massive documentation, Marie Schulte-Langforth, a labor ministry specialist on protective legislation for women workers, affirmed that equality and special treatment were by no means incompatible. However, Teetz represented a truly "unusual case" (*Sonderfall*). She was physically able to do the work required on board a ship and entitled to a job. Drafting specific legislation to regulate women's employment in the maritime industry was not necessary, and most women needed no instruction to realize that work on large fishing boats was not for them. Teetz's case was unique, an exception to this rule, and the Transport and Traffic Workers' Union was informed that if it did not clear the decks for Teetz, it could anticipate massive intervention by the labor ministry on her behalf.[8] With support from women leaders within the SPD, Schulte-Langforth's threat worked. By March 1953—as the Bundestag was debating "money-for-children" and rapidly approaching the deadline for specifying the dimensions of women's equality in a revised Civil Code—Teetz was back at sea, pursuing her "irrepressible desire" and earning a living.[9]

Although Teetz was the only West German woman to work as a sea captain in the late forties and early fifties, she was not the only woman to work. Her experience was exemplary not because throngs of women shared her professional ambitions but because it illuminated larger dimensions of the West German state's attempts to negotiate the boundaries between the drive to get women into nontraditional occupations under the Nazis and the Allies in the forties and the return to a normal labor market in the fifties, between equality and special treatment, between women's rights and women's protection, between women's bodies and women's work, between women's productive and reproductive labor. The Basic Law had ensured all women equal rights with men, but as Selbert had insisted, recognizing equal rights was completely consistent with acknowledging that women and men were different. How that difference translated into women's work in the home was at issue in debates over family policy and reform of the Civil Code. How it translated into women's rights in the paid workplace was the question that had been raised explicitly in Teetz's case and that would be answered for hundreds of thousands of others in state policies aimed at protecting working women.

The relentless emphasis on the indispensability of women's work as housewives and mothers in the debates over family policy and family law did not prevent many women—married and unmarried—from going out to work in the first years of the Bonn Republic. Their numbers began to increase in 1948 with the introduction of the Deutschmark. With the collapse of the black market and the end to the postwar subsistence economy, more women sought jobs that paid wages.[10]

Finding work was not always easy. In some heavy industrial districts women confronted unemployment rates of twice the national average. Those who had been granted exemption from labor mobilization under the Allies because of their responsibilities for dependents also now swelled the ranks of job-seekers; often with little or no work experience outside the home, they fared poorly in a tight labor market. Together with female expellees, they were overrepresented among the unemployed.[11] But the number of women job-seekers unable to find work after currency stabilization was generally lower than labor ministry officials had predicted, and increases in unemployment paralleled increases in employment; there were more jobs, but there was also a growing number of women looking for work.

When women found jobs, it was not, as some critics of women's work alleged, at the expense of men. Allied proposals for increasing the employment of women in jobs typically held by men, particularly by expanding training opportunities, had remained vaguely formulated and not systematically implemented before 1948. Indeed, six months before currency reform the Allies began to back off from early calls for women's mobilization into nontraditional employment; training women for jobs that were fit for men returning from prisoner-of-war camps was seen to be unwise, because "it would not make for stability if women were employed on jobs for which unemployed men would be equally suitable." The market, not Allied policy, should define women's opportunities, and by early 1948 the Allies emphasized that with regard to training and mobilizing women workers, "our policy must inevitably be subordinated to economic considerations."[12] Even though the Allies perceived that it was not only market forces but also many male trade unionists who opposed the "idea of women entering other than traditional occupations," they were not willing to undertake concerted action to overcome this prejudice.[13]

What the Allies were loath to do, German labor ministry officials, particularly those responsible for enforcing the protective legislation that limited the hours and conditions of women's employment, had always viewed with enormous skepticism. Before 1948, they aggressively opposed all Allied attempts to coax women into "men's jobs." They acted no differently once they were freed completely from Allied supervision and it became their responsibility to oversee developments in the labor market on their own.[14] Protective legislation that had barred women from certain jobs, suspended first by the Nazis to meet the needs of the war economy and held in abeyance by the Allies to respond to the shortage of adult men after the war, was still considered necessary to circumscribe women's work with the return to normal times after currency reform. There was no longer any reason to force women into occupations for which men were available and which women did not want; the war and postwar years were seen as a mandated experiment that had changed no one's priorities. Käthe Gaebel, writing in the labor ministry's official publication, concluded that "young women approach 'new' occupations only very hesitantly, their parents even more so, and the masters not infrequently withdraw an apprenticeship once offered, if there is no young man assigned to it." The division between women's and men's work, explained Gaebel, was defined by "the bodily performance capacity of the woman," which simply put some jobs out of her reach.[15]

In the view of labor ministry officials, not only biology but also the destiny it entailed placed limits on women's labor-force participation. Counselors in the state-run labor exchanges that tracked unemployment and that brought job-seekers together with employers looking for workers were reminded that when they sought suitable employment for women, not only a woman's individual wishes but also her "personal ties and obligations" must be taken into account. These ties and obligations subjected her to particular physical and psychological demands, and job counselors and placement officers must remember that women were constantly weighing competing strategies of how best to fulfill the needs of their families. Not for men but for women, there "always exists alongside the world of work a second world of personal obligations, from which she can and will not extract herself." If a woman worked for wages, it was because such work was the way in which she could best serve her family. Although it was never discussed explicitly, men apparently worked because they were men. The female job-placement counselors, assigned exclusively to female job-seekers, were advised to recall that they and their clients bore the "same double burden of obligations." Finding the right job for women meant attempting to reconcile the "contradictory demands of occupational life and multifaceted family life," a challenge not faced when placing a man.[16]

Elaborating on these general outlines, a local employment office in Lower Saxony instructed its officials to take into consideration the "otherness (*Andersartigkeit*) of women's work." From the initial interview through final placement, a woman required special treatment because, unlike a man, she "is not born into the life of work." Only a small number of women would work their entire lives; the others would see wage work as a necessary evil to be tolerated as a transitional stage. Labor-exchange officials were also advised to distinguish carefully between the legitimate and illegitimate unemployed. A woman fell into the former category only if "she had nothing tying her to the home." A woman with family obligations could not be unemployed; she already had one full-time job. The "life of work" she was "born into" was one of unpaid housewifery and motherhood, not one of work for wages. To be sure, under the existing economic conditions a mother might have to work, but it was worth evaluating critically whether she might lack "the will and the physical strength" for this second shift.[17] Such attitudes ensured that state policy did absolutely nothing to loosen the confines of a labor market rigidly segmented by sex, and it was into such a labor market that women came in the fifties. Indeed, by acknowledging this reality, women trade unionists sought to reassure men that women would not be competing for jobs with their male comrades.[18]

A sex-segregated labor market did not translate into a shortage of jobs for women. Fears early in the decade that the economy might rapidly reach a "saturation point" for female labor, leaving women job-seekers out of work, proved unfounded.[19] The combination of the influx of foreign capital initiated by the Marshall Plan and the "Korea boom," the increase in demand for West German goods as the United States economy diverted some of its resources to war in the Far East, generated more and more jobs for women and men.[20] By 1953, West German economists predicted the imminent end of unemployment; by the mid-fifties, they proclaimed that it had arrived. Women's labor-force participation rates increased much more rapidly than men's. Between 1947 and 1955, nearly two million women entered the labor force. While total employment had grown by 28 percent, the number of women working for wages had increased by over 48 percent.[21]

By the mid-fifties, the problem that labor-exchange officials confronted was no longer how best to allocate scarce jobs among a surplus of would-be workers but rather how best to meet the continued demands for labor by mobilizing the silent reserve of adult women who allegedly resisted work outside the home. Employers were advised to expect a certain resentment on women's part as once again they were called upon to make up for labor scarcities. Memories of the deployment of women's labor during the war were still vivid, and labor ministry officials reported women's concerns that the jobs offered them would not be tailored to their particular needs and aspirations.[22]

Whether more motivated by necessity or desire, by 1961, 48.9 percent of all women between the ages of 15 and 60 were engaged in paid employment. Although those decrying the dangers of working mothers in debates over family allowances viewed this development with consternation, these employment levels marked a return to pre–World War II trends, not a startling departure from well-established patterns. The figures for 1961 were still slightly lower than those reached in the full-employment economy of Nazi rearmament in 1939 and no higher than those recorded in 1925. But for commentators in the first postwar decade, the most common point of reference remained the low level of 1950. From this vantage point, the number of working women was increasing dramatically, not picking up where long-term trends had left off before the decade of economic disruption brought on by the war and the postwar crisis. For contemporary observers, it was still more alarming that among those women who worked for wages or salaries, some 2.3 million—about one in four of all employed women—were mothers of children under fourteen, and they feared that this figure was on the rise. The working mother employed outside the home, labeled an anomaly in discussion of "money-for-children" and family law reform, could be found on the assembly line, at the typewriter or stenographer's pad, or behind the retail counter.[23]

Even under conditions approaching full employment, sex-segregated labor markets diverged little from patterns firmly established in the twenties. Female employment in agriculture declined dramatically— from 35.2 percent of all working women in 1950 to 19.7 percent in 1961—as did employment in domestic service—from 9 to 3.4 percent over the same period. This decline represented the flip side of the increase in women working in certain "women's industries," such as textiles, leather-working, and clothing, where women had always outnumbered men, and in some other industries—food processing and electrotechnical manufacturing—where female employment increased, but the jobs done by women and men remained sharply differentiated. Still more important was the expansion of employment opportunities in the tertiary sector, particularly retail sales and commerce. It was in the service sector that female employment increased most rapidly, from 31 percent of all working women in 1950 to 44 percent in 1961, and that vocational training programs for women workers expanded most rapidly. The removal of women from the isolated workplace of household service or agriculture meant that the visibility of women's wage labor increased more dramatically than the number of women working.[24] In the professions, women continued to dominate education and health services, though administrative posts remained all but the exclusive preserve of men.

As the shifts in the location of women's employment indicate, there was nothing particularly traditional about some sectors where women were overrepresented; women often entered new areas because men had left for better jobs or because unskilled labor was in high demand. What was traditional was that no matter where women worked, their wages

were below men's, they were crammed into the lowest-paying job classifications, and they remained concentrated in a limited spectrum of employment possibilities to an extent far greater than men.[25]

Analysts of sex-segregated employment patterns within the labor
ministry continued to explain the apparently immutable distinction between men's and women's work as a reflection of differences in women's
and men's capacities, defined primarily by women's bodily constitution.
Writing in the labor ministry's official monthly publication in 1957,
Maria Tritz echoed the language used to exclude women from joining
Anneliese Teetz in the maritime industry. Tritz observed that women
were smaller, more sensitive to heat, foul odors, poisons, and standing
for long periods; they had a narrower grasp and hands that were
more sensitive and flexible. Their dexterity, patience, and adaptability,
their talents at counting and sorting, their capacity for repetitive
work, while barring them from some jobs, made them particularly well
suited for other employment—spinning the finest threads, making the
thinnest wires, putting the filaments into electric light bulbs, working
on the assembly line. It was up to employers to adjust the workplace to
the "peculiar quality" (*Eigenart*) of the female worker in order to
minimize threats to her health while maximizing her productivity.[26]
To be sure, this catalogue of natural capacities was not uniquely
German. However, its proclamation in the labor ministry's official publication was stunning evidence that the state would reiterate and
reinforce entrenched attitudes rather than challenging or calling them
into question.

Natural capacities also continued to register clearly in wage differentials for women and men.[27] When individual women went to court to
challenge this, claiming that it violated the Basic Law's promise of equality, the courts conceded their point, thus also acknowledging the political pressure of middle-class feminists, women within the SPD and the
trade union movement, and at least the public pronouncements of their
male colleagues.[28] By 1955, a number of lower-court decisions on appeal had percolated up to the Federal Labor Court (Bundesarbeits-
gericht), the final arbiter of cases involving labor relations.[29] This body
upheld judgments granting women and men the same wages when they
did the same work. It unequivocally rejected employer arguments that
mandating wage equality represented an unjustified intervention by the
state into private contractual relations, which threatened the competitive position of West German industry. The court was also not convinced by employers' remarkably candid explanation that paying a

woman less than a man in the same job was justified precisely because she worked a second shift at home. Because she carried a double burden, employers reasoned, a woman would not appear at the workplace as refreshed and ready to work as a man, resulting in productivity declines that were further aggravated because a woman's thoughts would wander from one workplace to the other. Employers also proclaimed their altruistic intentions in maintaining wage inequality, a policy they argued was preferable to those proposals "inimical to women" (*frauenfeindlich*) to pay women and men the same, because wage equality would result in massive layoffs of women workers.[30]

The court determined that if women workers and the constitution had any enemies, it was trade unions and employers who negotiated contracts specifying different hourly wages for women and men in the same jobs. However, what this ruling gave with one hand, it took away with the other, by providing advice on how employers might circumvent the very principle that it claimed to uphold: employers would be completely within their rights, the court held, if they described in detail what belonged to a specific job classification and differentiated between "heavy" and "light" work. In the court's formulation, "Should such a method result in women being paid less because it is precisely women who do light work or predominantly light work, then there could be no legal objections."[31] With this mechanism, wage inequalities were easily maintained, as women were relegated to jobs classified as "light" work. Women trade unionists protested that physical strength was by no means the best criterion for determining the difficulty of a job and argued that not all skills used to justify higher wages were learned in exclusively male apprenticeships.[32] But the court's counsel that it was up to management and labor to determine standards for measuring comparable work provided no clear guidelines and was not systematically followed. Across all sectors of the economy, women continued to be employed in the lowest wage categories in numbers much larger than men. Even in those industries where women and men did the same work, collective-bargaining agreements negotiated between management and male-dominated trade unions reflected pronounced gender-specific differentials.[33]

What most distressed analysts of women's growing labor-force participation was that no matter how light or how heavy, women's wage labor would unavoidably complicate women's weightiest job of all. Woman as real or potential mother was at the center of debates over how state policy could mandate what employers might not otherwise do—tailor the workplace to woman's nature. This was the one arena where state policy attempted directly to regulate women's wage work in the fifties.

Even before the full employment levels of the mid-fifties, the increased visibility of women's wage labor intensified concerns about women's perceived needs. The fact that by and large women were not entering jobs dominated by men was little comfort to factory inspectors, trade unionists, labor ministry officials, and parliamentary representatives who zealously advocated protection for women workers. At issue was not just women's exclusion from certain jobs in heavy industry or, as in Teetz's case, at sea, because in an increasingly rationalized economy there were few occupations for which brute force was a necessary qualification. Rather, explained the champions of protective legislation, women needed special treatment in all forms of employment because they had specific physiological characteristics and because they worked a second shift. As more women entered wage labor, it was essential that they find employment opportunities adapted to these differences. State intervention was justified because the insatiable demand of an expanding economy might not otherwise accommodate these needs. The hothouse economic growth of the Nazi years was a case study in how the abuses of the labor market lay not in its apparent ability to bar women from certain occupations but rather in its potential to drive women into jobs for which they were not suited because of their bodies. Enforcing tough protective legislation would ensure that this did not happen.[34]

For social policy-makers, concerns about women's work for wages *outside* the home were always directly linked to conceptions of women's place *within* the home. Protective legislation that acknowledged women's biological difference uncritically accepted women's socially constructed responsibilities to children, husbands, and other relatives dependent on unpaid domestic labor; it spared women from certain kinds of work in order to save them for work of a different sort.[35]

There was a broad political consensus that though equality guaranteed women the right to work, economic prosperity and higher wages for men would allow mothers of school-aged children to stay at home. In the discussions of "money-for-children," the question was not whether mothers should stay out of the wage-labor force but what it would take to make stay-at-home mothers a reality; the answer was a male wage, bolstered by social insurance and family allowances. Protective legislation was the political response to the needs of women denied these sources of financial stability for whom wage work might remain essential. For those women who did not have adequate providers, who worked two jobs instead of one, protective legislation represented the state's attempt to allow them to manage their double burden.

Labor ministry officials, the community of occupational medical practitioners, Communists, Social, Christian, and Free Democrats, women trade unionists, and female factory inspectors supported these practices and in no way saw them as inconsistent with the constitutional guarantee of women's equality and the promise of individual fulfillment. Like the drafters of the Basic Law, they emphasized that the social and political equality they legislated must fully acknowledge a woman's special needs and not violate woman's nature. Left open was the question of where nature ended, where politics and society began.

Nowhere was the link between production and reproduction clearer, nowhere were the boundaries of natural difference less at issue, nowhere was the state's regulation of the conditions of women's work more extensive than in the 1952 Law for Protection of Mothers (*Mutterschutzgesetz*). Maternity legislation for women workers in Germany—like other forms of protective legislation regulating and limiting women's participation in wage work—dated back to Bismarck's social legislation of the 1870s and 1880s. Nonetheless, before the First World War provisions for maternity leaves of up to eight weeks and restrictions on pregnant women's work had remained principles few women could afford to practice as long as there was no system to compensate them fully for wage losses suffered during absences from the job. Also, exclusion of agricultural and domestic workers denied coverage to the large numbers of women who worked in those sectors. It was only in the last years of the Weimar Republic that the terms of maternity care were significantly revised. Time away from work could be extended to twelve weeks. In addition, in 1929 payments from health insurance to women workers during maternity leaves were increased from 50 percent to 75 percent of basic wages. Still, most pregnant women did not take advantage of these measures. The level of compensation was not high enough to allow them to stop working before or to keep them from resuming work as soon as possible after giving birth. Women in domestic service and agricultural work—chief employers of female labor—were still excluded altogether.

The Nazis paid little attention to improving maternity benefits for women workers as long as they could afford to remain ideologically committed to the idea that women should devote themselves exclusively to the work of reproduction and leave the labor force permanently. Only

in 1942—under the very different circumstances of the wartime economy and intensified attempts to coax women into wage labor—did the
Nazis introduce a new law. This measure dramatically extended coverage, most importantly by including women in the agricultural sector and
by authorizing payments in the full amount of wages for six weeks before and six weeks following birth. The assurance that taking off from
work would result in no loss in wages meant that for the first time, many
working women could actually afford to claim the benefits to which they
were legally entitled. At the same time, the Nazi law made claims contingent on the fulfillment of explicitly racialist criteria.[36] It aimed at
meeting a racialist, pronatalist agenda, while simultaneously mobilizing
women for the wartime economy.

With the end of the war, the Allies suspended payments under the law
on grounds that its intention was National Socialist in origin and more
practically because of the impossible demands it placed on a health
insurance system seriously weakened by war and defeat. Although
West German labor officials and the courts maintained that pregnancy
still constituted prima facie grounds for protection from dismissal, the
Allies left the specific formulation of a new law to the first German
parliament.[37]

"One of the problems that we have to solve," the SPD's Liesel Kipp-
Kaule explained in 1950 as she presented her party's proposals for re-
instituting the Law for Protection of Mothers in the Bundestag, "is
the woman question." Kipp-Kaule spoke with conviction, having found
her own answers by working her way up from a job as a seamstress in
the garment trades to a position after the war as a specialist in the problems of youth and women in the Union of Textile and Garment Workers.
She warned against the traditional response to the "woman question"
offered by the "propertied circles of our nation [who] were always prepared to do something in the arena of social policy when it was a matter
of representing their interests in the battlefield." Rather, it was up to the
parliament of a new West Germany to take progressive action without
such ulterior motives.[38] Highly critical of the Allied decision to suspend
the payments provided by the 1942 law, Kipp-Kaule expressed her anger
"that it should be women who first should feel that we lost the war."[39]
It was the Bundestag's responsibility to redress this injustice by reinsti-
tuting the protection of pregnant women without further ado.

Social Democrats demanded that a new law fully reinstitute the 1942
provisions; it should protect pregnant women workers from being fired,
exclude them from certain jobs deemed too taxing, limit their hours of

work, grant them six weeks' leave at full pay before and after giving birth, and guarantee them the right to return to their workplace after the end of the maternity leave. New mothers who wanted to breast-feed should also be granted additional work-breaks for this purpose, though the law made no provision for how infants would reach their mothers at work. Beyond this, the SPD called for dramatically expanding the number of women entitled to maternity benefits by extending benefits to *all* pregnant women—whether workers for wages or unpaid workers in the home.

Although SPD supporters of a new law conceded that the racialist content of the Nazi precedent was totally unacceptable, they argued that there was no denying that under the Nazis "mothers enjoyed a high degree of protection"; however horrifying a totalitarian dictatorship had been in other respects, at least it had acted to protect pregnant women workers.[40] In proposing new legislation, the SPD claimed a position of authority based on its historic ties to the trade unions' fight for laws regulating the safety of the workplace and its long-standing commitment to promoting the special concerns of working women. In this sense, Social Democrats could argue that the Nazis had only appropriated and perverted a Social Democratic tradition, which the SPD now forcefully sought to reclaim.[41]

Social Democratic advocates of a new maternity law also justified their proposals by pointing to the increased number of women who would be driven into the labor force by the high costs of economic rebuilding after the war; they demanded that Germany subscribe to the principles laid down in the 1919 agreement of the International Labor Organization that had proposed guidelines for the treatment of pregnant working women, and they called for Germany to restore its reputation as a leader in the area of progressive social welfare legislation. Finally, they emphasized that special treatment for pregnant women would bring workplace practice into line with the Basic Law's Article 6, the constitutional guarantee that "every mother has a right to protection and care by the community."[42]

Article 3, the Basic Law's promise of women's equal rights, was never invoked in debates over how best to protect maternity, though there were other types of protective legislation where balancing equality and special treatment was at issue. For example, provisions introduced in the war and extended into the postwar years in some states granted a monthly day off to women who worked at least forty-eight hours weekly and had responsibilities at home as well. Like the improved provisions of the maternity law, these measures also dated from the wartime economy, but under the Nazis time off had been unpaid; in the postwar period, some states determined that women who qualified for the day off should also receive their wages. Justified as essential for maintaining the "national health" (*Volksgesundheit*) after the war and a necessary response to the difficult circumstances of the late forties, many trade unionists were loath to relinquish the "housework day" (*Hausarbeitstag*) once it was in place.[43]

This provision, available only to women workers, came under attack from some trade unionists and middle-class feminists who contended that it hurt working women more than it helped. They argued that identifying unpaid household labor as an exclusively female responsibility sanctioned not immutable biological difference but social convention and tradition; it was in conflict with the constitutional promise of women's equality with men. Women workers should join men in the common struggle for a shorter work week for all employees, not for special measures that prompted charges that women received a dozen additional days of paid leave annually.[44]

Some employers also challenged the provisions and took their case to court, arguing that giving female employees a paid day off violated the Basic Law's prescription of equality. A year before it advised employers to eliminate wage categories of women's and men's work, the Federal Labor Court upheld the right of a single woman employed in a hosiery factory to the "housework day." Her employer held that because she was not married and lived in a furnished room, she had no more claim to a monthly paid day off than male employees living in the same circumstances, but the court judged differently. In its decision, it determined that granting women equality would be meaningless if it left them worse off than they had been before. In addition, equality must accommodate not only biology but also those differences defined "sociologically or functionally," or more broadly, "generally recognized in the division of labor between the sexes." Even when a woman did not have specific responsibility for others in a family, she had a different role and a different relationship to the household. Whether single or married, the court judged, men did no housework; whether single or married, women did. Thus, "there exists a difference in the circumstances of daily life that permits a differential legal treatment of the employed woman vis-à-vis the employed man." Employers who sought to cut costs with the ostensible excuse of realizing equality were reminded that "the housework day for women was put into effect in order to provide some compensation for women's double burden from occupation and household management."[45] In its assessment of women's claims to equal wages, the court maintained that relegating women to the lower-paid ranks of those doing light work did not violate the principle of equality; neither did acknowledging the weight of the double burden, as its evaluation of the "housework day" made clear. The common thread tying together these decisions was the court's explicit identification of women as a different category of worker, one that diverged from a male norm.[46]

Although the courts were called upon to decide whether biology or society made women into unpaid workers in the home, no one questioned that these powerful forces made women into mothers, or that granting pregnant women special treatment might violate the Basic Law's promise of equal rights to women. Elisabeth Selbert had addressed this issue head on in the debates of the Parliamentary Council. A conception of equality that "acknowledge[d] difference" incorporated a recognition of the particular demands of motherhood. CDU critics of Selbert's equal-rights language at the time charged that unequivocal guarantees of equality would threaten the protection of mothers in the workplace. Complete equal rights would mean "protecting 'male motherhood' "; because this was nonsensical, placing women on completely equal footing with men would mean eliminating their claims to special treatment. If men could not be mothers, and women and men were equal in all respects, then mothers could claim no special treatment. Selbert countered that the protection of motherhood in no way privileged women; rather, it represented only "compensation for the burdens . . . that arise because of a woman's natural obligations as mother."[47]

Once the SPD's proposals for new provisions to grant pregnant women special treatment on the job began to make their way through parliamentary channels, it was clear that protecting motherhood was a political demand that no one would oppose. The official publication of the business community quickly dissociated itself from those "propertied circles" who sought to exploit women, not to help them, and claimed that "German employers have always made it their honorable obligation to bestow a particular measure of *social protection* upon wage-earning women and mothers."[48] While generally accepting the SPD's position, the CDU/CSU echoed complaints from its agrarian and middle-class constituents that the rural and home workplace was of a different sort; protecting women working in these contexts, they alleged, would give advantages to some working mothers at the expense of others and would represent an unbearable expense for the employers of domestic servants. There was also concern that in the home workplace, a pregnant domestic servant might present threats to the moral upbringing of young children; protecting one woman's family did not justify the moral endangerment of another's. Behind such objections was the class divide that had long distinguished the interests of women who were workers and women who were employers.[49]

Ultimately, Social Democrats pushed through their measure by compromising on some particulars. They tabled the demand that *all* women be entitled to benefits but won on the inclusion of women employed in agriculture. Accepting the political expedience of defining special provisions for domestic workers, they agreed that women in these jobs could be laid off after the fifth month of their pregnancy. Still, once fired, they could claim their wages, paid out of health-insurance funds, and like other pregnant workers they were entitled to a paid maternity leave. Their inclusion in the law in any form extended coverage to an important sector of female employment for the first time.

"You know," proclaimed Kipp-Kaule as the Bundestag prepared to pass the legislation, "that hundreds of thousands of women have waited two years for this moment, and will all be thankful to us that they are no longer subject to the arbitrary measures of administrative officials, health-insurance offices, and employers."[50] Kipp-Kaule's overly optimistic assessment reflected her exuberance at her party's imminent political victory, but there was no question that the Law for Protection of Mothers did much to address the needs of pregnant women workers. On balance, it embodied a significant expansion of Weimar measures and more comprehensive provisions than its Nazi predecessor.

A closer look at the debates over the law reveals that it also did much else. Without exception, supporters of *Mutterschutz* agreed that working women might need protection from arbitrary treatment by employers, but equally important was the "rising generation" (*Nachwuchs*) that needed protection from the dangers of working women. The potentially deleterious effects of wage work on expectant mothers translated immediately into a "damaging influence on the physical development of the young generation." Kipp-Kaule estimated that in the Kaiserreich, the inadequacy of pre- and postnatal care for working mothers resulted in seventeen million infant deaths.[51] Such figures took on particular significance in an atmosphere clouded by fears of the tremendous burdens already placed on women's health by the crises of the war and postwar years, a declining birth rate, and the widely accepted relationship between population growth and economic reconstruction.

Proponents of the new law were at considerable pains to emphasize why it was different from its Nazi precedent. The Nazi law showed no genuine concern for women but instead was a weapon in the "battle for births," intended to supply the war economy's demand for "cannon fodder."[52] Such policies were common to all totalitarian states, proponents of the West German alternative argued. The specter of communist regimes, where protective legislation ruthlessly forced women to expand the population while they toiled in jobs for which they were ill-suited, once again hovered in the background. East Germans might claim that they sought to permit women to be both workers and mothers, but through the lens of the Cold War, West Germans could see only a perversion of equality in policies that granted women "equal rights to be exploited and left with no protection"; maternity provisions intensified the double burden rather than diminishing it.[53]

Still, despite all disclaimers, concerns about population size were explicit in West German discussions of mother's work. It was not Wuermeling but the former Social Democratic mayor of Berlin, Louise Schroeder, who justified protection for working mothers, "not just [as] a question of labor protection; rather it is a matter of population policy that will benefit all people," especially given the war's demographic legacy.[54] The combination of the war's devastation, the incomparably straitened economic circumstances faced by many women, and the need "more than ever for a healthy rising generation" made strict enforcement of mothers' protection essential, because "the rising generation of a nation . . . must not be endangered."[55]

The Law for Protection of Mothers acknowledged that mothers might have to produce outside the home, particularly in the postwar period of recovery as they helped rebuild what the bombs had destroyed. To help rebuild a "healthy generation," women in wage work might also have to reproduce while earning their pay. The law adopted by the parliament in 1952 represented society's concern that they be able to fulfill both tasks; it ensured that women involved in production would still be able to carry out their responsibilities for reproduction. Women workers appeared in the debates around the law not as individuals who chose to work and bear children, but rather as a disadvantaged group, forced out to work while fulfilling their obligations as mothers at considerable risk to their own health, and more importantly, to the health of the next generation. It was precisely for this reason that employers should not use the costs of special treatment for their women workers as a justification for paying female employees less. The *Mutterschutzgesetz* not only addressed the needs of women but also benefited children, "the rising generation [that] is a social responsibility."[56]

These larger themes could be read between the lines of the *Mutterschutzgesetz*, and they were fully articulated in commentaries on the law. The best known of these, Gustav-Adolf Bulla's massive treatise on the legal provisions regulating women's wage work, the standard source on the subject, explained that "the survival of a nation (*Volk*), its health, and its capacity to perform is influenced to a large degree by the active care that it bestows upon its women as the bearers of new life." Protecting mothers' work was not only an "ethical command" but was also the "fundamental prerequisite for sustaining and renewing the nation."[57] A detailed explanation of the law prepared for the German Federation of Trade Unions by Thea Harmuth and Emmy Theuerkauf expressed similar sentiments, justifying the law as an indication of "respect for woman as the carrier of life," but not in the manner of totalitarian states in pursuit of population expansion. Rather, the West German measure met the needs of the woman employed outside the home, "who maintains the health of the family and also the entire people through her double burden as mother and working woman."[58]

Laws are probably never implemented according to lawgivers' intentions, and the Law for Protection of Mothers was no exception. Because the law was under the supervision of the labor ministries of individual state governments, its enforcement and oversight have left a paper trail in official sources from which we can reconstruct the discrepancy between its letter and spirit and its interpretation by employers, workers, and the state factory inspectors charged with ensuring compliance. "Money-for-children" was likely to disappear into the paycheck of a male wage earner without an archival trace; how it affected the lives of the individual families who received it is only open to conjecture. The Civil Code's detailed description of a wife's unpaid domestic labor and its guarantee of a father's last word in irreconcilable marital disputes were of enormous symbolic significance, but these provisions were rarely invoked in divorce proceedings. To be sure, this book argues that both family law and family policy were important because they illuminate the political reconstruction of gender relations in West Germany after the war; they reveal much about how "politics construct[ed] gender and gender construct[ed] politics" in the Federal Republic's first decade.[59] Analyzing debates around the Law for Protection of Mothers also serves this purpose, but the law directly affected many employers and working women in ways that family law and family policy did not. A range of sources provides unusually rich glimpses into the ways in which paper prescriptions were actually understood and carried out.[60]

Factory inspectors' accounts of the reception and implementation of the law made it immediately apparent that not everyone agreed that mothers needed protection. Even a decade after the law's passage, not all employers perceived an "honorable obligation" on their part to provide special treatment for their pregnant employees; in particular, small-scale factory owners, retailers, and employers of agricultural and domestic labor simply chose not to inform their workers of the benefits to which they were entitled or failed to register pregnant women who worked for them.[61]

Reports also record frequent expression of fears that barring women from certain types of work only resulted in employers' reluctance to hire any women of child-bearing age. There were some indications that bosses found reasons to fire single women workers when they married, rehiring them with short-term provisional contracts that were not covered by the law and firing them should they become pregnant. In other instances, employers sought to avoid the law's consequences by demanding written agreement from single women workers that they would be subject to immediate dismissal should they marry; only such measures could prevent women from disingenuously exploiting the law by taking a job after they knew they were pregnant in order to reap the law's benefits with no intention of returning to work after their maternity leave elapsed.[62] Still other women, employers charged, simply exploited the law's protection to be obstreperous and lazy on the job, because they knew they could be fired only with great difficulty.

Common complaints from employers also included claims that they could not comply with the law because their production permitted no alternative jobs for those whom the law prohibited from certain types of work. Restrictions on night work prompted similar objections from industries that operated on round-the-clock shifts, restaurants, bars, and firms confronting excessive demand and asking for overtime from all employees. Other businesses—beauty shops and retailers—worried that their customers would take offense at the sight of a pregnant woman, while owners of movie theaters expressed concern that pregnant employees would no longer fit into required uniforms. Less motivated by ostensibly aesthetic or moral considerations, still other bosses encouraged women to accept dismissal in order to establish eligibility for unemployment support—though by this action, workers waived all claims to the more substantial payments and the right to return to their workplace guaranteed by the law. Once fired, the law allowed only a week for appeals, and employers gambled that women would fail to make this deadline.

Employers were not alone in their attempt to circumvent the law; women workers also frustrated well-meaning factory inspectors by revealing that they did not always share the Bundestag's conception of what was in their best interest. Women's resistance to reporting a pregnancy immediately might sometimes have reflected "false modesty," as one factory inspector speculated,[63] but more often, silence could be explained by rational calculation. Because health-insurance payments during the maternity leave were based on average wages for the thirteen weeks before stopping work, women feared that a change of jobs or reduction of hours would mean lower wages and consequently lower payments. This financial concern, not women's "lack of consideration for their own health and that of the child," as one factory inspector maintained, created an unintended alliance between women and employers in their attempts to circumvent some provisions of the law.[64] Women resisted their restriction from certain kinds of work, the mandatory reduction of the work week to forty-five hours, and prohibition of work past eight P.M., which excluded them from shift differentials. They also complained that forfeiting the camaraderie of coworkers for new surroundings might have immeasurable psychic costs.

Maintaining high wage levels for as long as possible prompted women who worked for piece rates to intensify their efforts and those working for hourly wages to increase their overtime. The same objective could be achieved by the pregnant home-worker by enlisting other family members to credit her for their production in the months prior to giving birth. A troubled factory inspector could bemoan the fact that "in the first instance, the expectant mother does not think about her health and the health of the child, but rather exclusively about her earnings,"[65] but for women workers, such action was intended to increase benefits under the law. Achieving this goal also led women to report pregnancies only when it was absolutely essential—either when they were clearly visible or when the maternity leave began, six weeks before the anticipated due date—to avoid potential transfer to a different job with lower wages. Employers who charged that this practice constituted "deceitful fraud" learned that according to the law, pregnant women *should* report their condition but were under no binding obligation to do so. Even establishing that women took up work only after they were pregnant was no cause for dismissal. Verifying such charges was necessarily complicated, and women workers could insist on ignorance of their condition and still claim protection from the law.[66]

Additional problems of enforcement came from women's resistance to mandated extra break times; factory inspectors reported that many women objected to potentially lengthening the workday with unpaid time on the job, thus cutting into the hours available for their household labor. For the same reason, women expressed a preference to work longer hours for five days instead of the eight-and-one-half-hour days called for by the law; shorter workdays meant stretching a forty-five-hour week into Saturday morning, time needed for their second shift.

The task of overseeing and guarding against attempts to circumvent the law was the special preserve of the relatively few women employed by state labor ministries as factory inspectors. Just as women officials were assigned as counselors for women job-seekers in state-run labor exchanges, so too it was primarily women who investigated other women's conditions of work. Factory inspectors were responsible for identifying potential threats to occupational health and safety. Unlike their male colleagues, the women in these jobs typically had a background in social work, not engineering; their expertise lay in identifying the particular problems of women workers, not in knowing when steam engines might explode. Their duties were tremendously expanded by the passage of the 1952 law.[67]

Particularly time-consuming were detailed examinations of cases in which pregnant women had been fired and claimed protection from dismissal or employers requested exemptions from the law and permission to fire a particular employee. Although unauthorized layoffs were explicitly prohibited, even a pregnant woman could be fired "in an exceptional case," subject to the approval of the state labor ministry.[68] Precisely what this meant was far from clear, and it was the responsibility of the factory inspectors and ultimately their superior, the labor minister, to make this determination.

Factory inspectors were zealous in their efforts to resolve disputes, and there is substantial evidence of their success at achieving reconciliations between workers and employers through direct intervention at the workplace. In other cases, the two sides failed to reach a verbal compromise, and full-scale investigations ensued. In these cases, factory inspectors systematically followed up complaints from both fired workers and outraged employers, questioning all parties involved at the workplace and making on-site inspections of the home and work conditions of the women involved. The record of their attempts to mete out just solutions provides exceptional insights into the lives and working conditions of the women they scrutinized and the ways they believed they could best protect mothers. In their decisions, they entered into an economic, moral, and legal calculus that reveals much about the conceptions of women's status, the sexual division of labor, and gender relations, which they read out of the law.

In theory, a pregnant woman could be fired only when the economic interests of the employer far outweighed those of the worker. What if the employer faced an economic downturn or even a complete shutdown of operations? In such instances, factory inspectors often reminded employers that it was the intention of the law to prevent pregnant women from confronting particular economic hardship. A pregnant woman would be unable to find another job, and employers were informed that by hiring a woman, they had assumed a "business risk" that denied them rights to fire her should she become pregnant.[69] Determining an employer's obligations involved careful consideration of the firm's balance sheet, on the one hand, and the economic circumstances of the worker, on the other, in order to measure which was "economically the stronger partner." Typically, it was the woman denied the "protection of marriage," one who had recently married and was still securing essentials for her new household, or one whose husband was not in regular work who was guaranteed the law's protection—even if it meant keeping her on the payroll after a plant had completely shut down operations. When factory inspectors determined that women were in homes with male providers, when the employer's familial status was no less precarious than the worker's, or when the factory inspector judged that the employee was enjoying luxuries not appropriate for her social status—a new radio, or too many nights out dancing—or was neglecting her responsibilities to children she already had, the firm might well find that its interests won greater consideration.[70]

Inspectors also had to evaluate allegations of insubordination and impropriety, which, employers claimed, could be threats to authority in the firm and thus to the firm's economic performance. Assessing competing economic interests was again crucial. The twenty-three-year-old unmarried cook in a small community tavern might stretch her employer's tolerance by breaking too many dishes and referring to a regular customer as "the asshole with the butcher's platter," but her single status, her mother's shaky economic circumstances, and the "honest and believable" impression she made on the factory inspector saved her from being fired.[71] And a woman married to a disabled barrelmaker, the mother of two children aged eleven and eight, kept her job in a radio-parts company despite her employer's charges that she incessantly re-counted intimacies from her private life, including sexual-performance evaluations of her first husband compared with her second ("who can do it much better") and tales of evenings when the children were asleep and she had intercourse with her husband "in the kitchen [and] on the sofa, in a variety of ways." The woman's categorical denial of all charges and the absence of witnesses to confirm the boss's allegations undercut the case against her and ensured her job security and a paid maternity leave.[72]

Potentially as important as a woman's economic circumstances and credibility was her psychological state. There was general agreement that pregnancy transformed both the body and the mind. A worker fired because she had stolen soap from the store where she was employed as a packer was reinstated because she suffered from a "pregnancy psycho-sis" and had only taken the soap "when she really liked it, and it was something special." Pregnancy brought on an "unrestrainable desire for particularly good smells" and also might prompt a woman to take ac-tions for which she could not be held responsible, "suspend[ing] legal culpability altogether." It was, the labor minister reminded her em-ployer, "legally established that pregnant women, even those in well-ordered marital circumstances . . . out of their desire to care for their offspring adequately, often uncontrollably grasp at the most incredible means and steal in order to obtain what they consider necessary for the child."[73]

In similar cases, factory inspectors reiterated that pregnancy caused greater sensitivity to "alarm and anger"; pregnant women were often unable "to control themselves from pursuing irrational resolutions and desires once formulated, and they lose a clear perception of the conse-quences of their decisions." Pregnancy might bring on attacks of raven-ous hunger, which could easily lead to lavish expenditures, and even "fits of kleptomania." Employers were instructed to remember that "just at the time when they're pregnant, women are often unaware of the impact of their words and deeds."[74]

Becoming pregnant while unmarried was certainly no grounds for an employer's moral condemnation, nor did it justify firing a woman "with-out the protection of marriage." In language that became almost for-mulaic in such cases, employers were informed that "all motherhood—the married as well as the unmarried—stands under the protection of

the community according to Article 6 of the Grundgesetz." Those who
charged that protecting unmarried mothers was perhaps permissible under a Nazi law aimed at population expansion at all costs but not in a
new Germany of "propriety and morality," or who claimed that a pregnant widow should not be tolerated in a "Christian cultural nation,"
quickly learned that they were mistaken.[75] They need only recall "that
with their primordial feeling for life, our forefathers said of pregnant
women that they were of a *blessed* body and of *good* hope. Even if these
very vivid expressions have increasingly been driven from our language
by the materialism of our lives, it is nonetheless indisputable that everyone who confronts a woman in whom a new life grows will meet her
with adoration and empathy."[76]

As in their determinations of the "economically stronger partner,"
factory inspectors also measured which party was morally more vulnerable. Thus, a factory inspector was dispatched to investigate a movie-
theater owner's charges that his employee had not only allowed her
dachshund to defecate freely throughout the theater but more importantly had turned her small apartment in the theater into a "love nest"
where she entertained young men after work hours and even during
screenings. Exhaustive interviews with the boss, the employee, and the
neighbors convinced the factory inspector that in fact there was no evidence that the pregnant worker had pursued intimacy at the expense of
"good moral principles . . . and on the contrary her reputation in the
neighborhood is up until now quite good."[77]

A factory inspector determined that it was the psychological impact
of her mother's death and an unsatisfactory change of jobs that had led
a "solid and homey" sales representative with sixteen years of service to
the firm to seek solace in the arms of an older married man, formerly a
trusted coworker, who had offered his help after her mother's death and
then had become her lover. He claimed that he could not fulfill his
pledge to get a divorce because of his wife's refusal to end the marriage,
further complicating the worker's life. These elements completely over-
shadowed the employer's charges that the woman's affair represented a
"moral derailment of the most massive proportions," and her excellent
work record provided further grounds for overruling her dismissal.[78]
Also worthy of protection was the worker whose female employer, the
owner of a small trucking firm, had all but encouraged her to flirt with
the company's drivers by giving her a room on the first floor where she
daily came in contact with them. It was, the factory inspector judged,
the boss's neglect of the "moral degeneration of the drivers" and the

"morally endangered" condition of the worker, not her "fresh and indecent" behavior and "very loose lifestyle," as the boss alleged, that was subject to censure by the factory inspector.[79]

Judgments that favored women on the basis of such calculations prompted angered responses from employers who charged that any unmarried mother "was fully responsible for what she allowed herself,"[80] or who asked rhetorically if the maternity law justified all actions and sanctioned "moral lapses of the coarsest sort."[81] The answer was no, as a retail sales clerk learned when her firing was upheld after two years of hearings and court appearances. Her alleged offense was appearing at work with a swimsuit on under her clothes and offering to show it to a recently married male coworker. A second infraction involved entertaining a young male apprentice under her supervision with "amorous bedroom stories" and inviting him to inspect her upper body closely for any signs of pregnancy. In her case, her "jokes . . . so immodest that they could hardly be repeated at a men's bowling night" exceeded the limits even of a "pregnancy psychosis," and her fate was sealed when the factory inspectors determined that her fiancé's financial circumstances were solid.[82] This evidence of her future economic security made it possible to allow her to be fired for her impropriety.

No more sympathy was shown to a worker in a long-playing record manufacture who was witnessed as she interrupted the inventory in the warehouse by sitting on a coworker's lap and kissing him, then encouraging him to go to her colleague, "who has larger bosoms than I." According to the testimony of witnesses, the coworker had followed her instruction, laying the other woman on a worktable and kissing her breasts, while the first woman encouraged her to "feel what big balls [he] has." For the factory inspector, such behavior warranted dismissal, despite the woman's pregnant condition, and her appeals to the local labor court were unsuccessful.[83]

Just as unworthy of special dispensation in the eyes of the factory inspector was the salesperson in a small firm that manufactured bandages and orthopedic supplies. Her boss charged that she was after his son's inheritance, and in pursuit of this goal she had seduced him during working hours. For the employer, proof positive of her deceitful intentions was her failure to fulfill her "obligation" to provide his son with a condom, "to press it in his hand." These allegations prompted the worker's rejoinders that romantic interludes with the young man were not on company time; they had been confined to breaks and reflected no seduction, but rather mutual desire. Charges that she had used her sexual wiles as an older woman were groundless; her partner was only one year her junior and his social advantage as the boss's son surely more than compensated for their age difference. In rejecting her arguments, the labor minister avoided the question of who had seduced whom but did hold the woman responsible for providing her coworkers with a bad example and for endangering the "cleanliness and morality of the workplace in the rudest possible fashion." Her gender meant that she was more mature than her partner, and it was consequently her duty to "see to it that [her] workplace remained clean."[84] She was left to ponder this judgment, pregnant and without her old job or maternity benefits.

In another case, not an employee's morals but her accusations that her employer was "more like a slave-trader than a socially concerned entrepreneur" exceeded the tolerable changes in a pregnant woman's "spiritual constitution."[85] So too did the repeated insubordination of the unmarried worker in a small greenhouse and flower shop, who, according to her boss's account, ended a verbal exchange with him by calling him "'a bum' and 'Schweinehund,'" and inviting him to "'shut your trap, you [Sie] idiot.'" "'You're a crazy Heini, thrice over crazy. . . . You're as dumb as shit, you're a bum, you idiot, you Polish pig, you Russkie.'" When she returned the next day, ready to resume work, her boss told her she was fired. As he advised, the factory inspector was not taken in by the woman's "madonna-like" appearance; rather, the official investigation determined that the worker "belongs to those elements who are convinced that the state or other people ought to take care of them." That the father of her child was in secure economic circumstances might make firing her easier, but in any event, she had "only herself to blame for an outcome that was unfavorable to her." In a series of appeals that ultimately reached the Federal Labor Court, the woman found no greater sympathy; the employer's decision was upheld.[86]

In assessing conflicting claims, factory inspectors and the labor minister sorted through evidence and weighed competing interests. On occasion they also interpreted the intention of the Basic Law. The constitution's promise to protect every mother could be invoked in defense of unmarried mothers on some occasions, but a thirty-four-year-old typist-stenographer, who had been employed for seven years in the office of a cabinet-level ministry in Bonn, learned that she was not entitled to such benevolent treatment. Her relationship with a white-collar worker in the same ministry was no secret; in a notarized statement, she had identified him as the father of her two children. Expecting a third, she had applied for a larger apartment in the ministry-controlled housing where she lived. The father of her children, twenty years her senior, was married, but not to her. It was ostensibly this that prompted not only the ministry's rejection of her appeal for a larger apartment but also demands for her immediate dismissal.

Protesting both decisions, the worker argued that her case was exemplary of the plight of single women whose would-be husbands "now rested on the battlefields of the Second World War while single women . . . struggle for a solution to give meaning to their lives." For her, meaning lay in motherhood. Waiting for children until her lover could marry her was not an option; she might already be too old to fulfill her wish for a family. Women over thirty, she argued were "medically 'old' to be giving birth for the first time" and might run the risk of serious complications. The difficulties accompanying the birth of her first child only confirmed her belief that she had acted correctly by postponing pregnancy no longer. Why should she, who had the "courage—in full consciousness of her actions—to bear the cross of unmarried motherhood," not enjoy the protection guaranteed by the law to all mothers?

According to her employer, factory inspectors, and the labor minister, the answer was simple: married and unmarried pregnancies were to be treated equally, but in this case, something else was at issue—the constitutional guarantee of the protection of a legal marriage. Although her lover had been estranged from his wife since 1948, seven years later he was still legally married. It was not the state's responsibility to "make possible the legalization of a relationship initiated in the confusion of the postwar period," and the woman's behavior was nothing less than a "conscious attack on the institution of marriage." Her claims to the protection of the constitution were not compelling, "because no marriage relation exists that is in need of protection." It was her lover's legal marriage that the state was obliged to protect, not her relationship with him. No marriage was beyond repair until it dissolved completely, she was reminded, and "in any event, in this instance his marriage cannot be denied the protection of the state." She was explicitly informed that her adulterous actions—not the fact of her unmarried motherhood—constituted a "special case," justifying her firing. By the time this judgment was reached, she had given birth to her third child. A mother who had more than fulfilled her obligation to keep the German nation from "dying out," who was "rich in children" and had amply provided for the "rising generation," she found herself without a husband, a job, housing, or the protection of the state.[87]

As these cases indicate, the Law for Protection of Mothers was subject to more than one interpretation. Kipp-Kaule's confident pronouncement that the law would free pregnant women workers from all arbitrary treatment was at odds with the patently arbitrary fashion in which the law could be applied by individual factory inspectors. When the *Mutterschutzgesetz* was put into practice not all working mothers were protected, and for factory inspectors and the labor ministry more than the care of pregnant women was at stake. To be sure, in the majority of cases, employers accepted the law, and pregnant women received benefits without having to establish their moral character or their economic neediness. When conflicts arose, however, the law was open to interpretations not fully anticipated or prescribed by legislators in Bonn. It was in these instances that employers, factory inspectors, the courts, and pregnant women revealed their understanding of the legislation's meanings and limits.

From these judgments, there emerges a consensus that pregnant women needed protection because their physical and psychological capacities were diminished. Pregnancy explained a variety of shortcomings and excesses; it created dependence, and dependence entitled pregnant women to protection. Protection was not to be taken for granted. Where the claims of employers and workers clashed, pregnant women could establish their cases only by submitting to explorations of how they lived, worked, and played; much more than their on-the-job performance was assessed. In theory, employers were legally barred from asking questions about the private lives of their workers; in practice, factory inspectors made the private public, posing such questions as a legitimate part of their attempts to protect pregnant women. The evidence that they unearthed is an exceptionally rich historical source; it vividly illuminates how legal structures made it possible for some women workers to challenge their employers and defend their rights successfully. It also testifies strikingly to how state officials assumed the authority to examine a female worker's personal circumstances because of their commitment to ensuring her rights.

When factory inspectors judged that a woman's behavior went beyond what was excusable because of the psychological transformation accompanying pregnancy, in itself an arbitrary construct, pregnant women workers might find themselves without the law's protection.

Judgments indicated that when ignorance, innocence, disability, and dependence accompanied pregnancy, they were good excuses; knowledge and self-assertion were not. The law potentially extended significant benefits to pregnant women: it could keep them from being fired, it guaranteed that they could return to their jobs, and it gave them their wages during twelve weeks away from work. But the law could also be used to underscore certain conceptions of women workers' subordination, power relations within the workplace, class structure, and female moral propriety. For women workers, these elements were linked. Proper behavior encompassed moral dimensions, and women's sexuality and sexual knowledge—or ignorance—made them immediately subject to particular scrutiny.

Factory inspectors also revealed their conviction that the law embodied a conception of the family. Their deliberations reflected the belief that morally and economically, pregnant women were best protected not by the state but by marriage. The most effective way to lighten the double burden was to eliminate it—by leaving women at home with children, supported by an adequate male wage. Women who did not conform to this norm—who were denied the "protection of marriage," tied to a husband whose wages were inadequate, financially responsible for parents or other dependents, or on shaky economic legs at the beginning of a marriage—constituted precisely the group most in need of special consideration. However, a woman married to man with an income deemed sufficient to maintain a family might no longer receive the state's protection should her interests conflict with those of her employer. And a woman who questioned the sanctity of marriage or challenged it by her actions forfeited all claims to protection as a mother.

The political theorist Zillah Eisenstein observes that legislation intended to meet women's gender-specific needs is not "inherently problematic or progressive. It is made so by its aim and its political context."[88] The aim of West German protective legislation for women workers in the fifties, the most important instance of the state's attempt to regulate women's work outside the home directly, was to acknowledge women's difference. In the political context of the postwar era, that difference was virtually synonymous with a woman's ability to bear children and her natural obligations as a mother; this was what defined her need for special treatment in the workplace. Anneliese Teetz was neither pregnant nor a mother, but it was the shape of her pelvis—her reproductive future— that was crucial for evaluating her ability to pilot a ship. Although by

1962, seventy-five percent of the 9.4 million women employed in West Germany had no children under fourteen,[89] in the discussion of how the state should regulate women's wage workplace, problems of working *women* were reduced to the problems of working *mothers*, and problems of working mothers were problems of the *Volk.*

Once again all but completely lost in the shuffle—as they had been in debates over "money-for-children" and proposals for family-law reform—were divorced women with children, mothers who had never married, and women workers—married and unmarried—who were not mothers. Although in the late forties and early fifties, it was particularly the needs of these groups that initially focused attention on women's growing labor-force participation, by the end of the decade their fate had been categorized as a short-term legacy of the war. In the most widely cited study of working mothers in the late fifties, conducted under the supervision of Elisabeth Pfeil, a sociologist who also served as part of the family ministry's scientific advisory committee, mothers in "incomplete families" were not even considered.[90]

Caught between demands for the labor required to build a healthy economy and the labor needed for "building a healthy generation," the political discussion of women's work was filled with tensions not easily reconciled. Nowhere was this more clearly articulated than in the programmatic demands of the women activists within the trade-union movement and the SPD, who claimed to represent the interests of all working women. They emphasized that women wage earners were there to stay, a constant in an industrial society. They stressed that the promise of women's equal rights in a new Germany must include better educational opportunities, greater access to a broad range of occupations, wage equality, and a forty-hour week. They argued that even those women who left the labor force to care for children would return once their children were grown and demanded that in such cases women's claims to social insurance not be diminished because of such family-related interruptions in their careers.[91] They also demanded dramatically expanded representation in all decision-making bodies—from firm-level works councils and communal government to the national Federation of Trade Unions and the Bundestag. The protocols of women's caucuses, created after the war within individual trade unions and at the regional and national levels, provide ample evidence of a broad vision of a future society transformed by the active participation of women at all levels.[92]

But while women trade union activists called for improved access to jobs, they also insisted that vocational training for young women include better instruction for their future work as housewives and mothers. Demands for legal safeguards of women's status "measured by their importance in the national economy" were tempered by avowals that "we do not wish to be blue-stockings"—a reference to those chimerical middle-class feminists who allegedly championed a brand of equality that would force women to be like men. While they called for a new social order where male-female relationships would be partnerships and where fathers would be actively involved in child-rearing, they continued to emphasize that "the power most particular to a woman's soul is the power to sacrifice," and this power revealed itself most fully in motherhood.[93]

Aggressively debunking those studies that concluded that women's paychecks went for furs and other luxuries, advocates for working women emphasized that mothers might have to work; they stressed that working women toiled for wages to meet their families' needs, not to fulfill individualistic desires. However, even as they reminded young women that Article 3 ensured them the "same occupational opportunities as young men," they completely endorsed the proviso that equality be limited by a woman's "bodily constitution . . . before all else with regard to her natural obligations as mother of the future generation."[94] It was the responsibility of employers to accommodate the workplace to woman's "peculiar nature" (Wesensart)—defined in physiological, psychological, and spiritual terms—thus avoiding the East German example where nature was disregarded.[95] The solution was even more tightly controlled protective legislation that would take account of a woman's physical difference and "the motherly tasks and obligations that the woman has to fulfill for the family. . . . These facts will certainly no longer be disputed by anyone."[96]

Women trade unionists protested the lack of day-care facilities, but in the same breath they joined ranks with those critics of working mothers who emphasized that no day care was an adequate substitute for a mother's love and who argued that mothers needed the bond with their children as much as children needed a deep attachment to their mothers. Children of working mothers faced enormous potential problems, and the child separated too early from her or his mother was subject to all manner of neuroses and a range of nervous diseases.[97] Trade-union activists also accepted arguments that equated state-regulated day care with the attempts by communists to rob parents of their children while forcing women into wage labor. Lest there be any doubt, they cited the German Democratic Republic's Law for the Protection of Mothers and Children and the Rights of Women, put into effect in 1950, which called explicitly for the creation of nurseries and day-care centers as part of the first five-year plan.[98] Of course, communists were not alone in their attempts to undermine the family, and in strains familiar from the debates over "money-for-children," any mention of group day care was also associated with the Nazis, who shared with communists the goal of transforming children into loyal servants of the state. Initial proposals that the West German Law for Protection of Mothers include provisions for child-care facilities were dismissed as unfortunate reminders of National Socialist plans and were never seriously debated.[99]

The few women who were delegated to attend the congresses of the national Federation of Trade Unions were typically called on to make presentations that focused on how most effectively to create a social order that would grant women choices between wage work and motherhood, allowing women to shed the double burden. Addressing the first postwar national meeting of the women's caucuses of the trade union movement, Liesel Kipp-Kaule asked, "Where can we find a genuine mother today? Women who work come home tired at night without even a smile on their lips for their children. At home, housework is waiting for them. I would like to see . . . how we can once again become the human beings whom we have lost."[100] Male trade unionists and the Social Democratic leadership were far more likely to join women in search of "genuine mothers" in the home than in pursuit of equal wages and job opportunities for mothers and other women in the workplace. Women's demands received greatest support from their male comrades when they focused on the need for improved social services for families and secure incomes for male providers.[101]

A sociological study based on one thousand interviews with working mothers in West Berlin in 1956 confirmed that many women shared these objectives. Those questioned reported that they were working not for fast cars, cosmetics, or vacations in Majorca. Rather, most used their legally mandated paid days off for relaxing and "really getting enough sleep" at home, not trips to the sunny southern climes that were ubiquitous in the lyrics of popular songs in the fifties.[102] The earnings of these women were a "necessary supplement" to the family income, and while necessity might be an elastic concept, aspirations extended little beyond a modestly appointed household, perhaps including a refrigerator—that birthright of every West German, according to Ludwig Erhard—or a television set.

The interviewees were by no means ignorant of the weight of their double burden; more than half of those living in "complete" families reported that between their two workplaces, they were busy for more than ninety hours a week, and another 31 percent worked between eighty and ninety hours, with variations directly related to family size. When asked how best to solve their problems, one-third unhesitatingly demanded higher wages, both in absolute terms and relative to men. Only one—"a mother in a good position with considerable help in the management of her household and the care of her children"— charged her "sex-comrades" with "begging for gifts" by asking for special treatment, exhorting them to "enter into the labor process just as completely as men." Far more common were calls for increased wages and job security for employed men so that "mothers won't be forced to take up employment," improvements in "money-for-children," including extension of payments at least to the second child, and the desire to "have more time for our children" by eliminating night work, shortening the workday by getting rid of unpaid lunch breaks, and guaranteeing Saturdays off.[103] Interviews with young women workers in the fifties and early sixties echoed these views. Those questioned articulated a general frustration with available training programs and job opportunities and hopes that marriage would provide an alternative to paid employment. Behind this conception of a world of options and choices, championed by trade unionists and assumed by sociologists, was the same vision of the "normal family" that was at the basis of family policy and family-law reforms as a choice that should be available to all women.[104]

While East Germany continued to provide a convenient negative point of reference, a model of how not to regulate women's work-force participation and a society where the "normal family" was not even an ideal, it did offer at least a partial solution to West Germany's dilemma of how to fill the growing demand for labor without fully mobilizing the silent reserve. More than ninety percent of the population increase in West Germany in the decade after 1950 consisted of returning expellees and those choosing to leave the east, and one-third of them came from the German Democratic Republic.[105] Indeed, it was not lost on women trade unionists that East German women with extensive vocational training and skills could cross the border and enter jobs for which West German women did not have the requisite qualifications.[106]

By the late fifties, the West German government also began exploring potential sources of "guest workers" (Gastarbeiter) from other countries, because of the general consensus that the limits of mobilizing married women had been reached. Foreigners living in West Germany in

178 Protecting Motherhood

1961 numbered roughly 686,000. Twenty years later, the figure had increased nearly sevenfold. In 1961, only 2.5 percent of workers in West Germany were foreigners; little over a decade later, they made up slightly more than 10 percent of the labor force.[107] Expanding part-time work for women was another alternative, though when working mothers were asked about this option in the mid-fifties they overwhelmingly rejected it, for the obvious reason that reduced hours meant reduced wages.[108] Nonetheless, from 1960 to 1984 the percentage of women working part time more than doubled—from 14 percent to 33 percent—and part-time jobs were held almost exclusively by women. By the mid-eighties, 90 percent of those working under twenty hours weekly—and thus not entitled to the medical, unemployment, and retirement benefits of full-time employment—were women. Women's demand for part-time jobs far exceeded the supply.[109]

To be sure, the political categories for assessing women's labor force participation did not remain constant. In the sixties, Soviet scientific achievements awakened West German fears of the "educational catastrophe" (*Bildungskatastrophe*) that began to compete with fears of the declining birth rate, intensifying pressures to expand women's educational opportunities and job qualifications. Not only the "political standing of the nation" but also its "spiritual potential," argued Georg Picht, an educational expert and a philosopher of religion who wrote extensively on these problems, depended on how well the population was schooled. While foreign workers could fill some of a growing economy's labor needs, they were not the well-educated domestic work force West Germany wanted to meet the demands of a "technological age."[110] Still, not until the late seventies did the state introduce initiatives to put "girls in men's jobs" (*Mädchen in Männerberufen*), returning to the agenda proposed but never systematically implemented by the Allied forces of occupation three decades earlier.[111] It is beyond the scope of this book to evaluate the success of these programs at dissolving gender-based wage differentials and the lines dividing a sex-segmented labor market, but at the very least, such initiatives indicate that in the sixties and seventies, state labor-market policy aimed explicitly at improving women's minds.[112] In the fifties, by contrast, it was primarily aimed at maintaining women's bodies.

The Law for Protection of Mothers and other forms of state intervention to regulate women's wage workplace in the Federal Republic's first decade were not solely responsible for positioning women at the crossroads of production and reproduction. The West German state did not

invent a labor market segmented by sex nor did it create firmly entrenched social attitudes that located a woman's destiny in her body.
Where the state did intervene to regulate women's labor force participation, however, it did not challenge established patterns and attitudes;
rather, it reinforced them. There is no question that for the women
who fought hard for women's special treatment in the workplace, protective legislation represented a significant victory. Nor do the cases of
firings appealed under the *Mutterschutzgesetz* summarized here leave
much doubt that for those women who had access to this protection, it
met some of the needs of working women with responsibility for
dependents.[113] But in the political climate of the fifties, protective legislation also protected much else: it protected conceptions of women's
work and the sexual division of labor; it protected an elevated image of
a nuclear family, best supported by a male wage; it protected pronatalist
sentiments; it protected notions of sexual difference, grounded not only
in biology but also in society, function, and accepted practice; and it protected conceptions of women's natural obligations as wives and mothers. This larger ideological context restricted the possibilities for formulating additional policies that would permit women to be both mothers
and workers.

Anneliese Teetz's "entire hope" was the Basic Law's promise of equality for women. Where the state protected women workers in the fifties,
however, it was not, as Teetz put it, because "in reality the two sexes are
really not so different," but precisely because women were not like men.
It is particularly telling that when the standard legal commentary on the
Basic Law, completed in the late fifties, took up the topic of protective
legislation for women workers in its volume on "The Constitution of the
Economy and Work," it addressed protective measures not under the
right to work or the right to equality, but rather under the elaboration
of Article 6, the protection of marriage, family, and motherhood. The
special treatment of all working women was collapsed into the protection of motherhood. As the author explained, "The protection of mothers . . . serves population policy. . . . By keeping mothers healthy, it pro-
motes the healthy and hearty rising generation, needed for maintaining
the nation."[114] In the fifties, women as workers could claim protection
because they were also potential mothers. The "Constitution of the
Economy and Work" for women was inseparable from the constitution
of their bodies.

CHAPTER SIX

Women's Equality
and the Family's Protection

The Family Law Reform of 1957

In mid-January 1954, Marie-Elisabeth Lüders, the oldest member of the Bundestag, a long-time feminist activist, and a member of the FDP, wrote to Erna Scheffler, the only woman justice on the Federal Constitutional Court. On Lüders's mind was the continued commitment of the Adenauer government, the overwhelming majority of the CDU/CSU, and some of her own political colleagues to the patriarchal provisions of the Civil Code. She freely vented her frustration to Scheffler.[1]

Lüders was not confronting these issues for the first time. She had celebrated her seventy-fifth birthday the previous June, and her involvement with the organized women's movement stretched back into the Kaiserreich. She credited her father, a high-ranking Prussian civil servant, with encouraging her not to abandon her intellectual aspirations, and by her early thirties, she became one of the first women to earn a doctorate from a German university, concentrating her studies in "state sciences" (*Staatswissenschaften*). Involved in organizing social-work services for women and children during the First World War, she also became politically active and entered the Weimar constitutional assembly and the Reichstag as a delegate of the liberal German Democratic party. Here, in her own words, she lived out her conviction that "in the long term we can help woman to emancipation not through individual social work but through fundamental regulation at the level of law."[2]

The Nazi seizure of power abruptly interrupted Lüders's political career, and unlike many other Weimar bourgeois feminists she found no basis for accommodation with National Socialism. Legally prohibited from public speaking and writing, she was arrested by the Gestapo in 1937 and released after four months in prison only because of the protest of international women's organizations on her behalf. Bomb attacks drove her from Berlin at the end of the war, but she returned in the late forties, throwing herself into the renewal of public political life. A member of the newly founded FDP, she served the party first in the communal government in Berlin and after the 1953 elections took a seat in the Bundestag.[3]

Among the causes Lüders had championed in Weimar was the reform of marriage and family law, and it was no surprise that she was vitally interested in pursuing this issue in a democratic West Germany. Reflecting in 1950 on her own experience in the twenties, she mused that "back then the women were so credulous that they accepted that in principle (*grundsätzlich*) and in reality meant the same thing." In retrospect, it was clear that the Weimar constitution's guarantee of equal rights to women "in principle" had not led to instituting equality in practice and had created a loophole for justifying maintenance of the patriarchal provisions of the family law and for impeding reform initiatives. In a new Germany an unqualified language of equality would provide the legal basis for securing women's rights in all areas. "Children who have been burned fear fire, even when they are no longer children"; it was up to the Bundestag to extinguish the blaze of legal patriarchy once and for all.[4] Lüders's confidence that history would not repeat itself explained her enormous distress and disappointment when a majority in the Bundestag still apparently supported the ultimate authority of husbands and fathers. She described the collapse of parliamentary debate over marriage-law reform in the spring of 1953 as "the greatest political defeat of my long political life."[5]

In the meantime, Lüders hoped judges might prove themselves wiser than parliamentarians. Following the Bundestag's inability to meet the April 1953 deadline for revising the Civil Code, it was left to the courts to fill the void while waiting for more precise guidelines from the government and the legislature. The initial misgivings of some judges about their authority to interpret the Basic Law's prescriptions in the absence of such guidance were dismissed by the Federal High Court of Justice (Bundesgerichtshof). In a series of advisory decisions, the high court acknowledged that lawyers and judges were not empowered to shape a new Civil Code; in the German codified-law tradition, it was the court's duty to administer justice, not define it. Nonetheless, the Basic Law stated explicitly that with or without specific instruction from the legislature, the constitutional promise of women's equality applied to both public and private spheres as of April 1953. While the courts awaited action by the Bundestag, it was up to judges to "realize the equal rights of the sexes along the lines of the law shaped by judicial decisions (*Richterrecht*) in the Anglo-Saxon tradition."[6]

The high court reminded judges that there were precedents. After the end of the post–World War I currency inflation, the judiciary had intervened to regulate the revaluation of debts. The inflation had undermined the principles of "equity and good faith" (*Treu und Glauben*), and the legislature had not regulated how financial obligations should be renegotiated after stabilization of the currency. To be sure, a marriage contract was not a contract between debtor and creditor, but the justices pointed to parallels between restoring order after the disruption of war and inflation and restoring order after the disruption of the unlawful National Socialist regime.[7]

The Basic Law's emphasis on the separation of powers was another clear indication that the courts were not only entitled but obliged to step in. A "patriarchal form of state" might exclude such a system of checks and balances, but without this, "in the modern mass state, there was a constant danger of slipping into a totalitarian state." It was essential to prevent the "agglomeration of power in the hands of a single bearer of authority." The allusion to the recent past of National Socialism was unmistakable. To be sure, by accepting these expanded responsibilities, the courts confronted circumstances "only barely tolerable and exceptionally critical for the rule of law," the German tradition of *Rechtsstaat,* but by acting, the judiciary would not usurp the legislature's authority but rather would create the "security of law" within which the Bundestag could continue to pursue its task.

The court acknowledged the range of opinion about the meaning of equal rights for women and men. On one side stood those who explicitly rejected all arguments that would subordinate women's equality to the alleged needs of the family. They dismissed clerical claims to find a justification for hierarchical families in a preordained, God-given natural order; appeals to scripture belonged to a "metajuridical" realm, not the this-worldly order of the "bourgeois law's Civil Code." On the other side were those who saw hierarchy within the family as essential to preserving this fundamental social institution. Negotiating between these conflicting viewpoints was clearly no simple matter; so far, the Bundestag had found it impossible. But acknowledging this difficulty did not absolve judges from fulfilling the obligations of their office and offering their best-informed legal opinion. The government's draft proposals for reform and parliamentary discussion to date could guide, but need not bind or limit, their deliberations.[8]

By December 1953, a case challenging the judiciary's authority to define the meaning of equality in the absence of legislative guidelines had reached the level of the Federal Constitutional Court, offering this body, including Scheffler, the chance to add its weighty opinion. A lower court had determined that the Parliamentary Council was not entitled to set a deadline for completing revisions of the Civil Code; this represented an intolerable threat to the "security of law." Because the separation of powers dictated that the definition of equality must come from the legislature, not the judicial branch, the old provisions of the family law should remain in effect until the Bundestag completed its work of revision.

In its decision, the Constitutional Court dismissed attempts to second-guess the Parliamentary Council. Surely the courts' obligation to realize "material justice"—including the full equality of women and men—outweighed any potential threats to the "security of law." The "experience of the past" and the "vivid memories of the catastrophes brought on by the unlawful National Socialist state" dictated that sex, along with "origin, race, language, residence, faith, religious or political conviction," be forcefully rejected as potential bases for any discriminatory treatment. The relationship intended by the Parliamentary Council between equality and the protection of the family was just as unambiguous: "In marriage and the family as well, husband and wife have equal rights."

Determining what that meant without exact guidance from the legislature need not create uncertainty or "legal chaos." In such instances it was the constitutional responsibility of the courts to fill the gap; the body of case law that had emerged since April was a clear indication that judges were up to the task. The Constitutional Court also invoked the recent past of the National Socialist regime as evidence that "law-makers could also legislate injustice." Its decision affirmed that equality did not mean "comparable worth" or senseless "leveling" (*Gleichmacherei*), polemical concepts that had no tangible legal content. Rather, citing Selbert's comments in the debates of the Parliamentary Council, the justices reasoned that equality had meaning only if coupled with the recognition of difference. As Selbert had prescribed, this recognition meant that in the context of family law, "objective biological or functional" differences that defined a "division of labor"

(*Arbeitsteilung*) necessitated "particular legal regulation," such as "measures for the protection of the woman as mother, [and] differentiation of the types of work [of wives and husbands] for the community of the family."

The high court reminded judges that West Germans already agreed in large measure about the meaning of the "equal rights of the sexes constituted by the Basic Law," ensuring that the courts' work of "interpretation and filling holes" need not be based on "the arbitrary decision of a judge, determined by politics or ideology." It was only in questions of the "family leadership" of husbands and fathers that "convictions diverged in sharp, and, so it seems, irreconcilable ways." Here the courts must be prepared to offer an opinion and to do what was necessary to realize the legal principle explicit in the Basic Law's promise of equality, while lawgivers continued to strive for consensus.[9]

The collapse of Bundestag deliberations over family-law reform and the prospect of a significantly expanded mandate for the courts led at least one middle-class feminist in the FDP, Herta Ilk, to fear the worst. Ilk had left the legal profession in 1929 when she married, combining her new occupation with voluntary work for the Red Cross and a range of women's organizations, and after 1945, political activity in the FDP. Perhaps it was her own brief career before the bar that prompted her concerns that placing definitions of equality in the hands of male-dominated courts instead of parliament might be disastrous, because judicial opinion would be clouded by judges' unwillingness to "surrender any of their rights" as part of a collective patriarchy. But her party colleague Lüders accepted the assessment of the SPD's Frieda Nadig that by taking their chances in court, "married women have scarcely anything to lose; their status can't become worse than it currently is according to the precepts of the Civil Code."[10]

Although the Federal Constitutional Court's decision had briefly provided some basis for Nadig's views, Lüders was writing to Scheffler to communicate her astonishment and outrage that the CDU was still holding on to the principle of patriarchal authority, justifying its position by invoking conceptions of functional difference. She could find no more informed and sympathetic an audience for her complaints. A leading feminist jurist, Scheffler too had long been involved in the struggle for a reform of the patriarchal Civil Code. Fifteen years younger than Lüders, Scheffler had abandoned her hope to become a professional singer for a career only slightly less improbable for a daughter of the bourgeoisie in the Kaiserreich; she had studied law, completing her dissertation on the eve of the First World War. Working first as a lawyer, then as a judge in the twenties, she had been laid off after the Nazis came to power because of her gender and because her father, dead since she was eleven, was Jewish. For the Nazis, her Christian conversion and upbringing could not dilute her blood, nor could anything alter her sex. After surviving the Thousand Year Reich, she had once again worked as a judge, first in Berlin, then in Düsseldorf, where she moved with her husband, also a jurist, when he was appointed to the regional superior court.[11]

Scheffler's remarks on the reform of the Civil Code at the 1950 meeting of the national lawyer's association (Juristentag) had dramatically enhanced her reputation. Her speech summarized a feminist agenda that had existed since the 1890s, including demands for an end to all forms of patriarchal authority in laws governing marriage and family relations. The functional difference between women and men might lead to a sexual division of labor according to which husbands worked outside, wives within, the home, but this difference could not justify the legal subordination of wife to husband or mother to father; "the wife's 'occupation' (Beruf) as housewife and mother has absolutely nothing to do with equal rights." Scheffler insisted that the "real, bodily, spiritual, and social difference between man and woman leads logically according to law just as little to legal inequality as differences in faith, origin, race, or occupational status (Berufsstand)." Should only one person hold ultimate authority within marriage, she joked, then "following the principle of equality, for the next two thousand years it should be the wife, after the past two thousand years when the husband had the last word."[12] Scheffler's high profile as an intelligent and articulate expert on these questions combined with her established history of persecution by the Nazis were credentials that contributed to her selection for a twelve-year term on the new Federal Constitutional Court. She was the only woman chosen. Half the court's members were elected by the Bundestag, the other half by the Federal Council. According to a political compromise worked out between the governing coalition and the SPD at the time of the court's creation, each party was permitted to select eight justices. Another eight seats were set aside for individuals with no party affiliation. Scheffler held one of these, and her candidacy, initially put forward by the SPD and the state government of North Rhine–Westphalia, won general acceptance.[13]

Writing in a law journal in May 1953, Scheffler detailed her conviction that the courts should bring some order to the rhetorical disarray of parliamentary diatribes over the meaning of equality in marriage and family law. Those who claimed that the constitutional guarantee of equal rights for women was limited by the Basic Law's pledge to protect the family missed the point, Scheffler explained. Citing the liberal Catholic social theorist Walter Dirks, she emphasized that "the law-giver intends to place only the marriage and family under the protection of the state in which husband and wife have equal rights." At the most fundamental level this meant acknowledging that there was no justification for granting husbands and fathers any form of ultimate authority over wives and mothers; the positions fervently defended by Adenauer's government quite simply violated the constitution. Claims that loosening the bonds of patriarchal authority would fuel the divorce rate were unfounded; conflicts over authority became relevant only after marriages fell apart, not before. In addition, "the increase in the number of divorces took place under patriarchal law, and the husband's privilege to have the final say was not capable of avoiding conflicts."[14] Scheffler's participation in the judgment of the Federal Constitutional Court in December had allowed her the unique opportunity as a feminist jurist to translate at least some of these legal principles into legal practice; her voice was clearly audible in the court's decision.

By the time Lüders exploded to Scheffler, it was obvious to both that Adenauer's government endorsed a significantly different interpretation of the consequences of "objective biological and functional difference." Although in its draft proposals brought to the newly elected Bundestag, the government stressed the need for husband and wife to seek consensus when they disagreed, when their efforts failed, "according to the natural and Christian conceptions of order, the decision devolves upon the husband." As for disputes over children's welfare, the government also refused to budge from its insistence on a father's final say. Leaving resolution of conflicts to the courts, the alternative put forward by the FDP and advocated by Scheffler and other liberal jurists as well, would invite marriage partners to take their disagreements outside of marriage, only intensifying conflict. This, in turn, would violate the constitutional protection of the family by further estranging mothers from fathers. A father's predominance was justified only when it was essential for the protection of the family, but in such instances it was indispensable.[15]

Perhaps, Lüders observed, the functional difference between woman and man that was so important to Adenauer's government was a man's "brute force," a "functional superiority of the husband" that could resolve any difference of opinion within a marriage and that the state apparently wanted to secure in the law. As an embittered Lüders confided to Hildegard Krüger, another feminist jurist, the government's notion seemed to be that through the "successful beating of his wife a husband irrefutably proves his functional superiority." Though such conceptions had little to do with what was "desirable in a Christian marriage," they seemed to inform Adenauer's government. It was possible, Lüders added, that her inability to follow this argument lay in the "functional difference" of her mind. To Scheffler, she lamented that "the saddest of all . . . is that the respect for the constitution even among the highest representatives of the Ministry of Justice is so limited—and thus, is steadily reduced among the population." She encouraged Scheffler to "be prepared for an ongoing struggle."[16]

The "ongoing struggle" extended into the late fifties in the courts and in the parliament. From the bench and within the Bundestag, West German jurists and politicians continued to contest the boundaries between equality and difference. In the first decade of the Federal Republic's history, the debates over the revision of family law revolved endlessly around the tensions between the Basic Law's guarantee of women's equality in Paragraph 2 of Article 3 and the guarantee of the protection of the family in Article 6. In its 1953 decision, the Federal High Court had referred to those who feared that "marriage and family are to a particularly great degree endangered, because in large part there are no firm, self-evident, general conceptions of their essence, meaning, and spiritual content."[17] Defining women's equality was directly linked to filling this void.

While the Bundestag continued its deliberations, judges took seriously their charge to provide a framework for interpreting the meaning of the Basic Law. Central in the cases that came before them was determining which "biological or functional" differences between women and men legally justified different treatment. Where the parliament had neared consensus before April 1953, the courts did nothing to muddy the waters. Their judgments underscored the conception that in the "normal marriage," the marriage that "corresponds to the natural order" and God's will,

> the husband is in the world of work, he is the provider for the family; the wife works in and cares for the home and kitchen, she is housewife, companion, mother, educator of the children. This [form of] marriage is not backward and outdated, and it never will be. It corresponds to the eternal natural essence of marriage, to the biological inequality of husband and wife, and for the most part to their desires and wishes as well.[18]

Even where such scriptural overtones were absent, judges consistently upheld the parliament's view that a wife's household labor was the equivalent of a husband's work for wages outside the home.

These lofty principles took on practical relevance in cases where ex-husbands attempted to deny ex-wives financial support or a share of the property accumulated in marriage, maintaining that if women were truly equal, then they should fend for themselves once they were divorced. Those women, the courts determined, who within marriage had devoted "their entire labor power to their natural obligations as mothers," need not pursue other employment once a marriage ended. "According to the western occidental conception of marriage and family, the mother is by nature given the obligation to raise the children and to surround them continually with care in the first years of life." It followed that in a western occidental divorce, a mother's tasks should be no different. Indeed, caring for children was not only a mother's right but also her obligation. Even when a grandmother was available and offered to help with children, no mother should have to "place [her] children in care."[19] Completely supporting these judgments, the Federal High Court added that when a wife worked for wages outside the home while still doing housework, it was her right to surrender a smaller percentage of her money wages for her family's support, a form of material compensation for her uncompensated second shift.[20] For the courts no less than for the Bundestag, the unpaid work of wife and mother was work that had measurable value; equality did not mean redefining the sexual division of labor, but it did mean acknowledging the vital economic significance of women's unpaid work.

Where the Bundestag was most divided, there was also no unanimity among judges, though in most cases the courts confirmed the unconstitutionality of legislating the final authority of husbands and fathers.[21] Thus, for example, a husband who came to West Germany at the war's end, fleeing his former home in Soviet-occupied Poland, could not command his wife, residing after the war in East Germany, to join him, nor could her refusal be construed as grounds for divorce. In both Germanys, the court determined, the legal provision giving the husband the last word over his wife was no longer binding. Choice of a place of residence must reflect the interests of both marriage partners. Whatever advantages the plaintiff's wife might reap from life in the west, in this case the wife had an understandable attachment to the place where her mother and sister also lived and where she was only a relatively short distance from her pre-1945 home. While emphasizing her equal rights, the court also underscored her difference; precisely because she was a woman, she was more fearful of change and more dependent on familial and local ties. Having never experienced life in the west, the court maintained, the woman could not fully appreciate what drew her husband irreversibly in that direction, but this was no reason to disregard her wishes or to subordinate her will to her husband's.[22]

When asked if a father could still veto a mother's choice of names for their daughter, the regional court in Frankfurt was ready to say no. The first syllable of the name Ulrike, claimed the outraged father, "a high-ranking academic civil servant" who was separated from the girl's mother, was a "dark, ugly la-la word of Mongol origin, while the other syllables invoked unfortunate memories of the name of the legal agent of the mother." The father's preference was for names from mythology—Minerva, Vesta, or Diana—but ultimately he had accepted the name Gerda Agathe. The mother claimed that for the father, what was in a name was not the child's welfare but an opportunity to harass her. For her, the father's compromise solution—Rotlind Maria—was no more acceptable than Minerva. The court granted that before 1 April 1953, the final determination of the girl's name would have rested legally with the father, but the child was born two years later, after women had become equal with men in all respects. Realizing women's equality within marriage meant granting a mother equal right to make decisions that clearly affected her child's welfare. A name was hardly a simple matter of aesthetics, as a lower court had determined, but rather "of significance for the entire life of the bearer." Gerda Agathe was at one time acceptable to both parents; justice, the child's welfare, and a mother's equal rights were served by prefixing a third name, Ulrike, to these two.[23]

Maternal rights were also upheld in cases where fathers sought to override a mother's choice of occupation for their child. The father of a son, sent by his mother to learn the trade of cabinetmaker, could not force the boy to join him in his chimney-sweeping firm. Nor could a father compel his daughter to pursue training in domestic service, if she and her mother preferred that she study to become a secretary and stenographer.[24] Such weighty decisions required consultation and agreement between parents even when they were estranged and living apart, as was typically the case when conflicts over a child's welfare came before the courts.

Still, balancing these judgments were others that maintained that paternal authority was essential for realizing the constitutional guarantee of the family's protection; the ultimate authority of fathers conformed with the "occidental tradition" and the "dominant conception in all parts of the population that the father represents the family group."[25] In one case, a Catholic mother who arranged to baptize her daughter in her faith without consulting the child's Protestant father was informed that if her husband objected, she could not justify her action by appealing to the principle of equal rights. No more compelling for the court was the mother's argument that she was primarily responsible for the child's welfare because the father's work kept him away from home most of the day. A parent's contribution to a child's upbringing could not be measured temporally. "Equal rights within the marital union for life did not mean uniformity [Gleichschaltung] without authority and internal order." The Basic Law's promise to protect the institution of marriage and the family superseded "the recognition of the individual rights of those who stand within this institution"; a father could override a mother's judgment.[26]

In other cases, the court ventured well beyond defining equality within marriage and revealed a remarkable willingness to charge in where even the Bundestag chose not to tread. In a case that reached the Federal Constitutional Court in 1957, two male plaintiffs, one of whom died during the appeals process, argued that the criminalization of male, but not female, homosexual activity violated the Basic Law because it amounted to treating women and men differently. The court was also asked to decide whether more severe punishments for male homosexuals introduced in 1935 were products of National Socialist "racial teaching" (Rassenlehre). Although on this issue, the court granted that Nazi revisions had come in the aftermath of the assassination of Ernst Röhm, leader of the Nazi paramilitary organization (Sturmabteilung), and the Nazis' "destruction of homosexual groups within the NSDAP that had been politically close to him," it determined that these harsher penalties were nonetheless consistent "with the fundamental principles of a free democratic state." Not all laws introduced by the Nazis were indelibly tainted by the "National Socialist body of thought [Gedankengut]."[27] Apparently, the same ambivalent relationship to the most recent German past that had allowed lawmakers to borrow from Nazi schemes for family allowances and the protection of mothers also prevailed when it came to learning from the Nazis how more effectively to criminalize certain forms of sexual activity. Male homosexuals were among the victims of Nazi terror for whom there would be no restitution in the fifties.[28]

To evaluate the plaintiffs' charge of violations of the Basic Law's Article 3, the court solicited expert assistance; it commissioned a panel of psychologists and sociologists, who were asked to offer their opinion on the sexual drives and activities of women and men, the significance of the "large *Frauenüberschuss* and the frequency of common household arrangements of two or more women" for understanding "lesbian love" (*die lesbische Liebe*) in postwar West Germany, and the potential dangers to society presented by male homosexuality and lesbianism. At issue was once again what constituted sexual difference and what circumstances justified legal penalties for men that did not apply to women. In this case, however, the court was asked not whether sexual differences justified male privilege but rather whether it justified women's exemption from criminal sanctions applicable only to men.

Helmut Schelsky, truly a sociologist for all seasons, had followed his investigations of the postwar German family with a major study of the sociology of sexuality and was among those called on to testify.[29] In his work on the family, Schelsky had relentlessly attacked feminists and other critics of the patriarchal order who advocated a "false emancipation." In his testimony before the Federal Constitutional Court, the same themes resounded. Schelsky asserted that the growing public and professional status of women made lesbianism no less dangerous than male homosexuality. Once lesbians were supervisors, they would be just as likely as men to exploit their positions "to seduce their subordinates for lesbian friendly relationships." Still, mitigating circumstances included the fact that "for a large portion of women, there would be a stronger family connection and a greater need for privacy, so that on balance, their lesbian activity should not be subject to the same criminal penalties as those [that applied] to male homosexuals"; lesbianism represented "a less serious social danger." Lesbians were also more likely to keep their relationships private, "entering less frequently into public," and they would be less inclined to "build cliques or to tend to other asocial forms and to prostitution."[30]

Figuring even more prominently in the court's final decision was the opinion of psychiatric and medical experts, who emphasized that male and female sexuality differed fundamentally because of the nature of men's and women's respective contributions to "generative continuity." For men, it lasted but a moment. Becoming a father was accomplished not through the "generative-vegetative effort," but through "social efforts." For women, in contrast, motherhood began at the moment of conception. "Procreation and becoming a father are thus not connected in the same way as conception and becoming a mother." Unlike a man, the court determined, a woman "is intuitively reminded by her body that burdens accompany sexual activity." From fundamental physiological difference stemmed different psychological attitudes toward sexuality. It was possible that women in lesbian relationships would "instinctively" tend in a "womanly-motherly" direction, pushed by their "organism," while for men these inclinations did not exist. The linkage woman-mother thus even defined the sexuality of those women whose sexual activity could not lead to conception.

"As different sexual beings," the court concluded, "man and woman are also able to practice same-sex immoral activity [*gleichgeschlecht-liche Unzucht*] only in the form that their sex makes possible."[31] Men were "set free" sexually and suffered from an "excess of drives," as was evident in their ability to be aroused more rapidly and, relative to women, more often, and to engage in sexual behavior that was "aggressive [and] demanding." This in turn led to the "characteristic experience of pleasure [*Lusterleben*] of male sexuality," greater tendencies toward promiscuity, limited abilities to form lasting relationships, and the danger of pursuing sex merely for "lustful gain." Women, no matter what the object of their lust, apparently used different balance sheets. They were more inclined toward abstinence, more interested in "friendships with women" than in the "purely sexual," and, in general, more willing to "accept [and] sacrifice." This also created problems, unique to women, in locating clear boundaries between women's friendships and love relationships, greatly complicating enforcement of sanctions against lesbianism.

In the court's view, criminalizing only male homosexual activity was not a violation of the Basic Law's guarantee of equal rights. Equal treatment was justified only in cases where women and men were subject to the same circumstances, not where "the peculiarity of woman as sexual being and the peculiarity of man as sexual being so fundamentally and decisively determine the facts that the comparable element, the abnormal turn of desire to one's own sex, retreats from view, and lesbian love and male homosexuality appear as noncomparable in a legal sense." In citing precedents that had established the limits of "biological or functional difference," the court pointed out that neither the woman worker, whose hours of work were restricted, nor the "woman who becomes a mother" had any "legal advantages or disadvantages" because of state-mandated measures not applied to men. By acknowledging the significance of their difference, the law did not deny the equality of women and men; rather, it recognized the demands of biological and social motherhood. Similarly, it was men's difference in function and biology that justified criminalizing their homosexual activity, protecting society from dangers that lesbianism simply could not present.[32]

A woman's modesty and "patient sacrifice" were also among the natural characteristics that justified a double standard in laws obliging husband and wife to "provide for the cleanliness of marriage." In a case that reached the Federal High Court, a husband who was sentenced to six months in jail for photographing his wife as she engaged in "immoral activity" with the male employee of a trucking firm and another woman claimed that his wife was equally guilty of violating laws prohibiting such practices and equally liable to be behind bars. Why should husbands alone wield the scrub brush of morality? Why in this instance should equal rights find a limit at the prison gate? "Naturally given fundamental differences demand different treatment" was the court's response. Again, the Law for Protection of Mothers and other measures regulating women's wage workplace provided the most compelling legal precedents. In addition, because a woman "is generally more restrained in sexual matters" and "tends in her love life more to solid bonds than a man," she ran a far smaller risk of "threatening the moral order." The state's interest in protecting marriage, whose "maintenance was essential for the permanence of the state and whose continued cleanliness is of particular significance for the moral order indispensable for the state," placed a particular obligation on the husband "according to nature." "He is entrusted not only with protecting the honor of his wife. He is also expected to pledge himself to preserve the moral order within marriage."

In its decision, the court directly addressed any concerns that its judgment undermined the principle of women's equality. A sexual double standard was not justified because a wife had a subordinate legal status. On the contrary, both "spiritually and economically" women had experienced significant improvements in recent times. Still, when it came to upholding the moral order, whether within marriage or within society, there was no denying that woman's "weaker nature" and the "fundamental difference between the sexes that rests on a natural foundation" made women more needy of protection, more dependent, and consequently less liable for the moral endangerment of marriage.[33]

The constitutionality of a sexual double standard was also at issue in cases challenging the claims for legal compensation by the woman "of

good reputation" (*unbescholten*), whose honor was endangered by a fiancé who had intercourse with her and then broke off the engagement.
In these cases, the courts were divided. Some judgments maintained that
sex before marriage had gender-specific "physical and psychic" consequences; recognizing this difference implied no double standard but
rather meant acknowledging that for men, "in general sexual intercourse does not lead to a circumstance that requires compensation."[34]
The Basic Law did not intend to legislate the "schematic equivalence" of
women and men; biological differences translated for women into a
greater need for protection of "sexual honor."[35] Freed from the physical
burdens potentially accompanying intercourse, men were also immune
to the "spiritual change" that occurred in a woman and that justified the
conclusion that "for centuries these things have simply been different
and have been judged differently for women and men."[36]

There was no clear consensus on this question, however, and another
court, asked to investigate a similar case, read the historical record differently. The judge maintained that since the passage of the Civil Code
fifty-four years earlier, women's status had changed enormously. "Today's generation of women is in a purely physical sense different from
that at the turn of the century. . . . A certain approximation [by women]
of men's physical appearance has occurred." Psychological changes accompanied these physical developments, and today's woman was "physically more independent, more objective, less sensitive, more balanced,
more humorous, more certain of her personality, and more deliberate
than [the woman] of a half-century ago." To judge this new woman as
particularly "needy of protection" (*schutzbedürftig*) was to ignore the
"revolution" that had taken place. This revolution had also affected sexuality, and "one of the most notable trends of the twentieth century is
the decrease in male sexual activity and related to that the increase in
female." Compensation for threats to the honor of women "of good
reputation" was no more justified than similar treatment for men.[37] Another judge added that as the equal of man, a "woman is completely capable of assessing the consequences of such a step [premarital inter-
course] and of acting accordingly; she herself has to bear responsibility
for preserving her sexual honor."[38]

Still, such decisions emphasizing women's increased autonomy and
sexual activity were exceptions. Even in most cases where the courts
challenged male privilege and upheld a more expansive interpretation of
women's equal rights, it was not because they shared the opinion that
the differences between women and men were diminishing at a revolu-

tionary pace. Rather, more often than not it was precisely a woman's difference that defined the bases for granting her claims to equality. A wife's refusal to change her place of residence should be respected because she was more dependent on familiar surroundings and less open to change. A woman's claims to spousal support or property accumulated in marriage was justified because of her gender-specific contribution to supporting the household. And it was a woman's "conscientiousness and aptitude" in her "educational tasks" as a mother that gave her equal rights to determine a child's welfare. In most cases where the courts upheld women's demands for the equality guaranteed them by the Basic Law, it was not because judges recognized women as individuals who stood fully equal with men before the law but because the courts acknowledged women's "functional or biological" difference as wives and mothers.

Of course, difference was also the basis for women's claims to special treatment, and the courts concurred completely with the Bundestag that protecting real and potential mothers did not violate the constitutional principle of equality. Rather, such protection was a way to acknowledge the "biological peculiarity" of women.[39] Women, "biologically peculiar" in comparison with a male norm, were disadvantaged; protective legislation ensured women's equality by compensating for this. It gave women no privilege.[40] For lesbians and heterosexual women alike, a woman's biologically determined identity as a potential mother and the social expectations that this identity entailed shaped her entire being and structured her sexual activity. Whether on the factory floor or in the pornographer's studio, women's difference from men was significant and defined a need for special protection. By allowing for different treatment of different circumstances, the Federal Constitutional Court had created a form into which the legal system effortlessly poured the contents of biology and the force of "centuries-old tradition," dissolving nature into society.

These court judgments provide a tantalizing and frustrating source for the social historian for whom the outcome of a case is potentially less interesting than the personalities involved in the proceedings and the circumstances that lead individuals to request a third party to arbitrate their disagreements. Such glimpses behind the scenes are blocked by strict German laws of privacy. All personal details are carefully purged in the published record of the courts, and archives allow no access to cases from the fifties, where plaintiff and defendant might still be alive. Still, the courts' willingness to fill the void left by the absence of legislative action does provide fascinating testimony to the willingness of German jurists to take on the unusual task of interpreting the Basic Law. The cases they were asked to adjudicate also provide intriguing if anecdotal evidence that in the lives of at least some Germans, much more than a symbol was at stake in the Basic Law's mandate of equal rights for women.

In addition, the court cases are important because they served as a point of reference in ongoing parliamentary debates and because they further illuminate the conceptions of equality and difference that prevailed in postwar West Germany. Reflecting in 1953 on the courts' opportunity to act where the Bundestag had not, Scheffler admitted to a "sense of relief that the boundless debates over equal rights of recent years have for the time being been removed from the ideological-political discussion" and transferred to an arena of dispassionate legal calculation, where, she averred, judges would provide a clear and objective perspective.[41] At the other extreme were those judges, like Harald Schlüter, who opposed the rights of the courts to move into the space created by the legislature's silence and who expressed fears that the result would be "as many lawgivers as there are judges." Without explicit guidance, each judge would "interpret the law according to his conscience and conviction. Because there is no law, these are shaped by his personal opinion; he could only judge according to the picture of equal rights that he carries within himself."[42] The range of legal interpretation ultimately offered by the courts reveals that they were not all operating with the same scales of justice. However, on balance the record of judicial decisions also indicates that the pictures of equal rights that judges carried within themselves were confined to a fairly narrowly circumscribed "ideological-political" spectrum, differing little from the conceptions in the hearts and minds of Bonn lawgivers.

Early in 1954, Lüders had expressed her hopes that "the more the courts recognize the unrestricted equality of [women's] rights, the fewer are the chances that our opponents will be able to change this later on."[43] Close to four years' worth of judicial opinion did provide advocates of a more expansive definition of equality with some support, but those who sought in legal precedent a clear-cut case for eliminating all sanction of patriarchal authority were disappointed. Like scriptural exegesis, the record of judicial decisions provided something for everyone.

With no clear instruction for specific revision from the bench, the Bundestag continued to play out the drama of family-law reform according to a familiar script that allowed for little improvisation. Wuermeling set the dominant tone for the CDU/CSU, representing the government's position and the views of the conservative Catholic clergy. Adenauer's family minister claimed as allies the pope and all other advocates of the "occidental conception of marriage" in arguing that an "ordered society" could not exist without authority. What was true of society was true of society's most fundamental building block, the family. The reluctance of postwar Germans to accept legislated hierarchy reflected an understandably allergic response to unfortunate experiences with the authoritarian state in the Third Reich, but "democracy also requires authority," and authority, properly constituted, was completely consistent with equality.

According to Wuermeling, his views were amply supported by the work of postwar German sociologists. He freely paraphrased Schelsky's thesis that women had experienced the expansion of their responsibilities in the war and postwar years not as "an enlargement of their personal sphere of freedom or a better possibility for personal improvement and development" but rather as a forced emancipation that brought only additional work and worry. No wife or mother sought this form of equality, and after the disruptions of the forties it was time for Germany to get back on course. For Wuermeling, the only conceivable alternatives to the government's call for well-ordered relations within marriage and society were an "egotistical individualism"—equality run amok that would result in the "dwarf family" (*Zwergfamilie*) as selfishness led to family size limitation—or "state socialism," where equality meant little more than forcing "healthy girls into child-bearing services" and into the wage-labor force. Against the background of ongoing debates over "money-for-children" and fears that Germany was "dying out," it was obvious that "egotistical individuals" were more likely women than men, and that their actions had consequences not only for individual welfare, but for the future of the *Volk*.

Once again, the evils of "state socialism" were clearly visible to the east. Quoting at length from the German Democratic Republic's 1950 Law for the Protection of Mothers and Children and the Rights of Women, Wuermeling elaborated on the disastrous consequences of a social order where a state-mandated double burden drove a stake deep into the "heart of the family," the mother, who was expected to accomplish the impossible. "Ultimately there is no achievement of equal rights for women in society without their involvement on an equal basis in the economy." Wuermeling quoted this view of the head of the East German state, Otto Grotewohl, to illustrate the false equality "from which we should want to spare all of our women." "Where this leads in the final analysis," Wuermeling warned, "is the coal mine or the uranium mine."[44] In the west, women should spend their time rocking the cradle, not breaking rocks below the earth's surface. Providing a supporting chorus for these views, Helene Weber continued to offer living proof that some women were also willing to support the legal subordination of wives to husbands. Weber admitted that as a woman, it required the "courage of a lion" to defend this position, but she drew her strength from the thousands of "simple women of the people" whose interests she claimed to defend, the silent majority not represented by Social Democrats or liberals and content with the rule of the father.[45]

The SPD, joined by Lüders and other Free Democrats, with a wide array of middle-class women's groups in the wings, continued to fire back that equality within marriage allowed for no subordination of wives to husbands and charged the conservative coalition with advocating nothing less than a "return to patriarchy." For opponents of the Adenauer government's proposals, Wuermeling provided a convenient focus for attacks on the party in power. He was depicted as more "propaganda minister" than "family minister," and his remarks were taken as a measure of how unnecessary it had been to create his post in Adenauer's cabinet. Legislating patriarchal authority, argued the FDP's Herta Ilk, was legislating women's inferiority within marriage.[46] This did nothing to preserve the family; rather, it was most frequently deployed by husbands who were already estranged from their wives in marriages near dissolution. A father's rights simply became a vehicle for male rage, a weapon to crush a wife's opposition, forcing marital conflict to escalate and catching children in the cross-fire. In a "normal marriage," decisions would be made jointly; the government's proposal would lead not to a proper exercise of male authority but to its abuse in marriages gone sour.[47] Resolving differences of opinion, argued Ilk, was the "fundamental core of *democracy*." For children, the parents' example should provide the earliest introduction to this rule, and by legislating hierarchical parental relations, the Bundestag would make this impossible.[48] With unmistakable sarcasm, Lüders reassured Wuermeling that he need fear "no preparations of a war with the amazons"; women would always be inferior to the "brute force" of men. But surely it was time to concede that women together with many men were winning the intellectual battle for the achievement of true equality, which had raged since the late nineteenth century.[49]

Social Democrats and liberal feminists also insisted that associating advocates of unrestricted equality with the policies of the East German ruling party, the SED, was totally unfounded red-baiting, the product of Wuermeling's imagination. Writing in the SPD's monthly newspaper for women, *Gleichheit,* one woman advised Bonn lawmakers that only by granting women full equal rights would they most effectively enlist both sexes in the battle against communism.[50] In their opposition to Wuermeling, socialists emphasized that they were allied not with Otto Grotewohl but with such middle-class organizations as Protestant Women's Work in Germany.

Among the SPD's allies was also Margot Kalinke, who represented the conservative German party as well as the Association of Female Salaried Employees. As she had in the initial debates over family law reform, she broke ranks with many of her parliamentary colleagues, consistently emphasizing that women's experience in the war and postwar years and women's increased involvement in wage labor should register in a law that guaranteed women's rights within marriage. For the Bundestag to resurrect an order founded in the past was to deny the "raw reality" of women's lives and to "hide [our] heads in the sand." More than any other parliament, the West German Bundestag had to "solve the problems of the postwar period and the postwar generation . . . and to consider the problem of equal rights in the context of the changed world."[51] Kalinke's break with the majority of her party was a further indication of how isolated Helene Weber had become as a female advocate of female subordination and evidence of how bonds of gender pulled together the handful of women delegates to the parliament, a group apparently not among the "simple women of the people" for whom Weber claimed to speak.

The only indication of any shift in firmly established fronts was the CDU's public concession that not all of its members shared the majority opinion.[52] In contrast to the Catholic church, the official representatives of German Protestantism had steadfastly opposed the legal sanction of a husband's authority over his wife and conceded that within their ranks no unanimity existed on how best to resolve parental disputes over children's welfare. Since the early fifties, the conservative coalition had also confronted far more vocal criticism from women within the CDU, who rejected the majority support for all forms of patriarchal authority.[53]

Elisabeth Schwarzhaupt was particularly well qualified to represent both sources of dissent. After studying law in the twenties, she practiced in a counseling center for women in Frankfurt originally established by feminist political activists. Here she worked particularly with battered and divorced women, and through this experience gained firsthand knowledge of the consequences for women of a patriarchal family law that gravely disadvantaged wives. Her brief career as a judge was ended by the Nazi seizure of power. After 1935 she found employment in Berlin as an adviser to the national office of the Protestant church, where she continued working after the war. She also took over the leadership of Protestant Women's Work in Germany, the national umbrella organization for church-affiliated women's organizations. In this capacity, she played a crucial part in formulating that body's critical responses to the Adenauer government's proposals for upholding patriarchal authority in the first round of Bundestag debates. Initially undecided between membership in the CDU or the FDP, she opted in 1952 for the Christian Democrats, convinced that Catholic interests should not be allowed to claim an exclusive hold on Christian politics. When she was elected to the Bundestag a year later, she did not abandon her earlier demands for a broad conception of women's equality within marriage, and her party, acknowledging that she represented both Protestant interests and the pressures of organized women's groups within their own ranks, gave her ample opportunity to voice her opinion.[54]

While agreeing that in most marriages the wife would more readily sacrifice her individual concerns and independence for the good of the family, Schwarzhaupt rejected proposals to legislate a wife's subordination to her husband. Echoing the national position papers of the Protestant church on key provisions of family law reform, she argued that "the question is, what can the state as lawgiver determine?" Her response was that state authority ended where the private realm of the family began. "Neither an imposed equality nor an imposed patriarchy" could be legislated for the family; determining relations between wife and husband, mother and father, was their business, not the state's.[55]

Within the parameters defined by these opposing stances, lawgivers hammered out details on specific issues.[56] Social Democrats continued to call for allowing married couples to choose either the wife's or husband's last name or to symbolize their union by joining their names with a hyphen. With little support from Free Democrats, however, they confronted unified resistance from the conservative coalition that maintained that for a married couple to use the husband's family name represented no disadvantage for the woman and corresponded to a "primordial custom" still overwhelmingly accepted among the West German population. Recognizing that it stood no chance of winning

against these odds, the SPD ultimately accepted the government's alternative, allowing a married woman to request that her maiden name be
added by a hyphen to her husband's name, though this would be an exception to the rule.[57]

On a range of other provisions, the Bundestag developed in detail the
broad areas of agreement sketched out by 1953. There was little difficulty in determining definitions of wives' and mothers' work, spousal
support, and rights to property accumulated within marriage. These
concerns were related. The recognition that "in the final analysis housework too is like the work of the firm in which raw materials are transformed into finished products" was the justification for establishing unpaid domestic labor as the basis for the non-wage-earning wife's claims
to property within marriage and spousal support and marital property
in the event of divorce. A wife's unpaid work made a husband's wage
work possible; "if there were no women," quipped Lüders, "men
couldn't do their work, and that holds, for example, for most representatives to parliament as well."[58] Thus, what ex-wives could demand
from ex-husbands was not "alms" but their fair share of the material
wealth accumulated in marriage.[59] All political parties also ultimately
accepted the formulation that "in general, the wife fulfills her obligation
to contribute to the support of the family by running the household," a
task that she carried out on her "own accountability" (*in eigener Verantwortung*), not as the agent of the husband, as the 1900 Civil Code
had specified. Women thus had the "power of the keys" (*Schlüsselge-
walt*), the right and obligation to manage the household.

In the law's final version, a wife's right to work outside the home was
limited by the fulfillment of her "obligations to marriage and family."
Assessing how well a married woman did her job was not the prerogative of her husband, as had been the case under the Civil Code; rather,
it "must be judged from a purely objective perspective." Still, explicitly
linking women's work for wages with the responsibilities of wives and
mothers was essential for those "many cases . . . where because of an
exaggerated standard of living both spouses are employed to the detriment of the children."[60] Again, there were clear echoes of the debates
over "money-for-children" and evocations of fears of those mothers
who pursued the temptations of the "luxury dog," the automobile, and
the television set. The law reminded women of their priorities. When
Helene Weber fretted over rebellious teens, the so-called *Halbstarken*,
when she blamed their problems not on "bad movies" but on "parents
who paid no heed to which movies their children see," she also left no

doubt about which parent bore the greater responsibility for the "degeneration of youth" and the "disintegration of the family." These problems could not be solved by "pursuing [youth] with a policeman's billy club" but only by reminding those responsible that raising children was part of the work of the household, and that the work of the household was a mother's work.[61] As a representative of the justice ministry put it, the state had no intention of intervening in the particular laws governing any specific marriage, but the state should not hesitate to offer an "ideal model [*Leitbild*] of the division of tasks in marriage and the family,"[62] a model that embodied conceptions of both difference and equality.

Nonetheless, where marriage partners could not agree, according to the government's proposals, difference continued to create a basis for hierarchy. The issues that had divided Bonn lawmakers, the legal community, organized women's groups, and the national representatives of the Protestant and Catholic churches in the spring of 1953 continued to divide them in the spring of 1957. For the large majority within the CDU/CSU, the "Christian occidental" tradition and nature still fully justified such authority. In addition, the law should have a "pedagogical effect," in this case educating husband and wife to reach accord before relying on a father's final authority; were no other arbiter available, the parents' incentive to negotiate would be increased. A father should be "entrusted" with this ultimate authority "not only because he is of the male sex" but because such an investment of authority would protect the family, that "sociological twosome," and "bring into harmony" Article 3 and Article 6 of the Basic Law.[63] Compromise proposals that irreconcilable marital differences could be settled by court intervention were equated with the Third Reich's attempts to invade the privacy of the family. Fathers might abuse their authority on occasion, but, stressed the CDU's Eduard Wahl, this abuse did not justify "castrating" the family.[64] There could scarcely be a more graphic expression of where authority should lie.

The conservative coalition also underscored connections between a strong German nation and strong German patriarchs. Referring to recent parliamentary discussions of rearmament and military conscription, Wahl reminded his colleagues that women were excluded from conscription, and only men were responsible for certain "protective function[s]." Even as volunteers, women were prohibited from using weapons. Women could be drafted no more than men could claim the "housework day." Wahl concluded that a woman's need for protection—whether by the military or by laws regulating her workplace—in no way diminished her equal "dignity as an individual."[65]

It was not up to the Bundestag to judge whether "since the end of the century [Germany] has entered into a new phase in the cultural history of the world [*Weltkulturgeschichte*], and whether the emancipation of women [that ends] with winning women's equal rights has rocked these general sociological conceptions of the Christian western world." On this question, argued the Christian Democrat Hermann Kopf, the jury was still out. Legislators should not attempt to shape a "distant future" but to provide order to the present, and it was still safe to say that "even where this patriarchal system that we have had in the west for 3,000 years has been shaken . . . [it] is still rooted so firmly in the practices and customs and views of our nation [*unseres Volkes*] . . . that from this perspective it is justified to grant the father rights to make final decisions."[66] In Wahl's words, "with the stroke of a pen the lawgiver cannot simply set aside what has developed over centuries."[67] Neither pens nor any other sharp instruments should menace male authority.

No less well rehearsed, opponents of the government completely rejected these vestiges of patriarchal authority as unconstitutional and found support for their view in many court judgments that reached the same conclusion. As a final Bundestag vote on paternal rights neared, Lüders articulated what was fully apparent: "We all know exactly what's at stake. We all know exactly what we want. We all know exactly one another's arguments, and we know how to evaluate them. . . . Why should we spend the time saying the same thing in a more or less well-formulated fashion?"[68]

It remained only to count the votes. By a margin of twelve, the Bundestag granted wives equal rights with their husbands in matters concerning their relationships. When women became mothers and children's welfare was at stake, however, two of the CDU/CSU representatives who had broken with their party returned to the fold. They were joined by a handful of Free Democrats who disregarded their party delegation's decision to oppose the measure unanimously and by others who were willing to grant fathers rights that they denied husbands.[69] By a majority of twenty votes, the ultimate authority of fathers was confirmed. With a solemnity appropriate to a process that had stretched out to fill nearly eight years, the CDU's Richard Jaeger, presiding vice-president in the Bundestag and the father of five children whose welfare he now could ultimately determine, declared: "Ladies and gentlemen, the

Bundestag has thus concluded one of the most significant legislative votes for implementing the Basic Law."[70]

"Do you really want it to come to a legal suit over the law's constitutionality? Don't we have every reason to want to avoid a legal struggle over the constitution?" In the spring of 1957 a majority in the Bundestag had chosen not to heed Frieda Nadig's warning that a vote to uphold paternal authority in the family would force a confrontation in the courts.[71] Justice's sword was not particularly swift, but two years after the Bundestag's decision, Nadig's prediction came true. The Federal Constitutional Court "castrated" the family, declaring unconstitutional the legal sanction of a father's ultimate determination of his children's welfare. Neither as family father nor as Christian Democratic lawmaker was Jaeger to have the last word about family law in the fifties. With the encouragement of Lüders and other feminists, a number of "wives and mothers of minor children" charged that to grant paternal authority in this form was a violation of their constitutional rights.[72]

Defending the law passed by the Bundestag before the court, the Ministry of Justice maintained that it was completely consistent with the "objective biological or functional differences between husband and wife," the need to ensure a stable family order, and the "custom and actual practice in most families." Despite lower-court decisions to the contrary, the Basic Law had left to lawmakers, not judges, the duty "to set standards of measurement" for assessing the meaning of equality within marriage. Giving fathers the last word did not disadvantage mothers; rather it established the conditions for their full "self-realization" within stable families. Empowering the courts to settle marital disputes would only provide parents with "encouragement not to air their differences of opinion within the bosom of the family."

In the court's rejection of these arguments, the views of liberal feminists were ably presented by Erna Scheffler. The judgment unhesitatingly affirmed the appropriateness of a legally sanctioned sexual division of labor within marriage, which relegated wives and mothers to the home while husbands and fathers fulfilled their familial obligations through their economic activity; based on "biological or functional" difference, this represented no disadvantage or subordination for married women. But in decisions involving the welfare of children, no difference justified giving fathers priority over mothers. Appeals to natural law were not compelling, given the "multiplicity of natural-law theories" in existence.

The debates of the Parliamentary Council again served as a crucial touchstone for fathoming the true meaning of the Basic Law. In the court's decision, Walter Strauss, the state secretary in the Ministry of Justice who had represented the government's position in defense of patriarchal authority before the Bundestag in May 1957, got to hear the voice of the Walter Strauss of old, the CDU representative to the Parliamentary Council who in January 1949 had been assigned the task of justifying his party's conversion, in response to mounting pressure, to Selbert's language of women's equal rights. The court reminded him and his party that on this occasion he had expressed his colleagues' surprise at the public charges of their equivocation on women's rights, dismissing all doubts that the CDU supported anything but women's complete equality:

> [A]t least since 1918 the equal rights of man and woman have sunk into our blood and flesh. We have been of one mind about the fundamental principle from the beginning. It is something [we] take for granted. Especially the past years have made apparent to every man including the bachelors that the tasks of the woman are almost more difficult—physically as well—than those of the man. Most German women have already been active in occupations for years, just like men, but in addition to the tasks of the man they have also had the tasks of [running] the household and educating the children. . . . As a consequence there can be no doubt—with the exception of some backwoods bumpkins [*Hinterwäldlern*]—not even among the bachelors, that we must recognize and demand the complete equal rights of woman in every respect, not just in terms of her civil rights and obligations as a citizen [*staatsbürgerliche Rechte*], and whatever inconsistencies exist, we must remove them.[73]

A decade later, the court asserted that those inconsistencies included any legal recognition of a father's ultimate authority over a mother in questions of their children's welfare. Equal parental rights were also fully in accord with the demands presented by middle-class feminists since the turn of the century and with the Parliamentary Council's pledge to move beyond the Weimar constitution's restricted notion of women's equality. Since 1953, there was ample legal precedent, and cases overturning paternal authority outnumbered those upholding it. Citing figures provided by Lüders in the Bundestag debates,[74] the court also emphasized that fears of judicial intervention in family affairs were wildly exaggerated and without foundation in legal practice. Not only did granting fathers a tie-breaking vote "legally strengthen the position of the father [which is] already de facto stronger; moreover, it weakens the status of the mother precisely in that area—motherhood—where her essence is most deeply rooted and where she realizes herself." Giving

mothers rights did not undermine the family; rather, the "principle of
the Basic Law is the equal rights of parents." By refusing to give both
parents these rights, the Bundestag violated not only women's equality
but also the constitutional guarantee of the family's protection.[75]

Critics of a mother's equal rights continued to protest that the Federal
Constitutional Court's judgment endangered the institution of marriage. The Catholic legal expert F. W. Bosch reassured women that by
granting wives control over the household, the revised family law had
already accorded them extensive power in crucial areas affecting children's welfare. Arguably, a mother's rights now extended to determining "whether the newborn should be breast-fed or bottle-fed; which toys
the child should get for Christmas and birthday and which clothes;
which friends could visit the child at home; whether the child would be
cared for at home by the mother or someone else; whether the education
of the child should take place at home or in a boarding school." Surely
this catalogue included many "fundamental decisions" where the rights
of mothers were already firmly established. In practice, it meant that for
every hundred decisions the mother made, the father would "be on only
once or twice."[76]

In addition, Bosch objected that the court had rushed to judgment in
the summer months, while most jurists were on vacation, and had made
little effort to poll legal opinion. If ten experts were required to offer advice on the difference between male and female homosexuality, Bosch
asked rhetorically, then why should the court choose to scrutinize the
question of parental authority any less thoroughly? Even more fundamentally, how could the court admit the existence of "biological or functional difference" that justified regulating women's working conditions
and granting even unmarried women the "housework day" while declaring certain rights for fathers to be unconstitutional? How could the
court invoke sexual difference to justify "women's privileges" in some
cases, despite the constitutional call for equality, while completely rejecting its significance in others?[77]

The answer the court had provided was the same one advanced by a
sizable minority in the parliament—women and men were different, and
that difference could justify a sexual division of labor in some areas, but
determining children's welfare was not among them. What the concerted efforts of Social Democrats, many women within the CDU, and
all but a handful of Free Democrats had failed to accomplish in the halls
of parliament, the justices of the Federal Constitutional Court had
achieved from the bench. Outraged over the sanction of paternal authority in the law adopted by the Bundestag in 1957, Lüders had contrasted

the "songs of praise about the virtue and value of the housewife and mother, which continually emerge in the German world, particularly from men," with the German male's apparent willingness to disenfranchise mothers precisely in the arena most important to them, their relationship to their children.[78] Through her presence on the Federal Constitutional Court, Scheffler had contributed to granting Lüders some satisfaction and to bringing the ideological claims of a mother's elevated status into line with the legal principle of a mother's elevated rights.

The court decision of July 1959 effectively recapitulated a decade-long political debate over the structure of families, the limits of women's equality, and the significance of "biological or functional difference." That "ongoing political struggle" that Lüders had announced to Scheffler in 1954 and that for feminists of her generation dated back to the 1890s had reached a certain closure. Proposals for another complete overhaul of West German family law did not appear again until the late sixties and early seventies in a very different political context.[79]

When compared with the family law of 1900 and the unsuccessful attempts to achieve women's equality within marriage in the 1920s, the new law and the court's 1959 addendum marked a significant step toward the establishment of a legal basis for wives' and mothers' claims to equal rights with fathers and husbands. These changes in the legal status of married women had no noticeable influence on the inclination of husbands or wives to take one another to court to resolve disputes they could not settle themselves. Fears that the option of appealing to an outside arbiter would undermine marital stability and heighten antagonism between spouses proved to be unfounded, as opponents of patriarchal authority had predicted. Where the new law was of greatest practical significance was in regulating property settlements and financial arrangements in marriages that ended in divorce; in this area, women's position was greatly strengthened.[80]

However, compared with the justifications for demanding women's equality articulated in the late forties, the decade-long parliamentary discussion of women's equal rights focused on a relatively narrow range of issues. The extent of women's participation in wage work in the war and the immediate postwar years and their other contributions to maintaining Germany in hard times had been central to demands for lodging women's equality in the Basic Law. By the late fifties, the equality most frequently discussed in the Bundestag encompassed only the work of the married woman in the home. Battles over wage inequities and labor-market segmentation by sex were not perceived to be constitutional battles. No business of parliament, they were the preserve of the "social partners"—organized capital and labor—and labor courts that in 1955 sanctioned translating "women's and men's work" into "light and heavy work." As one female trade unionist observed, legally identifying the husband as the principal wage-earner in a "normal marriage" provided convenient justification for long-standing practices of calculating wages for women workers according to a separate standard of measurement.[81] Where the Bundestag insisted that women's work was to be legally recognized as equal in value to that of men was in that workplace where it was unremunerated—the home. Notwithstanding the alleged psychic rewards of maternal rights and the authority to run the household on her "own accountability," the imputed pay accorded a wife by equating her household labor with a husband's work outside the home was doled out only when the marriage dissolved.

The model (*Leitbild*) of marital relations endorsed by the Bundestag in 1957 was completely consistent with the model of the family endorsed in debates over "money-for-children." On this, there was consensus. The point at which Adenauer's government, the majority of the CDU/CSU coalition, some Free Democrats, the Catholic church, and a broad spectrum of the academic community diverged from their detractors was not in their opinion of where women should work but in their conceptions of the rights and responsibilities that came with their job. Crucial in championing or restricting women's rights was determining what would best protect the family.

The family thus defined a contested terrain where the defenders of hierarchy and authority confronted advocates of shared rights and equality. Everyone agreed about ends; the family was the basic building block of society, it was endangered, and state policy was a legitimate tool to ensure its protection. And by the late fifties, there was also no argument about what family was at issue; the "half," "incomplete," and "mother-families" that had been the source of such concern and preoccupation in the forties did not appear when the Bundestag gave the family legal definition in the fifties. Where consensus collapsed was over how properly constituted families could best be sustained.

In the final version of the family law, Lüders and Scheffler, the embodiment of a German tradition of liberal feminism, joined forces with Social Democrats to achieve one vision of the "equality of worth [which] acknowledges difference," which Selbert had called for in 1949; that vision was completely consistent with a legal order that fully legitimated a normative vision of the home as woman's most important workplace. The fiercest political battles over the meaning of women's equality during the Adenauer era were over the ideal conception of the family, where women were defined not as individuals but in terms of their relationships to others—to men and children as wives and mothers.

Epilogue

"No Experiments!" This was the simple advice broadcast by a stern-faced Konrad Adenauer from electoral posters plastered everywhere by the CDU and CSU as West Germans once again prepared to elect a national government in September 1957 (fig. 28). The ruling coalition asked voters to assess its record of economic, social, and political accomplishment, to choose between what had worked and uncertainty, between the success of Erhard and the "social market economy" and the promises of Social Democratic "functionaries," an easily deciphered code that associated the SPD with the "Apparatchiks" running the "planned economy" in East Germany (fig. 29).

Election results registered overwhelming support for "Adenauer and His Team." West German Communists no longer existed as a domestic political bogeyman; the KPD, only a marginal presence in the fifties, was formally prohibited in 1956, ostensibly because it represented a threat to the free democratic order in West Germany. The virtual disappearance of other small parties from the political landscape benefited both Social Democrats and the conservative coalition, and the SPD broke the 30 percent barrier for the first time in the postwar era. Still, once the ballots were counted it was the CDU/CSU that emerged with an absolute majority of the popular vote and in the Bundestag. Only three months after the parliament had locked fathers' rights into the revised family law, Adenauer, the "demagogic patriarch," as he was called with grudging admiration by Rudolf Augstein, publisher of the weekly

211

newsmagazine *Der Spiegel,* was also granted the last word. This was a judgment that the Constitutional Court could not overturn.[1]

The governing coalition's exhortation that West Germans should abide no experiments came after nearly a decade in which experimentation was the norm. Under the umbrella of the "social market economy," West Germans had, as Ralf Dahrendorf expressed it, "plunged into economic light,"[2] overcoming almost all remnants of Weimar-era ambivalence toward competitive capitalism based on private ownership and free enterprise. Long torn between east and west, after 1945 the western portion of that "country in the middle of Europe" was fully integrated into a western political, economic, and military alliance. The division of the world into east and west provided one clear answer to the "German Question," an answer Adenauer was ready to accept in return for the recognition of the Federal Republic's claims to sovereign status and equal rights in the international political arena. Despite the continued enthusiasm of many Germans for Hitler and National Socialism minus defeat in war, West Germany was also founded on a set of democratic political institutions far more solid and far more widely accepted than those that had collapsed in the crises of Weimar.

The basis of the broad popular support for these changes was sustained, unprecedented economic growth, the West German *Wirtschaftswunder,* the economic miracle. Relative and absolute increases in economic welfare were the principal source of political stability in the fifties.[3] Behind the "sparkle" of the economic miracle many still lived in the shadow of poverty, and the distribution of economic wealth became even more inequitable, but most West Germans were willing for the rich to get richer as long as many poor could escape the endless round of uncertainty and insecurity that had long defined the lives of most German working people. Overrepresented among those who found the exit from poverty more difficult were single women and their dependents, but as one social commentator wrote in the late fifties, the problems of the "woman standing alone" (*alleinstehende Frau*) and the *Frauenüberschuss* were the problems of those "who are totally ignored."[4] The CDU/CSU claimed responsibility for economic prosperity and for the reform of the social-insurance system that extended security into old age, and its record contributed significantly to its electoral success.

This book has argued that when it came to the political discussion of women's status and the structure of families, the Adenauer era created little political space for experimentation of any kind. Rather, the family was assumed to be among the few stable social institutions connecting

Germany's past to its present. It deserved restoration and protection but not rethinking; it constituted the solid foundation on which experimentation in other areas was possible.

In the late forties and early fifties, the repeated emphasis on the indestructibility of the German family, saved by German mothers first from Nazi intervention, then from Allied bomb attacks, then from the hardships of occupation, masked enormous fears about the future of postwar society. When the Parliamentary Council began debate over the Basic Law in 1948, initial drafts included no specific mention of women's rights and no explicit call for the protection of marriage, family, and motherhood. Both concerns were pushed into the final version of the West German constitution, framing extensive discussions of "woman's place" in the first decade of the Federal Republic's history. These debates illuminated a general uncertainty about the boundaries between public and private, state and society, women and men, sets of relationships thrown into disarray by National Socialism, war, and the postwar crisis.

To be sure, neither leveled cities nor the family and "woman's place" could be exactly restored or reconstructed according to prewar blueprints. The "normal family" of a heterosexual couple financially supported by a male wage seldom existed in the Kaiserreich or Weimar; few families could survive on one income, and households headed by women who had dependents and were widowed, never married, or divorced were no unique product of the Second World War. At least for the working class, the family assumed in state social policy of the fifties could not be *re*established because it had never existed.[5] Still, this utopian vision of "normalcy," the expression of a longing for security, remained at the basis of West German social policy. Women were at its center, promised true equality in stable families. Here was where women's contribution to reconstruction should take place.

Debates around women's status and the family, that "vestige of stability," provided a context for the delineation of other strong ideological ties binding West Germany to the past. Perhaps most striking were the elements of pronatalism that were constants in discussions of how to protect families, mothers, and women employed outside the home. Although a steady flow westward of East Germans and other eastern European immigrants amply supplemented the domestic labor supply for the economic miracle, the political discussion of the family expressed worries that Germans might not recover from the demographic devastation of the war and might resume prewar trends of family size limitation. Although elaborated in greatest detail by Franz-Josef

Wuermeling, the connections between a healthy economy, a self-supporting welfare state, large families, good mothers, and national vitality were not advanced only by the conservative Catholic family minister. Social Democrats were just as concerned about the "rising generation" and the equation of population growth with economic success when they advocated the Law for Protection of Mothers, and they joined in selectively adapting some National Socialist measures aimed at securing women's reproductive future as parts of a salvageable past.

Through the medium of pronatalism, it was also possible for racialist and eugenic themes, elevated to the level of public policy under the Nazis, to resurface. Anti-Slavic and anti-Asian prejudices merged under the guise of Cold War anticommunism. Comparing demographic trends in east and west, Wuermeling concluded that "the communist-ruled eastern nations have many more children than we do. If we are to be a people that dies out, and there's every indication that we're headed in that direction, then the ever-growing national power [*Volkskraft*] of the east—entirely independent of political systems and military security—will crush us in the future and will take from our families the room for home and hearth."[6]

In this remarkable inversion of Nazi ideology, it was the peoples of the east, not Germans, who became a *Volk ohne Raum,* threatening the democratic west. Strong families producing healthy children offered the best defense against this potential invasion from the populous east, the most effective bulwark against the spread of communism. Unless the Federal Republic escaped the "psychic and biological decline" that translated into declining birth rates, Wuermeling warned, it must abandon all illusions of being part of a "center of occidental culture."[7] It was impossible not to hear overtones of the Thousand Year Reich in such justifications of policies intended to promote West Germans' *Wille zum Kind.*[8]

Social Democrats did not subscribe to this rhetoric. Their proposals to give all families equal support, to extend maternity benefits to all pregnant women, and to insist on the rights of all mothers, whether married or not, challenged the majority position of the CDU/CSU. The SPD offered a broader vision of women's equal rights, questioned the government's claims that the market economy would necessarily be social, and scrupulously avoided the racialist overtones of Adenauer's family minister. Still, it is remarkable that these themes of declining national vigor and prolific "eastern peoples," so ubiquitous under the Nazis, should be revived so quickly, rehabilitated with such apparent ease, and subjected to no systematic scrutiny or analysis in the fifties.[9] From the perspective of the postwar decade, the links between race and reproduction, women's bodies and national strength, population size and population quality were not National Socialist in origin, and they did not disappear in Germany with the demise of the Thousand Year Reich. No exclusive property of the warfare state of the thirties, they reemerged as part of the welfare state in the fifties.

Where the categories for discussing women and the family in the postwar decade diverged decisively from the thoroughgoing and fundamental racialism of the thirties was in their reliance on a relentless, sometimes startlingly economistic rhetoric.[10] Whether in justifying family allowances or proclaiming married women's equality with their husbands, it was the economic value of women's labor in the home that was emphasized when making claims on the state as the guarantor of women's rights. The politics of equality in difference was founded on the material equivalence of men's paid and women's unpaid labor—reckoned to the last pfennig. In *The Feminine Mystique,* Betty Friedan, writing in 1963 of middle-class housewives in the United States, described the "problem that has no name," the "voice within women that says: 'I want something more than my husband and children and my home.' "[11] In the fifties, West German social policy affecting women and the family provided the work of housewife and mother with many names, saturating it with meaning, and underscoring that it was a right, a duty, and an obligation—not a problem.

The emphasis on the value of women's unpaid labor in postwar West Germany was appropriate to a nation that found itself in the throes of economic reconstruction according to a capitalist blueprint. West Germans proclaimed that what they most needed in the collective project of building anew was hard work. Not politics but productivity would allow them to redeem themselves and to gain distance from their own recent history. What the psychologists Alexander and Margarete Mitscherlich described as the "inability to mourn," West Germans' apparent lack of interest in directly assessing their responsibility for National Socialism, included a massive self-investment in the "expansion and modernization of our industrial potential right down to the kitchen utensils." Creating for the future was a way to forget the National Socialist past. "Entrepreneurial spirit," "restoring what has been destroyed"—such values and objectives cleared the way for a path to selective memory.[12] When the family, not class, was identified as the locus of individual social mobility, when human capital was just as vital to economic prosperity and growth as the capital invested in factories, women too had their work cut out for them; "kitchen utensils" were the tools of their trade, not mere metaphor. In the late forties, the *Trümmerfrau* took on enormous symbolic proportions, representative of a Germany clearing away its troubled past; in the fifties, the work of the German woman became no less significant once she moved from bombed-out buildings to protected homes. Her *deutsche Qualitätsarbeit* was now measured in the "rising generation" and the strength of family ties.

The constant emphasis on women's non-monetary contributions to economic development was potentially at odds with exhortations for women to be consumers. Erhard's "will for consumption" (*Wille zum Verbrauch*) collided head-on with Adenauer's *Wille zum Kind* when the lures of the consumer economy enticed mothers into wage work and away from reproducing Germany's future. West Germans' reluctance to accept unbridled consumerism resounded in ideological formulations that assigned mothers the duty of patrolling the border between legitimate need and illegitimate desire. This theme ran throughout discussions of "money-for-children" and surfaced as well in the revised family law's provision that the natural obligations of housewife and mother set limits to a woman's right to work outside the home. In describing "woman's place," West Germans were at pains to illustrate that they were neither fascists nor communists; by insisting that mothers must defend against the dangers of a mass-consumption society, they indicated that despite their commitment to competitive capitalism, they were also not Americans.

The political discussion of women's work outside the home articulated fears not only about declining birth rates and latch-key children but also about the accelerated movement of wage-earning women out of domestic service, the agricultural sector, and family-owned businesses to the department store, the secretarial pool, and the factory. By taking the 1950 census as a point of reference—the absolute low point of female labor-force participation in the twentieth century because of the disruption and social dislocation of the war and postwar period[13]—contemporary critics decried what they saw to be the dramatic increase in women's employment in the following decade. Had they focused instead on occupational census figures for 1925, 1939, or even the depression year 1933, they would have determined that by 1961, women's labor-force participation rates only slightly exceeded the level of 1933 and had not yet returned to the level of the late thirties. Seen from this perspective, the postwar debate about women's work was actually concerned less with the fact that some women worked for wages than with *where* they worked and the sorts of work they did.[14]

In Germany, the work of many married women had never been restricted to their jobs as wives and mothers. In 1933, 29.2 percent of all married women were in employment. The figure for 1939 at the beginning of wartime mobilization was 32.5 percent. It fell to 25.0 percent in 1950, the low point in the twentieth century, and by 1961 it increased to 32.8 percent. The big jump in the postwar decade obscured the fact that the fifties witnessed not a dramatic new tendency but a resumption of prewar trends.[15] However, before the fifties married women's work was primarily in the rural sector or elsewhere as "family assistants" in their husbands' or fathers' businesses, where it did not raise the same concerns about the future of the next generation. Indeed, in the pronouncements of conservatives since the Kaiserreich, in the Nazi ideology of "blood and soil," and in Wuermeling's rhetoric, it was precisely the peasant family farm that produced a bountiful harvest of crops, children, and moral values.[16] In the discussion of women's work in the fifties, juggling the double burden apparently presented no particular problem when home and workplace were one. It was only when women worked *ausserhäuslich*—literally, outside the home—that their work warranted intense scrutiny because it threatened women's reproductive lives, and it was here that women—married and single—worked in numbers greater than ever before in the fifties.

The alarm over women's work outside the home thus also articulated continued anxieties over the consequences of industrial, capitalist economic development. These concerns dated back to the late nineteenth century and were only partly obscured by the Nazis' rhetorical elevation of the artisan and the peasant and the dramatic dislocation of the war and postwar crises. They reemerged in postwar sociologists' paeans to the stability of families where wives and mothers made essential contributions to economic growth through their work in the home, a model of social organization located in an imagined preindustrial past. In the war and postwar years, social theorists and policy-makers found the proof that this family form was still robust—transformed, but still alive and well—within an advanced industrial present. Describing mothers' work outside the home as a short-term necessity in the wake of the war's destruction obscured the extent to which it was part of a long-term sectoral shift, accelerated in West Germany in the context of the economic miracle.

This book has emphasized the narrow range of political rhetorics available in postwar West Germany for describing women's abilities and rights, women's needs and how best to address them. Like every other aspect of formal political life in the fifties, the categories available for addressing these topics were structured and limited by a virulent, pervasive anticommunism. More than in other western European countries or the United States, the influence of the Cold War on West Germany was direct, explicit, and profound, only intensifying a domestic anticommunism that had been part of German political life since the Russian Revolution of 1917 and that had even deeper lineages in pre–World War I antisocialism. After 1945, West Germany's very geographic dimensions were defined piecemeal, determined by the international division between east and west; its self-definition was bound up with the alternative system imposed on those other Germans in the Soviet zone. Particularly for the ruling CDU/CSU, this larger political dimension merged with much older strains of a Christian politics of the family, which located Germany firmly in a Christian *Abendland*. This was a strong ideological mix that made immediately suspect any alternative languages of women's equality, which could be associated with the policies implemented in East Germany. In a world divided along lines of longitude, demands for women's rights and definitions of women's needs were measured on the yardstick of the "false," "mechanical" equality that brutally leveled difference. The politics of women and the family that prevailed not only drew boundaries between women and men but also fortified the boundary between east and west. In the process, other conceptions were pushed aside, clearing the ideological path along which West German women were to find their way home to their natural obligations in "normal families."

On this terrain, advocates of women's rights were still able to win some victories. The final form of the revised family law and the Federal Constitutional Court decision of 1959 represented triumphs in a fight that had engaged politically active middle-class women and Social Democrats since the 1890s. The long prehistory of this struggle was effectively represented by the confrontation in the 1957 debates between Helene Weber, seventy-six, the embodiment of the conservative Catholic women's movement, and Marie-Elisabeth Lüders, who would turn seventy-nine a month after the law passed. In the 1952 Law for Protection of Mothers, Social Democrats successfully reinstituted and expanded policies that they too had championed since the turn of the century. A political language of families' claims on the state, laid out explicitly in debates over "money-for-children," established categories of entitlement and rights that could be used in the sixties and seventies to make additional demands for improvement in this program and for expansion of benefits in other areas, such as subsidies for education and housing.

In the political context of the fifties, however, the equal rights of husbands and wives were seen to be completely consistent with the explicit relegation of women to an unpaid workplace in the home. Feminists and Social Democrats eschewed the language of *Abendland* and a preordained natural order. But if they rejected this metaphysical rhetoric, those who fought for a more expansive conception of women's equality did not dispute that German women were still defined by at least two of the three K's of Weimar and the Third Reich. For Social Democrats and liberal feminists, *Kirche* was rejected, but *Küche* and *Kinder* were still firmly in place. They maintained that accepting these roles should not deny a woman status as a *Kamerad*, as fully the equal of a man. In similar categories, the Law for Protection of Mothers extended some benefits to working women while implicitly reminding them that the best protection was a male wage and associating any demands for child care with a one-way ticket to the destruction of the family in the soulless communist collective. Once the structure for the family-allowance system was in place, battles were not over its heavily gendered foundation but over how to expand its coverage so that all women could be mothers and all mothers would devote themselves fully to their primary responsibilities. Once women's claims on the state had been defined in specific ways, schemes for meeting them were limited as well.

For Social Democrats, the 1957 campaign slogan, "Security for Everyone," included the promise to provide "Security for the Family," expressed clearly in an electoral poster that pictured a cherubic child, curls tousled by the breeze, reaching for the house keys that her father playfully offered her while an adoring mother looked on (fig. 30). This was not the "mother-family," still defended by Selbert in the debates of the Parliamentary Council, and certainly not the family of Bebel, Engels, and Zetkin, the proletarian family in which capitalism had created equality by leaving women as free as men—free to sell their wage labor and freed from ownership of the means of production. That family lived in the German Democratic Republic, where for women a perverted version of equality forced them to work at two jobs. Postwar Social Democrats would not be outdone in their insistence that east was east, and west was west. With Otto Grotewohl and the Socialist Unity Party proclaiming that women would achieve complete political and social equality only through complete participation in wage labor, it was more important than ever for the SPD to formulate non-Marxist answers to the "woman question."

The 1959 Godesberg Program, the end point in the long process of the SPD's self-examination that led away from a party of the working class (*Klassenpartei*) to a party of the people (*Volkspartei*), from a party in opposition to a party with aspirations to govern, expressed a clear commitment to protect the family and to remain vigilant in pursuing social policies that would prevent "mothers of preschool- and school-aged children from being forced to seek paid employment for economic reasons." With this, the SPD proclaimed that once and for all it had vanquished CDU charges that Social Democrats "pursue no policies that favor families [*familienfreundlich*]." No less than Christian Democrats, socialists were the family's friend, not its enemy. Only in the family could the "need for personal relationships be fulfilled." The family was not merely an institution for economic survival—such "materialistic" conceptions might prevail in the east, but not in the west—but a repository of priceless ideals. It was clear that if fathers held house keys, the keys to this treasure chest of traditional values lay securely in the hands of wives and mothers.[17] In crucial respects, such programmatic declarations accomplished exactly what Social Democrats wanted; in their articulation of what constituted the "normal family," they made the party virtually indistinguishable from the governing coalition.

Middle-class women's organizations, the heirs to the bourgeois feminist tradition, and women activists within the trade union movement and the SPD were no more effective in offering other visions. Although by the late fifties women within the SPD and middle-class feminists overcame some of their long-standing mutual antagonism and joined forces behind anchoring married women's equality in the revised Civil Code, this shared reform objective also solidly tied the interests of women to the interests of families. In the late forties, potentially distinct political agendas were defined by demands for acknowledging women's increased social and economic importance expressed in a language of equal rights and demands for acknowledging that families were at risk expressed in a language of protection. However, once equality was entwined with difference, it proved to be a short step from woman to wife, and the move from there to mother and family was virtually axiomatic. Women's rights became inseparable from the rights of families.

A rhetoric of individual rights had never been central to the politics of German liberalism or to the bourgeois feminist movement, and the fifties was no time for its efflorescence in Germany. Rather, in the political context of that decade individualism was linked to exaggerated expectations and materialism, which drew women away from children, hearth, and home. Other languages for formulating the relationship between equality and difference seemed to lead either to the uranium mines or to "dwarf families," abandoned by ambitious career women in pursuit of individual fulfillment.

This is not to dispute the significance of women's political activism in the postwar years. Throughout the fifties, women most articulately defended their own interests, and their political engagement tipped the balance at key points. Particularly for women who had come to political maturity in Weimar and who were the most influential leaders in postwar political battles, the fifties offered many opportunities to return to an agenda they had been forced to abandon by the Nazis. Without their concerted effort, it is easy to envision that the Basic Law's Article 3 would not have included the pledge of women's equal rights and that the revised family law of 1957 would have diverged little from that adopted by the Reichstag more than sixty years earlier. But women remained a marginal presence at the national political level in the state, in trade unions, and in political parties that remained overwhelmingly dominated by men. When women organized outside of these structures in nonpartisan lobbying organizations or in caucuses within individual trade unions and political parties, they outlined strategies for expanding women's social, economic, and political opportunities, but their chances to move from there to determine national priorities remained limited.

Even in 1957 after the CDU/CSU's electoral landslide, women activists within the coalition were unsuccessful at translating their claims that the government depended on the gender gap into demands for a woman cabinet minister.[18] Four years later, the continued pressure from women within the CDU/CSU and, ultimately, an impromptu sit-in in Adenauer's office instigated by eighty-year-old Helene Weber brought Elisabeth Schwarzhaupt into the cabinet. Even then, Schwarzhaupt did not replace Wuermeling, as many had hoped. She also did not become justice minister, as Helene Weber had proposed, because, according to Adenauer, an upcoming reform of the criminal code would exceed a woman's capacities. Rather, Schwarzhaupt became the head of a newly created Ministry of Health. Apparently, what made women too caring

and thus incapable of pushing through the "tough criminal law" that
Adenauer wanted suited them well for taking the nation's pulse.
Schwarzhaupt, reluctant to take a post for which she had no experience,
ultimately accepted the appointment to ensure that a woman would finally enter the highest levels of the state, though she conceded she was
only a "token" (*Alibifrau*) at the head of a ministry that had never before existed.[19]

With little institutional leverage or political power, West German
women who were active in formal politics ultimately exerted far less influence over defining and addressing women's needs than West German
men. Although much of this book analyzes how men formulated policies
affecting women, it also argues that in the process men were defining
themselves and outlining their vision of the nation. The constant refrains
of security and protection that ran through much of the political discussion of women's status implied that in a new Germany, there would be
protectors. "Protection," as the political theorist Carole Pateman puts it,
"is the polite way to refer to subordination."[20] Accompanying the construction of woman as "protected/dependent/subordinate" is the construction of man as protector/independent/superior. The relentless
emphasis on the metaphor of protection in the fifties only belied the
doubts and anxieties of men who had been unable to protect women and
the family in the Second World War. The CDU's argument in the final
1957 debates over the reformed family law that male authority in the
family could be justified in terms of the "protective function of the man"
in defending the nation articulated this clearly. Men, not "pistol-
packing mamas" (*Pistolenweiber*), the products of an equality that leveled difference in the east, should bear arms. Strong patriarchs were
back in uniform; strong patriarchs should also rule at home. In defense
of the nation and in defense of the family, men had responsibilities that
justified rights and privileges.

Hildegard Krüger, the feminist legal expert, responded in character-
istically acerbic fashion a year later in an extraordinary legal commentary on the family law:

> How is it possible to dare to speak at all about the protective function of the
> man who is subject to military service in light of the German women raped,
> frozen, trampled, and butchered on the streets of east and middle Germany,
> gassed in concentration camps, burned and wounded in Hamburg, Dresden,
> and in the cities of the Rhine and Ruhr? . . . Have we forgotten that the Ger-
> man woman, without being liable for military service, attempted to exercise
> her protective function by taking part in the resistance at the risk of her life,
> by improving the fate of foreign workers and prisoners by providing them . . .

with asylum, by hiding Jews and Communists and by sharing starvation rations with them? . . . Have we forgotten that it was women who despite the dangers of rape and forced labor illegally crossed borders in order to get bedding and civilian clothing for the men, completely collapsed—collapsed in body and soul—who came back from internment or prison?

Men, concluded Krüger, had no more protected German women in the forties than they could protect German women in the event of an atomic war.[21] Her powerful rhetoric was exceptional in the late fifties, and even Krüger's feminist colleagues in the legal community found her analysis to be "polemical."[22] Nonetheless, it did indicate that at least one West German woman had deep and painful memories of what many West German men were eager to forget, what they sought to bury beneath economic prosperity, normal times, and the legal construction of the "normal family," where men would once again provide women with security and protection.

Forgetting the past of National Socialism, war, and destruction proved easier than shoring up the perceived erosion of patriarchal authority or creating circumstances that would leave men protecting women with wages as well as armaments while women found satisfaction at home. Even in the late fifties, the Federal Constitutional Court reminded the CDU/CSU and Adenauer, the "father of the entire German people" as he was introduced at one 1957 campaign rally, that fathers would not have the last word about children's welfare.[23] A spate of publications in the late fifties and early sixties echoed Alexander Mitscherlich's conclusion that Germans were *On the Way to a Fatherless Society* (*Auf dem Weg zur vaterlosen Gesellschaft*). The problem was not just one of "incomplete" families and the *Frauenüberschuss*. In more or less anguished terms, Mitscherlich and many others described the larger context of the long-term transition from an agrarian society to a society dominated by "mass production and a complicated mass administration, the sundering of home and workplace, and the transition from an independent producer to the occupational status [*Stand*] of worker and white-collar employee, who receives wages and purchases consumer goods."[24] Sociological studies of the family from the early fifties repeated the same themes. These developments represented a decided decline in the authority of fathers; here was the flip side of anxieties about the increased employment of women outside the home. A world without fathers was a world where mothers no longer did their most important job. In the fifties, the politics of women and family underscored these fears but did little to allay them.

The difficulties of "representing difference as a relation of equality"[25] are enormous and by no means uniquely German. What this book argues is that demands for women's equality and rights and demands for recognition of women's capacities depend on the political rhetorics available in a particular historical context. This book has described a peculiarly German response to a not peculiarly German problem. It has emphasized that in the postwar period, the combination of Cold War anticommunism and the abandonment of socialist theory to East Germany combined with the political predominance of Christian Democracy and zealous pursuit of capitalist economic reconstruction to close off any space for a language of women's individual rights. It has argued that the relative weakness of organized feminism and its marginal opportunities to shape and implement public policy restricted alternative conceptions. It has illuminated the significance of postwar social theory that proclaimed an end to classes and trumpeted the family's resilience rather than offering tools to analyze the family as the locus of conflicting interests. And it has stressed how the postwar welfare state was based both on a productive and a reproductive order. This book has sought to sort out these paving stones in a postwar West German *Sonderweg,* to suggest why certain questions commanded so much attention and were addressed in certain ways while others were not even posed.

The ideological settlement achieved by the late fifties proved to be fragile. Fathers, left uncertain even in the era of the "demagogic patriarch," Konrad Adenauer, found themselves attacked in the late sixties and early seventies in terms far harsher than anything the first postwar decade had to offer. Breaking explicitly with the male-dominated parliamentary politics of the SPD and the student movement, an autonomous women's movement directly challenged the key assumptions about the sexual division of labor and the reproductive order at the basis of postwar policies affecting women and the family; it set in place a political language of women's individual rights to control their reproductive futures, focusing on the politics of abortion. Feminists also called for a drastic overhaul of the legal regulation of marriage and the family introduced in the Adenauer era, including abolition of language explicitly delegating women to be workers in the home. The generational nature of this new wave of feminist politics was unmistakable, and women who were children of the "women of the rubble" attacked not only patriarchs but what they perceived to be the limited vision of their foremothers.[26]

In addition, particularly in the late sixties and seventies, a Social Democratic–Free Democratic coalition government created a political environment more open to demands for social services for children, the elderly, and the disabled, relieving women of some of their caring work; it also introduced measures to improve women's educational and training opportunities, expanding their job prospects. By the early eighties, the Greens pushed for far more, bringing an explicitly emancipatory, feminist agenda into the arena of national electoral politics and placing even greater pressure on Social Democrats to advance meaningful reform proposals.

To offer this brief outline for a history of the shifting boundaries of "woman's place" in the sixties and seventies is not to conclude that the conservative fifties gave way to enlightened progress in the decades that followed, to advance a "Whig interpretation" of West German women's history. Indeed, the gains in women's educational and employment opportunities and the expanded conception of women's emancipation achieved since the sixties suffered from the one-two punch of economic crisis in the late seventies and the return to power of Christian Democrats in 1982. Although the CDU of the eighties was not the CDU of the fifties and was at great pains to show that it too had learned from the women's movement, the party's praise for the "gentle might of the family," for "mothers who remain mothers," and a "future [that] must be shaped by motherly virtue" revealed that at least some ideological mainstays remained in place. The movement by parts of West German feminism to a "culture of femininity" and an emphasis on a "politics of difference" also called for comparison with political rhetorics in Germany's past and indicated that in the eighties, organized feminism by no means spoke with a single voice.[27]

To ask how the "woman question" will be posed against this background in a Germany where the twain of East and West has not only met but been joined, a Germany beyond the Cold War, is to move even further beyond the scope of this study. Historians are wise to leave predictions about the future to others, but triumphalist assessments that the postwar period is finally at an end obscure the extent to which Germans are once again embarking on a process of reconstruction in the wake of a war, though this time no armistice was signed and the conflict was one in which ideology was the dominant weapon. It is safe to say that the politics of women's status, the family, the relationship between equality and difference, the limits to women's rights, the extent of women's responsibilities—concerns that loomed large in the post–World War II fifties—will be crucial to German self-definition in the post–Cold War nineties. This book's analysis of how West Germans approached the politics of *Frau* and family in the Federal Republic's first decade may thus offer one interpretation of precedents for such discussions and indicate how a larger political context can profoundly structure policies addressing these ostensibly non-political concerns.

Writing in 1958, Helge Pross, a thirty-one-year-old researcher working in Frankfurt with Max Horkheimer and Theodor Adorno at the Institute for Social Research, reflected on "The Societal Status of Woman in West Germany." Pross, who would go on to a career as a professor of sociology in Giessen and Siegen, one of the few women to achieve this status in a profession resolutely discouraging to women in high places, offered exceptional insights into the politics of gender in postwar West Germany. "It seems," Pross began,

> that asking about the social status of woman in the Federal Republic today is about the same as rummaging around idly in an antiques store for social problems. After all, the advocates of the new German conservatism assure us that men and women in the Federal Republic in fact have the same rights and the same practical responsibilities, that the exceptional underprivileged status of women has been ended, and that their social situation is no longer determined by their sex. [They claim that] the freedom for self-determination is achieved, the autonomy of the female individual [is] possible; it only remains for the woman herself to determine how she will shape her social and occupational existence.

Lest the irony of her rhetoric be missed, Pross quickly added that "the popularity that this widely held view enjoys does not make it any more true." While she acknowledged that parliament had achieved women's legal equality, she insisted that the "social and economic liberation" of women lagged far behind these legal norms. To be sure, in some sense women and men were equal—equally vulnerable to the threat of atomic war or to the dangers of totalitarianism. Where their inequality remained most pronounced was in the workplace. Here the demands placed on women and men were no different. The "protection and regard" that women had once enjoyed as part of the "bourgeois concept of femininity," a compensation of sorts for their socially underprivileged status, did not exist for the ever-growing number of women for whom "work outside the home is long since a necessity. If the civilized needs of humanity are to be filled," contended Pross, "then it is totally impossible to achieve this without women's wage work."

Because they confronted discrimination at every turn, Pross found it unremarkable that women should respond to these enormous obstacles by resigning themselves to their fate and internalizing conceptions of their own limited ability. The alternative of marriage offered no necessary "security for the rest of time" and was no alternative for the "millions of adult women . . . who simply cannot marry." Little better off was the woman "who fights for her career, is informed about politics, and confesses that she is not very interested in small children. . . . Society has forever had an aversion to such self-reliant, economically independent single women," in other eras burned as witches or dismissed as "blue-stockings" or "old maids."

The exclusion of women from positions of responsibility, the true realization of their equality, Pross concluded, was to the detriment not only of women but of all humanity. Where the "male leadership" could lead was apparent: "It has thrown us into catastrophes and maneuvered us into dangers that threaten everyone's existence. On the other hand, it has been shown that women when they grow into bigger tasks are able to fulfill these in a humane and well-informed fashion, provided that they are not constantly consumed in petty battles against prejudice and permanently excessive demands." Pross held out little hope for her alternative vision. "The conservative society of the Federal Republic, with its backwoods intellectual climate, its orientation toward the past, and its exclusive interest in material progress, will not voluntarily be god-father to any further liberation."[28]

This book began with the voice of Agnes von Zahn-Harnack, the voice of a past that echoed throughout the fifties. Her prediction in the late forties that the "question of the relation of the sexes to each other" would preoccupy postwar West Germans was accurate. A range of state policies affecting women and the family provided one set of answers in the first decade of the Federal Republic's history. They were not answers that satisfied Helge Pross, but her voice, the voice of a future that took shape a decade later in a reformulated feminism, was one not heard frequently in the Adenauer era.[29] When Bonn lawmakers turned to the ivory tower for auguries and advice, it was not to hear the trenchant critique of Pross or other opinions from the Institute for Social Research, but to Helmut Schelsky and those who offered reassurances that families properly supported would allow women to work where they worked best. And when they listened to feminists, it was to Lüders and others who insisted that women had a right to work while accepting that married women should exercise such a right only when it did not conflict with their work at home. Like West German men, West German women benefited from economic expansion and political stability in the fifties; they too could bask in the glow of the economic miracle, far from memories of Weimar's endemic crises, National Socialism, war, and defeat. But in other respects, Pross rightly emphasized that postwar West German society at best half filled woman's glass, that the economic miracle was not so miraculous for women. In the process of political self-definition that marked West Germans' exit from the ruins of the Third Reich, "woman's place" was reasserted and reified, not redefined.

Notes

INTRODUCTION

1. Agnes von Zahn-Harnack, "Um die Ehe (1946)," in *Agnes von Zahn-Harnack: Schriften und Reden 1914 bis 1950,* ed. Marga Anders and Ilse Reiche, 49.

2. "Agnes von Zahn-Harnack (1884–1950)," in *Frauen in Wissenschaft und Politik,* ed. Dorothea Frandsen, Ursula Huffmann, Annette Kuhn, 48–50.

3. See the useful reflections on these processes in Margaret R. Higonnet and Patrice L.-R. Higonnet, "The Double Helix," in *Behind the Lines: Gender and the Two World Wars,* ed. Margaret Randolph Higonnet et al., 31–47.

4. I borrow the expression "political reconstruction of the family" from Juliet Mitchell, *Psychoanalysis and Feminism*, 231.

5. Gabriele Strecker, *Überleben ist nicht genug: Frauen 1945–1950*, 53.

6. The quotations are from Bernhard Winkelheide, *VDBT*, [1.] Deutscher Bundestag, 162. Sitzung, 13 September 1951, 6959; and Winkelheide, "Warum Familienausgleichskassen?" *Soziale Arbeit* 1 (1951): 100. For a summary of Social Democratic views, see Louise Schroeder, "Kinderbeihilfe," *Soziale Arbeit* 1 (1951): 97–100.

7. On film, see the important work of Heide Fehrenbach, "The Fight for the 'Christian West': German Film Control, the Churches, and the Reconstruction of Civil Society in the Early Bonn Republic," 39–63.

8. See the useful introductions in Angela Delille and Andrea Grohn, eds., *Perlonzeit: Wie die Frauen ihr Wirtschaftswunder erlebten*, and Ingrid Laurien, " 'Wie kriege ich einen Mann'? Zum weiblichen Leitbild und zur Rolle der Frau in den Fünfziger Jahren," 32–44.

9. For introductions to the literature on the nineteenth and early twentieth centuries, see the bibliography in John C. Fout, ed., *German Women in the Nineteenth Century: A Social History*, 385–95; the recent overview, Ute Frevert, *Women in German History: From Bourgeois Emancipation to Sexual Liberation;* and Helena Cole, with the assistance of Jane Caplan and Hanna Schissler, *The History of Women in Germany from Medieval Times to the Present: Bibliography of English-Language Publications*. Recent work on the post–1945 period concentrates heavily on the years 1945–1949, and in Chapter 1, I draw on it extensively. For the 1950s, however, there is still very little. In addition to Delille and Grohn, see idem, *Blick zurück aufs Glück: Frauenleben und Familienpolitik in den 50er Jahren*. Angela Vogel also provides useful overviews in two articles, "Familie" and "Frauen und Frauenbewegung," both in *Die Bundesrepublik Deutschland: Geschichte in drei Bänden*, ed. Wolfgang Benz, vol. 2.

10. See, e.g., Theodor Eschenburg, *Jahre der Besatzung, 1945–1949*, and Hans-Peter Schwarz, *Die Ära Adenauer: Gründerjahre der Republik, 1949–1957*, parts of a massive multivolume history of the Federal Republic; or Dennis L. Bark and David R. Gress, *A History of West Germany*, vol. 1. Somewhat better in this respect are the two volumes by Christoph Klessmann, *Die doppelte Staatsgründung: Deutsche Geschichte, 1945–1955* and *Zwei Staaten, eine Nation: Deutsche Geschichte, 1955–1970*.

11. See, e.g., Marianne Weber, *Ehefrau und Mutter in der Rechtsentwicklung: Eine Einführung*.

12. Jean H. Quataert, "A Source Analysis in German Women's History: Factory Inspectors' Reports and the Shaping of Working-Class Lives, 1878–1914," 99–121; and idem, "Social Insurance and the Family Work of Oberlausitz Home Weavers in the Late Nineteenth Century," in Fout, *German Women in the Nineteenth Century*.

13. See Young Sun Hong, "The Politics of Welfare Reform and the Dynamics of the Public Sphere: Church, Society, and the State in the Making of the Social-Welfare System in Germany, 1830–1930"; and on SPD policies in

Weimar, David Crew, "German Socialism, the State and Family Policy, 1918–1933."

14. Elaine Tyler May, *Homeward Bound: American Families in the Cold War Era,* 14.

15. Helmut Schelsky, *Wandlungen der deutschen Familie in der Gegenwart: Darstellung und Deutung einer empirisch-soziologischen Tatbestandsaufnahme,* 13.

16. Joan Wallach Scott, "Rewriting History," in Higonnet et al., *Behind the Lines,* 30.

17. Jane Jenson, "Both Friend and Foe: Women and State Welfare," in *Becoming Visible: Women in European History,* 2d ed., ed. Renate Bridenthal, Claudia Koonz, and Susan Stuard, 535–56; and the insightful survey of recent literature on the United States in Linda Gordon, "The New Feminist Scholarship on the Welfare State," in *Women, the State, and Welfare,* ed. Linda Gordon, 9–35.

18. The point eludes Sylvia Ann Hewlett in her invocation of western European examples to highlight her critique of the inadequacy of state support for families in the United States. See Hewlett's *A Lesser Life: The Myth of Women's Liberation in America.*

CHAPTER ONE

1. Gerhard Baumert, with the assistance of Edith Hünniger, *Deutsche Familien nach dem Kriege,* 209–12. Baumert's study was part of a massive, multivolume sociological investigation of Darmstadt undertaken between 1949 and 1951. A slightly different version of the same case is presented in Gerhard Baumert, *Jugend der Nachkriegszeit: Lebensverhältnisse und Reaktionsweisen,* 24.

2. Ulrich Albrecht, Elmert Altvater, Ekkehart Krippendorff, eds., *Zusammenbruch oder Befreiung? Zur Aktualität des 8. Mai 1945.*

3. For one particularly moving account, see "The Story of Ruth," as told by Ruth Nebel to Sylvia Kramer, in *When Biology Became Destiny: Women in Weimar and Nazi Germany,* ed. Renate Bridenthal, Atina Grossmann, and Marion Kaplan, 334–49. Also, Marion Kaplan, "Sisterhood under Siege: Feminism and Anti-Semitism in Germany 1904–1938," ibid., 174–96; and idem, "Jewish Women in Nazi Germany: Daily Life, Daily Struggles, 1933–1939," *Feminist Studies* 16 (1990): 579–606. Useful as well are Gerda Szepansky, *Frauen leisten Widerstand: 1933–1945 (Lebensgeschichten nach Interviews und Dokumenten);* idem, ed., *"Blitzmädel," "Heldenmutter," "Kriegerwitwe": Frauenleben im zweiten Weltkrieg;* and Claudia Koonz, *Mothers in the Fatherland: Women, the Family, and Nazi Politics,* which provides excellent accounts of the experience of Jewish women and women in the resistance.

4. Es sind die blauen, sonnerfüllten Tage
    versunken und verweht,—kaum weiss *ich* wie.
    Kaum, dass ich ihren Hauch im Herzen trage.
    Wir liebten sie. Und weinen nicht um sie.

Die Nächte voller Sterne, voller Liebe
sind Träume nun aus einer andren Zeit.
Und wenn es draussen immer Frühling bliebe—
weit sind sie—Gott alleine weiss, wie weit.
Wohl ist es Tag—doch grau ist rings die Erde.
O, wohl ist Nacht—doch ohne jeden Stern.
Und Gott, mit unverstandener Gebärde,
ist, wie er sonst uns nahe war, so fern.

" 'Wer sich dem Reich verschrieb, ist ein Gezeichneter': Erinnerungen einer Frau vom Jahrgang 1924," in *Ein Volk, ein Reich, ein Glaube? Ehemalige Nationalsozialisten und Zeitzeugen berichten über ihr Leben im Dritten Reich*, ed. Lothar Steinbach, 69.

5. For example, Koonz's account of her interview with Gertrud Scholtz-Klink, in Koonz, *Mothers in the Fatherland*, xiv-xxxv.

6. Nora Möding, " 'Ich muss irgendwo engagiert sein—fragen Sie mich bloss nicht, warum': Überlegungen von Mädchen in NS-Organisationen," in *"Wir kriegen jetzt andere Zeiten": Auf der Suche nach der Erfahrung des Volkes in nachfaschistischen Ländern*, ed. Lutz Niethammer and Alexander von Plato, 277; Christoph Klessmann, "Untergänge-Übergänge: Gesellschaftsgeschichtliche Brüche und Kontinuitätslinien vor und nach 1945," in *Nicht nur Hitlers Krieg: Der Zweite Weltkrieg und die Deutschen*, ed. Christoph Klessmann, 83; and in general, on women's different experience of time in war, see the reflections of Higonnet and Higonnet, "The Double Helix," esp. 46.

7. "Die Struktur und Lage der Bochumer Industrie unter besonderer Berücksichtigung der Nachkriegsverhältnisse," 1947, prepared by the Industrie- und Handelskammer of Bochum, NWHStA, NW43/459; and the general description of conditions in Hans-Ulrich Sons, *Gesundheitspolitik während der Besatzungszeit: Das öffentliche Gesundheitswesen in Nordrhein-Westfalen, 1945–1949*, 75–119.

8. *Christ und Welt* 2 (7 July 1949): 6; Richard Detje et al., *Von der Westzone zum kalten Krieg: Restauration und Gewerkschaftspolitik im Nachkriegsdeutschland*, 97; Möding, " 'Ich muss irgendwo engagiert sein,' " 290; and idem, "Kriegserfahrungen von Frauen und ihre Verarbeitung," in *Über Leben im Krieg: Kriegserfahrungen in einer Industrieregion 1939–1945*, ed. Ulrich Borsdorf and Mathilde Jamin, 59.

9. Hilde Thurnwald, *Gegenwartsprobleme Berliner Familien: Eine soziologische Untersuchung an 498 Familien*, 10.

10. Quoted uncritically in Colin Townsend and Eileen Townsend, *War Wives: A Second World War Anthology*, xi. This book equates the suffering of British and German women during the war by juxtaposing their accounts without commentary, thus failing to make any attempt at differentiating between "victims" and "perpetrators."

11. Particularly important are the results of an extensive oral history project focusing on the Ruhr working class. See Lutz Niethammer, ed., *"Die Jahre weiss man nicht, wo man die heute hinsetzen soll": Faschismus-Erfahrungen im Ruhrgebiet*; idem, ed., *"Hinterher merkt man, dass es richtig war, dass es schief-

gegangen ist": *Nachkriegs-Erfahrungen im Ruhrgebiet;* Lutz Niethammer and Alexander von Plato, eds., *"Wir kriegen jetzt."* Also useful are Sibylle Meyer and Eva Schulze, *Wie wir das alles geschafft haben: Alleinstehende Frauen berichten über ihr Leben nach 1945;* idem, *Von Liebe sprach damals keiner: Familienalltag in der Nachkriegszeit;* insightful on the problems of periodization, idem, " 'Als wir wieder zusammen waren, ging der Krieg im Kleinen weiter': Frauen, Männer und Familien in Berlin der vierziger Jahre," in Niethammer and Plato, *"Wir kriegen jetzt,"* 305–26; Elke Nyssen and Sigrid Metz-Göckel, " 'Ja, die waren ganz einfach tüchtig'—Was Frauen aus der Geschichte lernen können," in *"Das Schicksal Deutschlands liegt in der Hand seiner Frauen": Frauen in der deutschen Nachkriegsgeschichte,* ed. Anna-Elisabeth Freier and Annette Kuhn, 312–47; Gudrun König, " 'Man hat vertrennt, vertrennt und wieder vertrennt': Erinnerungen an den Nachkriegsalltag," in ibid., 386–407; Gisela Dischner, ed., *Eine Stumme Generation berichtet: Frauen der dreissiger und vierziger Jahre;* Irmgard Weyrather, *"Ich bin noch aus dem vorigen Jahrhundert": Frauenleben zwischen Kaiserreich und Wirtschaftswunder;* Charles Schüddekopf, ed., *Der alltägliche Faschismus: Frauen im Dritten Reich;* Inge Stolten, ed., *Der Hunger nach Erfahrung: Frauen nach 1945;* and idem, *Das alltägliche Exil: Leben zwischen Hakenkreuz und Währungsreform.*

12. See the fascinating discussion in Annemarie Tröger, "German Women's Memories of World War II," in Higonnet et al., *Behind the Lines,* 285–99; also, the highly suggestive analysis of Ulrich Herbert, " 'Die guten und die schlechten Zeiten': Überlegungen zur diachronen Analyse lebensgeschichtlicher Interviews," in Niethammer, *"Die Jahre weiss man nicht,"* 67–96, esp. 93; idem, "Good Times, Bad Times: Memories of the Third Reich," in *Life in the Third Reich,* ed. Richard Bessel, 97–110; and Dan Diner, "Between Aporia and Apology: On the Limits of Historicizing National Socialism," in *Reworking the Past: Hitler, the Holocaust, and the Historians' Debate,* ed. Peter Baldwin, 139.

13. See, e.g., Maria Jochum, "Frauenfrage 1946," 29.

14. Report prepared by Rita Ostermann, 4 June 1947, German Political Branch, Political Division, PRO, FO 1050/1210.

15. Meyer and Schulze, *Wie wir das alles geschafft haben,* 178.

16. See Annette Kuhn, "Frauen suchen neue Wege der Politik," in *Frauen in der deutschen Nachkriegszeit,* vol. 2, ed. Annette Kuhn, 12–35; idem, "Power and Powerlessness: Women after 1945, or the Continuity of the Ideology of Femininity," 42–45; Barbara Henicz and Margrit Hirschfeld, "Die ersten Frauenzusammenschlüsse," in Kuhn, *Frauen in der deutschen Nachkriegszeit 2*: 94–101; Andrea Hauser, "Alle Frauen unter einem Hut?—Zur Geschichte des Stuttgarter Frauenausschusses," in ibid., 102–09; Henicz and Hirschfeld, "Der Club Deutscher Frauen in Hannover," in ibid., 127–34; Henicz and Hirschfeld, " 'Wenn die Frauen wüssten, was sie könnten, wenn sie wollten': Zur Gründungsgeschichte des Deutschen Frauenrings," in ibid., 135–56; Andrea Hauser, "Frauenöffentlichkeit in Stuttgart nach 1945—Gegenpol oder hilflos im Abseits?" in Freier and Kuhn, *"Das Schicksal Deutschlands,"* 51–89; Nora Möding, "Die Stunde der Frauen? Frauen und Frauenorganisationen des bürgerlichen Lagers," in *Von Stalingrad zur Währungsreform: Zur Sozialgeschichte des Umbruchs in Deutschland,* ed. Martin Broszat, Klaus-Dietmar Henke, and

234Notes to Pages 13–17

Hans Woller, 619–47; and Jutta Beyer and Everhard Holtmann, " 'Auch die Frau soll politisch denken'—oder: 'Die Bildung des Herzens': Frauen und Frauenbild in der Kommunalpolitik der frühen Nachkriegszeit 1945–1950," 385–419.

17. Timothy W. Mason, *Sozialpolitik im Dritten Reich: Arbeiterklasse und Volksgemeinschaft*, 18; Stolten, *Das alltägliche Exil*, 130. See also Hermann Lübbe, "Der Nationalsozialismus im deutschen Nachkriegsbewusstsein," 585.

18. Jürgen Habermas, "A Kind of Settlement of Damages (Apologetic Tendencies)," 26.

19. Thurnwald, *Gegenwartsprobleme Berliner Familien*, 180.

20. Herbert, " 'Die guten und die schlechten Zeiten,' " 92; and idem, "Zur Entwicklung der Ruhrarbeiterschaft 1930 bis 1960 aus erfahrungsgeschichtlicher Perspektive," in Niethammer and Plato, *"Wir kriegen jetzt,"* 26.

21. On antinatal policies aimed at those deemed unfit, see in particular Gisela Bock, *Zwangssterilisation im Nationalsozialismus: Studien zur Rassenpolitik und Frauenpolitik*; idem, "Antinatalism, Maternity and Paternity in National Socialist Racism," in *Maternity and Gender Policies: Women and the Rise of the European Welfare States, 1880s–1950s*, ed. Gisela Bock and Pat Thane; idem, "Racism and Sexism in Nazi Germany: Motherhood, Compulsory Sterilization, and the State," in Bridenthal et al., *When Biology Became Destiny*; and in general, Robert Proctor, *Racial Hygiene: Medicine under the Nazis*, 95–117, and Michael Burleigh and Wolfgang Wippermann, *The Racial State: Germany, 1933–1945*, 253–59.

22. Timothy W. Mason, "Women in Germany, 1925–1940: Family, Welfare and Work, Part I," 95–96; Jill Stephenson, *Women in Nazi Society*, 40–41, 46–47; Dorothee Klinksiek, *Die Frau im NS-Staat*, 87–92; D. V. Glass, *Population Policies and Movements in Europe*, 269–313; Garbriele Czarnowski, *Das kontrollierte Paar: Ehe- und Sexualpolitik im Nationalsozialismus*, 101–10 and passim; and Proctor, *Racial Hygiene*, 118–30.

23. Glass, *Population Policies*, 306–12; Mason, "Women in Germany, Part I," 95; Stephenson, *Women in Nazi Society*, 46.

24. Mason, "Women in Germany, Part I," 97.

25. Glass, *Population Policies*, 281–86, 305–13; and Mason, "Women in Germany, Part I," 102–05.

26. Anne-Katrin Einfeldt, "Auskommen—Durchkommen—Weiterkommen: Weibliche Arbeitserfahrungen in der Bergarbeiterkolonie," in Niethammer, *"Die Jahre weiss man nicht,"* 276–77.

27. Detlef J. K. Peukert, *Inside Nazi Germany: Conformity, Opposition, and Racism in Everyday Life*, 70–71; and Hans Dieter Schäfer, *Das gespaltene Bewusstsein: Deutsche Kultur und Lebenswirklichkeit 1933–1945*, 118–20.

28. Mason, "Women in Germany, Part I," 100; and idem, "Women in Germany, 1925–1940: Family, Welfare, and Work, Part II," 23–24. For a suggestive analysis of the potential gap between promise and practice in the implementation of welfare policies for the family, see Adelheid Gräfin zu Castell Rüdenhausen, " 'Nicht mitzuleiden, mitzukämpfen sind wir da!' Nationalsozialistische Volkswohlfahrt im Gau Westfalen-Nord," in *Die Reihen fast*

geschlossen: Beiträge zur Geschichte des Alltags unterm Nationalsozialismus,
ed. Detlev Peukert and Jürgen Reulecke, with assistance of Adelheid Gräfin zu
Castell Rüdenhausen, 223–44.

29. "Die Frau in den Haushalt, der Mann an die Arbeitsstätte," *Völkischer
Beobachter,* 1 November 1933, quoted in Stephenson, *Women in Nazi Society,*
87; see also ibid., 81–84, 135, 137–38; Klinksiek, *Die Frau,* 100–111; and
Karen Hagemann, *Frauenalltag und Männerpolitik: Alltagsleben und gesellschaftliches Handeln von Arbeiterfrauen in der Weimarer Republik,* 458–64.

30. On these developments in Weimar, see Renate Bridenthal, "Beyond
Kinder, Küche, Kirche: Weimar Women at Work," 148–66; and on the thirties,
Mason, "Women in Germany, Part II," 8–9; Stefan Bajohr, *Die Hälfte der Fabrik: Geschichte der Frauenarbeit in Deutschland 1914 bis 1945;* Dörte Winkler, *Frauenarbeit im "Dritten Reich";* and Annemarie Tröger, "The Creation
of a Female Assembly-Line Proletariat," in Bridenthal et al., *When Biology Became Destiny,* 237–70.

31. Mason, "Women in Germany, Part II," 7–8; and in general, Dörte Winkler, *Frauenarbeit,* 38–65, 194–95; and David Schoenbaum, *Hitler's Social
Revolution: Class and Status in Nazi Germany, 1933–1939,* 185.

32. Ulrike Ludwig-Bühler, "Im NS-Musterbetrieb: Frauen in einem Textilunternehmen an der Schweizer Grenze," in Niethammer and Plato, *"Wir
kriegen jetzt,"* 85.

33. Leila Rupp, " 'I Don't Call that *Volksgemeinschaft*': Women, Class and
War in Nazi Germany," in *Women, War, and Revolution,* ed. Carol R. Berkin
and Clara M. Lovett, 37–53.

34. Mason, *Sozialpolitik im Dritten Reich,* 28–29; Bernd Martin and Alan
S. Milward, eds., *Agriculture and Food Supply in the Second World War;* John
E. Farquharson, *The Western Allies and the Politics of Food: Agrarian Management in Postwar Germany,* 16–17, 20–22; and Karl Brandt, in collaboration
with Otto Schiller and Franz Ahlgrimm, *Management of Agriculture and Food
in German-Occupied and Other Areas of Fortress Europe: A Study of Military
Government.*

35. Jill Stephenson, "War and Society in Württemberg, 1939–1945: Beating
the System," 89–105; Ian Kershaw, *Popular Opinion and Political Dissent in
the Third Reich: Bavaria 1933–1945,* 281–330; Rupp, " 'I Don't Call that
Volksgemeinschaft' "; Lutz Niethammer, "Heimat und Front: Versuch, zehn
Kriegserinnerungen aus der Arbeiterklasse des Ruhrgebietes zu verstehen," in
Niethammer, *"Die Jahre weiss man nicht,"* 200–201, 222–24; and in general,
Bernd-A. Rusinek, " 'Maskenlose Zeit': Der Zerfall der Gesellschaft im Krieg,"
in Borsdorf and Jamin, *Über Leben im Krieg,* 184–86; Ulrich Heinemann,
"Krieg und Frieden an der 'inneren Front': Normalität und Zustimmung, Terror
und Opposition im Dritten Reich," in Klessmann, *Nicht nur Hitlers Krieg,* 39–
43; Ute Frevert, "Frauen an der 'Heimatfront,' " ibid., 61–65; and Gabriele
Rosenthal, ed., with the assistance of Christiane Grote, *"Als der Krieg kam,
hatte ich mit Hitler nichts mehr zu tun": Zur Gegenwärtigkeit des "Dritten
Reiches" in Biographien.* For a fascinating analysis of how crisis situations
alter the significance and perception of women's work, see Temma Kaplan,

"Women and Communal Strikes in the Crisis of 1917–1922," in Bridenthal et al., *Becoming Visible*, 429–49; and idem, *Red City, Blue Period: Social Movements in Picasso's Barcelona*, 118–24.

36. Quoted in Schoenbaum, *Hitler's Social Revolution*, 288; see the similar formulation in Baumert, *Deutsche Familien*, 6–7.

37. Jill Stephenson, " 'Emancipation' and its Problems: War and Society in Württemberg 1939–45," 345–65; Margot Schmidt, "Im Vorzimmer: Arbeitsverhältnisse von Sekretärinnen und Sachbearbeiterinnen bei Thyssen nach dem Krieg," in Niethammer, *"Hinterher merkt man,"* 228–29; and Niethammer, "Heimat und Front," 223.

38. Ulrich Herbert, *Fremdarbeiter: Politik und Praxis des "Ausländer-Einsatzes" in der Kriegswirtschaft des Dritten Reiches*, 46–48, 64, 142; and Ingrid Schupetta, *Frauen- und Ausländererwerbstätigkeit in Deutschland von 1939 bis 1945*.

39. Margot Schmidt, "Krieg der Männer—Chance der Frauen? Der Einzug von Frauen in die Büros der Thyssen AG," in Niethammer, *"Die Jahre weiss man nicht,"* 156; and Beatrix Hochstein, *Die Ideologie des Überlebens: Zur Geschichte der politischen Apathie in Deutschland*, 170–72.

40. Rupp, " 'I Don't Call that *Volksgemeinschaft*,' " 39–40; Dörte Winkler, *Frauenarbeit*, 102–21, 134–53, 156–57; Mason, "Women in Germany, Part II," 16; Bajohr, *Die Hälfte der Fabrik*, 178–87; Ludwig Eiber, "Frauen in der Kriegsindustrie: Arbeitsbedingungen, Lebensumstände und Protestverhalten," in *Bayern in der NS-Zeit*, vol. 3, ed. Martin Broszat, Elke Fröhlich, and Anton Grossmann, 570–644; Leila Rupp, *Mobilizing Women for War: German and American War Propaganda, 1939–1945*, 115–36; Ursula von Gersdorff, *Frauen im Kriegsdienst, 1914–1945*, 305–06, 342–44; and Herbert, "Zur Entwicklung der Ruhrarbeiterschaft," 33.

The uncritical celebration of women's willingness to sacrifice themselves, proclaimed by Nazi propaganda, resounds in some recent treatments as well. See, e.g., Klaus-Jörg Ruhl, *Unsere verlorenen Jahre: Frauenalltag in Kriegs- und Nachkriegszeit 1939–1949 in Berichten, Dokumenten und Bildern*, 9.

41. Baumert, *Jugend der Nachkriegszeit*, 37.

42. Lutz Niethammer, "Privat-Wirtschaft: Erinnerungsfragmente einer anderen Umerziehung," in Niethammer, *"Hinterher merkt man,"* 52–53. See similar accounts in Sibylle Meyer and Eva Schulze, " 'Alleine war's schwieriger und einfacher zugleich': Veränderungen gesellschaftlicher Bewertung und individueller Erfahrung alleinstehender Frauen in Berlin 1943–1955," in Freier and Kuhn, *"Das Schicksal Deutschlands"*, 358; and idem, " 'Als wir wieder zusammen waren, ging der Krieg im Kleinen weiter': Frauen, Männer und Familien in Berlin der vierziger Jahre," in Niethammer and Plato, *"Wir kriegen jetzt,"* 308.

43. Klessmann, *Die doppelte Staatsgründung*, 39–44; Marion Frantzioch, *Die Vertriebenen: Hemmnisse, Antriebskräfte und Wege ihrer Integration in der Bundesrepublik Deutschland*; Siegfried Bethlehem, *Heimatvertreibung, DDR-Flucht, Gastarbeiterzuwanderung: Wanderungsströme und Wanderungspolitik in der Bundesrepublik*, 21–106; and in general, on the expellees, Rainer Schulze, Doris von der Brelie-Lewien, and Helga Grebing, eds., *Flüchtlinge und Vertrie-*

bene in der westdeutschen Nachkriegsgeschichte: Bilanzierung der Forschung und Perspektiven für die künftige Forschungsarbeit; Wolfgang Benz, ed., *Die Vertreibung der Deutschen aus dem Osten: Ursachen, Ereignisse, Folgen;* and Alexander von Plato, "Fremde Heimat: Zur Integration von Flüchtlingen und Einheimischen in die Neue Zeit," in Niethammer and Plato, *"Wir kriegen jetzt."* On the so-called displaced persons, see Wolfgang Jacobmeyer, *Vom Zwangsarbeiter zum heimatlosen Ausländer: Die Displaced Persons in Westdeutschland 1945–1951.*

44. The literature on Allied deliberations on the "German Question" is massive. For introductions, see Josef Becker, "Die Deutsche Frage in der nationalen Politik 1941–1949," in *Vorgeschichte der Bundesrepublik Deutschland: Zwischen Kapitulation und Grundgesetz,* ed. Josef Becker, Theo Stammen and Peter Waldmann, 9–60; Theo Stammen, "Das alliierte Besatzungsregime in Deutschland," in ibid., 61–92; and Rolf Steininger, *Deutsche Geschichte 1945–1961: Darstellung und Dokumente in zwei Bänden,* vol. 1, which provides an extensive guide to further reading.

45. Meyer and Schulze, " 'Alleine war's schwieriger,' " 358–59; Möding, "Die Stunde der Frauen?" 620; and report of Arbeitsamt Recklinghausen, August 1947, NWHStA, NW62/17–18. On German reactions to occupation in general, see Josef Foschepoth, "Zur deutschen Reaktion auf Niederlage und Besatzung," in *Westdeutschland 1945–1955: Unterwerfung, Kontrolle, Integration,* ed. Ludolf Herbst, 151–65; and Barbara Marshall, "German Attitudes to British Military Government 1945–1947," 655–84.

46. Doris Schubert, *Frauen in der deutschen Nachkriegszeit* 1: 157–62, 196–97; Marita Krauss, " '. . . es geschahen Dinge, die Wunder ersetzten': Die Frau im Münchner Trümmeralltag," in *Trümmerleben: Texte, Dokumente, Bilder aus den Münchner Nachkriegsjahren,* ed. Friedrich Prinz and Marita Krauss, 30–37; Gunther Volz, "Trümmermode und New Look: Kleidung und Mode in München 1945–1949," in ibid., 81–86; the excerpts from women's magazines in Anette (*sic*) Kuhn and Doris Schubert, *Frauen in der Nachkriegszeit und im Wirtschaftswunder 1945–1960,* 21–23; and in general, Michael Wildt, *Der Traum vom Sattwerden: Hunger und Protest, Schwarzmarkt und Selbsthilfe,* 25–63, 85–91, 101–13.

47. Wolfgang Protzner, "Vom Hungerwinter bis zum Beginn der 'Fresswelle,' " in *Vom Hungerwinter zum kulinarischen Schlaraffenland: Aspekte einer Kulturgeschichte des Essens in der Bundesrepublik Deutschland,* ed. Wolfgang Protzner, 21–22.

48. "Die sozialen und gesundheitlichen Verhältnisse der Duisburger Bevölkerung," February 1947, NWHStA, NW43/463, 8. See also the comprehensive treatment of provisioning problems in Anna-Elisabeth Freier, "Überlebenspolitik im Nachkriegsdeutschland," in Kuhn, *Frauen in der deutschen Nachkriegszeit* 2: 39–92; and the documentary accounts in Klaus-Jörg Ruhl, ed., *Frauen in der Nachkriegszeit 1945–1963,* 16–17, 24–30; and Doris Schubert, *Frauen in der deutschen Nachkriegszeit* 1: 136–77.

49. Included in a report from the head of the welfare office in Gladbach to the Sozialminister of North Rhine–Westphalia, 29 May 1947, NWHStA, NW42/232; and in general, Hochstein, *Die Ideologie des Überlebens,* 248–55.

The phrase "epoch of calories" comes from Edith Oppens, "Ruhelose Welt," in Oppens et al., *Die Frau in unserer Zeit*, 39.

50. "Die Notlage der Bevölkerung in Duisburg," Stadt Duisburg to Sozial-minister of North Rhine–Westphalia, 18 June 1947, NWHStA, NW42/232; and Niethammer, "Privat-Wirtschaft," 60–66; Thurnwald, *Gegenwartsprobleme Berliner Familien*, 51–52, 76–77; Baumert, *Jugend der Nachkriegszeit*, 89–90; Manfred J. Enssle, "The Harsh Discipline of Food Scarcity in Postwar Stuttgart, 1945–1948," 481–502; James A. Diskant, "Scarcity, Survival and Local Activism: Miners and Steelworkers, Dortmund 1945–8," 555; Jörg Roesler, "The Black Market in Post-war Berlin and the Methods Used to Counteract It," 92–107; Karl-Heinz Rothenberger, *Die Hungerjahre nach dem Zweiten Weltkrieg: Ernährungs- und Landwirtschaft in Rheinland-Pfalz 1945–1950*, 125–40; Rainer Hudemann, *Sozialpolitik im deutschen Südwesten zwischen Tradition und Neuordnung 1945–1953: Sozialversicherung und Kriegsopferversorgung im Rahmen französischer Besatzungspolitik*, 82–106; and Günter J. Trittel, *Hunger und Politik: Die Ernährungskrise in der Bizone (1945–1949)*.

51. Thurnwald, *Gegenwartsprobleme Berliner Familien*, 59.

52. Ibid., 267–68, 297, 356.

53. Stephenson, " 'Emancipation' and its Problems," 355–56.

54. Thurnwald, *Gegenwartsprobleme Berliner Familien*, 146–47. See also Niethammer, "Privat-Wirtschaft," 20–33.

55. Baumert, *Deutsche Familien*, 65; and for a fictionalized account that vividly captures this aspect of postwar life, Heinrich Böll, *Haus ohne Hüter*.

56. Report of Gesundheitsamt Neuss, 24 May 1947, NWHStA, NW42/232 (published in Ruhl, *Frauen in der Nachkriegszeit*, 34); Gesundheitsamt Krefeld, 27 May 1947, NWHStA, NW 42/232; and other contemporary sources in Kuhn and Schubert, eds., *Frauen in der Nachkriegszeit*, 13–16. See also Isa Gruner, *Kinder in Not*, 41; and Plato, "Fremde Heimat," 204–05.

57. Ingrid Schmidt-Harzbach, "Eine Woche im April. Berlin 1945: Vergewaltigung als Massenschicksal," 51–62.

58. Niethammer, "Privat-Wirtschaft," 31.

59. Frevert, *Women in German History*, 258; Annemarie Tröger, "Between Rape and Prostitution: Survival Strategies and Chances of Emancipation for Berlin Women after World War II," in *Women in Culture and Politics: A Century of Change*, ed. Judith Friedlander et al., 97–117; Erika M. Hoerning, "Frauen als Kriegsbeute: Der Zwei-Fronten-Krieg: Beispiele aus Berlin," in Niethammer and Plato, *"Wir Kriegen jetzt andere Zeiten"*, 327–44; and Norman Naimark, " 'About the Russians and About Us': The Question of Rape and Soviet-German Relations in the East Zone."

60. Report from a social worker in Düren, 27 May 1947, NWHStA, NW42/232.

61. Ausschuss der deutschen Statistiker für die Volks- und Berufszählung 1946, *Volks- und Berufszählung vom 29. Oktober 1946 in den vier Besatzungszonen und Gross-Berlin: Berufszählung, Textteil*, 19; Schubert, *Frauen in der deutschen Nachkriegszeit* 1: 75–76; and Gewerbeaufsichtsamt Siegen to Regierungspräsident Arnsberg, 7 September 1946, NWStAM, Regierung Arnsberg, I GA, Nr. 385.

62. "Lohnordnung und Arbeitslenkung," *Arbeitsblatt für die britische Besatzungszone* 2 (1948): 333; Werner Abelshauser, *Wirtschaft in Westdeutschland 1945–1948: Rekonstruktion und Wachstumsbedingungen in der amerikanischen und britischen Zone*, 109; and in general, Petra Drohsel, *Die Lohndiskriminierung der Frauen: Eine Studie über Lohn und Lohndiskriminierung von erwerbstätigen Frauen in der Bundesrepublik Deutschland 1945–1984*, 39–79.

63. A. Morgan to E. Barber, Manpower Division, [British] Zonal Executive Offices, Lemgo, 5 March 1946, PRO, FO 1051/599. See also the documentation provided by Schubert, *Frauen in der deutschen Nachkriegszeit* 1: 272–89; report of factory inspector's office in Lower Saxony, 3 April 1948, NdsHStA, Nds. 1310, Acc. 53/72, Nr. 18, Bd. 2; and series of reports from local factory inspectors in NWStAM, Regierung Arnsberg, I GA, Nr. 386 and 426.

64. Länderrat Unterausschuss Arbeitslenkung, meeting of 3 June 1946, BA, Z1/926.

65. "Women's Employment in the British Zone of Occupation of Germany," 17 June 1948, prepared after visits to North Rhine–Westphalia, Lower Saxony, Hamburg, Schleswig-Holstein, and the British sector of Berlin, PRO, FO 1051/87; Charles D. Winning, Director, Regional Government Coordinating Office, to Erich Rossmann, Secretary General, Länderrat, 6 January 1947, BA, Z1/933; and Elizabeth Holt, Educational and Cultural Division, OMGUS, to Manpower Division, 3 June 1949, BA, RGO 260/OMGUS, 7/43–3/9.

66. E. V. Eves, [British] Manpower Division, to Philip Nicholls, 19 March 1948, PRO, FO 1051/596.

67. Thurnwald, *Gegenwartsprobleme Berliner Familien*, 18. In addition to Schubert, *Frauen in der deutschen Nachkriegszeit*, see idem, " 'Frauenmehrheit verpflichtet': Überlegungen zum Zusammenhang von erweiterter Frauenarbeit und kapitalistischem Wiederaufbau in Westdeutschland," in Freier and Kuhn, *"Das Schicksal Deutschlands,"* 231–65; Annette Kuhn, "Die vergessene Frauenarbeit in der Nachkriegszeit," in ibid., 170–201; and Freier, "Überlebenspolitik im Nachkriegsdeutschland," 39–92.

68. Interview of Halbfell, Labor Minister for North Rhine–Westphalia, with Mrs. B. P. Boyes, 19 May 1948, NWHStA, NW37/647, Bd. I.

69. Boyes, "Women's Employment in the British Zone of Occupation of Germany," 17 June 1948, PRO, FO 1051/87. See also Klaus Scherpe, ed., *In Deutschland unterwegs: Reportagen, Skizzen, Berichte 1945–1948*, 35–42, 45–49.

70. M[aria] Tritz, "Zeitbedingte Aufgaben des Fraueneinsatzes," *Arbeitsblatt für die britische Zone* 1 (1947): 90–92.

71. R. W. Luce, Manpower Division, Berlin to [British] Military Governor, 17 February 1948, PRO, FO 1051/596; and Luce to Educational Advisor, 12 January 1948, PRO, FO 1050/1179. On the relatively limited ability of the Allies to influence structural change in other parts of German society, see in general the essays in Ian D. Turner, ed., *Reconstruction in Post-War Germany: British Occupation Policy and the Western Zones, 1945–55;* and James M. Diehl, "Change and Continuity in the Treatment of German *Kriegsopfer*," 170–87.

72. Thurnwald, *Gegenwartsprobleme Berliner Familien*, 102.

73. Meyer and Schulze, *Wie wir das alles geschafft haben*, 24.

74. Hermann Korte, "Bevölkerungsstruktur und -entwicklung," in Benz, *Die Bundesrepublik Deutschland* 2: 15.

75. Ausschuss der Deutschen Statistiker für die Volks- und Berufszählung 1946, *Volks- und Berufszählung vom 29. Oktober 1946 in den vier Besatzungszonen und Gross-Berlin: Volkszählung, Textteil*, 36–37, 44–45, 58–59; and Adelheid zu Castell, "Die demographischen Konsequenzen des Ersten und Zweiten Weltkrieges für das Deutsche Reich, die Deutsche Demokratische Republik und die Bundesrepublik Deutschland," in *Zweiter Weltkrieg und sozialer Wandel: Achsenmächte und besetzte Länder*, ed. Waclaw Długoborski, 129, 135. The 1946 figures are for all of Germany. The 1950 figure, which is only for the Federal Republic, had claims to far greater accuracy.

76. Helga Prollius, "Ein Königreich für einen Mann?" 3, published in Kuhn and Schubert, *Frauen in der Nachkriegszeit*, 53.

77. "Die Notlage der Bevölkerung in Duisburg," Stadt Duisburg to Sozialminister of North Rhine–Westphalia, 18 June 1947, NWHStA, NW42/232; see also *Living Conditions in Germany 1947: A Survey by the Hilfswerk of the Evangelical Churches in Germany*, 27; and Merith Niehuss, "Zur Sozialgeschichte der Familie in Bayern," 928–29.

78. Meyer and Schulze, *Wie wir das alles geschafft haben*, 12.

79. Idem, *Von Liebe sprach damals keiner*, 76. And in general, Albrecht Lehmann, *Gefangenschaft und Heimkehr: Deutsche Kriegsgefangene in der Sowjetunion*, 140–51; Arthur L. Smith, *Heimkehr aus dem Zweiten Weltkrieg: Die Entlassung der deutschen Kriegsgefangenen;* and *Die Sexualität des Heimkehrers: Vorträge gehalten auf dem 4. Kongress der Deutschen Gesellschaft für Sexualforschung in Erlangen 1956.*

80. Meyer and Schulze, *Von Liebe sprach damals keiner*, 32. See also Herbert, "Zur Entwicklung der Ruhrarbeiterschaft," 31; and in general, the exceptionally useful discussion in Meyer and Schulze, " 'Als wir wieder zusammen waren.' "

81. Thurnwald, *Gegenwartsprobleme Berliner Familien*, 53–54; and Rothenberger, *Die Hungerjahre*, 175–76.

82. "Notlage der Bevölkerung, Berichte der Familienfürsorgerinnen" (Wuppertal), 7 June 1947, NWHStA, NW42/232.

83. Thurnwald, *Gegenwartsprobleme Berliner Familien*, 192; and for many similar reports for 1947 from social workers in North Rhine–Westphalia, NWHStA, NW42/232.

84. Evelyn Kühn, "Die Entwicklung und Diskussion des Ehescheidungsrechts in Deutschland: Eine sozialhistorische und rechtssoziologische Untersuchung," 159; Vogel, "Familie," 99; and Statistisches Bundesamt, *Die Frau im wirtschaftlichen und sozialen Leben der Bundesrepublik* (1952), 15.

85. Elsa Grallert, "Die Frau im sozialen und wirtschaftlichen Leben der Bundesrepublik," *Wirtschaft und Statistik* 3 (1951): 265.

86. *Constanze*, no. 21, 1948, quoted in Angela Seeler, "Ehe, Familie und andere Lebensformen in den Nachkriegsjahren im Spiegel der Frauenzeitschriften," in Freier and Kuhn, *"Das Schicksal Deutschlands,"* 101–02; and Roderich von Ungern-Sternberg, "Ehe und Ehezerrüttung, Geburten, Bevölkerungsgrösse und Eliteschwund," 589–92.

87. Meyer and Schulze, *Wie wir das alles geschafft haben*, 52–53; also Gruner, *Kinder in Not*, 50–51.

88. Baumert, *Deutsche Familien*, 145–46.

89. Report dated 6 June 1947, NWHStA, NW42/232.

90. Schelsky, *Wandlungen der deutschen Familie in der Gegenwart*, 282.

91. Gerhard Wurzbacher, *Leitbilder gegenwärtigen deutschen Familienlebens*, 188.

92. Statistisches Bundesamt, *Die Frau im wirtschaftlichen und sozialen Leben der Bundesrepublik* (1956), 4, 6–7.

93. Baumert, *Deutsche Familien*, 176–77. In general, see also Seeler, "Ehe, Familie und andere Lebensformen"; Meyer and Schulze, *Wie wir das alles geschafft haben;* Vogel, "Familie," 100; and the contemporary sources published in Kuhn and Schubert, *Frauen in der Nachkriegszeit*, 55–57.

94. Ludwig von Friedeburg, *Die Umfrage in der Intimsphäre*, 24, 27. The survey was conducted by the Institut für Demoskopie.

95. Elisabeth Noelle and Erich Peter Neumann, *The Germans: Public Opinion Polls 1947–1966*, 67.

96. Friedeburg, *Die Umfrage in der Intimsphäre*, 19–20; and Noelle and Neumann, *The Germans*, 64. On the sexual reform discussion and the organized political pressure for the repeal of the criminal statute prohibiting abortion in Weimar, see Atina Grossmann, "Abortion and Economic Crisis: The 1931 Campaign Against Paragraph 218," in Bridenthal et al., *When Biology Became Destiny*, 66–86; idem, "The New Woman and the Rationalization of Sexuality in Weimar Germany," in *Powers of Desire: The Politics of Sexuality*, ed. Ann Snitow, Christine Stansell, and Sharon Thompson, 153–71; idem, " 'Satisfaction Is Domestic Happiness': Mass Working-Class Sex Reform Organizations in the Weimar Republic," in *Towards the Holocaust: The Social and Economic Collapse of the Weimar Republic*, ed. Michael M. Dobkowski and Isidor Wallimann, 265–93.

97. A useful summary of this literature is provided by Dieter Wirth, "Die Familie in der Nachkriegszeit: Desorganisation oder Stabilität?" in Becker et al., *Vorgeschichte der Bundesrepublik Deutschland*, 193–216. See also Ingrid N. Sommerkorn, "Die erwerbstätige Mutter in der Bundesrepublik: Einstellungs- und Problemveränderungen," in *Wandel und Kontinuität der Familie in der Bundesrepublik Deutschland*, ed. Rosemarie Nave-Herz, 118–22.

98. Niethammer, "Privat-Wirtschaft," 46–48, 54, 93–94; see also Friedrich H. Tenbruck, "Alltagsnormen und Lebensgefühle in der Bundesrepublik," in *Die zweite Republik: 25 Jahre Bundesrepublik Deutschland—eine Bilanz*, ed. Richard Löwenthal and Hans-Peter Schwarz, 289–310.

99. Möding, " 'Ich muss irgendwo engagiert sein,' " 283, 292–93; idem, "Die Stunde der Frauen?" 646; and Barbara Willenbacher, "Zerrüttung und Bewährung der Nachriegsfamilie," in Broszat et al., *Von Stalingrad zur Währungsreform*, 595–618.

100. Such rhetorical questions abound in the reports of social workers and health officials in Ruhr cities in 1947; see NWHStA, NW42/232 and NW42/463.

101. Oppens, "Ruhelose Welt," 36.

102. Margot Schmidt, "Im Vorzimmer," 192; Niethammer, "Heimat und Front," 225–26.

103. Quoted in Walter Lafeber, ed., *The Origins of the Cold War, 1941–1947: A Historical Problem with Interpretations and Documents,* 154–55.

104. There is a vast literature on West Germany's position in the geopolitical wranglings of the immediate postwar years. For an introduction, see Josef Foschepoth and Rolf Steininger, eds., *Die britische Deutschland- und Besatzungspolitik 1945–1949;* John Gimbel, *The American Occupation of Germany: Politics and the Military, 1945–1949;* and the sources cited above in note 44.

105. Werner Abelshauser, *Wirtschaftsgeschichte der Bundesrepublik Deutschland (1945–1980),* 46–48; idem, "Probleme des Wiederaufbaus der westdeutschen Wirtschaft 1945 bis 1953," in *Politische Weichenstellungen im Nachkriegsdeutschland 1945–1953,* ed. Heinrich August Winkler, 237–39; Nicholas Balabkins, *Germany Under Direct Controls: Economic Aspects of Industrial Disarmament, 1945–1948,* 179–80; Hans Möller, ed., *Zur Vorgeschichte der deutschen Mark: Die Währungsreformpläne 1945–1948;* and Christoph Buchheim, "Die Währungsreform 1948 in Westdeutschland," 190–231.

106. Klessmann, *Die doppelte Staatsgründung,* 191–93.

107. Quoted ibid., 190.

108. Niethammer, "Privat-Wirtschaft," 81.

109. Abelshauser, "Probleme des Wiederaufbaus," 282; and Protzner, "Vom Hungerwinter," 26.

110. Einfeldt, "Auskommen-Durchkommen," 282; Niethammer, "Privat-Wirtschaft," 82; idem, "Zum Wandel der Kontinuitätsdiskussion," in *Westdeutschland 1945–1955: Unterwerfung, Kontrolle, Integration,* ed. Ludolf Herbst, 81; and idem, " 'Normalisierung' im Westen: Erinnerungsspuren in die 50er Jahre," in *Ist der Nationalsozialismus Geschichte? Zur Historisierung und Historikerstreit,* ed. Dan Diner, 161–62; Hochstein, *Die Ideologie des Überlebens,* 255; and on the short-term negative effects of currency reform, particularly for the expellees, Ian Connor, "The Refugees and the Currency Reform," in Turner, *Reconstruction in Post-War Germany,* 301–26. On returning veterans in general, Smith, *Heimkehr aus dem Zweiten Weltkrieg;* and Lehmann, *Gefangenschaft und Heimkehr.*

111. Klessmann, *Die doppelte Staatsgründung,* 110; Dörte Winkler, "Die amerikanische Sozialisierungspolitik in Deutschland, 1945–1948," in Heinrich Winkler, *Politische Weichenstellungen,* 88–110; and for examples of those who argue that the United States imposed a new order on Germany, Tilman Fichter and Ute Schmidt, *Der erzwungene Kapitalismus: Klassenkämpfe in den Westzonen 1945–1948;* Eberhard Schmidt, *Die verhinderte Neuordnung 1945–1952;* and Theo Pirker, *Die verordnete Demokratie: Grundlagen und Erscheinungen der Restauration.*

112. See, e.g., Bertram Schaffner, *Father Land: A Study of Authoritarianism in the German Family;* R. Birley, Educational Advisor to [British] Military Governor, to Chief of Manpower, 13 January 1948, PRO, FO 1051/596; and the far more nuanced account of David Rodnick, *Postwar Germans: An Anthropolo-*

gist's Account. My search in the archives of the British forces of occupation in
the PRO and in OMGUS materials in the Bundesarchiv for signs of Allied attempts to block German reforms that would dramatically affect women's status,
a "verhinderte Neuordnung" of gender relations, produced nothing of significance. There are also no indications that the Allies had extensive programs that
they failed to implement because of German resistance. British and United States
forces of occupation provided informative reports on the reemergence of organized political life among German women, but there is no evidence of Allied attempts to influence the postwar West German discussion of gender relations.

CHAPTER TWO

1. The biographical sketch of Selbert in this and the preceding paragraph is
drawn from Deutscher Juristinnenbund, ed., *Juristinnen in Deutschland: Eine
Dokumentation (1900–1984)*, 95–102; the excerpts from an interview with Selbert by Marielouise Janssen-Jurreit, *Sexismus: Über die Abtreibung der Frauenfrage*, 307–13; Marianne Feuersenger, *Die garantierte Gleichberechtigung: Ein
umstrittener Sieg der Frauen*, 49–57; "Elisabeth Selbert (1896–1986)," in
Frandsen, Huffmann, and Kuhn, *Frauen in Wissenschaft und Politik*, 69–70;
and Anke Martiny, "Von der Trümmerfrau zur Quotenfrau: Vierzig Jahre
Gleichberechtigung im Lichte und im Schatten der Verfassung," 71–72.
2. In general, see Peter H. Merkl, *The Origin of the West German Republic;*
Volker Otto, *Das Staatsverständnis des Parlamentarischen Rates: Ein Beitrag
zur Entstehungsgeschichte des Grundgesetzes für die Bundesrepublik Deutsch-
land;* Werner Sörgel, *Konsensus und Interessen: Eine Studie zur Entstehung des
Grundgesetzes für die Bundesrepublik Deutschland;* Hans-Hermann Hartwich,
Sozialstaatspostulat und gesellschaftlicher Status quo; Friedrich Karl Fromme,
*Von der Weimarer Verfassung zum Bonner Grundgesetz: Die verfassungspoliti-
schen Folgerungen des Parlamentarischen Rates aus Weimarer Republik und nationalsozialistischer Diktatur;* Karlheinz Niclauss, *Demokratiegründung in
Westdeutschland: Die Entstehung der Bundesrepublik 1945–1949;* and Wolfgang Horn, "Demokratiegründung und Grundgesetz," 26–40. None of these
works deals more than peripherally with the debates over women's status. For
useful overviews that focus on Article 3, see Ines Reich-Hilweg, *Männer und
Frauen sind gleichberechtigt;* Anna Späth, "Vielfältige Forderungen nach
Gleichberechtigung und 'nur' ein Ergebnis: Artikel 3 Absatz 2 GG," in Freier
and Kuhn, *"Das Schicksal Deutschlands,"* 122–67; Renate Wiggershaus, *Geschichte der Frauen und der Frauenbewegung in der Bundesrepublik Deutschland und in der Deutschen Demokratischen Republik nach 1945*, 23–34; and
Feuersenger, *Die garantierte Gleichberechtigung*, 11–62.
3. Feuersenger, *Die garantierte Gleichberechtigung*, 50–51.
4. Noelle and Neumann, *The Germans*, 227. See also Elisabeth Noelle and
Erich Peter Neumann, *Jahrbuch der öffentlichen Meinung, 1947–1955*, 45.
5. Anna J. Merritt and Richard L. Merritt, *Public Opinion in Occupied Germany: The OMGUS Surveys, 1945–1949*, 307; see also Beyer and Holtmann,
" 'Auch die Frau soll politisch denken,' " 389; Clara Menck, "The Problem of
Reorientation," in *The Struggle for Democracy in Germany*, ed. Gabriel A.

Almond, 288; and survey of 29 May 1947, "The Role of Women in Occupied Germany," carried out by the U.S. occupation forces, BA, OMGUS, 5/296–1/1; and in general, Merkl, *Origin of the West German Republic*, 128–30.

6. There is an extensive literature on the party's early history. See, e.g., Kurt Klotzbach, *Der Weg zur Staatspartei: Programmatik, praktische Politik und Organisation der deutschen Sozialdemokratie 1945 bis 1965*, 17–153; Douglas A. Chalmers, *The Social Democratic Party of Germany: From Working-Class Movement to Modern Political Party*, 14–17; and the useful summary and extensive bibliography in Siegfried Heimann, "Die Sozialdemokratische Partei Deutschlands," in *Parteien-Handbuch: Die Parteien der Bundesrepublik Deutschland 1945–1980*, ed. Richard Stöss, 2: 2025–30, 2042–50, 2127–30.

7. On the early history of the CDU/CSU, see Geoffrey Pridham, *Christian Democracy in Western Germany: The CDU/CSU in Government and Opposition, 1945–1976*, 21–35, 40, 48–52; Rudolf Uertz, *Christentum und Sozialismus in der frühen CDU: Grundlagen und Wirkungen der christlich-sozialen Ideen in der Union 1945–1949*; Hans Georg Wieck, *Die Entstehung der CDU und die Wiedergründung des Zentrums im Jahre 1945*; Wolf-Dieter Narr, *CDU-SPD: Programm und Praxis seit 1945*, 73–103; Gerhard Schulz, "Die CDU: Merkmale ihres Aufbaues," in *Parteien in der Bundesrepublik: Studien zur Entwicklung der deutschen Parteien bis zur Bundestagswahl 1953*, ed. Max Gustav Lange et al., 3–153; and on the history of Christian socialism, Fritz Focke, *Sozialismus aus christlicher Verantwortung: Die Idee eines christlichen Sozialismus in der katholisch-sozialen Bewegung und in der CDU*.

8. In general, see Dorothee Buchhaas, *Gesetzgebung im Wiederaufbau: Schulgesetz in Nordrhein-Westfalen und Betriebsverfassungsgesetz*, 30–36; Friedrich Spotts, *The Churches and Politics in Germany*, 47–48, 51; Sörgel, *Konsensus und Interessen*, 167; Hans Braun, "Demographische Umschichtungen im deutschen Katholizismus nach 1945," in *Kirche und Katholizismus 1945–1949*, ed. Anton Rauscher, 15; Hans Maier, "Der politische Weg der deutschen Katholiken nach 1945," in *Deutscher Katholizismus nach 1945: Kirche, Gesellschaft, Geschichte*, ed. Hans Maier, 190–99; idem, "Die Kirchen," in Löwenthal and Schwarz, *Die zweite Republik*, 494–95; Burkhard van Schewick, *Die katholische Kirche und die Entstehung der Verfassungen in Westdeutschland 1945–1950*, 74–77; Klaus Gotto, "Die katholische Kirche und die Entstehung des Grundgesetzes," in Rauscher, *Kirche und Katholizismus, 1945–1949*, 88–108; Rudolf Morsey, "Katholizismus und Unionsparteien in der Ära Adenauer," in *Katholizismus im politischen System der Bundesrepublik 1949–1963*, ed. Albrecht Langer, 33–59; Karl Forster, "Der deutsche Katholizismus in der Bundesrepublik Deutschland," in *Der soziale und politische Katholizismus: Entwicklungslinien in Deutschland 1803–1963*, vol. 1, ed. Anton Rauscher, 211, 218, 250; and Werner K. Blessing, " 'Deutschland in Not, wir im Glauben . . . ': Kirche und Kirchenvolk in einer katholischen Region 1933–1949," in Broszat et al., *Von Stalingrad zur Währungsreform*, 96–104.

9. Gerold Ambrosius, *Die Durchsetzung der Sozialen Marktwirtschaft in Westdeutschland 1945–1949*.

10. In general, see Jörg Michael Gutscher, *Die Entwicklung der FDP von ihren Anfängen bis 1961*; and Dieter Hein, *Zwischen liberaler Milieupartei und*

nationaler Sammlungsbewegung: Gründung, Entwicklung und Struktur der Freien Demokratischen Partei 1945–1949.

11. On the Center, see Wieck, Die Entstehung der CDU; and on the German Party, Horst W. Schmollinger, "Die Deutsche Partei," in Stöss, Parteien-Handbuch 1: 1025–31.

12. Frank R. Pfetsch, "Die Gründergeneration der Bundesrepublik: Sozialprofil und politische Orientierung," 243–44; Renate Bridenthal and Claudia Koonz, "Beyond Kinder, Küche, Kirche: Weimar Women in Politics and Work," in Bridenthal et al., When Biology Became Destiny, 35.

13. See the references in note 16 to Chapter 1.

14. Harold Hurwitz, Die politische Kultur der Bevölkerung und der Neubeginn konservativer Politik, 161; and for the early fifties, Noelle and Neumann, Jahrbuch der öffentlichen Meinung, 45, 51.

15. Gerhard Leibholz and Hermann von Mangoldt, eds., Entstehungsgeschichte der Artikel des Grundgesetzes, 66.

16. Parlamentarischer Rat, Stenographischer Bericht, Zehnte Sitzung, 8 May 1949, 225.

17. Parlamentarischer Rat, Ausschuss für Grundsatzfragen (hereafter PR, AfG), 3. Sitzung, 21 September 1948, 45–46, BA, Z5/29. A complete set of these protocols is also available in the Parlamentsarchiv, Bonn.

18. On these topics, see, most recently, Koonz, Mothers in the Fatherland, 175–221; and Klinksiek, Die Frau, 68–99.

19. In general, see Jean H. Quataert, Reluctant Feminists in German Social Democracy, 1885–1917; Heinz Niggemann, Emanzipation zwischen Sozialismus und Feminismus: Die sozialdemokratische Frauenbewegung im Kaiserreich; Sabine Richebächer, Uns fehlt nur eine Kleinigkeit: Deutsche proletarische Frauenbewegung 1890–1914; Richard J. Evans, Sozialdemokratie und Frauenemanzipation im deutschen Kaiserreich; Mary Nolan, "Proletarischer Anti-Feminismus: Dargestellt am Beispiel der SPD-Ortsgruppe Düsseldorf, 1890–1914," in Frauen und Wissenschaft: Beiträge zur Berliner Sommeruniversität für Frauen, Juli 1976, 356–77; Bridenthal and Koonz, "Beyond Kinder, Küche, Kirche," 37–38; Renate Pore, A Conflict of Interest: Women in German Social Democracy, 1919–1933; Werner Thönnessen, The Emancipation of Women: The Rise and Decline of the Women's Movement in German Social Democracy 1863–1933; and Hagemann, Frauenalltag und Männerpolitik, 531–43.

20. Michael John, Politics and the Law in Late Nineteenth-Century Germany: The Origins of the Civil Code.

21. William H. Hubbard, Familiengeschichte: Materialien zur deutschen Familie seit dem Ende des 18. Jahrhunderts, 41–43, 51–53, 58; and Thilo Ramm, Familienrecht 1: 76–80.

22. Ramm, Familienrecht 1: 76–77; and on the eighteenth- and early nineteenth-century background, Ute Gerhard, Verhältnisse und Verhinderungen: Frauenarbeit, Familie und Rechte der Frauen im 19. Jahrhundert; and Christoph Sachsse and Florian Tennstedt, "Familienpolitik durch Gesetzgebung: Die juristische Regulierung der Familie," in Staatliche Sozialpolitik und Familie, ed. Franz-Xaver Kaufmann, 88–94.

23. Marianne Weber, *Ehefrau und Mutter in der Rechtsentwicklung: Eine Einführung*, 413; and in general, Ute Gerhard, " 'Bis an die Wurzeln des Übels': Rechtskämpfe und Rechtskritik der Radikalen," 80–82.

24. Ed. Heilfron, ed., *Die deutsche Nationalversammlung im Jahre 1919 in ihrer Arbeit für den Aufbau des neuen deutschen Volksstaates*, vol. 6, quotation from Quarck, 3818, and in general, 3804–25, meeting of 15 July 1919.

25. Quotations from *Verhandlungen des sechsunddreissigsten Deutschen Juristentages (Lübeck)* 2: 124.

26. Ibid., 99 (comments of Marianne Weber).

27. Ibid., 82 (comments of Schultz).

28. Dirk Blasius, *Ehescheidung in Deutschland 1794–1945: Scheidung und Scheidungsrecht in historischer Perspektive*, 164–87; and Helen L. Boak, "Women in Weimar Germany: The 'Frauenfrage' and the Female Vote," in *Social Change and Political Development in Weimar Germany*, ed. Richard Bessell and E. J. Feuchtwanger, 160–61.

29. Freiherr von Freytagh-Lorinhoven, quoted in Blasius, *Ehescheidung in Deutschland*, 175; and Werner Schubert, *Die Projekte der Weimarer Republik zur Reform des Nichtehelichen-, des Adoptions- und des Ehescheidungsrechts*.

30. Ramm, *Familienrecht* 1: 86.

31. Quoted in ibid.; and in general, Czarnowski, *Das kontrollierte Paar*.

32. Blasius, *Ehescheidung in Deutschland*, 188–223.

33. Janssen-Jurreit, *Sexismus*, 310.

34. Parlamentarischer Rat, Hauptausschuss, Bonn 1948/49 (hereafter PR, HA), 17. Sitzung, 3 December 1948, 206–207. (The protocols of the Hauptausschuss were printed. A complete set is available in the Parlamentsarchiv, Bonn.)

35. PR, AfG, 26. Sitzung, 30 November 1948, 53, BA, Z5/34.

36. See, e.g., Gerda Vey (Würzburg) to Herta Gotthelf of the SPD's executive committee, 8 September 1948, ASD, Bestand Schumacher, J60.

37. See Lüders's comments, *Verhandlungen des sechsunddreissigsten Deutschen Juristentages (Lübeck)* 2: 122–23. This had been a demand of the bourgeois women's movement since the late nineteenth century. See Weber, *Ehefrau und Mutter;* also her remarks in *Verhandlungen des sechsunddreissigsten Deutschen Juristentages (Lübeck)* 2: 94–105.

38. See Dehler's comments, PR, AfG, 26. Sitzung, 30 November 1948, 49, BA, Z5/34.

39. Albert Finck, "Um die Gleichberechtigung der Frau," in Parlamentarischer Rat, Drucksachen, PR. 12.48/345. Finck was a member of the Parliamentary Council.

40. PR, AfG, 26. Sitzung, 30 November 1948, 46–47, BA, Z5/34.

41. On Nazi policies toward the gypsies, see Peukert, *Inside Nazi Germany*, 210–212, 215–16.

42. Helene Weber's comments in PR, AfG, 27. Sitzung, 1 December 1948, 12, PA; Renner, PR, HA, 17. Sitzung, 3 December 1948, 206; and meetings of CDU/CSU delegation, 4 November 1948, in *Die CDU/CSU im Parlamentarischen Rat: Sitzungsprotokolle der Unionsfraktion*, ed. Rainer Salzmann, 128.

43. PR, AfG, 6. Sitzung, 5 October 1948, 55, BA, Z5/30; and PR, AfG, 27. Sitzung, 1 December 1948, 27, PA; and on measures in the German Democratic Republic, Gabriele Gast, *Die politische Rolle der Frau in der DDR*, 35.

44. PR, AfG, 27. Sitzung, 1 December 1948, 15, PA.

45. See *Anlage zum stenographischen Bericht der 9. Sitzung des Parlamentarischen Rates am 6. Mai 1949*, Parlamentarischer Rat, Bonn 1948/49, Schriftlicher Bericht zum Entwurf des Grundgesetzes für die Bundesrepublik Deutschland (Drucksachen Nr. 850, 854), 8 (written by Mangoldt).

46. Freier Gewerkschaftsbund Hessen, Frauensekretariat, to Konrad Adenauer, as head of the Parliamentary Council, 15 December 1948, BA, Z5/96.

47. Industriegewerkschaft Metall für die britische Zone und Bremen to Adenauer, 30 December 1948, BA, Z5/110.

48. Frauen-Ausschuss, Dunlop-Hanau to Parlamentarischer Rat, 13 January 1949, BA, Z5/112; also quoted in Reich-Hilweg, *Männer und Frauen*, 22, 147.

49. Theanolte Bähnisch for Frauenring der Britischen Zone to Parliamentary Council, 31 December 1948, BA, Z5/111.

50. Dorothea Groener-Geyer to Parliamentary Council, 2 January 1949, BA, Z5/111. Groener-Geyer's letter was cited explicitly by Selbert in the plenary debates; see PR, HA, 42. Sitzung, 18 January 1949, 539.

51. Finck, "Um die Gleichberechtigung der Frau," in Parlamentarischer Rat, Drucksachen, PR. 12.48/345.

52. PR, HA, 42. Sitzung, 18 January 1949, 538. See also remarks by Helene Weber, "Niederschrift über die Tagung des Frauenzonenausschusses der CDU für die Britische Zone unter Hinzuziehung der Vertreterinnen der Reichsarbeitsgemeinschaft der Frauenausschüsse aller Zonen und von Gästen in Recklinghausen am 19./20.2.1949," ACDP, IV-003-22/1.

53. Heuss's comments, PR, HA, 42. Sitzung, 18 January 1949, 542; and on the pressure from women within the FDP, Herta Ilk, "Über die Gleichberechtigung der Frau," in "Informationsmaterial zu Informationsdienst Nr. 62," Freie Demokratische Partei, Hauptgeschäftsführung, Munich, 15 January 1949, ADL, DA/117. Also Herta Ilk to Thomas Dehler, 10 January 1949, BA, NL Lüders/227. This group might well have included Heuss's own wife, Elly Heuss-Knapp. Heuss-Knapp was the daughter of the well-known liberal economist Georg Friedrich Knapp, and she had studied economics in Berlin. Active in the FDP in Württemberg-Baden after the war, she was a member of the state's parliament from 1946 to 1949. See Barbara Greven-Aschoff, *Die bürgerliche Frauenbewegung in Deutschland 1894–1933*, 79, 223 (n. 68).

54. PR, HA, 42. Sitzung, 18 January 1949, 539–41.

55. Theophil Kaufmann (CDU), PR, HA, 3 December 1948, 207–208.

56. PR, HA, 42. Sitzung, 18 January 1949, 541.

57. Greven-Aschoff, *Die Bürgerliche Frauenbewegung*, 38–39. And in general, Richard J. Evans, *The Feminist Movement in Germany 1894–1933*; Ann Taylor Allen, "Spiritual Motherhood: German Feminists and the Kindergarten Movement, 1848–1911," 319–39; idem, "German Radical Feminism and Eugenics, 1900–1918," 31–56; idem, *Feminism and Motherhood in Germany, 1800–1914*; Irene Stoehr, " 'Organisierte Mütterlichkeit': Zur Politik der

deutschen Frauenbewegung um 1900," in *Frauen suchen ihre Geschichte: Historische Studien zum 19. und 20. Jahrhundert,* ed. Karin Hausen, 221–49; idem, "Housework and Motherhood: Debates and Policies in the Women's Movement in Imperial Germany and the Weimar Republic," in *Maternity and Gender Policies: Women and the Rise of European Welfare States, 1880s–1950s,* edited by Gisela Bock and Pat Thane, 212–32; Amy Hackett, "Feminism and Liberalism in Wilhelmine Germany, 1890–1918," in *Liberating Women's History: Theoretical and Critical Essays,* ed. Bernice Carroll, 127–36; idem, "The German Women's Movement and Suffrage, 1890–1914," in *Modern European Social History,* ed. Robert Bezucha, 354–86; Christoph Sachsse, *Mütterlichkeit als Beruf: Sozialarbeit, Sozialreform und Frauenbewegung 1871–1929;* James C. Albisetti, *Schooling German Girls and Women: Secondary and Higher Education in the Nineteenth Century,* 168–203; Sonya Michel and Seth Koven, "Womanly Duties: Maternalist Politics and the Origins of Welfare States in France, Germany, Great Britain, and the United States, 1880–1920," 1089; and on this strain of feminism in nineteenth-century Europe, Karen Offen, "Defining Feminism: A Comparative Historical Approach," 119–57.

58. "Ausführungen der Gen. Bähnisch Hannover bei der Gründung des überparteilichen Frauenbundes Rendsburg 14.4.47," ASD, PV Akten, Alter Bestand, Nr. 0244. Bähnisch, a Social Democrat, played a leading role in this organizational initiative after the war. For indications of enthusiasm for this alternative among other women in the SPD, see the correspondence between Herta Gotthelf and the regional heads of SPD women's caucuses, ASD, Bestand Schumacher, J55.

59. "Wuppertal," *Genossin* 11 (1948): 117.

60. Gotthelf to Anna Stiegler (Bremen), 12 June 1947, ASD, Bestand Schumacher, J56. Also Margarete Starrmann to Gotthelf, 20 June 1937 [1947], ASD, Bestand Schumacher, J59; Rita Ostermann of the British occupation force's "Women's Affairs" division, to Mr. Ramsbotham, 4 April 1949, PRO, FO 1049/1844; and Ostermann to Peter Sally-Flood, 24 November 1949, PRO, FO 1049/1846.

61. Grete Schmalz (SPD Bezirk Niederrhein) to Gotthelf, 16 May 1947, ASD, PV Akten, Alter Bestand, Nr. 0244.

62. Herta Gotthelf, "Zum Geleit," *Genossin* 10 (1947): 1.

63. PR, HA, 42. Sitzung, 18 January 1949, 540.

64. Quataert, *Reluctant Feminists,* 91–93, 99–103; Thönnessen, *Emancipation of Women,* 97–106; Niggemann, *Emanzipation zwischen Sozialismus und Feminismus,* 44–47, 237–43; Richebächer, *Uns fehlt nur eine Kleinigkeit,* 141–50; Bridenthal and Koonz, "Beyond *Kinder, Küche, Kirche,*" 37–38; and Pore, *Conflict of Interest,* 75–77.

65. Gotthelf in "Protokoll der Bezirksfrauenkonferenz am 20. Februar 1947 in Dortmund," ASD, Bestand Schumacher, J63.

66. PR, HA, 42. Sitzung, 18 January 1949, 540.

67. PR, HA, 39. Sitzung, 14 January 1949, 488.

68. Hartwich, *Sozialstaatspostulat,* 37–38; Sörgel, *Konsensus und Interessen,* 176–78; and Susanne Miller, "Die SPD vor und nach Godesberg," in Löwenthal and Schwarz, *Die zweite Republik,* 381.

69. Sörgel, *Konsensus und Interessen,* 177–79; and Otto, *Das Staatsverständnis des Parlamentarischen Rates,* 76–77. For examples of petitions, see, e.g., Zentralkomitee zur Vorbereitung der Generalversammlungen des Katholischen Deutschlands to Parlamentarischer Rat, 25 November 1948; and Arbeitsgemeinschaft katholischer Frauen to Parlamentarischer Rat, 26 November 1948, both in BA, Z5/110.

70. Feuersenger, *Die garantierte Gleichberechtigung,* 60–61.

71. Helmut Klaas, ed., *Die Entstehung der Verfassung für Rheinland-Pfalz: Eine Dokumentation,* 20–21; and Otto, *Das Staatsverständnis des Parlamentarischen Rates,* 42–43.

72. Rudolf Morsey, "Helene Weber (1881–1962)," in *Zeitgeschichte in Lebensbildern,* ed. Jürgen Aretz, Rudolf Morsey, Anton Rauscher, 3: 223–34; Michael Phayer, *Protestant and Catholic Women in Nazi Germany,* 63, 68–69; Laura Gellott and Michael Phayer, "Dissenting Voices: Catholic Women in Opposition to Fascism," 94–97; and Feuersenger, *Die garantierte Gleichberechtigung,* 57–60.

73. Reprinted in Ossip K. Flechtheim, ed., *Dokumente zur parteipolitischen Entwicklung in Deutschland seit 1945,* vol. 2, part 1, 31. And in general, on the importance of the concept of *Abendland* as an integrative element for Christian Democracy, see Arnold J. Heidenheimer, *Adenauer and the CDU: The Rise of the Leader and the Integration of the Party,* 240; and Jost Hermand, *Kultur im Wiederaufbau: Die Bundesrepublik Deutschland 1945–1965,* 44–47, 84.

74. From the "Guiding Principles" of the CSU in 1945, quoted in Pridham, *Christian Democracy,* 29. In general, see Klaus Gotto, "Zum Selbstverständnis der katholischen Kirche im Jahre 1945," in *Politik und Konfession: Festschrift für Konrad Repgen zum 60. Geburtstag,* ed. Dieter Albrecht et al., 465–81; Otto, *Das Staatsverständnis des Parlamentarischen Rates,* 80, 84–85, 198–200.

75. Principles adopted in Frankfurt, September 1945, reprinted in Flechtheim, *Dokumente zur parteipolitischen Entwicklung in Deutschland,* vol. 2, part 1, 39; see also the Grundsatzprogramm of the CSU, ibid., 214–15; and in general, Narr, *CDU-SPD,* 175.

76. PR, AfG, 29. Sitzung, 4 December 1948, 96, BA, Z5/34.

77. PR, HA, 21. Sitzung, 7 December 1948, 240.

78. PR, AfG, 26. Sitzung, 30 November 1948, 60–61, BA, Z5/34.

79. Ibid., 59–60.

80. "Frankfurter Leitsätze," 1945, quoted in Flechtheim, *Dokumente zur parteipolitischen Entwicklung in Deutschland,* vol. 2, part 1, 40.

81. PR, HA, 21. Sitzung, 7 December 1948, 240, 242.

82. Ibid., 241.

83. Quoted in Feuersenger, *Die garantierte Gleichberechtigung,* 50; and "SPD Frauentag in Wuppertal," *Neuer Vorwärts* 1, no. 11 (11 September 1948), 6; and comments at SPD Reichsfrauenkonferenz, reported in *Genossin* 11 (1948): 123.

84. Quoted in Niclauss, *Demokratiegründung,* 179.

85. PR, HA, 21. Sitzung, 7 December 1948, 242.

86. PR, AfG, 29. Sitzung, 4 December 1948, 29, BA, Z5/35.

87. Ibid., 52.

88. Ibid., 14.

89. PR, HA, 21. Sitzung, 7 December 1948, 243.

90. On the fascinating use of metaphors of containment to describe both families and foreign policy in the fifties, see May, *Homeward Bound*.

91. Adolf Blomeyer, PR, AfG, 29. Sitzung, 4 December 1948, 18, BA, Z5/35.

92. Ibid., 36.

93. PR, HA, 7 December 1948, 21. Sitzung, 246. In general, Merkl, *Origin of the West German Republic*, 137.

94. PR, AfG, 29. Sitzung, 4 December 1948, 7, BA, Z/35; PR, HA, 21. Sitzung, 7 December 1948, 247.

95. PR, AfG, 29. Sitzung, 4 December 1948, 7–9, 61–65, BA, Z5/35. In general, see Gutscher, *Die Entwicklung der FDP*, 37–38; and the FDP's official position on this question in the "Bremer Platform" of 1949 in Flechtheim, *Dokumente zur parteipolitischen Entwicklung in Deutschland*, vol. 2, part 1, 282.

96. PR, HA, 21. Sitzung, 7 December 1948, 246.

97. Rudolf Morsey, "Adenauer und Kardinal Frings 1945–1949," 497–98; Hans-Peter Schwarz, *Adenauer* 1: 593–94.

98. Merkl, *Origin of the West German Republic*, 153–54; and Blessing, " 'Deutschland in Not,' " 106.

99. Leibholz and Mangoldt, *Entstehungsgeschichte der Artikel des Grundgesetzes*, 92–98.

100. By 1960, women constituted 45 percent of the labor force, and women's labor force participation rate was at 69.8 percent, 20 percent higher than the comparable figure in the West. See Herta Kuhrig and Wulfram Speigner, "Gleichberechtigung der Frau: Aufgaben und ihre Realisierung in der DDR," in *Wie emanzipiert sind die Frauen in der DDR?*, ed. Herta Kuhrig and Wulfram Speigner, 52.

101. Friedel Schubert, *Die Frau in der DDR: Ideologie und konzeptionelle Ausgestaltung ihrer Stellung in Beruf und Familie*, 50–54, 90–91; Gesine Obertreis, *Familienpolitik in der DDR 1945–1980*, 51–61 and passim; Gottfried Zieger, "Die Entwicklung des Familienrechts in der DDR mit Berlin (Ost)," in *Das Familienrecht in beiden deutschen Staaten: Rechtsentwicklung, Rechtsvergleich, Kollisionsprobleme*, 41–67; Hilde Benjamin, *Vorschläge zum neuen deutschen Familienrecht;* idem, "Familie und Familienrecht in der Deutschen Demokratischen Republik," 448–57; and in general, Ina Merkl, *. . . und Du, Frau an der Werkbank: Die DDR in den 50er Jahren*.

102. Quoted in Schewick, *Die katholische Kirche*, 130 (1 March 1950).

103. Hermann von Mangoldt, *Das Bonner Grundgesetz*, 71.

104. Ibid.

105. Renner (KPD), HA, 17. Sitzung, 3 December 1948, 209.

106. Hagemann, *Frauenalltag und Männerpolitik*, 531–43.

107. See Carole Pateman, "The Patriarchal Welfare State," in *Democracy and the Welfare State*, ed. Amy Gutman, 250.

108. Cynthia Harrison, *On Account of Sex: The Politics of Women's Issues, 1945–1968*, 7–23; and in general, Leila Rupp and Verta Taylor, *Survival in the Doldrums: The American Women's Rights Movement, 1945 to the 1960s;* and

Myra Marx Ferree, "Equality and Autonomy: Feminist Politics in the United States and West Germany," in *The Women's Movement of the United States and Western Europe: Consciousness, Political Opportunity, and Public Policy,* ed. Mary Fainsod Katzenstein and Carol McClurg Mueller, 172–95.

CHAPTER THREE

1. Klaje to Verfassungsgebender Rat [*sic*], 8 December 1948, BA, Z5/110.
2. *Frauenwelt,* Heft 13/1948, quoted in Seeler, "Ehe, Familie und andere Lebensformen," 102–106; and "Mutter der Mutterfamilie: Die Männer leben am Rande," *Der Spiegel,* 29 January 1949, 4–5. On Stöcker, see Ann Taylor Allen, "Mothers of the New Generation: Adele Schreiber, Helene Stöcker and the Evolution of a German Idea of Motherhood, 1900–1914," 418–38; and Amy Hackett, "Helene Stöcker: Left-Wing Intellectual and Sex Reformer," in Bridenthal et al., *When Biology Became Destiny,* 109–30.
3. Klaje to BMJ, 11 August 1951, BA, B141/2028.
4. Ulla Grum, " 'Sie leben froher—Sie leben besser mit Constanze': Eine Frauenzeitschrift im Wandel des Jahrzehnts," in Delille and Grohn, *Perlonzeit,* 139.
5. For a succinct discussion of the campaign, see Eschenburg, *Jahre der Besatzung,* quotations from 529–33.
6. Wolfram Müller-Freienfels, "Zur Kodifikation des Familienrechts," in *Seminar: Familie und Familienrecht,* vol. 1, ed. Spiros Simitis and Gisela Zenz, 126–31; and on the creation of the Bundesverfassungsgericht, Donald P. Kommers, *The Constitutional Jurisprudence of the Federal Republic of Germany,* 6, 46; idem, *Judicial Politics in West Germany: A Study of the Federal Constitutional Court;* and Michael Fronz, "Das Bundesverfassungsgericht im politischen System der BRD: Eine Analyse der Beratungen im Parlamentarischen Rat," 629–82.
7. Carol Smart, *The Ties that Bind: Law, Marriage and the Reproduction of Patriarchal Relations,* 47–48; Hilary Land, "Who Still Cares about the Family? Recent Developments in Income Maintenance, Taxation and Family Law," in *Women's Welfare, Women's Rights,* ed. Jane Lewis, 65.
8. Eschenburg, *Jahre der Besatzung,* 529–33; and Klaus Gotto, "Die deutschen Katholiken in der Adenauer-Ära," in *Katholizismus im politischen System der Bundesrepublik 1949–1963,* ed. Albrecht Langer, 17.
9. Jürgen Falter, "Kontinuität und Neubeginn: Die Bundestagswahl 1949 zwischen Weimar und Bonn," 236–63.
10. Gabriele Bremme, *Die politische Rolle der Frau in Deutschland: Eine Untersuchung über den Einfluss der Frauen bei Wahlen und ihre Teilnahme in Partei und Parlament,* 78, 239; and on the Weimar background, Boak, "Women in Weimar Germany," 157.
11. *Protokoll der Verhandlungen des Parteitages der Sozialdemokratischen Partei Deutschlands vom 21. bis 25. Mai 1950 in Hamburg,* 45.
12. *Gleichheit* 13 (1950): 207.
13. Koonz, *Mothers in the Fatherland,* 110; Bridenthal and Koonz, "Beyond Kinder, Küche, Kirche," 37, 42–43.

14. Bremme, *Die politische Rolle der Frau in Deutschland,* 131, 137; and Hannelore Mabry, *Unkraut ins Parlament: Die Bedeutung weiblicher parlamentarischer Arbeit für die Emanzipation der Frau,* 39–43.

15. "Aufzeichnung des Staatspräsidenten und CDU-Vorsitzenden von Württemberg-Hohenzollern, Dr. Gebhard Müller, über die Beratungen führender Unionspolitiker am 21. August 1949 in Rhöndorf," published in Rudolf Morsey, "Die Rhöndorfer Weichenstellung vom 21. August 1949," 521–22; and Günter Müchler, *CDU/CSU: Das schwierige Bündnis,* 93–94.

16. Adenauer to Verbandspräses Hermann-Josef Schmitt, 31 August 1949, in *Adenauer Briefe 1945–1951,* ed. Hans Peter Mensing, 99. See also Schwarz, *Adenauer* 1: 624–25.

17. *Verhandlungen des achtunddreissigsten deutschen Juristentages in Frankfurt a.M. 1950,* B2.

18. Gabriele Strecker, *Gesellschaftspolitische Frauenarbeit in Deutschland: 20 Jahre Deutscher Frauenring,* 79–80.

19. Gotthelf to Bähnisch, 28 April 1947, ASD, PV Akten, Alter Bestand, Nr. 0244.

20. John, *Politics and the Law in Late Nineteenth-Century Germany,* 3. In addition, for the national lawyers' association, debating family-law reform meant returning to the unfinished business of Weimar; reform of marriage and family law had been a central preoccupation of the judicial congress in the twenties.

21. *Verhandlungen des achtunddreissigsten deutschen Juristentages,* B1-B2.

22. Erna Scheffler, "Die Stellung der Frau in Familie und Gesellschaft im Wandel der Rechtsordnung seit 1918," in Frandsen, Huffmann, and Kuhn, *Frauen in Wissenschaft und Politik,* 88; and *Verhandlungen des achtunddreissigsten deutschen Juristentages,* B55.

23. Comments of Curtius, *Verhandlungen des achtunddreissigsten deutschen Juristentages,* B74.

24. "Stellungnahme des Rats der Evangelischen Kirche in Deutschland zu den Fragen der Revision des Ehe- und Familienrechts," addressed to Dehler [n.d., probably early 1952], PA, I/1035B.

25. "Entwurf eines Gesetzes über die Gleichberechtigung von Mann und Frau auf dem Gebiete des bürgerlichen Rechts und über die Wiederherstellung der Rechtseinheit auf dem Gebiete des Familienrechts (Familienrechtsgesetz)," Deutscher Bundestag, 1. Wahlperiode, Drucksache Nr. 3802, 46.

26. The quotations are respectively from *VDBT,* [1.] Deutscher Bundestag, 20. und 21. Sitzung, 2 December 1949, 624–25, and 627–28. See also Margot Kalinke, "Die Frau als Staatsbürgerin," *Frau im Beruf: Nachrichten des Verbandes der weiblichen Angestellten* 2, no. 9 (1952): 1–2.

27. Grete Thiele, *VDBT,* [1.] Deutscher Bundestag, 19. Sitzung, 1 December 1949, 567; also the petition of the Demokratischer Frauenbund, Landesorganisation Hessen, to the Bundestag, 31 August 1952, PA, II/409B2. The Demokratischer Frauenbund was closely tied to the German Communist party.

28. Katholiken-Ausschuss Hamburg to chair of the Bundestag Ausschuss für das Familienrechtsgesetz, 21 November 1953, PA, II/409B3; and Katholiken-Ausschuss in der Stadt Essen to Dehler, 13 January 1953, ibid.

29. Karl Weber, "Kurzprotokoll der 1. Sitzung des Unterausschusses 'Fa-

milienrechtsgesetz' des (23.) Ausschusses für Rechtswesen und Verfassungsrecht am 5. Februar 1953," 3, PA; and protocol of a meeting on family reform between representatives of BMI and BMJ, 12 May 1952, BA, B141/2060. The protocols of all parliamentary committees and sub-committees were mimeographed. A complete set is available in PA.

30. *Verhandlungen des achtunddreissigsten deutschen Juristentages*, B7.

31. Much of the preliminary discussion of reform was sparked by a widely distributed white paper (*Denkschrift*), commissioned by the BMJ and written by Maria Hagemeyer, a Catholic and a legal expert. It was released in 1951. See "Denkschrift über die Anpassung des geltenden Familienrechts an den Grundsatz der Gleichberechtigung von Mann und Frau (Art. 3 Abs. 2 GG) erforderliche Gesetzesänderungen," PA, I/1035B; also Dehler to Adenauer, 15 June 1951, BA, B141/2055. For a sampling of responses, see *Informationen für die Frau*, no. 2 (1952).

32. See the summary of reform proposals in Hagemeyer, "Denkschrift."

33. See Gotthelf's remarks to the SPD party congress in Dortmund, *Neuer Vorwärts*, 3 October 1952, 11.

34. "Zur Eherechtsreform," *Gleichheit* 15 (1952): 12.

35. Hildegard Krüger, "Gedanken zur Familienrechtsreform," 543; also Emmy Meyer-Laule (SPD) and Herta Ilk (FDP), *VDBT*, [1.] Deutscher Bundestag, 239. Sitzung, 27 November 1952, 10060, 10064; and Dorothea Karsten, the specialist for women's affairs in the BMI, memo of 12 July 1952, BA, B106/3432.

36. "Stenographisches Protokoll über die 4. Sitzung des Unterausschusses 'Familienrechtsgesetz' des Ausschusses für Rechtswesen und Verfassungsrecht," 11 February 1953, 17, PA, I/1035A1.

37. Ibid., 12.

38. *VDBT*, [1.] Deutscher Bundestag, 239. Sitzung, 27 November 1952, 11060.

39. "Frau und Familie," *Gleichheit* 15 (1952): 329.

40. Quotations are from, respectively, "Hirtenwort der deutschen Erzbischöfe und Bischöfe zur Neuordnung des Ehe- und Familienrechtes," 30 January 1953, signed by Frings, PA, I/1035B; and Idamarie Solltmann quoted in Franz Josef Finke, "Das neue Familienrecht im Entwurf," *Das Parlament* no. 35 (1952), 2–3, 6.

41. "Absage an 'Sozialisierung' der Familie," *Westfalenpost*, 14 January 1953; and Vorsitzender der Fuldaer Bischofskonferenz (Frings) to Dehler, 12 January 1952, BA, B141/2057, republished in *Informationen für die Frau*, no. 2 (1952).

42. "Daten zum Leben von Frau Dr. Luise Rehling," a brief obituary in *Informationen für die Frau*, no. 6 (1964).

43. *VDBT*, [1.] Deutscher Bundestag, 239. Sitzung, 27 November 1952, 11058.

44. Ibid., 11059. This was a defining characteristic of a democratic political order.

45. Comments of Wahl, *Verhandlungen des achtunddreissigsten deutschen Juristentages*, B78. And on the Nazi "women's labor service," Jill Stephenson, "Women's Labor Service in Nazi Germany," 241–65; and Lore Kleiber,

" 'Wo ihr seid, da soll die Sonne scheinen!'"—Der Frauenarbeitsdienst am Ende der Weimarer Republik und im Nationalsozialismus," in *Mutterkreuz und Arbeitsbuch: Zur Geschichte der Frauen in der Weimarer Republik und im Nationalsozialismus*, ed. Frauengruppe Faschismusforschung, 188–214.

46. See, e.g., Helene Weber, *VDBT*, [1.] Deutscher Bundestag, 266. Sitzung, 13 May 1953, 13051; Udo Wengst, *Beamtentum zwischen Reform und Tradition: Beamtengesetzgebung in der Gründungsphase der Bundesrepublik Deutschland, 1948–1953*, 295; Hildegard Krüger, "Die Rechtsstellung der Beamtin," *Informationen für die Frau*, no. 4 (1952): 3–7; and Scheffler's comments at *Verhandlungen des achtunddreissigsten deutschen Juristentages*, B12.

47. Wilhelm Poetter, "Ein Wort zur Besinnung im Streit über die Gleichberechtigung von Mann und Frau," *Rheinisches Monatsblatt* (January 1952), republished in *Informationen für die Frau*, no. 1, Anlage C (1953): 1.

48. See, e.g., Herta Ilk, *VDBT*, [1.] Deutscher Bundestag, 239. Sitzung, 27 November 1952, 11063–64.

49. *VDBT*, [1.] Deutscher Bundestag, 44. Sitzung, 2 March 1950, 1490.

50. "Entwurf eines Gesetzes über die Gleichberechtigung von Mann und Frau," Deutscher Bundestag, [1.] Wahlperiode, Drucksache Nr. 3802, 6–7, 46–48.

51. *VDBT*, [1.] Deutscher Bundestag, 239. Sitzung, 27 November 1952, 11054.

52. Emmy Diemer to Dehler, 26 November 1953, ADL, DA/119.

53. See notes on a meeting between representatives of the BMJ and BMI, 20 May 1952, BA, B106/3432.

54. "Denkschrift des Deutschen Frauenrings zum Kabinettsentwurf eines Gesetzes über die Gleichberechtigung von Mann und Frau auf dem Gebiete des bürgerlichen Rechts und über die Wiederherstellung der Rechtseinheit auf dem Gebiete des Familienrechts (Familienrechtsgesetz)," 23 December 1952, written by Waldemar Wolle and Hildegard Wolle-Egenolf; also Deutscher Frauenring to Adenauer, 1 September 1952, BA, NL Lüders/225; "Niederschrift über die Tagung mit den zentralen Frauenorganisationen am 10. und 11.6.1952," organized by BMI, BA, NL Lüders/224; Dorothea Karsten memo on the meeting, 11 June 1952, BA, B106/3432; Deutscher Frauenring to BMJ, 15 October 1951, BA, B141/2028; and Deutscher Akademikerinnenbund to Bundesrat, August 1952, BA, NL Lüders/224.

55. "Kurzbericht über die Tagung des Bundesfrauenausschusses, Königswinter 5./6. Juli 1952," ACDP, IV-003-22/1; the report of the Presse- und Informationsamt der Bundesregierung on the same meeting, BA, B136/540; and the notes of Regierungsrat Tauche, 8 July 1952, BA, B106/3432. See also, the article by Else Bröckelschen, a member of the CDU parliamentary delegation, "Über die Gleichverantwortung der Frau," *Informationen für die Frau*, no. 2, Anlage C (1952): 6; and Ingeborg Marx, "Gleichberechtigung im Eherecht: Richtige und falsche Auffassungen," *Sonderbeilage: Frau in der Union*, Informations-Dienst der Christlich-Demokratischen und Christlich-Sozialen Union Deutschlands, no. 61, 2 August 1952, copy in BA, NL Lüders/227.

56. Evangelische Frauenarbeit in Deutschland, 1 June 1951, BA, B106/43313; also Evangelische Frauenarbeit in Deutschland to Bishop Dibelius, re-

printed in *Informationen für die Frau*, no. 2, Anlage D (1952): 16–19; and Dibelius, as head of the Rat der Evangelischen Kirche in Deutschland, to Dehler, 22 March 1952, ibid. The legal committee of Evangelische Frauenarbeit was headed by Elisabeth Schwarzhaupt, a member of the CDU, elected to the Bundestag in 1953, and in 1961 the first woman to be named to a cabinet post as Minister of Health. See "Elisabeth Schwarzhaupt (1901–1986)," in Frandsen, Huffmann, and Kuhn, *Frauen in Wissenschaft und Politik*, 100.

57. Käte Burchard to Dehler, 15 August 1952, BA, B141/2031.

58. Melitta Schöpf to Dehler, 8 January 1953, BA, B141/2022.

59. See the report of Maria Hagemeyer's meeting with a commission of legal experts, created by the Fulda Conference of Bishops, to explore family-law reform proposals, 9 November 1950, BA, B141/2017.

60. Memo from Massfeller (BMJ), 3 November 1951, BA, B141/2055.

61. Bosch to Maria Hagemeyer, 17 September 1951, BA, B141/2029; and F. W. Bosch, *Familienrechtsreform*, 57 and passim.

62. Bosch, "Zum Stand der Erörterungen über eine Familienrechtsreform," *Deutsche Tagespost*, 29 December 1952; and idem, *Familienrechtsreform*. See also Ivo Zeiger, "Gleichberechtigung der Frau," *Stimmen der Zeit*, no. 150 (1951/52): 113–22, 176–86; Günter Beitzke, "Gleichberechtigung und Familienrechtsreform," *Juristenzeitung* 7 (1952): 744–46; and Bosch's remarks, *Verhandlungen des achtunddreissigsten deutschen Juristentages*, B61–62.

63. Memo on this meeting, 4 April 1952, from Finke, BMJ, BA, B141/2057; and "Stellungnahme des Rats der Evangelischen Kirche in Deutschland zu den Fragen der Revision des Ehe- und Familienrechts" (undated, probably 1952), PA, I/1035B; also, Frings to Dehler, 15 April 1952, BA, B141/2057; in response to Dehler's letter of 2 February 1952, PA, I/1035B.

64. Spieler to Herrn Staatssekretäre, reporting the cabinet meeting of 15 July 1952, BA, B136/540; also Dehler's notes on the cabinet meeting of 24 June 1952, dated 27 June 1952, BA, B141/2060; his memo on the intervention of the Fulda Bishop's Conference, 25 June 1952, BA, B136/540; and his summary of his response in a personal letter to Adenauer, 10 July 1952, ADL, DA/117.

65. Adenauer to Bundesminister and Chef des Bundespräsidialamtes, 2 September 1952, BA, B106/3432; and Spieler's draft memo, BA, B136/540.

66. "230. Kabinettssitzung am Freitag, den 27. Juni 1952," in *Die Kabinettsprotokolle der Bundesregierung*, vol. 5 (1952), ed. Kai von Jena, 408; Dehler's notes on this meeting, dated 27 June 1952, BA, B141/2060; and his response to Staatssekretär of Bundeskanzleramt, articulating his objections to Adenauer's position, 4 July 1952, ibid. Spieler moved on to a seat on the Bundesgerichtshof in 1954.

67. Hermann Glaser, *Kulturgeschichte der Bundesrepublik Deutschland* 2: 18.

68. "235. Kabinettssitzung am Dienstag den 15. Juli 1952," in Jena, *Die Kabinettsprotokolle 5*: 454–55; Dorothea Karsten for BMI, 12 July 1952, BA, B106/3432; and Adenauer's reiteration of his position in a letter to cabinet members, 2 September 1952, BA, B106/3432.

69. *VDBT*, [1.] Deutscher Bundestag, 239. Sitzung, 27 November 1952, 11052.

70. Ibid., 11062.

71. For a sample of responses from women's organizations, see "Stellung-nahme zur Ehe- und Familienrechtsreform," *Informationen für die Frau*, no. 2 (1952): 3–19; ibid., no. 7 (1952); and the extensive collection of petitions from organizations and individuals in PA, I/1035B; also the memo on the meeting of the Bundesfrauenausschuss of the CDU, 5–6 July 1952, BA, B136/540; Walter Dirks, "Soll er ihr Herr sein? Die Gleichberechtigung der Frau und die Reform des Familienrechts," 825–37.

72. Meyer-Laule, *VDBT*, [1.] Deutscher Bundestag, 239. Sitzung, 27 November 1952, 11060; and Nadig, ibid., 11062.

73. Ibid., 11065.

74. Krüger, "Gedanken zur Familienrechtsreform," 543; and idem, "Die Nichtverwirklichung der Gleichberechtigung im Regierungsentwurf zur Fami-lienrechtsreform," *Juristenzeitung* 7 (1952): 613–17; also the angry protest over Adenauer's action, Deutscher Frauenring to Adenauer, 1 September 1952, BA, NL Lüders/225.

75. "Zur Eingabe der Fuldaer Bischofskonferenz an den deutschen Bundes-tag zur Reform des Ehe- und Familienrechts," 21 April 1953, ADL, A5/5; also "Protokoll der Frauenausschuss-Sitzung im Bad-Hoffen/Rhein am 20./ 21.9.52," ADL, A5/2.

76. See, e.g., the comments of Helene Weber, *VDBT*, [1.] Deutscher Bundes-tag, 239. Sitzung, 27 November 1952, 11071; also "Die katholische Frauenbe-wegung in der sich wandelnden Zeit," 25–27 July 1952, summary in BA, B211/ 112; "Bericht über die Generalversammlung des katholischen deutschen Frauen-bundes," *Informationen für die Frau*, no. 7 (1952): 4–5; and petitions of the Katholischer Deutscher Frauenbund, Rheydt, 19 June 1952, BA, B141/2031; and Katholiken-Ausschuss Hamburg, 15 November 1952, HStAS, EA1/4/1380/2.

77. "Hirtenwort der deutschen Erzbischöfe," 30 January 1953, PA, I/ 1035B; and Vorsitzender der Fuldaer Bischofskonferenz [Frings] to Deutscher Bundestag, 30 January 1953, BA, NL Lüders/224.

78. "Protokoll der 250. Sitzung des Ausschusses für Rechtswesen und Ver-fassungsrecht am 15. April 1953," 9.

79. "Protokoll der 256. Sitzung des Ausschusses für Rechtswesen und Ver-fassungsrecht am 8. Mai 1953," 9–10, 15. The reference is probably to Hans Globke, one of Adenauer's closest advisors, who was among the commentators on the Nuremberg Laws of 1935. Glaser, *Kulturgeschichte* 2: 22. See the gen-erally sympathetic account in Klaus Gotto, ed., *Der Staatssekretär Adenauers: Persönlichkeit und politisches Wirken Hans Globkes*. The "declaration of war" was attributed explicitly to Gisela Praetorius in her speech to the fourth national congress of the CDU in April 1953. See *Deutschland, sozialer Rechtsstaat im geeinten Europa*, 168–73.

80. Walter Strauss for BMJ, "Protokoll der 239. Sitzung des Ausschusses für Rechtswesen und Verfassungsrecht am 27. Februar 1953," 7.

81. Annemarie Heiler (CDU), *VDBT*, [1.] Deutscher Bundestag, 258. Sit-zung, 26 March 1953, 12522; Hans Ewers (DP), ibid., 12523.

82. "Protokoll der Bundesfrauen-Ausschusssitzung [FDP] in Bonn, am 16./ 17.4 1953," ADL, A5/5; also Ilk to heads of women's organizations in the FDP,

11.3.53, in "FDP, Bundesfrauensekretariat, Rundschreiben Nr. 13/53," 25 March 1953, ADL, A5/6; and Vereinigung weiblicher Juristen und Volkswirte, e.V., 9 May 1953, Rundschreiben Nr. 15, BA, NL Lüders/224.

83. "Protokoll der 256. Sitzung des Ausschusses für Rechtswesen und Verfassungsrecht am 8. Mai 1953," 9.

84. Club berufstätiger Frauen, Karlsruhe, e.V., to Dehler, 26 November 1953, ADL, DA/119; also Marie-Elisabeth Lüders to Brinkert, 10 March 1953, ADL, A5/73; Heidi Flitz (Wilhelmshaven) to Lüders, 25 November 1953, BA, NL Lüders/224; and Landesgruppe der FDP, Landesverband Hamburg, December 1952, BA, NL Lüders/226.

85. Bremme, *Die politische Rolle der Frau in Deutschland*, 90–98.

86. "Bericht über den Lehrgang 'Die Frau in der Gemeinde' vom 28.10.–3.11.53 in Haus Schwalbach," BA, NL Lüders/188. There is a revealing collection of assessments of the election outcome by local-level women activists in the SPD, ASD, PV Akten, Alter Bestand, Nr. 0283. See also Lotte Böhne, head of the Club berufstätiger Frauen in Karlsruhe, to Dehler, 26 November 1953, ADL, DA/119.

87. Bremme, *Die politische Rolle der Frau in Deutschland*, 93–94. See also "Hirtenwort der deutschen Bischöfe zur Bundestagswahl am 6. September 1953," in *Katholische Kirche im demokratischen Staat: Hirtenworte der deutschen Bischöfe zu wichtigen Fragen der Zeit und zu den Bundestagswahlen 1945 bis 1980*, ed. Alfons Fitzek, 90–93. And on the background of Catholic women's organizations in Weimar, Phayer, *Protestant and Catholic Women in Nazi Germany*; Gellott and Phayer, "Dissenting Voices," 91–114; and Doris Kaufmann, "Vom Vaterland zum Mutterland: Frauen im katholischen Milieu der Weimarer Republik," in *Frauen suchen ihre Geschichte: Historische Studien zum 19. und 20. Jahrhundert*, ed. Karin Hausen, 250–75.

88. "Des Papstes Garde," *Der Spiegel*, 15 September 1954: 8–15.

89. See Wuermeling, "Letzter Appell an Bonn," *Rheinischer Merkur*, 9 April 1949; Süsterhenn to Wuermeling, 7 April 1949, ACDP, I-221-004; Wuermeling to Frings, 2 May 1949, ibid.; and Wuermeling to Maassen, 30 April 1949, ibid.

90. Waldemar Wolle und Hildegard Wolle-Egenolf, "Der Gleichberechtigungsgrundsatz von Mann und Frau (Art. 3 Abs. 2 des Bonner Grundgesetzes) im neuen deutschen Familienrecht" (n.d.), BA, B141/2026. Wolle and Wolle-Egenolf were also the authors of the official response of the Deutscher Frauenring to the government's draft. See above, note 54. Also the critical assessment of Wuermeling by Lisa Albrecht and Adolf Menzel, *VDBT*, [1.] Deutscher Bundestag, 44. Sitzung, 2 March 1950, 1480, 1488–89.

91. Quotations from Hans Heinrich, "Wuermelings Sittengesetz gegen Gleichberechtigung," *Frankfurter Rundschau*, 29 October 1953.

92. Franz Josef Wuermeling, "Für den Schutz der Familie," *Union in Deutschland*, no. 86, 4 November 1953, copy in ACDP, I-221-004; also transcript of interview with Nordwestdeutscher Rundfunk, 10 November 1953, ACDP, I-221-017.

93. *Rheinischer Merkur*, 1 July 1950, quoted in Gunther Mai, *Westliche Sicherheitspolitik im Kalten Krieg: Der Korea-Krieg und die deutsche Wiederbewaffnung 1950*, 103.

94. Quotations, from 1948 and 1946 respectively, are in Gottfried Niedhardt and Normen Altmann, "Zwischen Beurteilung und Verurteilung: Die Sowjetunion im Urteil Konrad Adenauers," in *Adenauer und die Deutsche Frage,* ed. Josef Foschepoth, 102.

95. Hans-Jürgen Schröder, "Kanzler der Alliierten? Die Bedeutung der USA für die Aussenpolitik Adenauers," in *Adenauer und die Deutsche Frage,* ed. Josef Foschepoth, 118–45; and in general, Josef Foschepoth, "Westintegration statt Wiedervereinigung: Adenauers Deutschlandpolitik 1949–1955," in ibid., 29–60; and Hermann-Josef Rupieper, *Der besetzte Verbündete: Die amerikanische Deutschlandpolitik 1949–1955,* 41–139.

96. "Denkschrift des deutschen Frauenrings," PA, I/1035B.

97. Headline of report of a meeting of Catholic journalists in early 1953, "Absage an 'Sozialisierung' der Familie," *Westfalenpost,* 14 January 1953.

98. Schröder, "Kanzler der Alliierten?" 126.

99. Quoted in Mai, *Westliche Sicherheitspolitik im Kalten Krieg,* 135–39. In general, see Klessmann, *Die doppelte Staatsgründung,* 210–12, 232–34; and Bark and Gress, *A History of West Germany* 1: 258–60; and Klaus von Schubert, *Wiederbewaffnung und Westintegration: Die innere Auseinandersetzung um die militärische und aussenpolitische Orientierung der Bundesrepublik, 1950–1952,* 62–73.

100. Quoted in Bark and Gress, *A History of West Germany,* 1: 279–80.

101. Beitzke, "Gleichberechtigung und Familienrechtsreform," 744–46; Hans Schneider, "Zwischenbilanz im Gleichberechtigungsstreit," *Juristenzeitung* 8 (1953): 590–92; Hans Heinrich, "Wuermelings Sittengesetz gegen Gleichberechtigung," *Frankfurter Rundschau,* 29 October 1953.

102. Benno Mugdan, *Die gesamten Materialien zum bürgerlichen Gesetzbuch für das deutsche Reich* 4: 1284, protocols of Bundestag sessions of 24–25 June 1896.

103. Ibid., 1309–1310.

104. The charges are made in Beitzke, "Gleichberechtigung und Familienrechtsreform," 744–46.

105. Greve, "Stenographisches Protokoll der 8. Sitzung des Unterausschusses 'Familienrechtsgesetz' des Ausschusses für Rechtswesen und Verfassungsrecht, Bonn, Freitag, den 13. Februar 1953," 6, PA, I/1035A2. See also Elsbeth Weichmann, "Um die Gleichberechtigung," *Gleichheit* 13 (1950): 143–44.

106. For interesting parallels on the other dimensions of SPD policy, see Klaus Erdmenger, "Adenauer, die Deutsche Frage und die sozialdemokratische Opposition," in Foschepoth, *Adenauer und die Deutsche Frage,* 176.

CHAPTER FOUR

1. Foschepoth, "Zur deutschen Reaktion auf Niederlage und Besatzung," 161.

2. G[erhard] van Heukelum, "Staatliche Kinderbeihilfen: Ein Vorschlag," *Arbeitsblatt* (1949): 213–14; memo from Goldschmidt, BMA, reporting on meeting of an expert commission convened to discuss family allowances, 21 December 1949, BA, B153/733.

3. On the development of this concept under the Nazis, see Joan Campbell, *Joy in Work: The National Debate, 1800–1945*, 340–41; and Tröger, "The Creation of a Female Assembly-Line Proletariat," 259–61.

4. "Niederschrift über die vom Unterausschuss Kinderbeihilfen des Ausschusses für Arbeit und Sozialpolitik des Bundesrates einberufene Konferenz am 21.12.49," NWHStA, NW42/547; also Heukelum to Labor Minister Anton Storch, 7 December 1949, BA, B153/733.

5. Reinhold Schillinger, *Der Entscheidungsprozess beim Lastenausgleich 1945–1952;* Peter Paul Nahm, "Lastenausgleich und Integration der Vertriebenen und Geflüchteten," in Löwenthal and Schwarz, *Die zweite Republik,* 817–42; Peter Paul Nahm, *Der Lastenausgleich;* and Werner Abelshauser, *Die langen Fünfziger Jahre: Wirtschaft und Gesellschaft der Bundesrepublik Deutschland 1949–1966,* 33–42. The quotation is from Gerd Bucerius, "Rechnung für Hitlers Krieg: Lastenausgleich—die grösste Vermögensabgabe der Geschichte," *Die Zeit,* 13 April 1979, republished in Klessmann, *Die Doppelte Staatsgründung,* 493–95.

6. Gerhard Mackenroth, "Die Reform der Sozialpolitik durch einen deutschen Sozialplan," 56, 58.

7. *VDBT,* [1.] Deutscher Bundestag, 162. Sitzung, 13 September 1951, 6575.

8. Jacob Schiefer, representative of the Labor Ministry of North Rhine–Westphalia, in "Niederschrift über die vom Unterausschuss Kinderbeihilfen"; also his "Denkschrift über das Verhältnis der Alfu und Wohlu zum Lohn in Bezug auf ein Gesetz zur Gewährung von Kinderbeihilfe" (10 October 1949), BA, B153/733; Jacob Schiefer, "Kommt eine staatliche Kinderbeihilfe?" *Arbeit und Sozialpolitik* 3, no. 21 (1949): 1–5; and in general, Walter Auerbach, "Ein Übergangsgesetz über die Gewährung von Kinderbeihilfen," *Bundesarbeitsblatt* (1950): 11–14; a summary of proposals prepared in BMA, draft copy dated 19 February 1952, BA, B153/761; and Fritz Emil Bünger, *Familienpolitik in Deutschland: Neue Erkenntnisse über den Einfluss des sogenannten "Giesskannenprinzips" auf die Wirksamkeit sozialpolitischer Massnahmen,* 14.

9. Winkelheide, *VDBT,* [1.] Deutscher Bundestag, 60. Sitzung, 28 April 1950, 2202.

10. Winkelheide, *VDBT,* [1.] Deutscher Bundestag, 162. Sitzung, 13 September 1951, 6570–71.

11. Hammer, *VDBT,* [1.] Deutscher Bundestag, 60. Sitzung, 28 April 1950, 2204.

12. Memo from BMF, 15 December 1950, prepared by Rompe, BA, B153/733.

13. "Protokoll über die 149. Sitzung des Ausschusses für Sozialpolitik am Freitag, den 19. September 1952," 3. Höffner was coauthor of a white paper on the reform of social security, commissioned by Adenauer. See Hans Achinger, Joseph Höffner, Hans Muthesius, Ludwig Neundörfer, *Neuordnung der sozialen Leistungen.*

14. *VDBT,* [1.] Deutscher Bundestag, 60. Sitzung, 28 April 1950, 2197–2206; also ibid., 162. Sitzung, 13 September 1951, 6569–78; and on BMF's position, the memos from Wilhelm Herschel, BMA, 26 April 1950, and Jüngst,

18 November 1950, BA, B153/733; Schäffer (BMF) to BMA, 22 January 1951, ibid; and "Zur Frage der staatlichen Kinderbeihilfen," *Der Arbeitgeber* no. 12 (1951): 8–9.

15. Ludwig Erhard, quoted in *Dritter Parteitag der Christlich-Demokratischen Union Deutschlands, Berlin, 17.–19. Oktober 1952*, 202; echoed by the CDU's Peter Horn, "Kurzprotokoll der 151. Sitzung des Ausschusses für Sozialpolitik am Freitag, den 3. Oktober 1952," 12.

16. Hammer, *VDBT*, [1.] Deutscher Bundestag, 60. Sitzung, 28 April 1950, 2204; and 162. Sitzung, 13 September 1951, 6575; also Wilhelm Polligkeit, "Kurzprotokoll der 67. Sitzung des Ausschusses Nr. 21—Ausschuss für Sozialpolitik—am Donnerstag, den 4. Januar 1951," 4.

17. Hammer, *VDBT*, [1.] Deutscher Bundestag, 60. Sitzung, 28 April 1950, 2204.

18. Brauksiepe, *Dritter Parteitag der Christlich-Demokratischen Union Deutschlands*, 67–68.

19. Willi Richter, chair of the Bundestag committee on Social Policy, *VDBT*, [1.] Deutscher Bundestag, 60. Sitzung, 28 April 1950, 2198; also Richter in *Protokoll: Ausserordentlicher Bundeskongress des Deutschen Gewerkschaftsbundes, Essen, 22. und 23. Juni 1951*, 67; and Ludwig Preller in *Protokoll der Verhandlungen des Parteitages der sozialdemokratischen Partei Deutschlands vom 21. bis 25. Mai 1950 in Hamburg*, 197. The support of the national trade-union movement for family allowances was cited repeatedly in the SPD's defense of these proposals.

20. Karl Osterkamp from the Wirtschaftswissenschaftliches Institut of the trade unions, "Kurzprotokoll der 148. Sitzung des Ausschusses für Sozialpolitik am Freitag, den 12. September 1952," 19; Emma Schulze, from Arbeiterwohlfahrt, ibid., 16; Ludwig Preller, "Protokoll über die 149. Sitzung des Ausschusses für Sozialpolitik am Freitag, den 19. September 1952," 13; and Karl Osterkamp and Heinz Beykirch, "Soziallohn oder Kinderbeihilfen," *Mitteilungen des wirtschaftswissenschaftlichen Instituts der Gewerkschaften*, 4–10.

21. Margarete Glinka, "Die heilende Kraft des mütterlichen Lebensbezirks," *Gleichheit* 15 (1952): 247–49.

22. On the structure of tax deductions, see Walter Bogs, et al., *Soziale Sicherung: Sozialenquête in der Bundesrepublik Deutschland*, 315–17.

23. This position is summarized in "Kurzprotokoll der 148. Sitzung des Ausschusses für Sozialpolitik am Freitag, den 12. September 1952," 16–24; see also Clara Döhring, "Wann endlich allgemeine Kinderbeihilfen?" *Gleichheit* 15 (1952): 6–8.

24. Döhring, "Kurzprotokoll der 151. Sitzung des Ausschusses für Sozialpolitik am Freitag, den 3. Oktober 1952," 10; and for the views of middle-class feminists supporting this position, Edith Hinze, "Was denken die Frauen über Familienausgleichskassen?" *Bundesarbeitsblatt* (1952): 263–65; Hinze for the Berliner Frauenbund 1945, to Bernhard Winkelheide, 9 September 1952, BA, NL Lüders/188; "Berliner Frauen zum Familienlastenausgleich," *Der Arbeitgeber*, no. 13 (1952): 493–94; and resolution of Frauenparlament Württemberg, 17 September 1950, PA, I/1053B.

25. Gregor Dettermann, *VDBT*, [1.] Deutscher Bundestag, 60. Sitzung, 28 April 1950, 2197; and "Probleme der Kinderbeihilfen (Familienausgleichs-

kassen)," *Bundesarbeitsblatt* (1952): 210, which provides a summary of this and all other proposals.

26. Wilhelm Herschel of BMA, as reported in a memo from Jüngst, 29 June 1953, BA, B153/738.

27. M. Rainer Lepsius, "Die Entwicklung der Soziologie nach dem zweiten Weltkrieg," in *Deutsche Soziologie seit 1945: Entwicklungsrichtungen und Praxisbezug,* ed. Günther Lüschen, 38; and Johannes Weyer, *Westdeutsche Soziologie 1945–1960: Deutsche Kontinuität und nordamerikanischer Einfluss,* 26.

28. Jüngst, BMA, 21 October 1953, report of Schelsky's speech to Deutscher Fürsorgetag, 15–17 October 1953, BA, B153/739.

29. Helmut Schelsky, "Die Aufgaben einer Familiensoziologie in Deutschland," 222–23.

30. Helmut Schelsky, "Die gegenwärtige Problemlage der Familiensoziologie," in *Soziologische Forschung in unserer Zeit,* ed. Karl Gustav Specht, 293–94. In his *Wandlungen der deutschen Familie in der Gegenwart,* probably the most influential analysis of the family in this period, Schelsky fully developed his position. Schelsky was also part of an advisory board that counseled the Ministry of Family Affairs on social policies affecting the family. See "Kinder haben—das darf keine Strafe sein!" *Das Parlament,* 23 November 1955, 3. Useful critical analyses of Schelsky are Heidi Rosenbaum, *Familie als Gegenstruktur zur Gesellschaft;* Yvonne Schütze, "Mütterliche Erwerbstätigkeit und wissenschaftliche Forschung," in *Frauensituation: Veränderungen in den letzten zwanzig Jahren,* ed. Yvonne Schütze and Ute Gerhard, 117–19; and Yvonne Schütze, *Die gute Mutter: Zur Geschichte des normativen Musters "Mutterliebe,"* 104–09.

31. Helmut Schelsky, "Die Gleichberechtigung der Frau und die Gesellschaftsordnung," *Sozialer Fortschritt* 1 (1952): 131.

32. Ibid.

33. Ibid.; and in general, idem, *Wandlungen der deutschen Familie in der Gegenwart,* 335–46; and idem, "Die gelungene Emanzipation," 360–70. See the critical response of Käthe Feuerstack, "War die Frauenbewegung familienfeindlich? Eine notwendige Auseinandersetzung," *Sozialer Fortschritt* 1 (1952): 264–67.

34. Schelsky, "Aufgaben," 219.

35. Helmut Schelsky, "Die Wandlungen der deutschen Familien in der Gegenwart und ihr Einfluss auf die Grundanschauungen der Sozialpolitik," *Sozialer Fortschritt* 1 (1952): 284, 287.

36. Schelsky elaborated on these themes at length later in the fifties. See, e.g., "Die Jugend in der industriellen Gesellschaft und die Arbeitslosigkeit," in *Arbeitslosigkeit und Berufsnot der Jugend,* vol. 2, ed. Helmut Schelsky, 297–98; idem, "Die Bedeutung des Schichtungsbegriffes für die Analyse der gegenwärtigen deutschen Gesellschaft (1952)," in *Auf der Suche nach der Wirklichkeit: Gesammelte Aufsätze,* 331–36; and idem, "Gesellschaftlicher Wandel (1956/61)," in ibid., 342, 348. His studies of the postwar family constituted the starting point for this theory, which prompted considerable contemporary discussion. See, e.g., Ralf Dahrendorf, *Society and Democracy in Germany,* 114–20; and Baumert, *Jugend der Nachkriegszeit,* 39–40; also Axel Schildt,

Notes to Pages 120–122

"Gründerjahre: Zur Entwicklung der westdeutschen Gesellschaft in der 'Ära Adenauer,' " 27–29; and Josef Mooser, "Abschied von der 'Proletarität,' " in Conze and Lepsius, *Sozialgeschichte der Bundesrepublik Deutschland,* 143–86; and in general, Hans Braun, "Helmut Schelskys Konzept der 'nivellierten Mittelstandsgesellschaft' und die Bundesrepublik der 50er Jahre," 199–223.

37. Schelsky, "Aufgaben," 225–26.

38. Lepsius, "Entwicklung," 33. See Gerhard Mackenroth, *Bevölkerungslehre: Theorie, Soziologie und Statistik der Bevölkerung.*

39. Mackenroth, "Reform," 39–75; "Niederschrift über die Sitzung des Arbeitsstabes Kinderbeihilfen am 18. Januar 1951," BA, B153/733.

40. Mackenroth, "Reform," 49.

41. Ibid., 59.

42. Achinger, Höffner, Muthesius, Neundörfer, *Neuordnung;* on the influence of the so-called Rothenfelser Denkschrift, see Hans Günter Hockerts, *Sozialpolitische Entscheidungen im Nachkriegsdeutschland: Alliierte und deutsche Sozialversicherungspolitik 1945 bis 1957,* 291–95.

43. H[ans] Achinger, S. Archinal, and W. Bangert, *Reicht der Lohn für Kinder?*

44. Hans Achinger, "Kinderbeihilfen, volkswirtschaftlich betrachtet," *Bundesarbeitsblatt* (1950): 45.

45. Ibid., 44.

46. Hans Achinger, "Kinderbeihilfen als Teil der Familienpolitik," *Sozialer Fortschritt* 1 (1952): 28–30.

47. Friedrich Burgdörfer, *Volk ohne Jugend: Geburtenschwund und Überalterung des deutschen Volkskörpers,* 270–73; idem, "Bevölkerungspolitische Erwägungen zum Umbau der Sozialversicherung," 318–25; idem, *Bevölkerungsentwicklung im Dritten Reich: Tatsachen und Kritik;* idem, *Kinder des Vertrauens: Bevölkerungspolitische Erfolge und Aufgaben im grossdeutschen Reich;* Burgdörfer, Alfred Kühn, and Martin Staemmler, *Erbkunde, Rassenpflege, Bevölkerungspolitik: Schicksalsfragen des deutschen Volkes;* and in general, Jill Stephenson, " 'Reichsbund der Kinderreichen'· The League of Large Families in the Population Policy of Nazi Germany," 351–75; Karin Hausen, "Mother's Day in the Weimar Republic," in Bridenthal, Grossmann, and Caplan, *When Biology Became Destiny,* 135–46; Mason, "Women in Germany, Part I," 85–86; Czarnowski, *Das kontrollierte Paar;* Proctor, *Racial Hygiene;* and Paul Weindling, *Health, Race and German Politics Between National Unification and Nazism,* 416–23, 528–30. These themes were by no means unique to Burgdörfer in the early fifties. See, e.g., Roderich von Ungern-Sternberg and Hermann Schubnell, *Grundriss der Bevölkerungswissenschaft (Demographie),* 540–41; and Roderich von Ungern-Sternberg, "Bevölkerungspolitische Erwägungen zur Familiengrösse," *Gewerkschaftliche Monatshefte* 5 (1954): 430–34.

48. A typescript of Burgdörfer's analysis, commissioned by the Bavarian FDP, is in ADL, DA/1161. For an earlier formulation of the same theme, Burgdörfer, *Kinder des Vertrauens,* 12. On the antinatal dimensions of Nazi racial politics, see in particular Bock, *Zwangssterilisation im Nationalsozialismus;*

and idem, "Antinatalism, Maternity, and Paternity in National Socialist Racism."

49. Typescript in ADL, DA/1161; also, after the passage of the law in 1954, Burgdörfer, "Die Wandlungen in der Bevölkerung: Ist Bestandserhaltung gesichert?" in a special issue of *Das Parlament*, 31 August 1955, 3, introduced by the Minister for Family Affairs, Franz-Josef Wuermeling; and Burgdörfer, "Bemerkungen zum Ausgleich der Familienlasten," *Ärztliche Mitteilungen*, 20 March 1954, copy in ASD, Gesellschaft für sozialen Fortschritt, no. 48.

50. James Woycke, *Birth Control in Germany, 1871–1933*, 134; and Proctor, *Racial Hygiene*, 19–20.

51. Ferdinand Oeter, "Organischer Ausgleich der Familienlasten," *Bundesarbeitsblatt* (1950): 273–74.

52. Ferdinand Oeter, "Frondienstpflicht der Familie?" 441; and "Protokoll über die 149. Sitzung des Ausschusses für Sozialpolitik am Freitag, den 19. September 1952," 8–10. Like Schelsky, Oeter was brought onto the advisory board that counseled the Ministry of Family Affairs.

53. Oeter, "Ausgleich der Familienlasten—Eine notwendige Klärung," *Bundesarbeitsblatt* (1952): 308.

54. Ferdinand Oeter, *Soziale Sicherheit für Deutschland*, 47.

55. In addition to the works already cited, see H. Beckendorff, *Ausgleich der Familienlasten? Finanzwirtschaftliche Probleme einer Kinderbeihilfe*, 93.

56. Wurzbacher, *Leitbilder gegenwärtigen deutschen Familienlebens*, 181–82; and in general, the insightful, critical analysis of Josef Mooser, *Arbeiterleben in Deutschland, 1900–1970: Klassenlagen, Kultur und Politik*, 157, 159.

57. Marta Gieselmann, "Gedanken über die Hausarbeit," *Gleichheit* 15 (1952): 244–45. For a perceptive discussion of the historical lineages of this ideology, see Gisela Bock and Barbara Duden, "Arbeit aus Liebe—Liebe als Arbeit: Zur Entstehung der Hausarbeit im Kapitalismus," in *Frauen und Wissenschaft: Beiträge zur Berliner Sommeruniversität für Frauen, Juli 1976*, 118–99; and Clair (Vickery) Brown, "Home Production for Use in a Market Economy," in *Rethinking the Family: Some Feminist Questions*, ed. Barrie Thorne and Marilyn Yalom, 151–67. And for the economic analysis of unpaid housework in the very different context of Weimar, see Mary Nolan, " 'Housework Made Easy': The Taylorized Housewife in Weimar Germany's Rationalized Economy," 549–77; and Stoehr, "Housework and Motherhood."

58. See the interesting reflections connecting the search for security in foreign and domestic policy in the fifties in Hans Braun, "Das Streben nach 'Sicherheit' in den 50er Jahren: Soziale und politische Ursachen und Erscheinungsweisen," 279–306.

59. Gerda Wagner, "Die alleinstehende berufstätige Frau," *Informationen für die Frau*, no. 7, Anlage B (1952).

60. *VDBT*, 2. Deutscher Bundestag, 3. Sitzung, 20 October 1953, 18.

61. "Des Papstes Garde," *Der Spiegel*, 15 September 1954, 8–15; Jutta Akrami-Göhren, "Die Familienpolitik im Rahmen der Sozialpolitik mit besonderer Berücksichtigung der Vorstellungen und der praktischen Tätigkeit der CDU," 89–91; and the immediate negative response, Erich Ollenhauer, *VDBT*, [1.] Deutscher Bundestag, 4. Sitzung, 28 October 1953, 45.

62. Bundesgeschäftsstelle der Christlichen Demokratischen Union Deutschlands, ed., *Deutschland, sozialer Rechtsstaat im geeinten Europa,* 67; also the speeches by Johannes Albers and Gisela Praetorius on the relationship between family policy and domestic politics, ibid., 126–28, 168–73; and Wuermeling, "Zwei Notwendigkeiten der Familienpolitik," *Bulletin,* no. 31 (1954): 255.

63. E.g., Jüngst, BMA, memo of 21 January 1954 on meeting of the CDU/CSU committee called on to aid the government in drafting legislation for *Kindergeld,* BA, B153/739; Wuermeling's remarks, "Niederschriften über die Sitzungen der CDU-Fraktion des 2. Bundestages vom 18. Mai–17. Dezember 1954," meeting of 20 September 1954, typescript, 398, ACDP, 08/001/1006/3; Wuermeling, *VDBT,* 2. Deutscher Bundestag, 44. Sitzung, 23 September 1954, 2119; *Fränkische Nachrichten* (Tauberbischofsheim, Nordbaden), 21 June 1954, copy in ACDP, I-221-005; and in general, Dietrich Haensch, *Repressive Familienpolitik: Sexualunterdrückung als Mittel der Politik,* 74–75, 117–22.

64. Louise Schroeder for the SPD, *VDBT,* 2. Deutscher Bundestag, 21. Sitzung, 1 April 1954, 735; and Marie-Elisabeth Lüders for the FDP, ibid., 738.

65. Schellenberg, *VDBT,* 2. Deutscher Bundestag, 44. Sitzung, 23 September 1954, 2117.

66. See Anton Storch, Minister of Labor, presenting the government's position, *Protokoll: 3. ordentlicher Bundeskongress Frankfurt a.M., 4. bis 9. Oktober 1954* [DGB], 348.

67. Pitz, *VDBT,* 2. Deutscher Bundestag, 21. Sitzung, 1 April 1954, 736–37.

68. CDU/CSU-Fraktion des Deutschen Bundestages, "Kurzprotokoll über die Sitzung des Unterausschusses Familienausgleichkassen (sic) vom 4.3.1954," ACDP, VIII-005-059-2.

69. Arnd Jessen, "Der Aufwand für Kinder in der Bundesrepublik im Jahre 1954," in *Familie und Sozialreform,* 107–11.

70. Krone to Alex.-Paul Fröde, 10 March 1955, ACDP, VIII-005-059-2.

71. "Schriftlicher Bericht des Ausschusses für Sozialpolitik (28. Ausschuss) (zu Drucksache 708) über den von der Fraktion der SPD eingebrachten Entwurf eines Gesetzes über die Gewährung von Kinderbeihilfen (Kinderbeihilfegesetz) (Drucksache 318) und den von der Fraktion der CDU/CSU eingebrachten Entwurf eines Gesetzes über die Gewährung von Kindergeld und die Errichtung von Familienausgleichskassen (Drucksache 319)," *VDBT,* 2. Deutscher Bundestag, 23 September 1954 (Anlage C), 2139–47.

72. In 1961, payments were introduced for the second child in low-income families. See Akrami-Göhren, "Die Familienpolitik," 151–53, 277–90; and Volker Hentschel, *Geschichte der deutschen Sozialpolitik (1880–1980): Soziale Sicherung und kollektives Arbeitsrecht,* 204. Only in 1974 did an SPD-led government achieve what it had proposed more than twenty years earlier—the elimination of all income tax deductions for children and substantially increased flat-sum payments for all children.

73. "Kinder und Jugendliche in Familien," *Wirtschaft und Statistik,* n.s., 12 (1960): 215; Statistisches Bundesamt, *Bevölkerung und Kultur, Reihe 2: Natürliche Bevölkerungsbewegung, Sonderbeitrag: Kinderzahl der Ehen, Oktober 1962,* 19–21. On women in poverty, see Stephanie Münke, *Die Armut in der*

heutigen Gesellschaft: Ergebnisse einer Untersuchung in Westberlin, 62, 74; Edith Hinze, with the assistance of Elisabeth Knospe, *Lage und Leistung erwerbstätiger Mütter: Ergebnisse einer Untersuchung in Westberlin;* Ilse Elsner and Rüdiger Proske, "Der fünfte Stand: Eine Untersuchung über die Armut in Westdeutschland," 109–10; Detlef Fehrs, "Die wirtschaftlichen Verhältnisse der Sozialleistungsempfänger in der Bundesrepublik und in Berlin (West)," *Bundesarbeitsblatt* (1956): 811–12; and, "Die Rentnerhaushalte: Ergebnis der 1%-Wohnungserhebung 1960," *Wirtschaft und Statistik*, n.s., 14 (1962): 633–38.

74. Gerd-Rüdiger Rückert, "Die Kinderzahl der Ehen in der Bundesrepublik Deutschland im Intergenerationenvergleich," in *Soziale Strukturen und individuelle Mobilität: Beiträge zur sozio-demographischen Analyse der Bundesrepublik Deutschland*, ed. Heinrich Tegtmeyer, 334.

75. Wolfgang Köllmann, "Die Bevölkerungsentwicklung der Bundesrepublik," in Conze and Lepsius, *Sozialgeschichte der Bundesrepublik Deutschland*, 107, 110; and in general, Bruno Salzmann, "Fruchtbarkeitswandel und die Rolle der Politik," in *Beiträge aus der bevölkerungswissenschaftlichen Forschung: Festschrift für Hermann Schubnell*, ed. Sabine Rupp and Karl Schwarz, 65–74; Hermann Schubnell, *Der Geburtenrückgang in der Bundesrepublik Deutschland: Die Entwicklung der Erwerbstätigkeit von Frauen und Müttern;* and Nancy B. Tuma and Johannes Huinink, "Post-War Fertility Patterns in the Federal Republic of Germany," in *Applications of Event History Analysis in Life Course Research*, ed. Karl Ulrich Mayer and Nancy Brandon Tuma, 510. Chapter 5 addresses the patterns of women's employment outside the home.

76. The quotations are from Herta Gotthelf in *Protokoll der Verhandlungen des Parteitages der Sozialdemokratischen Partei Deutschlands vom 20. bis 24. Juli 1954 in Berlin*, 235; the *Grundsatzprogramm* proclaimed in 1959, *Protokoll der Verhandlungen des ausserordentlichen Parteitages der Sozialdemokratischen Partei Deutschlands vom 13.–15. November 1959 in Bad Godesberg*, 23, 257–58; and "SPD-Frauenprogramm," *Gleichheit* 20 (1957): 293.

77. "Objekt-Frau," *Gleichheit* 14 (1951): 110, and in general, Akrami-Göhren, "Die Familienpolitik," 109–12.

78. "Der Familienlastenausgleich: Erwägungen zur gesetzgeberischen Verwirklichung—Eine Denkschrift des Bundesministers für Familienfragen," November 1955, PA, II/201A; "Kurzprotokoll der 66. Sitzung des Ausschusses für Sozialpolitik am Freitag, den 18. November 1955"; also Wuermeling, "Keine Bevölkerungspolitik, sondern Familienpolitik," *Bulletin*, no. 231 (1955): 1967–68; and idem, "Kinder haben—das darf keine Strafe sein," *Das Parlament*, 23 November 1955, 3.

79. *VDBT*, 2. Deutscher Bundestag, 120. Sitzung, 15 December 1955, 6378; also Lisa Korspeter, ibid., 6403; and in general, Elfriede Eilers and Marta Schanzenbach, "Zur Nachkriegsgeschichte der Familienpolitik aus sozialdemokratischer Sicht," in *Sozialpolitik nach 1945: Geschichte und Analysen*, ed. Reinhart Bartholomäi, et al., 229–38.

80. See, e.g., "Frau, Familie und Sozialplan," *Gleichheit* 20 (1957): 330–32; "Die kinderreiche Familie und die Allgemeinheit," ibid.: 388–90; and *Protokoll*

der Verhandlung des ausserordentlichen Parteitages der Sozialdemokratischen Partei Deutschlands vom 13.–15. November 1959 in Bad Godesberg, 24, 257. The SPD's commitment to the family in the Godesberg program won high marks from the conservative Bund der Kinderreichen Deutschlands in its monthly paper, *Das Fundament*, May 1961.

81. Survey conducted by the Allensbacher Institut für Demoskopie, quoted in Hockerts, *Sozialpolitische Entscheidungen*, 424–25; Bark and Gress, *A History of West Germany* 1: 396; Jens Albers, "Germany," in *Growth to Limits: The European Welfare States Since World War II*, vol. 2, ed. Peter Flora, 13, 22–23, 148; Abelshauser, *Die langen Fünfziger Jahre*, 49; Hans Günter Hockerts, "Sicherung im Alter: Kontinuität und Wandel der gesetzlichen Rentenversicherung 1889–1979," in Conze and Lepsius, *Sozialgeschichte der Bundesrepublik*, 296–323; Peter J. Katzenstein, *Policy and Politics in West Germany: The Growth of a Semisovereign State*, 180–82; and Detlev Zöllner, "Germany," in *The Evolution of Social Insurance 1881–1981: Studies of Germany, France, Great Britain, Austria and Switzerland*, ed. Peter A. Köhler and Hans A. Zacher, 56–66.

82. Hentschel, *Geschichte der deutschen Sozialpolitik*, 168–72; Bundesminister für Arbeit und Sozialordnung, "Bericht der Bundesregierung über die Situation der Frauen in Beruf, Familie und Gesellschaft," Deutscher Bundestag, 5. Wahlperiode, Drucksache V/909, 133–34.

83. H. Schieckel, "Die soziale Unsicherheit der deutschen Frau," *Ehe und Familie im privaten und öffentlichen Recht: Zeitschrift für das gesamte Familienrecht* 2 (1953): 316–17.

84. Ibid. In general, see Hentschel, *Geschichte der deutschen Sozialpolitik*, 161, 172; Barbara Riedmüller, "Frauen haben keine Rechte: Zur Stellung der Frau im System sozialer Sicherheit," in *Die armen Frauen: Frauen und Sozialpolitik*, ed. Ilona Kickbusch and Barbara Riedmüller, 46; Renate Meyer-Harter, *Die Stellung der Frau in der Sozialversicherung: Lageanalyse und Reformmöglichkeit*, 28–31, 41–76; and Helgard Planken, *Die soziale Sicherung der nicht-erwerbstätigen Frau*.

85. Wilfrid Schreiber, *Existenzsicherheit in der industriellen Gesellschaft: Vorschläge zur "Sozialreform,"* 34; on Schreiber's influence on Adenauer, Hockerts, *Sozialpolitische Entscheidungen*, 310–17; and for a fully developed articulation of his views on *Kindergeld*, Wilfrid Schreiber, *Kindergeld im sozioökonomischen Prozess: Familienlastenausgleich als Prozess zeitlicher Kaufkraft-Umschichtung im Individual-Bereich*.

86. Schreiber, *Existenzsicherheit*, 34.

87. See the comments of the Labor Minister, Anton Storch, quoted in Abelshauser, *Die langen Fünfziger Jahre*, 141.

88. Jenson, "Both Friend and Foe," 541–45; idem, "The Liberation and New Rights for French Women," in Higonnet et al., *Behind the Lines*, 272–84; Marie-Monique Huss, "Pronatalism in the Inter-War Period in France," 39–68; Gabriele Bremme, *Freiheit und soziale Sicherheit: Motive und Prinzipien sozialer Sicherung dargestellt an England und Frankreich*, 177–203; Nicole Questiaux and Jacques Fournier, "France," in *Family Policy: Government and Families in Fourteen Countries*, ed. Sheila B. Kamerman and Alfred J. Kahn,

117–28; Karen Offen, "Body Politics: Women, Work and the Politics of Motherhood in France, 1920–1950," in Bock and Thane, *Maternity and Gender Policies*, 138–59; and the excellent study by Susan Gay Pedersen, "Social Policy and the Reconstruction of the Family in Britain and France, 1900–1945," 478–566.

89. See Pedersen, "Social Policy and the Reconstruction of the Family," 392–447; idem, "Gender, Welfare, and Citizenship in Britain during the Great War," 983–1006; idem, "The Failure of Feminism in the Making of the British Welfare State," 86–110; Jenson, "Both Friend and Foe"; Hilary Land, "Eleanor Rathbone and the Economy of the Family," in *British Feminism in the Twentieth Century*, ed. Harold L. Smith, 104–23; John Macnicol, *The Movement for Family Allowances, 1919–45: A Study in Social Policy Development;* Jane Lewis, "Dealing with Dependency: State Practices and Social Realities, 1870–1945," in *Women's Welfare, Women's Rights*, ed. Jane Lewis, 17–37; idem, "Models of Equality for Women: The Case of State Support for Children in Twentieth-Century Britain," in Bock and Thane, *Maternity and Gender Policies*, 73–92; Pat Thane, "Visions of Gender in the Making of the British Welfare State: The Case of Women in the British Labour Party and Social Policy, 1906–1945," in ibid., 93–118; the insightful treatment of the World War II context in Geoffrey Field, "Perspectives on the Working-Class Family in Wartime Britain, 1939–1945," 3–28; and in general, Peter Baldwin, *The Politics of Social Solidarity: Class Bases of the European Welfare State, 1875–1975.*

90. Rita Liljeström, "Sweden," in Kamerman and Kahn, *Family Policy: Government and Families in Fourteen Countries*, 19–48; Mary Ruggie, *The State and Working Women: A Comparative Study of Britain and Sweden;* Alva Myrdal, *Nation and Family: The Swedish Experiment in Democratic Family and Population Policy;* Ann-Sofie Ohlander, "The Invisible Child? The Struggle for a Social Democratic Family Policy in Sweden, 1900–1960s," in Bock and Thane, *Maternity and Gender Policies*, 60–72; and Lisbet Rausing, "The Population Question: The Debate of Family Welfare Reforms in Sweden, 1930–38," 521–56.

91. Max Horkheimer, ed., *Studien über Autorität und Familie;* Martin Jay, *The Dialectical Imagination: A History of the Frankfurt School and the Institute of Social Research 1923–1950*, 124–33; and Lepsius, "Entwicklung," 37–38. In the fifties, the one West German study of the "crisis of the family" that was deeply influenced by Adorno was Baumert, *Deutsche Familien*, but it had none of the resonance or influence of Schelsky's.

92. Wuermeling, "Keine Bevölkerungspolitik, sondern Familienpolitik!" 1967–68.

93. See, for example, "Zentrale Frauenkonferenz in Köln vom 29. bis 32. Mai 1953," *Gleichheit* 16 (1953): 221; Clara Döhring, "Kinderbeihilfen und ein sozial gerechter Lohn," ibid., 15 (1952): 297; and Marta Schanzenbach, *Protokoll der 1. Bundesfrauenkonferenz der Gewerkschaft Nahrung-Genuss-Gaststätten, Bielefeld, 16.–18. September 1955*, 15–18, where Schanzenbach virtually adopted Schelsky's analysis. This demand was repeated by socialist women and women trade unionists throughout the fifties.

94. A. Grossmann, "Vitamin Mutterliebe," *Gleichheit* 15 (1952): 355–56.

95. On this topic, see Hong, "Politics of Welfare Reform"; idem, "Femininity as a Vocation: Gender and Class Conflict in the Professionalization of German Social Work," in *German Professions, 1800–1950,* ed. Geoffrey Cocks and Konrad H. Jarausch, 232–51; and Sachsse, *Mütterlichkeit als Beruf.* The comparison with the United States, where middle-class women entered government service through their engagement in the politics of social-welfare reform, is instructive. In general, see Michel and Koven, "Womanly Duties," 1076–1108; Kathryn Kish Sklar, "A Call for Comparisons," 1109–14; and Gwendolyn Mink, "The Lady and the Tramp: Gender, Race, and the Origins of the Welfare State," in Gordon, *Women, the State, and Welfare,* 92–122.

96. Wagner, "Die alleinstehende berufstätige Frau."

97. Castell, "Die demographischen Konsequenzen," in Długoborski, *Zweiter Weltkrieg und sozialer Wandel,* 130; Bethlehem, *Heimatvertreibung, DDR-Flucht, Gastarbeiterzuwanderung;* Ulrich Herbert, *Geschichte der Ausländerbeschäftigung in Deutschland 1880 bis 1980: Saisonarbeiter, Zwangsarbeiter, Gastarbeiter,* 180–92; Köllmann, "Die Bevölkerungsentwicklung der Bundesrepublik," 77–78; and a rare contemporary commentary questioning the shortages of skilled labor, Kurt Fiebich, "Zur westdeutschen Bevölkerungssituation: Haben wir einen Facharbeitermangel zu erwarten?" *Gewerkschaftliche Monatshefte* 2 (1951): 607–17.

98. Denise Riley, *War in the Nursery: Theories of the Child and Mother,* 159. See also Angela Vogel, "Familie," 102.

99. Hans Köhler, a professor at the Free University in Berlin, at *Dritter Parteitag der Christlich-Demokratischen Union,* 52. The antifamily policies of communist states, particularly East Germany, were also attacked frequently in the publications of the conservative Bund der Kinderreichen Deutschlands; see, e.g., "Im Namen der Gerechtigkeit? Zehn Jahre Familiennot in der Zone der Unfreiheit," *Das Fundament* (November 1959), 5–6; and "Im Namen des Fortschritts? Entchristlichung der Familie in der Sowjetzone," ibid. (December 1959), 5–6.

100. Willi Albers, "Probleme der westdeutschen Familienpolitik," in *Leitbilder für Familie und Familienpolitik: Festgabe für Helga Schmucker zum 80. Geburtstag,* ed. Rosemarie von Schweitzer, 42. Albers was an active participant in the social-reform discussion of the fifties. See Albers, "Neuer Plan für einen Ausgleich der Familienlasten," *Sozialer Fortschritt* 3 (1954): 217–21; and idem, "Familie und Gesellschaft," *Sozialer Fortschritt* 8 (1959): 54–57. Similar sentiments ring through in Bünger, *Familienpolitik in Deutschland,* 47; Hans Harmsen, "Aussprache," in *Familie und Sozialreform,* 40–41; and Martin Donath, "Grundsatzreferat und Ausschussbericht," ibid., 11–27.

101. Wuermeling, "Weder Bevölkerungspolitik noch Geburtenbeschränkung," *Bulletin,* no. 152 (1958): 1563–64; also idem, "Sterbendes Abendland?" *Deutsche Tagespost,* 12 April 1955; idem, "Hilfe für die Familie," *Bulletin,* no. 144 (1954): 1289–91; idem, "Bevölkerungspolitik und Geburtenbeschränkung," *Zentralmitteilungsdienst: Familienbund der deutschen Katholiken* 5, no. 8 (1958), copy in ACDP, I-221-017; and "Familie und Staat," speech by Wuermeling, 15 September 1956, typescript in ibid.

102. Wuermeling, "Das muss geschehen! Die Familie fordert vom Bundestag," *Kirchen-Zeitung* (Cologne), 6 December 1953, quoted in Ingrid Langer,

"Die Mohrinnen hatten ihre Schuldigkeit getan . . . Staatlich-moralische Aufrüstung der Familien," in *Die fünfziger Jahre: Beiträge zu Politik und Kultur,* ed. Dieter Bähnsch, 121.

103. Wuermeling, "Der Sinn der Familienpolitik," *Bulletin,* no. 211 (1954): 1911–12.

104. For the discussion among socialist feminists in the 1970s, see the summary in Michèle Barrett, *Women's Oppression Today: Problems in Marxist Feminist Analysis,* 172–86. For examples of the German variant of this discussion, see Ilona Ostner, *Beruf und Hausarbeit: Die Arbeit der Frau in unserer Gesellschaft;* and many of the contributions to Sommeruniversität für Frauen e.V. Berlin, ed., *Frauen als bezahlte und unbezahlte Arbeitskräfte: Beiträge zur Berliner Sommeruniversität für Frauen, Oktober 1977.*

105. Arnd Jessen, *Was kostet dein Kind? Ein Vorschlag zur Einführung allgemeiner staatlicher Kinderbeihilfen.*

106. Jessen, "Der Aufwand für Kinder," 98, 144–45, 149; Theodor Hellbrügge, "Waisenkinder der Technik," 49–55.

107. Ludwig Erhard, "Einen Kühlschrank in jeden Haushalt," *Welt der Arbeit,* 16 June 1953, republished in idem, *Deutsche Wirtschaftspolitik: Der Weg der sozialen Marktwirtschaft,* 221; and idem, *Wohlstand für alle,* 234, 239, 241. The role of woman as consumer was a central part of the CDU's electoral campaign appeal to women in 1953. See Bremme, *Die politische Rolle der Frau in Deutschland,* 105–06. See also the useful theoretical insights of Batya Weinbaum and Amy Bridges, "The Other Side of the Paycheck: Monopoly Capital and the Structure of Consumption," in *Capitalist Patriarchy and the Case for Socialist Feminism,* ed. Zillah R. Eisenstein, 190–205.

108. Ludwig Erhard, "Familie und soziale Marktwirtschaft," *Das Fundament* (July–August 1957), 3. And in general, Abelshauser, *Die langen Fünfziger Jahre,* 56–57; Axel Schildt and Arnold Sywottek, " 'Wiederaufbau' und 'Modernisierung': Zur westdeutschen Gesellschaftsgeschichte in den fünfziger Jahren," 25–28; and Karin Jurczyk, *Frauenarbeit und Frauenrolle: Zum Zusammenhang von Familienpolitik und Frauenerwerbstätigkeit in Deutschland von 1918–1975,* 101–102.

109. For interesting comparisons with the United States in the fifties, see May, *Homeward Bound,* 18.

110. Otto von Usslar, "Massnahmen und Forderungen zum wirtschaftlichen Ausgleich der Familienlasten unter Berücksichtigung der Bevölkerungswissenschaft," 9.

111. The quotations are from, respectively, L. Kroeber-Keneth, *Frauen unter Männern: Grenzen und Möglichkeiten der arbeitenden Frau,* 39; Edo Osterloh (of the BMF), "Arbeit, Freizeit und Familie," *Bulletin,* no. 111 (1955): 923–24; Elisabeth Pfeil, *Die Berufstätigkeit von Müttern: Eine empirisch-soziologische Erhebung an 900 Müttern aus vollständigen Familien,* 230; and A. Mayer, "Doppelberuf der Frau als Gefahr für Familie, Volk und Kultur," 693. These themes were developed ad nauseam in a spate of other studies of married women's work in the fifties. See, e.g., Otto Speck, *Kinder erwerbstätiger Mütter: Ein soziologisch-pädagogisches Gegenwartsproblem;* A. Hedwig Hermann, *Die ausserhäusliche Erwerbstätigkeit verheirateter Frauen: Eine sozialpolitische*

Studie; Rolf Frohner, Maria von Stackelberg, Wolfgang Eser, *Familie und Ehe: Probleme in den deutschen Familien der Gegenwart;* Heinrich Greeven, ed., *Die Frau im Beruf: Tatbestände, Erfahrungen und Vorschläge zu drängenden Fragen in der weiblichen Berufsarbeit und in der Lebenshaltung der berufstätigen Frau;* Anton Christian Hoffmann and Dietrich Kersten, *Frauen zwischen Familie und Fabrik: Die Doppelbelastung der Frau durch Haushalt und Beruf;* and A. Mayer, *Emanzipation, Frauentum, Muttertum, Familie und Gesellschaft.*

112. Roderich von Ungern-Sternberg, "Mutterschaft und weibliche Berufstätigkeit," 344.

113. "Die Kinder von morgen," *Sozialer Fortschritt* 6 (1957): 234–35; Wolfgang Metzger, "Der Auftrag des Elternhauses," in *Familie im Umbruch,* ed. Ferdinand Oeter, 221; Albers, "Familie und Gesellschaft."

114. Oswald von Nell-Breuning, "Kommerzialisierte Gesellschaft," 32–45; Phillip Ludwig, "Probleme der Familienpolitik," *Soziale Welt* 8 (1957): 137; and Donath, "Grundsatzreferat und Ausschussbericht," in *Familie und Sozialreform,* 20.

115. Daniel Bell, *The End of Ideology: On the Exhaustion of Political Ideas in the Fifties;* and Raymond Aron, "The End of Ideology and the Renaissance of Ideas," in *The Industrial Society: Three Essays on Ideology and Development,* 92–183.

116. Schelsky's language continued to echo explicitly in the formulations of the family minister. See, e.g., "Denkschrift des Bundesministeriums für Familien- und Jugendfragen: Die wirtschaftliche Situation der Familien in der Bundesrepublik," [1961], BA, B191/124.

117. Rüdiger Proske, "Die Familie 1951: Eine Beschreibung ihrer wichtigsten Merkmale," 179.

CHAPTER FIVE

1. *Der Spiegel,* 23 April 1949, 5.

2. Teetz to Böckler, 8 July 1948, BA, B149/1124.

3. Petition to the Vereinigung weiblicher Bundestagsabgeordnete, 10 March 1950, ibid.

4. Report dated 13 February 1952, prepared by Herschel for BMA, providing account of interviews with trade union representatives in November 1951, ibid.

5. Protocol of Petitions-Ausschuss of the Bundestag, 29 September 1952, ibid.

6. Bundesministerium für Verkehr to BMA, 25 January 1951, ibid.

7. Dr. Härting, report of 12 November 1951; and "Niederschrift über die Sitzung vom 9.11.1951 im Bundesverkehrsministerium betr. Beschäftigung von Frauen in der Seeschiffahrt und Behandlung der Eingabe der Frau A. Teetz geb. Sparbier an den Deutschen Bundestag," ibid.

8. Schulte-Langforth, memo of 22 October 1952, ibid.

9. Schulte-Langforth to Petitions-Ausschuss des Bundestages, 9 March 1953, ibid.

10. E.g., report of Labor Minister for North Rhine–Westphalia, January 1948, and President for the Central Labor Office in the British Zone, 12 April 1948, both in NdsHStA, Nds. 1310, Acc. 53/72, Nr. 18, Bd. 2; report by Mrs. M. Taylor for British forces of occupation, on meeting with labor ministry officials in Hannover (9 April 1948), PRO, FO 1051/596.

11. E.g., report of president of Landesarbeitsamt, Bremen, to local labor exchanges, 25 August 1948, NdsHStA, Nds. 1310, Acc. 53/72, Nr. 18, Bd. 1; "Die Vermittlung für Frauen im Jahre 1948 im Bezirk des Landesarbeitsamts Niedersachsen," 12 February 1949, NdsHStA, Nds. 1311, Arbeitsamt Lüneburg, Acc. 100/69, Nr. 3; Heinrich Strathus, "Die voraussichtliche Auswirkungen der künftigen Währungsreform auf die Sozialausgaben in Bayern: Ein Gutachten für das Bayerische Staatsministerium der Finanzen," BA, Z40/324; Fritz Molle, "Die Frauenarbeitslosigkeit im Bundesgebiet," *Bundesarbeitsblatt* (1951): 280–82; Charlotte Richter, *Frauenarbeitsnot in Duisburg;* Bundesministerium für Arbeit, *Entwicklung, Stand und Gewicht der Frauenarbeitslosigkeit in der Bundesrepublik Deutschland;* and in general, Rhea Maxson, *The Woman Worker in Germany.*

12. Quotations from R. W. Luce, Manpower Division, [British] Headquarters, Berlin, to R. Birley, 19 January 1948, PRO, FO 1051/596; and Luce to Birley, 12 January 1948, PRO, FO 1050/1179. See also, R. Birley, Educational Advisor to the British Military Government, to Chief of Manpower, January 1948, PRO, FO 945/285.

13. Memo from Elizabeth Holt to J. Makiman, Manpower Division, OMGUS, BA, OMGUS, 7/43–3/9. For a useful summary of the theoretical literature on sex-segmented labor markets, see Angelika Willms-Herget, *Frauenarbeit: Zur Integration der Frauen in den Arbeitsmarkt,* 31–67.

14. Margarete Brendgen, "Neue Wege der weiblichen Berufsberatung," *Arbeitsblatt für die britische Zone* 1 (1947): 354–57; idem, *Frau und Beruf: Beitrag zur Ethik der Frauenberufe unserer Tage;* and in general, Doris Schubert, *Frauen in der deutschen Nachkriegszeit* 1: 86–92, 272–93.

15. Käthe Gaebel, "Die Erwerbstätigkeit der Frau im Lichte der Statistik," *Arbeitsblatt für die britische Zone* (1948): 264–66; and "Protokolle der Arbeitstagung der Fürsorgerinnen, gemeinsam mit dem Bezirksfrauenausschuss des DGB-Landesbezirks Nordrhein-Westfalen am 6. Juli 1951," DGB Archiv, Werksfürsorge, 1957–1961.

16. Erna Hamann, "Arbeit und Arbeitsvermittlung der Frauen," *Arbeitsblatt* (1949): 468–69; idem, "Die Frau auf dem Arbeitsmarkt," ibid., 425; and Hilde Mohrmann, "Gedanken zur Berufsarbeit und zur Berufsbildung der Frauen," *Bundesarbeitsblatt* (1954): 723.

17. Arbeitsamt Lüneburg, "Jahresbericht der weiblichen Vermittlung des Arbeitsamts Lüneburg für das Jahr 1950," NdsHStA, Nds. 1311, Arbeitsamt Lüneburg, Acc. 100/69, Nr. 3.

18. Irmgard Enderle, "Die Neuerschliessung von Frauenberufen," *Gewerkschaftliche Monatshefte* 1 (1950): 87.

19. *Entwicklung, Stand und Gewicht,* 3.

20. Abelshauser, *Wirtschaftsgeschichte,* 63–70.

21. "Fast 18.3 Millionen unselbständiger Erwerbspersonen," *Bulletin*, no. 223 (1955): 1890; "Sozialpolitik 1955: Aus dem Rechenschaftsbericht des Bundesministeriums für Arbeit," *Bundesarbeitsblatt* (1956): 14–23; and in general, Maria Tritz, *Die Frauenerwerbsarbeit in der Bundesrepublik.*

22. See, e.g., M[aria] Tritz, "Die Reserve der weiblichen Arbeitskräfte," *Bundesarbeitsblatt* (1955): 896–99; and in general, the essays in Ruth Bergholtz, ed., *Die Wirtschaft braucht die Frau.* The term *silent reserve* was used frequently by contemporaries.

23. Angelika Willms, "Grundzüge der Entwicklung der Frauenarbeit von 1880 bis 1980," in *Strukturwandel der Frauenarbeit 1880–1980*, ed. Walter Müller, Angelika Willms, Johann Handl, 35; Hermann Schubnell, "Die Erwerbstätigkeit von Frauen und Müttern und die Betreuung ihrer Kinder," *Wirtschaft und Statistik*, n.s., 16 (1964): 445; Tritz, *Frauenerwerbsarbeit*, 17; and Ursula Lehr, *Die Frau im Beruf: Eine psychologische Analyse der weiblichen Berufsrolle*, 1–2.

24. Ursel Schulze, "Ausbildung und Stellung der Frau in den kaufmännischen Berufen," in Bergholtz, *Die Wirtschaft braucht die Frau*, 149–60; M[aria] Tritz, "Die Industriearbeiterin," *Bundesarbeitsblatt* (1957): 456–8; "Starke Zunahme der Frauenarbeit: Die beschäftigungspolitische Bedeutung des Textil- und Bekleidungsgewerbes," *Bulletin*, no. 148 (1955): 1247–48; M[argarete] Brendgen, "Die Frau in den kaufmännischen Berufen," *Bundesarbeitsblatt* (1954): 383; Christa Morawe, "Die Lage der älteren weiblichen Angestellten," *Bundesarbeitsblatt* (1955): 274; "Die Beschäftigungslage in der Bundesrepublik Deutschland im Rahmen der Wirtschafts- und Bevölkerungsentwicklung 1956," *Bundesarbeitsblatt*, Beilage zum 2. Juniheft (1957): 29; and Margot Schmidt, "Im Vorzimmer," 191–232.

25. Willms-Herget, *Frauenarbeit*, 139–50, 211–25; and Margarete Schrecker, *Die Entwicklung der Mädchenberufsschule*, 320–43.

26. Tritz, "Die Industriearbeiterin," 459; also P[aul] Hülsmann and J. Pilgram, "Bestgestaltung automatisierbarer Arbeitsformen der gewerblichen Frauenarbeit," *Bundesarbeitsblatt* (1955): 21–24; Paul Hülsmann, *Die berufstätige Frau: Arbeitsmedizinische Leitsätze;* Agnes Karbe and Maria Tritz, *Das Mädchen im Betrieb;* and on the articulation of such theories under the Nazis, Tröger, "The Creation of a Female Assembly-Line Proletariat," 249–58.

27. In general, see Drohsel, *Die Lohndiskriminierung der Frauen;* and Henry Braunwarth, *Die Spanne zwischen Männer- und Frauenlöhnen: Tatsächliche Entwicklung und kritische Erörterung ihrer Berechtigung*, 63–72.

28. See, e.g., Elisabeth Selbert, "Gleichberechtigung der erwerbstätigen Frau," *Gleichheit* 13 (1950): 215–16; Grete Schmalz, "Das Recht der Frau auf Arbeit und gerechten Lohn," *Gleichheit* 15 (1952): 299–300; and H. C. Nipperdey, *Gleicher Lohn der Frau für gleiche Leistung: Rechtsgutachten erstattet dem Bundesvorstand des Deutschen Gewerkschaftsbundes.*

29. U. Wittig, "Frauenlohn nach fünf Jahren Grundgesetz," *Bundesarbeitsblatt* (1954): 211–13; also Ilse Elsner, "Der Frauenlohn in unserer Zeit," in Bergholtz, *Die Wirtschaft braucht die Frau*, 31–56.

30. See the position paper prepared by Walter Jellinek for the Association of German Employer Associations (Vereinigung der Deutschen Arbeitgeberver-

bände) in 1950, NWHStA, RW177/40; Erich Molitor, "Zur Frage der Gleichbehandlung von Männern und Frauen," *Betriebs-Berater* (1952): 203–04; idem, "Die arbeitsrechtliche Bedeutung des Art. 3 des Bonner Grundgesetzes," *Archiv für die civilistische Praxis* 151 (1950/51): 385–415.

31. *Entscheidungen des Bundesarbeitsgerichts* 1: 268. The decision is from 15 January 1955, ibid., 259–73. See also decision of 6 April 1955, ibid., 349–59; and in general, Drohsel, *Die Lohndiskriminierung der Frauen*, 211; and Elsner, "Der Frauenlohn in unserer Zeit."

32. E.g., DGB Gewerkschaftsbrief, Frauen (June 1954), NWHStA, RW177/494; and Käte Sodann (of IG Druck und Papier), "Wie die 'Lohngleichheit' umgangen wird," *Gleichheit* 22 (1959): 413–14; Elsner, "Der Frauenlohn in unserer Zeit," 42–43; and in general, Braunwarth, *Die Spanne zwischen Männer- und Frauenlöhnen*, 120–26.

33. Jan Sierks, "Löst die analytische Arbeitsplatzbewertung die Lohngleichheit von Mann und Frau?" in Bergholtz, *Die Wirtschaft braucht die Frau*, 56–62; Anneliese Weber, "Zur Problematik der betrieblichen Frauenarbeit," *Gewerkschaftliche Monatshefte* 5 (1954): 688; Hans Rehhahn, "Zur Frage der Frauenlöhne," ibid., 6 (1955): 750–71. In 1958, women industrial workers earned 63.8 percent of the wages of men doing the same jobs, significantly less even than men in lower job classifications. In the same year, nearly one in two of all women wage-earners was in the lowest job classification, compared to only 15.7 percent of men. See Heinz-Herbert Noll, "Soziale Indikatoren für Arbeitsmarkt und Beschäftigungsbedingungen," in *Lebensbedingungen in der Bundesrepublik: Sozialer Wandel und Wohlfahrtsentwicklung*, ed. Wolfgang Zapf, 286, 295–96; and in general, Drohsel, *Die Lohndiskriminierung der Frauen*.

34. A useful collection of documents on these early discussions of protective legislation is provided by Doris Schubert, *Frauen in der deutschen Nachkriegszeit* 1: 272–311. See also the general discussion in Klaus Geratewohl, "Sonderarbeitsrecht der Frau," in Bergholtz, *Die Wirtschaft braucht die Frau*, 260–90.

35. See, e.g., "Arbeitsschutz für erwerbstätige Frauen," *Bundesarbeitsblatt* (1950): 387. Methodologically very useful on this topic are Marilyn J. Boxer, "Protective Legislation and Home Industry: The Marginalization of Women Workers in Late Nineteenth–Early Twentieth-Century France," 44–65; Mary Lynn McDougall, "Protecting Infants: The French Campaigns for Maternity Leaves, 1890s–1913," 79–105; Mary Lynn Stewart, *Women, Work, and the French State: Labour Protection and Social Patriarchy, 1879–1919;* Eileen Boris, "Homework and Women's Rights: The Case of Vermont Knitters, 1980–1985," 98–120; idem, "Regulating Industrial Homework: The Triumph of 'Sacred Motherhood,' " 745–63; Zillah R. Eisenstein, *The Female Body and the Law*, 195–218; Alice Kessler-Harris, *Out to Work: A History of Wage-Earning Women in the United States*, 180–214; Judith A. Baer, *The Chains of Protection: The Judicial Response to Women's Labor Legislation;* and for treatments of the ongoing discussion of this issue among feminist legal experts, Wendy W. Williams, "Equality's Riddle: Pregnancy and the Equal Treatment/Special Treatment Debate," 325–80; Lise Vogel, "Debating Difference: Feminism, Pregnancy, and the Workplace," 9–32; Herma Hill Kay, "Models of Equality," 39–88; and idem, "Equality and Difference: The Case of Pregnancy," 1–38. On

the German case, see Jean H. Quataert, "Source Analysis in German Women's History," 99–121, esp. 111. Quataert's article first called my attention to the potential value of the factory inspectors' reports on which I draw heavily in this chapter. See also idem, "Social Insurance and the Family Work of Oberlausitz Home Weavers in the Late Nineteenth Century," in Fout, *German Women in the Nineteenth Century*, 270–94.

36. The summary here is based on Bajohr, *Die Hälfte der Fabrik*, 298–309; Hagemann, *Frauenalltag und Männerpolitik*, 189–90; Dörte Winkler, *Frauenarbeit*, 155–56; and Gustav-Adolf Bulla, *Mutterschutzgesetz und Frauenarbeitsrecht*, 13–21.

37. Grete Schmalz, "Gesetzlicher Mutterschutz gestern und heute," *Gewerkschaftliche Monatshefte* 1 (1950): 283; and the reflections of British forces of occupation from 1946–47 in PRO, FO 1051/386.

38. Kipp-Kaule, *VDBT*, [1.] Deutscher Bundestag, 80. Sitzung, 27 July 1950, 2997–98. See also the testimony of Agnes Arndt, head of the women's division of the white-collar workers' union (Deutsche Angestellten Gewerkschaft), "Kurzprotokoll der gemeinsamen Sitzung der Ausschüsse Nr. 21—Ausschuss für Sozialpolitik—und Nr. 20—Ausschuss für Arbeit am Dienstag, den 19. September 1950," 4, HStAS, EA1/17 Bü 161.

39. Kipp-Kaule for IG Textil-Bekleidung-Leder, Hauptvorstand in the British Zone, to Education Branch, Women's Affairs, Berlin, 21 January 1948, PRO, FO 1051/386.

40. Maria Schott, Hauptverwaltung, Frauenreferat, IG Nahrung-Genuss-Gaststätten, to Herta Gotthelf, 8 August 1950, ASD, PV Akten, Alter Bestand, Nr. 01385.

41. "Mutterschutz," *Die Quelle* 2 (1951): 428–29; and Louise Schroeder, "Ein neues Mutterschutzgesetz," *Sozialer Fortschritt* 1 (1952): 18–19.

42. *VDBT*, [1.] Deutscher Bundestag 1949, Drucksache Nr. 1182.

43. See, e.g., the discussion of the law in North Rhine–Westphalia, where it was an initiative of the KPD, *Stenographischer Bericht über die 18.–23. Sitzung (6. Sitzungsabschnitt) des Landtages Nordrhein Westfalen am 26.–28. November 1947*, 179. And in general, Bulla, *Mutterschutzgesetz*, 543–749; and Doris Schubert, *Frauen in der deutschen Nachkriegszeit* 1: 93–98.

44. The controversy surrounding the "housework day" reemerged frequently at meetings of the women's caucuses within many trade unions throughout the fifties. See, e.g., *Protokoll: 2. Bundesfrauenkonferenz des Deutschen Gewerkschaftsbundes vom 12. bis 14. Mai 1955 in Dortmund*, 72–79; *Protokoll der 1. Bundesfrauenkonferenz der Gewerkschaft Nahrung-Genuss-Gaststätten, Bielefeld, 16.–18. September 1955*, 53–54; *Protokoll der zweiten zentralen Frauenkonferenz 1957 in Hannover, Industriegewerkschaft Chemie-Papier-Keramik*, 38–39; also "Der Hausarbeitstag—ein Problem!" *Frau im Beruf: Nachrichten des Verbandes der weiblichen Angestellten* 2, no. 3 (1952): 5–6; and "Streitobjekt 'Hausarbeitstag,'" ibid. 4, no. 4 (1954): 5.

45. Decision of 14 July 1954, *Entscheidungen des Bundesarbeitsgerichts* 1: 51–66, quotations on 54, 56; see also Eberhard Heyken, "Rechtsfragen des Hausarbeitstages und gleichgerichtete Massnahmen in anderen Ländern"; and

Hans Grewe, "Die arbeitsgerichtliche Rechtsprechung zum Gesetz des Landes Nordrhein-Westfalen über den Hausarbeitstag für erwerbstätige Frauen mit eigenem Hausstand."

46. Hildegard Krüger, "Hausarbeitstag trotz Gleichberechtigung?" *Der Betrieb* (1954), copy in DGB library, Düsseldorf. See also a standard textbook on labor law from this period, which discusses the woman worker in its section on "distinct forms of labor relations" (*besondere Formen des Arbeitsverhältnisses*) as a "deviation from the normal case." Alfred Hueck and Hans Carl Nipperdey, *Lehrbuch des Arbeitsrechts* 1: 653.

47. Selbert's comments are in PR, HA, 42. Sitzung, 18 January 1949, 539. See also the exchange between Mangoldt and Bergsträsser, PR, AfG, 26. Sitzung, 30 November 1948, 47, BA, Z5/34; and Elisabeth Selbert, "Um die Gleichberechtigung der Frau," Rundschreiben no. 1a, SPD, PV, Frauenbüro, 21 January 1949, ASD, PV Akten, Alter Bestand, no. 0128; and the court's confirmation of this position, *Neue juristische Wochenschrift* 7 (1954): 1298.

48. *Der Arbeitgeber,* 15 February 1951, 6.

49. Luise Rehling (CDU), *VDBT,* 80. Sitzung, [1.] Deutscher Bundestag, 27 July 1950, 2998–99; Luise Rehling, "Betrachtungen zum Mutterschutzgesetz," *Informationsdienst* (published by Frauenarbeitsgemeinschaft CDU/CSU Deutschlands), no. 8 (1951), NWHStA, RWV38/408; also Rehling, "Kurzprotokoll der gemeinsamen Sitzung des Ausschusses für Sozialpolitik, für Arbeit und für Fragen des Gesundheitswesens am Mittwoch, den 28. Februar 1951," 4 (copy in PA); petitions to the parliamentary committee responsible for the bill from Deutsch-Evangelischer Frauenbund, 29 December 1950, and Der Katholische Deutsche Frauenbund (n.d.), PA, I/257B; testimony of representatives of Vereinigung der Arbeitgeberverbände and Deutscher Bauernverband, "Kurzprotokoll der gemeinsamen Sitzung des Ausschusses Nr. 21—Ausschuss für Sozialpolitik—und Nr. 20—Ausschuss für Arbeit am Dienstag, den 19. September 1950," 3–4, HStAS, EA1/117 Bü 161; and Bundesministerium für Ernährung, Landwirtschaft und Forsten to BMA, 10 November 1950, BA, B149/10782. On the Weimar background of the organized representation of middle-class housewives' interests, see Renate Bridenthal, " 'Professional' Housewives: Stepsisters of the Women's Movement," in Bridenthal et al., *When Biology Became Destiny,* 153–73; and idem, "Class Struggle Around the Hearth: Women and Domestic Service in the Weimar Republic," in Dobkowski and Walliman, *Towards the Holocaust,* 243–64.

50. *VDBT,* [1.] Deutscher Bundestag, 180. Sitzung, 12 December 1951, 7529.

51. Kipp-Kaule, *VDBT,* [1.] Deutscher Bundestag, 80. Sitzung, 27 July 1950, 2997.

52. *Genossin* 12 (1949): 150–51, also quoted in Doris Schubert, *Frauen in der deutschen Nachkriegszeit,* 1: 292.

53. Charlotte Starck, Deutscher Gewerkschaftsbund, Landesbezirk Gross-Berlin, to Thea Harmuth, 3 November 1950, DGB Archiv, Familienrecht; "Das ganze Deutschland soll es sein: Gesamtdeutsche Frauenarbeitstagung der Sozialdemokratischen Partei Deutschlands in Berlin," *Neuer Vorwärts,* 5 September

1952, 8; *Von der NS-Frauenschaft zum Demokratischen Frauenbund* (published by the SPD); and in general, Stephanie Münke, "Frauenarbeit in der Sowjetzone," in Bergholtz, *Die Wirtschaft braucht die Frau*, 364–77; Louise Schroeder, "Sozialpolitik in der Sowjetzone," *Gleichheit* 16 (1953): 228–29; and Annemarie Heiler, "Die Frau im ostzonalen 'Gesetz der Arbeit,' " Frauenarbeitsgemeinschaft CDU/CSU Deutschland, Informationsdienst (July 1950), NWHStA, RWV38/408. And on the policies actually implemented in the German Democratic Republic, Friedel Schubert, *Die Frau in der DDR*, 52–53.

54. Schroeder, "Ein neues Mutterschutzgesetz," 19.

55. Schott to Gotthelf, 8 August 1950, ASD, PV Akten, Alter Bestand, Nr. 01385.

56. O. Radke, "Problem des Frauenlohnes," *Zentralblatt für Arbeitswissenschaft* 4 (1950): 166–68; see also Sahlberg, *Protokoll der 3. Landesbezirks-Frauenkonferenz des DGB Rheinland-Pfalz am 24. April 1955 in Koblenz*, 59.

57. Bulla, *Mutterschutzgesetz*, 40–41.

58. Emmy Theuerkauf and Thea Harmuth, *Mutterschutzgesetz: Gesetz zum Schutze der erwerbstätigen Mutter*, 20.

59. The phrase is borrowed from Joan Wallach Scott, "Women in History: The Modern Period," 156.

60. The cases presented here are drawn from the unusually extensive holdings of NWHStA for the years 1950 through 1955. Case records beyond 1955 were not open to me. My inspection of the available sources in many other state archives indicates that North Rhine–Westphalia was alone in thinking these materials might be of potential interest to historians; elsewhere, they have yet to be turned over to archives, or they simply no longer exist. I was able to evaluate about two hundred cases. Because it is impossible to know if all cases from this period were saved, there was no point in trying to construct a statistically valid sample; the cases I selected, however, seem representative. The sorts of circumstances they present appear regularly—though described only in vague, abbreviated, and anonymous terms—in the annual reports of other factory inspectors, summarized in *Jahresberichte der Gewerbe-Aufsicht: Bundesrepublik Deutschland und Land Berlin* (cited hereafter as *JGA*). The same general outlines are also apparent in some scattered files from the Labor Ministry of Baden-Württemberg. See HStAS, EA8/3900.2.1.A, EA8/3900/2.1.A.2, and EA8/2/2472. To preserve anonymity and comply with strict German laws protecting individuals still living and businesses still in existence, places of employment and names have been omitted in the presentation of cases.

61. The discussion here and in the following paragraphs draws heavily on the annual reports of factory inspectors, summarized in *JGA*. Figures for 1954 from North Rhine–Westphalia indicated that in the best instance, only 54.7 percent of working women who ultimately made claims for maternity benefits were reported by their employers to be pregnant. This compliance record was probably better than the national average; North Rhine–Westphalia was a heavily industrial state that prided itself on particularly conscientious enforcement of protective legislation. In areas dominated by small-scale manufacturing and agriculture, the reporting rates were well below this level. See *JGA 1954*, report for North Rhine–Westphalia, NRW 89.

62. See Thea Harmuth to members of the DGB Bundesfrauenausschuss, 19 November 1953, DGB Archiv, Kündigungsschutz, 1952–57.

63. *JGA 1953*, report for Bavaria, By 58.

64. *JGA 1955*, Bw 47.

65. *JGA 1952*, report for Baden-Württemberg, Bw 69.

66. The themes summarized in this and the preceding paragraph run throughout the *JGA* for the years 1950–60.

67. Complaints that their limited capacity was stretched enormously after the law went into effect abound in the *JGA*. Although information on the female factory inspectorate is scarce, I was able to learn much about their work in an interview with Gisela Nagel in June 1985. Nagel works in the office of occupational safety of the North Rhine–Westphalian Government President (Regierungspräsident) in Düsseldorf. She has been involved with various aspects of the enforcement of the *Mutterschutzgesetz* in that state since the late fifties.

68. Bulla, *Mutterschutzgesetz*, 250–52; Hans-H. Butz, *Das Mutterschutzgesetz in der Praxis: Systematische Übersicht unter besonderer Berücksichtigung der Rechtssprechung des Bundesarbeitsgerichts*, 28, 65; and the memo from the Labor Minister in Baden-Württemberg, 28 October 1952, HStAS, EA8/8/3900.2.1.A.

69. NWHStA, NW37/665.

70. NWHStA, NW37/685.

71. Ibid.

72. NWHStA, NW37/683. Case from 1952.

73. NWHStA, NW37/691. See also "Kündigung des Arbeitsverhältnisses der werdenden Mutter," *Bundesarbeitsblatt* (1950): 189–90.

74. NWHStA, NW37/680.

75. NWHStA, NW37/685, NW37/714, and NW37/660.

76. NWHStA, NW37/888. The report is from early 1954.

77. NWHStA, NW37/707.

78. NWHStA, NW37/708.

79. NWHStA, NW37/706.

80. NWHStA, NW37/682.

81. NWHStA, NW37/664.

82. NWHStA, NW37/708. The case is from 1954–55.

83. NWHStA, NW37/689. The case is from 1955.

84. NWHStA, NW37/679. The case is from 1955.

85. NWHStA, NW37/694. The case is from 1955.

86. NWHStA, NW37/678; and decision of 26 April 1956, *Entscheidungen des Bundesarbeitsgerichts* 3: 66–76.

87. NWHStA, NW37/663, Bd. II. The case is from 1954.

88. Eisenstein, *The Female Body and the Law*, 206. And in general, Alice Kessler-Harris, "The Debate Over Equality for Women in the Work Place: Recognizing Differences," 141–61; and Jane Jenson, "Representations of Gender: Policies to 'Protect' Women Workers and Infants in France and the United States before 1914," in Gordon, *Women, the State, and Welfare*, 152–77.

89. Schubnell, "Die Erwerbstätigkeit von Frauen und Müttern," 445.

90. Pfeil, *Die Berufstätigkeit von Müttern*.

91. Lucie Beyer, *Protokoll der 3. Frauenkonferenz der Industriegewerkschaft Metall für die Bundesrepublik Deutschland*, 96–97.

92. On the structure of these caucuses, see Hauptabteilung "Frauen" beim Bundesvorstand des Deutschen Gewerkschaftsbundes, *Jahres- und Geschäftsbericht 1950–1951*, 7–8, 54–64.

93. Käthe Feuerstack, *1. Bundesfrauenkonferenz Mainz, 27. bis 29. Mai 1952*, 157, 164.

94. Maria Böckling, "Zur Berufswahl der Mädchen des Entlassungsjahrganges 1960," *Frauen und Arbeit: Mitteilungsblatt der Hauptabteilung "Frauen" im DGB-Vorstand*, no. 8 (1959): 1.

95. Frau Dr. Ziegler, *Zweite zentrale Frauenkonferenz der Industriegewerkschaft Druck und Papier, 30. September bis 2. Oktober 1960 in Lahr*, 92–93.

96. "Verbesserung des Arbeitsschutzes: Eine Forderung des DGB für die berufstätige Frau," *Frauen und Arbeit: Mitteilungsblatt der Hauptabteilung "Frauen" im DGB-Bundesvorstand*, no. 10 (1958): 1–2. These undisputed "facts" usually had a medical basis, which was given considerable attention at meetings of women trade unionists throughout the fifties. See, e.g., Dietrich Schürmann, "Arbeitsschutz und Frauenarbeit aus der Sicht der Gewerbemedizin," in *Protokoll der 2. Frauenkonferenz der Industriegewerkschaft Metall für die Bundesrepublik Deutschland*, 102–20; Otto Graf, "Gesundheitliche Gefahren bei der Frauenerwerbsarbeit: Vorbeugung und Bekämpfung," in *Protokoll: 2. Bundesfrauenkonferenz des Deutschen Gewerkschaftsbundes*, 101–36; and Horst Schmidt, "Gesundheitliche Vorsorge—eine sozialpolitische Forderung unserer Zeit," in *Protokoll der 3. Frauenkonferenz der Industriegewerkschaft Metall für die Bundesrepublik Deutschland*, 124–25.

97. Marta Schanzenbach, *Protokoll der 1. Bundesfrauenkonferenz der Gewerkschaft Nahrung-Genuss-Gaststätten*, 15–17.

98. On these provisions, see Friedel Schubert, *Die Frau in der DDR*, 52–53; and the critical assessment in "Die 'Rechte' der Frau in der Ostzone," *Gewerkschaftliche Monatshefte* 2 (1951): 259–61. For an exceptional example of an analysis that identified positive aspects of East German policies toward women, see Katharina Petersen, "Einordnung der Frau in die Leistungsgesellschaft," ibid. 10 (1959): 706–708.

99. See Ilk for FDP, *VDBT*, [1.] Deutscher Bundestag, 80. Sitzung, 27 July 1950, 3001; also Sozialminister of NRW Düsseldorf, 15 January 1951, to BMA, BA, B149/10782. On the inadequacy of day care in West Germany well into the seventies, see "Bericht der Bundesregierung über die Situation der Frauen in Beruf, Familie und Gesellschaft," prepared by Bundesminister für Arbeit und Sozialordnung, 5. Deutscher Bundestag, Drucksache V/909, 28–31, 337; Harry G. Shaffer, *Women in the Two Germanies: A Comparative Study of a Socialist and a Non-Socialist Society*, 103; and Friedhelm Neidhardt, "Germany," in Kamerman and Kahn, *Family Policy*, 234–35. Quotation from " 'Das ganze Deutschland soll es sein': Gesamtdeutsche Frauenarbeitstagung der Sozialdemokratischen Partei Deutschlands in Berlin," *Neuer Vorwärts*, 5 September 1952.

100. *1. Bundesfrauenkonferenz Mainz, 27. bis 29. Mai 1952*, 185.

101. For good examples of these themes, see the speeches by Marta Schanzenbach, *Protokoll der 1. Bundesfrauenkonferenz der Gewerkschaft Nahrung-*

Genuss-Gaststätten, 6–20; Schanzenbach, *Protokoll: 2. Bundesfrauenkonferenz des deutschen Gewerkschaftsbundes vom 12. bis 14. Mai 1955 in Dortmund,* 165–99; Maria Weber, *3. Bundes-Frauenkonferenz: Deutscher Gewerkschaftsbund vom 25. bis 27. Mai 1959 in Bremen,* 44–45, 49–50; Weber, *Protokoll: 5. ordentlicher Bundeskongress Stuttgart, 7. bis 12. September 1959,* 88–90; Deutscher Gewerkschaftsbund, Der Bundesvorstand, Hauptabteilung Frauen, *Ergebnisse einer Befragung über die Belastung der erwerbstätigen Frauen durch Beruf, Haushalt und Familie;* and Maria Borris, "Aufgaben der Frau bei vermehrter Freizeit," in *Protokoll der zweiten zentralen Frauenkonferenz 1957 in Hannover, Industriegewerkschaft Chemie-Papier-Keramik,* 136.

102. See, e.g., Monika Sperr, *Schlager: Das grosse Schlager-Buch, Deutsche Schlager 1800–Heute,* 240, 256, 269, 274.

103. Hinze, *Lage und Leistung erwerbstätiger Mütter,* 44, 95–96, 224, 228, 234, 236, 239, 242; Hertha Siemering, "Erwerbstätige Mütter," *Soziale Welt* 9 (1958): 106–19.

104. Walter Jaide, "Selbsterzeugnisse jugendlicher Industriearbeiterinnen," in *Die junge Arbeiterin: Beiträge zur Sozialkunde und Jugendarbeit,* ed. Gerhard Wurzbacher et al., 104–106; Renate Wald, "Ausgewählte Monographien jugendlicher Arbeiterinnen," in ibid., 331; Elisabeth Pfeil, *Die 23jährigen: Eine Generationsuntersuchung am Geburtenjahrgang 1941,* 93; Elfriede Höhn, *Das berufliche Fortkommen von Frauen,* 12; and Hildegard Friese, *Beruf und Familie im Urteil weiblicher Lehrlinge: Eine empirische Untersuchung zur Mädchenbildung,* 51–54, 58, 71–73, 101–108.

105. Herbert, *Geschichte der Ausländerbeschäftigung in Deutschland,* 180–81; and in general, Bethlehem, *Heimatvertreibung, DDR-Flucht, Gastarbeiterzuwanderung;* and Köllmann, "Die Bevölkerungsentwicklung der Bundesrepublik," 68–76.

106. Albrecht (IG Metall), *3. Bundes-Frauenkonferenz,* 110–11; see also Rationalisierungs-Kuratorium der deutschen Wirtschaft, ed., *Frauenarbeit: Ergebnisse einer Befragung* (n.p., n.d. [1959]), 13.

107. Herbert, *Geschichte der Ausländerbeschäftigung in Deutschland,* 188; Ralf Rytlewski and Manfred Opp de Hipt, *Die Bundesrepublik Deutschland in Zahlen, 1945/49–1980: Ein sozialgeschichtliches Arbeitsbuch,* 47; Köllmann, "Die Bevölkerungsentwicklung der Bundesrepublik," 80–85; Kurt Fiebich, "Das deutsche Arbeitskräftepotential," *Gewerkschaftliche Monatshefte* 7 (1956): 604–11; and Jürgen Fijalkowski, "Gastarbeiter als industrielle Reservearmee? Zur Bedeutung der Arbeitsimmigration für die wirtschaftliche und gesellschaftliche Entwicklung der Bundesrepublik Deutschland," 399–456.

108. Hinze, *Lage und Leistung erwerbstätiger Mütter,* 293; Kläre Pohl, "Teilzeitarbeit für Frauen," *Bundesarbeitsblatt* (1955): 900; and Christa Jacobsohn, "Familiengerechte Frauenarbeit—ein gesamtgesellschaftliches Zeitproblem," 118–25.

109. Elisabeth Vogelheim, "Women in a Changing Workplace: The Case of the Federal Republic of Germany," in *Feminization of the Labor Force: Paradoxes and Promises,* ed. Jane Jenson, Elisabeth Hagen, and Ceallaigh Reddy, 107; Eva Kolinsky, *Women in West Germany: Life, Work and Politics,*

174–78; Noll, "Soziale Indikatoren," 246–47; Eva Jenkins, "Teilzeitarbeit: Eine Sackgasse," in *Vom Nutzen weiblicher Lohnarbeit*, ed. Gerlinde Seidenspinner et al., 197–236; and, the positive assessment of Rosmarie Nemitz, "Zur Entwicklung der Frauenarbeit," *Gewerkschaftliche Monatshefte* 10 (1959): 713, 715–16.

110. Quoted in Klessmann, *Zwei Staaten, eine Nation*, 261. See also Hermann Korte, *Eine Gesellschaft im Aufbruch: Die Bundesrepublik Deutschland in den sechziger Jahren*, 56–69.

111. Kolinsky, *Women in West Germany*, 100, 119; and Willms-Herget, *Frauenarbeit*, 233–34.

112. See the generally pessimistic assessments in Johann Handl, "Abbau von Ungleichheit im Beruf durch bessere Bildung? Eine sozialhistorische Betrachtung," in Müller, Willms, and Handl, *Strukturwandel der Frauenarbeit*, 183–215; Hanna Beate Schöpp-Schilling, "Federal Republic of Germany," in *Women in Fifteen Countries: Essays in Honor of Alice Hanson Cook*, ed. Jennie Farley, 133–34; Willms-Herget, *Frauenarbeit*, 266–67; Seidenspinner et al., *Vom Nutzen weiblicher Lohnarbeit*; and Karl Ulrich Mayer, "Sozialhistorische Materialien zum Verhältnis von Bildungs- und Beschäftigungssystem bei Frauen," in *Bildungsexpansion und betriebliche Beschäftigungspolitik: Aktuelle Entwicklungstendenzen im Vermittlungszusammenhang von Bildung und Beschäftigung*, ed. Ulrich Beck, Karl H. Hörning, Wilke Thomssen, 60–79; and Maria Borris, with the assistance of Peter Raschke, *Die Benachteiligung der Mädchen in Schulen der Bundesrepublik und Westberlin*.

113. A comparison with the United States, where similar measures were absent, is instructive. See Sheila B. Kamerman, Alfred J. Kahn, and Paul Kingston, *Maternity Policies and Working Women*, 29–46.

114. Johannes Denecke, "Mutterschutz und Jugendschutz," in *Die Grundrechte: Handbuch der Theorie und Praxis der Grundrechte*, ed. Karl August Bettermann, Hans Carl Nipperdey, and Ulrich Scheuner, vol. 3, part 1, *Die Wirtschafts- und Arbeitsverfassung*, 475–76.

CHAPTER SIX

1. Lüders to Scheffler, 15 January 1954, BA, NL Lüders/227.

2. Quoted in Deutscher Juristinnenbund, ed., *Juristinnen in Deutschland*, 90.

3. For biographical information on Lüders, see ibid., 87–93; "Marie-Elisabeth Lüders (1878–1966)," in Frandsen, Huffmann, and Kuhn, *Frauen in Wissenschaft und Politik*, 39–40; and Marie-Elisabeth Lüders, *Fürchte dich nicht: Persönliches und Politisches aus mehr als 80 Jahren, 1878–1962*.

4. *Verhandlungen des achtunddreissigsten deutschen Juristentages*, B68–69.

5. Lüders to Brinkert, 10 March 1953, ADL, A5/73.

6. Decision of 6 September 1953, *Entscheidungen des Bundesgerichtshofes in Zivilsachen*, 11: 53*; and in general, Jan Kropholler, *Gleichberechtigung durch Richterrecht: Erfahrungen im Familienrecht—Perspektive im Inter-*

nationalen Privatrecht; and Wolfgang Voegeli and Barbara Willenbacher, "Die Ausgestaltung des Gleichberechtigungssatzes im Eherrecht," 239–40.

7. Bundesgerichtshof judgment of 14 July 1953, *Der Deutsche Rechtspfleger,* Sonderheft (1954): 65–68. On the precedent-setting intervention of the courts into the revaluation of debts after the post–World War I inflation, see the lucid discussion in Michael L. Hughes, *Paying for the German Inflation,* 17–19.

8. *Entscheidungen des Bundesgerichtshofes in Zivilsachen* 11: 50*–51*, 57*–58*, 62*, 67*–68*.

9. *Entscheidungen des Bundesverfassungsgerichts,* judgment of 18 December 1953, quotations from 3: 232, 239–42; see also Bernhard Diestelkamp, "Kontinuität und Wandel in der Rechtsordnung, 1945 bis 1955," in Herbst, *Westdeutschland 1945–1955,* 89.

10. Ilk in "Protokoll der Bundesfrauen-Ausschusssitzung [FDP] in Bonn am 16./17.4. 1953," ADL, A5/5; and Nadig, *VDBT,* [1.] Deutscher Bundestag, 258. Sitzung, 26 March 1953, 12518.

11. See the obituaries in *Neue juristische Wochenschrift* 36 (1983): 1653–54; and *Juristenzeitung* 38 (1983): 721; also the biographical sketch, "Erna Scheffler (1893–1983)," in Frandsen, Huffmann, and Kuhn, *Frauen in Wissenschaft und Politik,* 75–77.

12. *Verhandlungen des achtunddreissigsten deutschen Juristentages,* B6, B25.

13. Kommers, *Judicial Politics in West Germany,* 121–28.

14. Erna Scheffler, "Zur Auslegung des Grundsatzes der Gleichberechtigung," *Deutsche Richter-Zeitung* 31 (1953): 85–88; also idem, *Die Stellung der Frau in Familie und Gesellschaft im Wandel der Rechtsordnung seit 1918.*

15. *VDBT,* 2. Deutscher Bundestag, Drucksache 224 (dated 29 January 1954), 59.

16. Lüders to Scheffler, 15 January 1954, and Lüders to Krüger, 15 January 1954, both in BA, NL Lüders/227.

17. *Entscheidungen des Bundesgerichtshofes in Zivilsachen* 11: 66*.

18. Oberlandesgericht Celle, decision of 1953, *Deutscher Rechtspfleger* (Sonderheft) (1954): 53.

19. Decision of Oberlandesgericht Frankfurt, 16 June 1953, *Neue juristische Wochenschrift* 6 (1953): 1104–05; Oberlandesgericht Düsseldorf, decision of 9 September 1953, *Deutscher Rechtspfleger* (Sonderheft) (1954): 72.

20. Bundesgerichtshof decision of 14 December 1956, reported in *Neue juristische Wochenschrift* 10 (1957): 537.

21. Kropholler, *Gleichberechtigung durch Richterrecht,* 13–14, 50–51.

22. Decision of Oberlandesgericht Celle, 13 May 1954, *Ehe und Familie im privaten und öffentlichen Recht: Zeitschrift für das gesamte Familienrecht* 1 (1954): 141–44 (cited hereafter as *FamRZ*). Edited by Catholic legal expert F. W. Bosch, this was a key journal for family law.

23. Decision of Oberlandesgericht Frankfurt, 17 December 1956, *FamRZ* 4 (1957): 55–56.

24. Decisions of Oberlandesgericht Celle, 10 February 1955 and 22 April 1955, *FamRZ* 2 (1955): 213–14.

25. Decision of Bayerisches Oberlandesgericht, 12 December 1957, *FamRZ* 5 (1958): 67–71.

26. Decision of 12 November 1956, Landesgericht Bad Kreuznach, *FamRZ* 4 (1957): 326–28. See also Kropholler, *Gleichberechtigung durch Richterrecht,* 50–51.

27. Decision of 10 May 1957, *Entscheidungen des Bundesverfassungsgerichts* 6: 394, 413, 419. See also decision of 13 March 1951, *Entscheidungen des Bundesgerichtshofs in Strafsachen* 1: 80–84; and other similar precedents in 1946 and 1947, *Neue juristische Wochenschrift* 1 (1947/48): 32.

28. Peukert, *Inside Nazi Germany,* 219–20; Erwin J. Haeberle, "Swastika, Pink Triangle, and Yellow Star: The Destruction of Sexology and the Persecution of Homosexuals in Nazi Germany," in *Hidden From History: Reclaiming the Gay and Lesbian Past,* ed. Martin Bauml Duberman, Martha Vicinus, George Chauncey, Jr., 365–79; Rüdiger Lautmann, " 'Hauptdevise: bloss nicht anecken': Das Leben homosexueller Männer unter dem Nationalsozialismus," in *Terror und Hoffnung in Deutschland 1933–1945: Leben im Faschismus,* ed. Johannes Beck et al., 366–90; Burkhard Jellonnek, *Homosexuelle unter dem Hakenkreuz: Die Verfolgung von Homosexuellen im Dritten Reich;* Heinz-Dieter Schilling, ed., *Schwule und Faschismus;* Hans-Georg Stümke, *Homosexuelle in Deutschland: Eine politische Geschichte,* 132–35; Hans-Georg Stümke and Rudi Finkler, *Rosa Winkel, Rosa Listen: Homosexuelle und "gesundes Volksempfinden" von Auschwitz bis heute,* 212–301, 356–67; Burleigh and Wippermann, *The Racial State,* 182–97; Claudia Schoppmann, *Nationalsozialistische Sexualpolitik und weibliche Homosexualität;* Peter Kröger, "Entwicklungsstadien der Bestrafung der widernatürlichen Unzucht und kritische Studie zur Berechtigung der §§ 175, 175a, 175b StGB de lege ferenda," 18–20, 54–63, 100; and Tobias Brocher et al., *Plädoyer für die Abschaffung des § 175,* 10–11. Only in 1985 after intense lobbying by the Green party were gay men added to the official litany of those with just claims to compensation for their persecution by the Nazis.

29. Helmut Schelsky, *Soziologie der Sexualität: Über die Beziehungen zwischen Geschlecht, Moral und Gesellschaft,* esp. 75–87.

30. *Entscheidungen des Bundesverfassungsgerichts* 6: 408–09.

31. Ibid., 424.

32. Ibid., 421–32. The court case cited determined that hours-of-work restrictions for women did not violate the Basic Law's equal-rights provisions. See decision of 25 May 1956, *Entscheidungen des Bundesverfassungsgerichts* 5: 9–12. And for precedents, decision of the Bundesgerichtshof, 22 June 1951, *Neue juristische Wochenschrift* 4 (1951): 810; and decision of Oberlandesgericht Braunschweig, 2 October 1953, *Neue juristische Wochenschrift* 6 (1953): 1929–31.

33. Bundesgerichtshof decision of 29 April 1954, *FamRZ* 1 (1954): 107–08.

34. Decision of 15 June 1954, Amtsgericht Stromberg-Hunsrück, *FamRZ* 2 (1955): 102–03.

35. Decision of Landesgericht Munich I, 25 September 1953, *FamRZ* 2 (1955): 103.

36. Amtsgericht Stromberg-Hunsrück, 15 June 1954, *FamRZ* 2 (1955): 102–03.

37. Decision of 30 March 1954, Amtsgericht Nuremberg, *FamRZ* 2 (1955): 102. See also the article by the judge in this case, Egon Arnold, "§ 1300 BGB und die Gleichberechtigung von Mann und Frau," *FamRZ* 2 (1955): 91–93; also Hans Dölle, "Die Gleichberechtigung von Mann und Frau im Familienrecht," *Juristenzeitung* 8 (1953): 356.

38. Decision of 24 May 1954, Landesgericht Hamburg, *FamRZ* 2 (1955): 102.

39. Decision of 10 May 1957, *Entscheidungen des Bundesverfassungsgerichts* 6: 422.

40. In general, see the discussion in Chapter 5 and the theoretical insights offered by Eisenstein, *The Female Body and the Law*.

41. Scheffler, "Zur Auslegung," 85.

42. Harald Schlüter, "Der Richter und die Frage der Gleichberechtigung," *Neue juristische Wochenschrift* 6 (1953): 809.

43. Lüders to Krüger, 15 January 1954, BA, NL Lüders/227.

44. *VDBT,* 2. Deutscher Bundestag, 15. Sitzung, 12 February 1954, 488–93.

45. *VDBT,* 2. Deutscher Bundestag, 206. Sitzung, 3 May 1957, 11776; 15. Sitzung, 12 February 1954, 512–15.

46. Ilk, *VDBT,* 2. Deutscher Bundestag, 15. Sitzung, 12 February 1954, 483; also, for the FDP, Dehler and Lüders, 483, 503–509; and 206. Sitzung, 3 May 1957, 11772; and for SPD, Metzger and Nadig, 15. Sitzung, 12 February 1954, 485–87, 494–97; and 206. Sitzung, 3 May 1957, 11777–78, 11786. See also Helene Wessel, "Der Stichentscheid des Mannes in christlicher Betrachtung," *Gleichheit* 20 (1957): 209. Wessel, one of the four women who participated in the Parliamentary Council, had left the Center party for the SPD.

47. These themes ran throughout position papers and petitions of middle-class women's organizations. See, e.g., Deutscher Frauenring, e.V., Frauenring Wuppertal, to Rechtsausschuss of the Bundestag, 13 February 1957, PA, II/409B2; Vereinigung weiblicher Juristen und Volkswirte e.V. to Familienrechtsausschuss of the Bundestag, 6 November 1956, PA, II/409B1; petition of Deutscher Frauenring, 18 January 1954, HStAS, EA1/4/1380/3; Deutscher Akademikerinnenbund, e.V., Zweiggruppe Karlsruhe to BJM, 4 June 1954, BA, B141/2024; Landesverband Hessen e.V. im Deutschen Hausfrauenbund to BJM, 9 February 1957, BA, B141/2025; and the many petitions, especially for early 1957, reprinted in *Informationen für die Frau,* the monthly publication of the Deutscher Frauenring.

48. Ilk in *Informationen für die Frau,* no. 2 (1957): 6–7.

49. *VDBT,* 2. Deutscher Bundestag, 15. Sitzung, 12 February 1954, 504.

50. Gudrun Fuhrmann, "Gleichberechtigung—eine Verpflichtung," *Gleichheit* 20 (1957): 24.

51. *VDBT,* 2. Deutscher Bundestag, 206. Sitzung, 3 May 1957, 11789–91; "Protokoll der 67. Sitzung des Unterausschusses 'Familienrechtsgesetz' des Ausschusses für Rechtswesen und Verfassungsrecht am Donnerstag den 15. November 1956," 8–9; and Feuersenger, *Die garantierte Gleichberechtigung,* 109–10.

52. Notes on the CDU/CSU Bundestag delegation meeting, 3 May 1957, the day of the final vote, ACDP, 08/001/1007/3, 197–201.

53. See above, Chapter 3, note 56. Also, e.g., Deutscher Hausfrauenbund, protesting CDU intransigence, 15 March 1954, *Informationen für die Frau*, no. 3, Anlage A (1954): 1; and Evangelische Frauenarbeit in Deutschland to members of Bundestag, 17 January 1957, BA, NL Lüders/226.

54. Deutscher Bundestag, Wissenschaftliche Dienste, Abteilung Wissenschaftliche Dokumentation, ed., *Abgeordnete des Deutschen Bundestages: Aufzeichnungen und Erinnerungen* 2: 241–63; and "Elisabeth Schwarzhaupt (1901–1986)," in Frandsen, Huffmann, and Kuhn, *Frauen in Wissenschaft und Politik*, 99–101.

55. *VDBT*, 2. Deutscher Bundestag, 206. Sitzung, 3 May 1957, 11787; also 15. Sitzung, 12 February 1954, 498–502. Echoing these positions, Anna Endres, "Zur Ehe- und Familienrechtsreform," *Informationen für die Frau*, no. 11 (1956): 3. And on the position of the national organization of the Protestant church, "Beschluss der Eherechtskommission der Evangelischen Kirche in Deutschland zur Eherechtsreform vom 24./25. September 1954," in *Familienrechtsreform: Dokumente und Abhandlungen*, ed. Hans Adolf Dombois and Friedrich Karl Schumann, 61–66.

56. Committee discussions are summarized in Deutscher Bundestag, 2. Wahlperiode 1953, Drucksache 3409, dated 12 April 1957.

57. Comments of Massfeller, BJM, "Protokoll der 55. Sitzung des Unterausschusses 'Familienrechtsgesetz' des Ausschusses für Rechtswesen und Verfassungsrecht am 28. September 1956," 8; and *VDBT*, 2. Deutscher Bundestag, 206. Sitzung, 3 May 1957, 11779. These provisions held up to legal challenge after the law's passage. See the decision of Oberlandesgericht Karlsruhe, 3 July 1958, *FamRZ* 5 (1958): 326–29; the decision of Bundesverwaltungsgericht, VII. Senat, 27 November 1959, *FamRZ* 7 (1960): 113–16; and Kropholler, *Gleichberechtigung durch Richterrecht*, 25–33.

58. "Protokoll der 4. Sitzung des Unterausschusses 'Familienrechtsgesetz' des Ausschusses für Rechtswesen und Verfassungsrecht am 19. April 1955," 13.

59. Herta Ilk's remarks, "Zweiter Teil des Protokolls der 21. Sitzung des Ausschusses für Rechtswesen und Verfassungsrecht am 12. Juli 1954," 6.

60. Comments of Massfeller, BJM, "Protokoll der 56. Sitzung des Unterausschusses 'Familienrechtsgesetz' des Ausschusses für Rechtswesen und Verfassungsrecht am 29. September 1956," 7–8.

61. "Protokoll der 56. Sitzung," 7; "Protokoll der 52. Sitzung," 17; and in general, Curt Bondy et al., *Jugendliche stören die Ordnung: Bericht und Stellungnahme zu den Halbstarkenkrawallen*.

62. Comments of Massfeller, BJM, "Protokoll der 56. Sitzung," 5.

63. Walter Strauss, BJM, *VDBT*, 2. Deutscher Bundestag, 206. Sitzung, 3 May 1957, 11789.

64. "Protokoll der 68. Sitzung des Unterausschusses 'Familienrechtsgesetz' des Ausschusses für Rechtswesen und Verfassungsrecht am 26. November 1956," 30.

65. *VDBT*, 2. Deutscher Bundestag, 206. Sitzung, 3 May 1957, 11792.

66. "Protokoll der 172. Sitzung des Ausschusses für Rechtswesen und Verfassungsrecht am 12. Dezember 1956," 12.

67. *VDBT*, 2. Deutscher Bundestag, 206. Sitzung, 3 May 1957, 11792.

68. Ibid., 11787.

69. Lüders to Stephan, 15 May 1957, BA, NL Lüders/226.

70. *VDBT*, 2. Deutscher Bundestag, 206. Sitzung, 3 May 1957, 11800.

71. Ibid., 11786; also Frieda Nadig, "Neuregelung des Familienrechts," *Gleichheit* 20 (1957): 242–44.

72. Lüders, *Fürchte dich nicht*, 189; and Feuersenger, *Die garantierte Gleichberechtigung*, 132–33.

73. Parlamentarischer Rat, Hauptausschuss, 42. Sitzung, 18 January 1949, 538–39, quoted in Bundesverfassungsgericht decision of 29 July 1959, *Entscheidungen des Bundesverfassungsgerichts* 10: 68. This was not the first time Strauss's words had been shoved in his face. Indeed, his remarks before the Parliamentary Council were cited frequently by liberal feminists and the courts, arguing for a broader interpretation of equal rights within marriage. See Bundesverfassungsgericht decision of 18 December 1953, *Entscheidungen des Bundesverfassungsgerichts* 3: 238; Lüders, *VDBT*, 2. Deutscher Bundestag, 15. Sitzung, 12 February 1954, 506–07; and Hildegard Krüger in her devastating critique of the 1957 law, published before the 1959 court decision. See Hildegard Krüger, Ernst Breetzke, and Kuno Nowack, *Gleichberechtigungsgesetz*, 133.

74. Lüders, *VDBT*, 2. Deutscher Bundestag, 206. Sitzung, 3 May 1957, 11778. See also Gethmann, head of the Vereinigung weiblicher Juristen und Volkswirte, e.V., to Lüders, 18 March 1957, reporting results of a survey of judges on this issue, BA, NL Lüders/226; and the report of the same organization in *Informationen für die Frau*, no. 2 (1957): 6. And in general, Barbara Willenbacher, "Thesen zur rechtlichen Stellung der Frau," in Gerhardt and Schütze, *Frauensituation*, 147.

75. Decision of 29 July 1959, *Entscheidungen des Bundesverfassungsgerichts* 10: 63–64, 67–71, 75, 78, 81–82; also Kommers, *Constitutional Jurisprudence*, 493–98. Other important legal decisions in the late fifties clearly restated this theme. See, e.g., the Federal Constitutional Court's decision declaring that joint-filing requirements for the income taxes of married couples where both spouses were employed, which subjected them to higher rates, were unconstitutional. Joint filing was rejected not on the basis of women's equal rights with men but because it was seen as a "tax penalty on marriage" (*Ehestrafsteuer*). See *Entscheidungen des Bundesverfassungsgerichts* 6: 71–81; Marie-Elisabeth Lüders, "Ehestrafsteuer," in FDP Bundesfrauenreferat, Rundschreiben Nr. 10.54, 29 September 1954, in ADL, A5/8; the collection of petitions from women's organizations attacking the law, "Zum Thema Steuerreform," *Informationen für die Frau*, no. 2, Anlage D (1953); and ibid., no. 4, Anlage C (1953); and the ministerial discussions within the BMF, in BA, B106/8168, Heft 1, Heft 2. In another case, the Federal Labor Court dismissed as "fundamentally inimical to marriage"—at odds with Article 6—not as a violation of women's rights—Article 3—laws that required female trainees in

state-run vocational programs to resign should they marry. Decision of 10 May 1957, *Entscheidungen des Bundesarbeitsgerichts* 4: 279–81.

76. F. W. Bosch, "Grundsatzfragen des Gleichberechtigungsgesetzes vor dem Bundesverfassungsgericht," *FamRZ* 6 (1959): 266.

77. F. W. Bosch, "Zum Urteil des Bundesverfassungsgerichts vom 29. Juli 1959," *FamRZ* 6 (1959): 406–16. See also Eduard Wahl, "Zur Verfassungs-mässigkeit des Stichentscheids des Vaters," *FamRZ* 6 (1959): 305–09.

78. Marie-Elisabeth Lüders, "Vorläufig letztes Rennen," *Was Frauen wissen wollen*, no. 8, 21 May 1957; see also the sharp exchange between the head of the national Protestant church organization and Lüders, 18 June 1957, and 3 July 1957, BA, NL Lüders/226.

79. See the general overviews provided by Jutta Limbach, "Die Entwicklung des Familienrechts seit 1949," in Nave-Herz, *Wandel und Kontinuität*, 11–35; Shaffer, *Women in the Two Germanies*, 28–33; and Sachsse and Tennstedt, "Familienpolitik durch Gesetzgebung," 94–100.

80. Dietrich Reinecke and Elisabeth Schwarzhaupt, *Die Gleichberechtigung von Mann und Frau nach dem Gesetz vom 18. Juni 1957*, 10.

81. Anneliese Weber, "Zur Problematik der betrieblichen Frauenarbeit," *Gewerkschaftliche Monatshefte* 5 (1954): 687; and in general, Christine Hohmann-Dehnhardt, "Gleichberechtigung via Rechtsnorm? Zur Frage eines Antidiskriminierungsgesetzes in der Bundesrepublik," in Schütze and Gerhard, *Frauensituation*, 167–68; Reich-Hilweg, *Männer und Frauen*; and Drohsel, *Die Lohndiskriminierung der Frauen*.

EPILOGUE

1. U. W. Kitzinger, *German Electoral Politics: A Study of the 1957 Campaign;* also, Hans-Peter Schwarz, *Die Ära Adenauer*, 363–74; and Gotto, "Die deutschen Katholiken," 28–30.

2. Ralf Dahrendorf, "Die neue Gesellschaft: Soziale Strukturwandlungen der Nachkriegszeit," in *Bestandsaufnahme: Eine deutsche Bilanz 1962*, ed. Hans Werner Richter, 215. Dahrendorf in turn borrows the phrase from Joseph Schumpeter. For an excellent analysis of the changing nature of West German industrial capitalism after 1945, see Volker R. Berghahn, *The Americanisation of West German Industry 1945–1973*.

3. See, e.g., Mooser, *Arbeiterleben in Deutschland*, 73–80; and Mary Fulbrook, "The State and the Transformation of Political Legitimacy in East and West Germany since 1945," 226, 240.

4. Heinz-Dietrich Ortlieb, "Glanz und Elend des deutschen Wirtschafts-wunders," in Richter, *Bestandsaufnahme*, 275–91; Ingeborg Marx, "Die Tot-geschwiegenen: Das Problem des Frauenüberschusses in der Bundesrepublik," *Frau im Beruf: Nachrichten des Verbandes der weiblichen Angestellten* 9 (1959): 40–41; Regina Bohne, *Das Geschick der zwei Millionen: Die alleinle-bende Frau in unserer Gesellschaft;* Lothar Franke, *Das tapfere Leben: Lebens-fragen alleinstehender Frauen und Mütter;* Meyer and Schulze, *Wie wir das alles geschafft haben;* and Herta Däubler-Gmelin and Marianne Müller, *Wir sind auch noch da! Ältere Frauen zwischen Resignation und Selbstbewusstsein*, 32–41.

5. See the survey in Heidi Rosenbaum, *Formen der Familie: Untersuchungen zum Zusammenhang von Familienverhältnissen, Sozialstruktur und sozialem Wandel in der deutschen Gesellschaft des 19. Jahrhunderts;* Hagemann, *Frauenalltag und Männerpolitik,* 23–132; and Lutz Niethammer and Franz Brüggemeier, "Wie wohnten Arbeiter im Kaiserreich?" 61–134.

6. Wuermeling in Nordwestdeutscher Rundfunk interview, typescript, 10 November 1953, in ACDP, I-221-017.

7. Account of a press conference by Wuermeling, "Das Problem eines Familienlastenausgleichs," *Bulletin,* no. 221 (1955): 1870.

8. See, e.g., "Familienpolitik," *Deutsche Zeitung,* 14 November 1953, clipping in HStAS, EA8/1/78.

9. See the interesting parallels with postwar West German silence on Nazi anti-Semitism in Max Miller, "Kollektive Erinnerungen und gesellschaftliche Lernprozesse: Zur Struktur sozialer Mechanismen der Vergangenheitsbewältigung," in *Antisemitismus in der politischen Kultur nach 1945,* ed. Werner Bergmann and Rainer Erb, 83.

10. In addition to the examples cited above, see, e.g., Helga Schmucker, "Auswirkungen des generativen Verhaltens der Bevölkerung auf die Lage der Familie und auf die Wirtschaft," in *Die ökonomischen Grundlagen der Familie in ihrer gesellschaftlichen Bedeutung,* ed. Gesellschaft für sozialen Fortschritt, 128–223. A comparison with the psychoanalytic terms that dominated the British approach to the postwar problems of women and children is illuminating. See Riley, *War in the Nursery;* John Bowlby, *Maternal Care and Mental Health;* and on the German reception of Bowlby in the sixties and seventies, Schütze, "Mütterliche Erwerbstätigkeit," 124.

11. Betty Friedan, *The Feminine Mystique,* 29.

12. Alexander Mitscherlich and Margarete Mitscherlich, *Die Unfähigkeit zu trauern: Grundlagen kollektiven Verhaltens,* 19; and Wilfried Röhrich, *Die Demokratie der Westdeutschen: Geschichte und politisches Klima einer Republik,* 21.

13. See, e.g., "Bericht der Bundesregierung über die Situation der Frauen in Beruf, Familie und Gesellschaft," a major study undertaken by the Bundestag, which takes 1950 as the point of reference, Deutscher Bundestag, 5. Wahlperiode, Drucksache V/909; and Willms-Herget, *Frauenarbeit,* 88, 118; also Schwarz, *Die Ära Adenauer,* 395; and Klessmann, *Zwei Staaten, eine Nation,* 34.

14. Willms, "Grundzüge der Entwicklung der Frauenarbeit," 35; Karl Ulrich Mayer, "German Survivors of World War II: The Impact on the Life Course of the Collective Experience of Birth Cohorts," in *Social Structures and Human Lives,* ed. Matilda White Riley in association with Bettina J. Huber and Beth B. Hess, 239; and in general, Abelshauser, *Wirtschaftsgeschichte,* 119–28.

15. Willms-Herget, *Frauenarbeit,* 88.

16. See, e.g., Wuermeling's speech to Deutsche Landjugend, "Zehn Jahre Deutsche Landjugend," *Bulletin,* no. 177 (1959): 1785–86.

17. *Protokoll der Verhandlungen des ausserordentlichen Parteitages der Sozialdemokratischen Partei Deutschlands vom 13.–15. November 1959,* 24; Marta Schanzenbach's comments in *Protokoll der Verhandlungen und Anträge*

*vom Parteitag der Sozialdemokratischen Partei Deutschlands in Hannover 21.
bis 25. November 1960,* 364–66; and the introduction to the vast literature on
this topic in Susanne Miller, *Die SPD vor und nach Godesberg;* and Klotzbach,
Der Weg zur Staatspartei, 449–54; and the critical assessment of Theo Pirker,
*Die SPD nach Hitler: Die Geschichte der Sozialdemokratischen Partei Deutsch-
lands 1945–1964.* None of these standard works pays any attention to the SPD's
answers to the "woman question." Regrettably, there is still no history of the
Social Democratic organization of women in this period.

18. See the protest in 1956 of conservative "family associations" to Adenauer over rumors that Wuermeling might be forced out of his post to make
room for a woman, ACDP, I-221-013. And on women's electoral behavior, Kitzinger, *German Electoral Politics,* 289.

19. Deutscher Bundestag, *Abgeordnete des Deutschen Bundestages* 2: 267;
Deutscher Juristinnenbund, ed., *Juristinnen in Deutschland,* 121–22; Feuersenger, *Die garantierte Gleichberechtigung,* 122–31; and Gabriele Bremme, "Die
Mitarbeit der Frau in der Politik," *Informationen für die Frau,* no. 4 (1958):
3–4.

20. Pateman, "The Patriarchal Welfare State," 238, 254.

21. Krüger, Breetzke, and Nowack, *Gleichberechtigungsgesetz,* 513–14.

22. Maria Hagemeyer, "Zum Gleichberechtigungsgesetz," *Informationen
für die Frau,* no. 5 (1958): 6.

23. Kitzinger, *German Electoral Politics,* 122, n. 1.

24. Alexander Mitscherlich, *Auf dem Weg zur vaterlosen Gesellschaft: Ideen
zur Sozialpsychologie,* 183; idem, "Der unsichtbare Vater: Ein Problem für Psychoanalyse und Soziologie," 188–201; Hans-Rudolf Müller-Schwefe, *Die Welt
ohne Väter: Gedanken eines Christen zur Krise der Autorität;* the discussion in
Reinhold Junker, *Die Lage der Mütter in der Bundesrepublik Deutschland: Ein
Forschungsbericht,* part 1, vol. 1, 3; and Walter Dirks, "Was die Ehe bedroht:
Eine Liste ihrer kritischen Punkte," 24.

25. Sally Alexander, "Women, Class and Sexual Differences in the 1830s
and 1840s," 146.

26. Frevert, *Women in German History,* 292; and Frigga Haug, "The
Women's Movement in West Germany," 50–74. In some respects, this represented a return to an agenda pursued in Weimar and silenced, first by the Nazis,
then by the politics of family and motherhood in the Adenauer era. See Grossmann, "Abortion and Economic Crisis"; idem, "The New Woman and the Rationalization of Sexuality"; and idem, " 'Satisfaction is Domestic Happiness.' "

27. Mechtild Jansen, "Der Einfluss der Frauenbewegung auf die politische
Kultur der Bundesrepublik," 299; idem, "Frauen und Politik: Die 'neue' Frauenpolitik der Bundesrepublik und das Agieren der Frauenbewegung," in *Frauen-
Widerspruch: Alltag und Politik,* ed. Mechtild Jansen, 11–44; Frevert, *Women
in German History,* 298–303; Haug, "The Women's Movement in West Germany," 71–72; Birgit Meyer, "Viel bewegt—auch viel erreicht? Frauengeschichte und Frauenbewegung in der Bundesrepublik," 832–42; Joyce M.
Mushaben, "Feminism in Four Acts: The Changing Political Identity of Women
in the Federal Republic of Germany," in *The Federal Republic at Forty,* ed. Peter
H. Merkl, 76–109; and on the revival of CDU/CSU *Familienpolitik* in the sev-

enties, Rainer Silkenbeumer, "Familie ist Trumpf—statt eines Vorworts," in *Geburtenrückgang: Risiko oder Chance*, ed. Rainer Silkenbeumer, 7–19; Albert Müller, "Ideologische Elemente, Ungereimtes und Widersprüchliches in der bevölkerungs- und familienpolitischen Diskussion," in ibid., 162–69; Roland Eckert et al., *Familie und Familienpolitik: Zur Situation in der Bundesrepublik Deutschland;* Heiner Geissler, ed., *Abschied von der Männergesellschaft;* and Elisabeth Beck-Gernsheim, *Vom Geburtenrückgang zur neuen Mütterlichkeit: Über private und politische Interessen am Kind*, 153–78.

28. Helge Pross, "Die gesellschaftliche Stellung der Frau in Westdeutschland," 26–33.

29. Author of an influential study of entrepreneurial elites in the sixties, Pross went on in the seventies to pursue a feminist agenda in her scholarship. See, e.g., Helge Pross, *Über die Bildungschancen von Mädchen in der Bundesrepublik;* idem, *Abtreibung: Motive und Bedenken;* idem, *Kapitalismus und Demokratie: Studien über westdeutsche Sozialstrukturen*, 68–85; idem, *Gleichberechtigung im Beruf? Eine Untersuchung mit 7000 Arbeitnehmerinnen in der EWG;* idem, *Die Wirklichkeit der Hausfrau: Die erste repräsentative Untersuchung über nichterwerbstätige Ehefrauen: Wie leben sie? Wie denken sie? Wie sehen sie sich selbst?;* Rosemarie von Schweitzer and Helge Pross, eds., *Die Familienhaushalte im wirtschaftlichen und sozialen Wandel: Rationalverhalten, Technisierung, Funktionswandel der Privathaushalte und das Freizeitbudget der Frau;* and Helge Pross, "Zu den Zielen und Methoden der soziologischen Frauenforschung," in Frandsen, Huffmann, and Kuhn, *Frauen in Wissenschaft und Politik*, 121–29.

Bibliography

PRIMARY SOURCES

ARCHIVAL SOURCES

Archiv der sozialen Demokratie, Bonn (ASD)
    Bestand Schumacher
    Gesellschaft für sozialen Fortschritt
    PV Akten, Alter Bestand
Archiv des Deutschen Liberalismus, Gummersbach (ADL)
    A5 Bundesfrauenausschuss und Bundesfrauenreferat
    DA Nachlass Thomas Dehler
Archiv für Christlich-Demokratische Politik, St. Augustin (ACDP)
    IV-003 Frauenvereinigung und Europäische Frauen-Union
    I-221 Franz-Josef Wuermeling
    VIII-005 Arbeitskreis IV, Arbeit und Soziales
    Niederschriften über Fraktionssitzungen
Bildarchiv preussischer Kulturbesitz, Berlin
Bundesarchiv, Koblenz (BA)
    B106 Bundesministerium des Innern (BMI)
    B136 Bundeskanzleramt
    B141 Bundesministerium für Justiz (BMJ)
    B149 Bundesministerium für Arbeit (BMA)
    B153 Bundesministerium für Familie und Jugend
    B191 Evangelische Arbeitsgemeinschaft für Familienfragen
    B211 Deutscher Frauenrat
    RG260/OMGUS
    Z1 Länderrat des amerikanischen Besatzungsgebiets
    Z5 Parlamentarischer Rat
    Z40 Zentralamt für Arbeit in der britischen Zone
    Nachlass Marie-Elisabeth Lüders (NL Lüders)
    Plakbestand

Deutscher Gewerkschaftsbund, Archiv, Düsseldorf (DGB Archiv)
    Hausarbeitstag, Berichte, Pressemeldungen, Gutachten, 1949–1960
    Familienrecht Kündigungsschutz, 1952–1957
    Werksfürsorge, 1957–1961
Hauptstaatsarchiv Stuttgart (HStAS)
    EA 1 Staatsministerium
    EA 2 Innenministerium
    EA 8 Ministerium für Arbeit, Gesundheit und Sozialordnung
Hoover Institution Archives, Stanford
    GE Poster Collection
Landesarchiv Berlin
    Rep. 240 Plakate
Niedersächsisches Hauptstaatsarchiv (NdsHStA)
    Nds. 1310 Landesarbeitsamt Niedersachsen-Bremen
    Nds. 1311 Arbeitsämter
Nordrhein-Westfälisches Hauptstaatsarchiv, Düsseldorf (NWHStA)
    NW37 Gewerbeaufsicht
    NW42–43 Ministerium für Arbeit, Gesundheit und Soziales
    NW45 Gewerbeaufsicht, Sozialversicherung und Soziales
    NW62 Arbeitsrecht und Arbeitsschutz
    RWV38 CDU Kreisverband Duisburg
    RW177 DGB Kreisausschuss Bochum
    RWB Bildbestand
    RWP Plakbestand
Nordrhein-Westfälisches Staatsarchiv Münster (NWStAM)
    Regierung Arnsberg Abt. I Sozialangelegenheiten
Parlamentsarchiv des Deutschen Bundestages, Bonn (PA)
    Gesetzesdokumentation, I/257, I/1035, I/1053, II/201, II/409
    Parlamentarischer Rat
    Protokolle der Ausschüsse des Bundestages
Public Records Office, Kew (PRO)
    FO Foreign Office, Control Commission for Germany, British Element, 945,
    1049–51
Zentrum für audio-visuelle Medien, Landesbildstelle, Berlin

JOURNALS AND NEWSPAPERS

*Der Arbeitgeber: Zeitschrift der Bundesvereinigung der deutschen Arbeitgeber-
    verbände* (1949–57)
Arbeitsblatt (1949)
Arbeitsblatt für die britische Zone (1947–48)
*Arbeit und Sozialpolitik: Mitteilungsblatt des Arbeitsministeriums Nordrhein-
    Westfalen* (1948–59)
Der Betriebs-Berater (1951–59)
Bulletin des Presse- und Informationsamtes der Bundesregierung (1951–60)
Bundesarbeitsblatt (1950–60)

Deutsche Richter-Zeitung (1953–60)
Der deutsche Rechtspfleger (Sonderheft, 1954)
Ehe und Familie im privaten und öffentlichen Recht: Zeitschrift für das gesamte Familienrecht (1954–62)
Frauen und Arbeit: Mitteilungsblatt der Hauptabteilung "Frauen" im DGB-Vorstand (1958–60)
Frau im Beruf: Nachrichten des Verbandes der weiblichen Angestellten (1951–58)
Frau und Politik: Mitteilungen und Berichte der Christlich-Demokratischen Union (1955–60)
Das Fundament: Überparteiliche Zeitung für Familienpolitik und Familienbildung (1957–63)
Genossin: SPD Informationsblatt für Funktionärinnen (1947–49)
Gewerkschaftliche Monatshefte (1950–60)
Gleichheit: Das Blatt der arbeitenden Frau (1950–60)
Informationen für die Frau (1952–65)
Jahresberichte der Gewerbe-Aufsicht, Bundesrepublik und Land Berlin (1950–62)
Juristenzeitung (1949–60)
Neue juristische Wochenschrift (1947/48–61)
Das Parlament (1951–55)
Die Quelle (1948–52)
Recht der Arbeit: Zeitschrift für Wissenschaft und Praxis des gesamten Arbeitsrechts (1950–61)
Soziale Arbeit (1951–59)
Sozialer Fortschritt (1952–63)
Soziale Welt (1950–60)
Was Frauen wissen wollen (1955–60)
Wirtschaft und Statistik (1949–65)

PUBLISHED PRIMARY SOURCES

Ausschuss der deutschen Statistiker für die Volks- und Berufszählung 1946. *Volks- und Berufszählung vom 29. Oktober 1946 in den vier Besatzungszonen und Gross-Berlin: Berufszählung, Textteil.* Berlin: Duncker & Humblot, n.d. [1946].
———. *Volks- und Berufszählung vom 29. Oktober 1946 in den vier Besatzungszonen und Gross-Berlin: Volkszählung, Textteil.* Berlin: Duncker & Humblot, n.d. [1946].
Bundesministerium für Arbeit. *Entwicklung, Stand und Gewicht der Frauenarbeitslosigkeit in der Bundesrepublik Deutschland.* Bonn: n.p., [1951].
Deutscher Gewerkschaftsbund, Der Bundesvorstand, Hauptabteilung Frauen. *Ergebnisse einer Befragung über die Belastung der erwerbstätigen Frauen durch Beruf, Haushalt und Familie.* Cologne: Bund-Verlag, 1961.
Deutscher Gewerkschaftsbund. *1. Bundesfrauenkonferenz Mainz, 27. bis 29. Mai 1952.* Düsseldorf: Gebr. Hermes, n.d.

———. *Protokoll: 2. Bundesfrauenkonferenz des Deutschen Gewerkschaftsbundes vom 12. bis 14. Mai 1955 in Dortmund.* Düsseldorf: Gebr. Hermes, n.d.

———. *3. Bundes-Frauenkonferenz: Deutscher Gewerkschaftsbund vom 25. bis 27. Mai 1959 in Bremen.* Bochum: Verlagsgesellschaft der IG Bergbau, n.d.

———. Hauptabteilung "Frauen" beim Bundesvorstand des Deutschen Gewerkschaftsbundes. *Jahres- und Geschäftsbericht 1950–1951.* Düsseldorf: Gebr. Hermes, n.d. [1952].

———. *Protokoll: Ausserordentlicher Bundeskongress des Deutschen Gewerkschaftsbundes, Essen, 22. und 23. Juni 1951.* Cologne: Bund-Verlag, n.d.

———. *Protokoll: 5. ordentlicher Bundeskongress Stuttgart, 7. bis 12. September 1959.* Cologne-Deutz: Druckhaus Deutz, n.d.

Deutschland, sozialer Rechtsstaat im geeinten Europa. 4. Bundesparteitag [Christlich-Demokratische Union], 18.–22. April 1953, Hamburg. Hamburg: Sator Werbe, n.d.

Dritter Parteitag der Christlich-Demokratischen Union Deutschlands, Berlin, 17.–19. Oktober 1952. Cologne: Kölnische Verlagsdruckerei, n.d.

Entscheidungen des Bundesarbeitsgerichts. Berlin: Walter de Gruyter & Co., 1955 ff.

Entscheidungen des Bundesgerichtshofes in Strafsachen. Detmold and Berlin: Carl Heymanns, 1951 ff.

Entscheidungen des Bundesgerichtshofes in Zivilsachen. Berlin: Carl Heymanns, 1954 ff.

Entscheidungen des Bundesverfassungsgerichts. Tübingen: J. C. B. Mohr (Paul Siebeck), 1954 ff.

Heilfron, Ed., ed. *Die deutsche Nationalversammlung im Jahre 1919 in ihrer Arbeit für den Aufbau des neuen deutschen Volksstaates.* Vol. 6. Berlin: Norddeutsche Buchdruckerei und Verlagsanstalt, n.d.

Jena, Kai von, ed. *Die Kabinettsprotokolle der Bundesregierung.* Vol. 5 (1952). Boppard am Rhein: Harald Boldt, 1989.

Living Conditions in Germany 1947: A Survey by the Hilfswerk of the Evangelical Churches in Germany. Stuttgart: n.p., 1947.

Parlamentarischer Rat, Hauptausschuss, Bonn 1948/49. n.d., n.p.

Protokoll der zweiten zentralen Frauenkonferenz 1957 in Hannover, Industriegewerkschaft Chemie-Papier-Keramik. Hannover: Buchdruckwerkstätte, n.d.

[Protokoll] Zweite zentrale Frauenkonferenz der Industriegewerkschaft Druck und Papier, 30. September bis 2. Oktober 1960 in Lahr. Stuttgart: Vereinsdruckerei Heilbronn, n.d.

Protokoll der 1. Bundesfrauenkonferenz der Gewerkschaft Nahrung-Genuss-Gaststätten, Bielefeld, 16.–18. September 1955. Hamburg: Hamburger Buchdruckerei und Verlagsanstalt Auerdruck, n.d.

Protokoll der 2. Frauenkonferenz der Industriegewerkschaft Metall für die Bundesrepublik Deutschland. Frankfurt am Main: Union-Druckerei und Verlagsanstalt, n.d. [1958].

Protokoll der 3. Frauenkonferenz der Industriegewerkschaft Metall für die Bundesrepublik Deutschland. Frankfurt am Main: Union-Druckerei und Verlagsanstalt, n.d. [1960].

Sozialdemokratische Partei Deutschlands. *Protokoll der Verhandlungen des Parteitages der Sozialdemokratischen Partei Deutschlands vom 21. bis 25. Mai 1950 in Hamburg.* 1950, reprint. Bonn–Bad Godesberg: Verlag J. H. W. Dietz Nachf., 1976.

———. *Protokoll der Verhandlungen des Parteitages der Sozialdemokratischen Partei Deutschlands vom 20. bis 24 Juli 1954 in Berlin.* Berlin-Grünewald: Graphische Gesellschaft Grünewald, n.d.

———. *Protokoll der Verhandlungen des ausserordentlichen Parteitages der Sozialdemokratischen Partei Deutschlands vom 13.–15. November 1959 in Bad Godesberg.* Hannover: Neuer Vorwärts, Nau & Co., n.d.

———. *Protokoll der Verhandlungen und Anträge vom Parteitag der Sozialdemokratischen Partei Deutschlands in Hannover 21. bis 25. November 1960.* Hannover: Neuer Vorwärts, Nau & Co., n.d.

Statistisches Bundesamt. *Bevölkerung und Kultur, Reihe 2: Natürliche Bevölkerungsbewegung, Sonderbeitrag: Kinderzahl der Ehen, Oktober 1962.* Stuttgart: W. Kohlhammer, 1966.

———. *Die Frau im wirtschaftlichen und sozialen Leben der Bundesrepublik.* Wiesbaden: Statistisches Bundesamt, 1952.

———. *Die Frau im wirtschaftlichen und sozialen Leben der Bundesrepublik.* Wiesbaden: Statistisches Bundesamt, 1956.

Verhandlungen des sechsunddreissigsten deutschen Juristentages (Lübeck). 2 vols. Berlin: Walter de Gruyter and Co., 1931.

Verhandlungen des achtunddreissigsten deutschen Juristentages in Frankfurt a.M. 1950. Tübingen: J. C. B. Mohr (Paul Siebeck), 1951.

Verhandlungen des deutschen Bundestags. Bonn: Universitäts-Buchdruckerei Gebr. Scheur, 1950 ff.

Von der NS-Frauenschaft zum Demokratischen Frauenbund. Schriftenreihe Tatsachen und Berichte aus der Sowjetzone [SPD]. Hannover: n.p., n.d. [1952].

SECONDARY SOURCES

Abelshauser, Werner. *Die langen Fünfziger Jahre: Wirtschaft und Gesellschaft der Bundesrepublik Deutschland 1949–1966.* Düsseldorf: Schwann, 1987.

———. "Probleme des Wiederaufbaus der westdeutschen Wirtschaft 1945 bis 1953." In *Politische Weichenstellungen im Nachkriegsdeutschland 1945–1953,* edited by Heinrich August Winkler. Göttingen: Vandenhoeck & Ruprecht, 1979.

———. *Wirtschaft in Westdeutschland 1945–1948: Rekonstruktion und Wachstumsbedingungen in den amerikanischen und britischen Zonen.* Stuttgart: Deutsche Verlags-Anstalt, 1975.

———. *Wirtschaftsgeschichte der Bundesrepublik Deutschland (1945–1980).* Frankfurt am Main: Suhrkamp, 1983.

Achinger, H[ans], S. Archinal, and W. Bangert. *Reicht der Lohn für Kinder?* Frankfurt am Main: Selbstverlag des Deutschen Vereins für öffentliche und private Fürsorge, 1952.

Achinger, Hans, Joseph Höffner, Hans Muthesius, and Ludwig Neundörfer. *Neuordnung der sozialen Leistungen.* Cologne: Greven, 1955.

Akrami-Göhren, Jutta. "Die Familienpolitik im Rahmen der Sozialpolitik mit besonderer Berücksichtigung der Vorstellungen und der praktischen Tätigkeit der CDU." Diss., Bonn University, 1974.

Albers, Jens. "Germany." In *Growth to Limits: The European Welfare States Since World War II*, edited by Peter Flora. Vol. 2, *Germany, United Kingdom, Ireland, Italy*. Berlin: Walter de Gruyter, 1988.

Albers, Willi. "Probleme der westdeutschen Familienpolitik." In *Leitbilder für Familie und Familienpolitik: Festgabe für Helga Schmucker zum 80. Geburtstag*, edited by Rosemarie von Schweitzer. Berlin: Duncker & Humblot, 1891.

Albisetti, James C. *Schooling German Girls and Women: Secondary and Higher Education in the Nineteenth Century*. Princeton: Princeton University Press, 1988.

Albrecht, Ulrich, Elmert Altvater, and Ekkehart Krippendorf, eds. *Zusammenbruch oder Befreiung? Zur Aktualität des 8. Mai 1945*. Berlin: Europäische Perspektive, 1986.

Alexander, Sally. "Women, Class and Sexual Differences in the 1830s and 1840s." *History Workshop*, no. 17 (1984): 125–49.

Allen, Ann Taylor. *Feminism and Motherhood in Germany, 1800–1914*. New Brunswick, N.J.: Rutgers University Press, 1991.

———. "German Radical Feminism and Eugenics, 1900–1918." *German Studies Review* 11 (1988): 31–56.

———. "Mothers of the New Generation: Adele Schreiber, Helene Stöcker, and the Evolution of a German Idea of Motherhood, 1900–1914." *Signs* 10 (1985): 418–38.

———. "Spiritual Motherhood: German Feminists and the Kindergarten Movement, 1848–1911." *History of Education Quarterly* 22 (1982): 319–39.

Ambrosius, Gerold. *Die Durchsetzung der Sozialen Marktwirtschaft in Westdeutschland 1945–1949*. Stuttgart: Deutsche Verlags-Anstalt, 1977.

Aron, Raymond. "The End of Ideology and the Renaissance of Ideas." In *The Industrial Society: Three Essays on Ideology and Development*. New York: Frederick Praeger, 1967.

Baer, Judith A. *The Chains of Protection: The Judicial Response to Women's Labor Protection*. Westport, Conn.: Greenwood Press, 1978.

Bajohr, Stefan. *Die Hälfte der Fabrik: Geschichte der Frauenarbeit in Deutschland 1914 bis 1945*. Marburg: Arbeiterbewegung und Gesellschaftswissenschaft, 1979.

Balabkins, Nicholas. *Germany Under Direct Controls: Economic Aspects of Industrial Disarmament, 1945–1948*. New Brunswick, N.J.: Rutgers University Press, 1964.

Baldwin, Peter. *The Politics of Social Solidarity: Class Bases of the European Welfare State, 1875–1975*. Cambridge: Cambridge University Pres, 1990.

Bark, Dennis L., and David R. Gress. *A History of West Germany*. Vol. 1, *From Shadow to Substance, 1945–1963*. Oxford: Basil Blackwell, 1989.

Barrett, Michèle. *Women's Oppression Today: Problems in Marxist Feminist Analysis*. London: Verso, 1980.

Baumert, Gerhard. *Jugend der Nachkriegszeit: Lebensverhältnisse und Reaktionsweisen.* Darmstadt: Eduard Roether, 1952.

Baumert, Gerhard, with the assistance of Edith Hünniger. *Deutsche Familien nach dem Kriege.* Darmstadt: Eduard Roether, 1954.

Beckendorff, H. *Ausgleich der Familienlasten? Finanzwirtschaftliche Probleme einer Kinderbeihilfe.* Berlin: Duncker & Humblot, 1953.

Becker, Josef. "Die Deutsche Frage in der nationalen Politik 1941–1949." In *Vorgeschichte der Bundesrepublik Deutschland: Zwischen Kapitulation und Grundgesetz,* edited by Josef Becker, Theo Stammen, and Peter Waldmann. Munich: Wilhelm Fink, 1979.

Becker, Josef, Theo Stammen, and Peter Waldmann, eds. *Vorgeschichte der Bundesrepublik Deutschland: Zwischen Kapitulation und Grundgesetz.* Munich: Wilhelm Fink, 1979.

Beck-Gernsheim, Elisabeth. *Vom Geburtenrückgang zur neuen Mütterlichkeit: Über private und politische Interessen am Kind.* Frankfurt am Main: Fischer, 1984.

Bell, Daniel. *The End of Ideology: On the Exhaustion of Political Ideas in the Fifties.* Glencoe, Ill.: The Free Press, 1960.

Benjamin, Hilde. "Familie und Familienrecht in der Deutschen Demokratischen Republik." *Einheit* 10 (1955): 448–57.

———. *Vorschläge zum neuen deutschen Familienrecht.* Berlin: Deutscher Frauen-Verlag, n.d. [1949?].

Benz, Wolfgang, ed. *Die Bundesrepublik Deutschland: Geschichte in drei Bänden.* Vol. 2, *Gesellschaft.* Frankfurt am Main: Fischer, 1983.

———, ed. *Die Vertreibung der Deutschen aus dem Osten: Ursachen, Ereignisse, Folgen.* Frankfurt am Main: Fischer Taschenbuch, 1985.

Berghahn, Volker R. *The Americanisation of West German Industry, 1945–1973.* Leamington Spa: Berg, 1986.

———. *Modern Germany: Society, Economy and Politics in the Twentieth Century.* 2d ed. Cambridge: Cambridge University Press, 1987.

Bergholtz, Ruth, ed. *Die Wirtschaft braucht die Frau.* Darmstadt: W. W. Leske, 1956.

Bethlehem, Siegfried. *Heimatvertreibung, DDR-Flucht, Gastarbeiterzuwanderung: Wanderungsströme und Wanderungspolitik in der Bundesrepublik.* Stuttgart: Klett-Cotta, 1982.

Beyer, Jutta, and Everhard Holtmann. " 'Auch die Frau soll politisch denken'— oder: 'Die Bildung des Herzens': Frauen und Frauenbild in der Kommunalpolitik der frühen Nachkriegszeit 1945–1950." *Archiv für Sozialgeschichte* 25 (1985): 385–419.

Blasius, Dirk. *Ehescheidung in Deutschland 1794–1945: Scheidung und Scheidungsrecht in historischer Perspektive.* Göttingen: Vandenhoeck & Ruprecht, 1987.

Blessing, Werner K. " 'Deutschland in Not, wir im Glauben . . . ': Kirche und Kirchenvolk in einer katholischen Region 1933–1949." In *Von Stalingrad zur Währungsreform: Zur Sozialgeschichte des Umbruchs in Deutschland,* edited by Martin Broszat, Klaus-Dietmar Henke, and Hans Woller. Munich: R. Oldenbourg, 1988.

Boak, Helen L. "Women in Weimar Germany: The 'Frauenfrage' and the Female Vote." In *Social Change and Political Development in Weimar Germany*, edited by Richard Bessell and E. J. Feuchtwanger. London: Croom Helm, 1981.

Bock, Gisela. "Antinatalism, Maternity and Paternity in National Socialist Racism." In *Maternity and Gender Policies: Women and the Rise of the European Welfare States, 1880s–1950s*, edited by Gisela Bock and Pat Thane. London: Routledge, 1991.

———. "Racism and Sexism in Nazi Germany: Motherhood, Compulsory Sterilization, and the State." In *When Biology Became Destiny: Women in Weimar and Nazi Germany*, edited by Renate Bridenthal, Atina Grossmann, and Marion Kaplan. New York: Monthly Review Press, 1984.

———. *Zwangssterilisation im Nationalsozialismus: Studien zur Rassenpolitik und Frauenpolitik*. Opladen: West-Deutscher Verlag, 1986.

Bock, Gisela, and Barbara Duden. "Arbeit aus Liebe—Liebe als Arbeit: Zur Entstehung der Hausarbeit im Kapitalismus." In *Frauen und Wissenschaft: Beiträge zur Berliner Sommeruniversität für Frauen, Juli 1976*. Berlin: Courage, 1977.

Bock, Gisela, and Pat Thane, eds. *Maternity and Gender Policies: Women and the Rise of the European Welfare States, 1880s–1950s*. London: Routledge, 1991.

Bogs, Walter, et al. *Soziale Sicherung: Sozialenquête in der Bundesrepublik Deutschland*. Stuttgart: W. Kohlhammer, 1966.

Bohne, Regina. *Das Geschick der zwei Millionen: Die alleinlebende Frau in unserer Gesellschaft*. Düsseldorf: Econ, 1960.

Böll, Heinrich. *Haus ohne Hüter*. Cologne: Kiepenheuer & Witsch, 1954.

Bondy, Curt, et al. *Jugendliche stören die Ordnung: Bericht und Stellungnahme zu den Halbstarkenkrawallen*. Munich: Juventa, 1957.

Boris, Eileen. "Homework and Women's Rights: The Case of Vermont Knitters, 1980–1985." *Signs* 13 (1987): 98–120.

———. "Regulating Industrial Homework: The Triumph of 'Sacred Motherhood.' " *Journal of American History* 71 (1985): 745–63.

Borris, Maria, with the assistance of Peter Raschke. *Die Benachteiligung der Mädchen in Schulen der Bundesrepublik und Westberlin*. Frankfurt am Main: Europäische Verlagsanstalt, 1972.

Borsdorf, Ulrich, and Mathilde Jamin, eds. *Über Leben im Krieg: Kriegserfahrungen in einer Industrieregion 1939–1945*. Reinbek bei Hamburg: Rowohlt, 1989.

Bosch, F. W. *Familienrechtsreform*. Siegburg: Reckinger & Co., 1952.

Bowlby, John. *Maternal Care and Mental Health*. Geneva: World Health Organization, 1952.

Boxer, Marilyn J. "Protective Legislation and Home Industry: The Marginalization of Women Workers in Late Nineteenth–Early Twentieth-Century France." *Journal of Social History* 20 (1987): 44–65.

Brandt, Karl, in collaboration with Otto Schiller and Franz Ahlgrimm. *Management of Agriculture and Food in German-Occupied and Other Areas of Fortress Europe: A Study of Military Government*. Stanford: Stanford University Press, 1953.

Braun, Hans. "Demographische Umschichtungen im deutschen Katholizismus nach 1945." In *Kirche und Katholizismus 1945–1949*, edited by Anton Rauscher. Munich: Ferdinand Schöningh, 1977.

———. "Helmut Schelskys Konzept der 'nivellierten Mittelstandsgesellschaft' und die Bundesrepublik der 50er Jahre." *Archiv für Sozialgeschichte* 29 (1985): 199–223.

———. "Das Streben nach 'Sicherheit' in den 50er Jahren: Soziale und politische Ursachen und Erscheinungsweisen." *Archiv für Sozialgeschichte* 18 (1978): 279–306.

Braunwarth, Henry. *Die Spanne zwischen Männer- und Frauenlöhnen: Tatsächliche Entwicklung und kritische Erörterung ihrer Berechtigung.* Cologne-Deutz: Bund, 1955.

Bremme, Gabriele. *Freiheit und soziale Sicherheit: Motive und Prinzipien sozialer Sicherung dargestellt an England und Frankreich.* Stuttgart: Ferdinand Enke, 1961.

———. *Die politische Rolle der Frau in Deutschland: Eine Untersuchung über den Einfluss der Frauen bei Wahlen und ihre Teilnahme in Partei und Parlament.* Göttingen: Vandenhoeck & Ruprecht, 1956.

Brendgen, Margarete. *Frau und Beruf: Beitrag zur Ethik der Frauenberufe unserer Tage.* Cologne: J. P. Bachem, 1947.

Bridenthal, Renate. "Beyond *Kinder, Küche, Kirche:* Weimar Women at Work." *Central European History* 6 (1973): 148–66.

———. "Class Struggle around the Hearth: Women and Domestic Service in the Weimar Republic." In *Towards the Holocaust: The Social and Economic Collapse of the Weimar Republic,* edited by Michael Dobkowski and Isidor Walliman. Westport, Conn.: Greenwood Press, 1983.

———. " 'Professional' Housewives: Stepsisters of the Women's Movement." In *When Biology Became Destiny: Women in Weimar and Nazi Germany,* edited by Renate Bridenthal, Atina Grossmann, and Marion Kaplan. New York: Monthly Review Press, 1984.

Bridenthal, Renate, and Claudia Koonz. "Beyond *Kinder, Küche, Kirche:* Weimar Women in Politics and Work." In *When Biology Became Destiny: Women in Weimar and Nazi Germany,* edited by Renate Bridenthal, Atina Grossmann, and Marion Kaplan. New York: Monthly Review Press, 1984.

Bridenthal, Renate, Atina Grossmann, and Marion Kaplan, eds. *When Biology Became Destiny: Women in Weimar and Nazi Germany.* New York: Monthly Review Press, 1984.

Bridenthal, Renate, Claudia Koonz, and Susan Stuard, eds. *Becoming Visible: Women in European History.* 2d ed. Boston: Houghton Mifflin, 1987.

Brocher, Tobias, et al. *Plädoyer für die Abschaffung des §175.* Frankfurt am Main: Suhrkamp, 1966.

Broszat, Martin, Klaus-Dietmar Henke, and Hans Woller, eds. *Von Stalingrad zur Währungsreform: Zur Sozialgeschichte des Umbruchs in Deutschland.* Munich: R. Oldenbourg, 1988.

Brown, Clair (Vickery). "Home Production for Use in a Market Economy." In *Rethinking the Family: Some Feminist Questions,* edited by Barrie Thorne and Marilyn Yalom. New York: Longman, 1982.

Buchhaas, Dorothee. *Gesetzgebung im Wiederaufbau: Schulgesetz in Nordrhein-Westfalen und Betriebsverfassungsgesetz.* Düsseldorf: Droste, 1985.

Buchheim, Christoph. "Die Währungsreform 1948 in Westdeutschland." *Vierteljahrshefte für Zeitgeschichte* 36 (1988): 190–231.

Bulla, Gustav-Adolf. *Mutterschutzgesetz und Frauenarbeitsrecht.* Munich: C. H. Beck, 1954.

Bünger, Fritz Emil. *Familienpolitik in Deutschland: Neue Erkenntnisse über den Einfluss des sogenannten "Giesskannenprinzips" auf die Wirksamkeit sozialpolitischer Massnahmen.* Berlin: Duncker & Humblot, 1970.

Burgdörfer, Friedrich. *Bevölkerungsentwicklung im Dritten Reich: Tatsachen und Kritik.* Heidelberg: Kurt Vowinckel, 1935.

———. "Bevölkerungspolitische Erwägungen zum Umbau der Sozialversicherung." *Archiv für Bevölkerungswissenschaft und Bevölkerungspolitik* 6 (1934): 318–25.

———. *Kinder des Vertrauens: Bevölkerungspolitische Erfolge und Aufgaben im grossdeutschen Reich.* Berlin: Zentralverlag der NSDAP, Franz Ehler, Nachf., 1940.

———. *Volk ohne Jugend: Geburtenschwund und Überalterung des deutschen Volkskörpers.* Berlin-Grünewald: Kurt Vowinckel, 1932.

Burgdörfer, Friedrich, Alfred Kühn, and Martin Staemmler. *Erbkunde, Rassenpflege, Bevölkerungspolitik: Schicksalsfragen des deutschen Volkes.* Leipzig: Quelle & Meyer, 1935.

Burleigh, Michael, and Wolfgang Wippermann. *The Racial State: Germany, 1933–1945.* Cambridge: Cambridge University Press, 1991.

Butz, Hans-H. *Das Mutterschutzgesetz in der Praxis: Systematische Übersicht unter besonderer Berücksichtigung der Rechtssprechung des Bundesarbeitsgerichts.* Düsseldorf: Verlag Handelsblatt, 1956.

Campbell, Joan. *Joy in Work: The National Debate, 1800–1945.* Princeton: Princeton University Press, 1989.

Castell, Adelheid zu. "Die demographischen Konsequenzen des Ersten und Zweiten Weltkrieges für das Deutsche Reich, die Deutsche Demokratische Republik und die Bundesrepublik Deutschland." In *Zweiter Weltkrieg und sozialer Wandel: Achsenmächte und besetzte Länder,* edited by Waclaw Długoborski. Göttingen: Vandenhoeck & Ruprecht, 1981.

Chalmers, Douglas A. *The Social Democratic Party of Germany: From Working-Class Movement to Modern Political Party.* New Haven: Yale University Press, 1964.

Cole, Helena, with the assistance of Jane Caplan and Hanna Schissler. *The History of Women in Germany from Medieval Times to the Present: Bibliography of English-Language Publications.* Washington, D.C.: German Historical Institute, 1990.

Connor, Ian. "The Refugees and the Currency Reform." In *Reconstruction in Post-War Germany: British Occupation Policy and the Western Zones, 1945–55,* edited by Ian D. Turner. Oxford: Berg, 1989.

Conze, Werner, and M. Rainer Lepsius, eds. *Sozialgeschichte der Bundesrepublik Deutschland: Beiträge zum Kontinuitätsproblem.* Stuttgart: Klett-Cotta, 1983.

Crew, David. "German Socialism, the State and Family Policy, 1918–1933." *Continuity and Change* 1 (1986): 235–63.

Czarnowski, Gabriele. *Das kontrollierte Paar: Ehe- und Sexualpolitik im Nationalsozialismus.* Weinheim: Deutscher Studien Verlag, 1991.

Dahrendorf, Ralf. "Die neue Gesellschaft: Soziale Strukturwandlungen der Nachkriegszeit." In *Bestandsaufnahme: Eine deutsche Bilanz 1962,* edited by Hans Werner Richter. Munich: Kurt Desch, 1962.

———. *Society and Democracy in Germany.* Garden City, New York: Anchor Books, 1969. Originally published as *Gesellschaft und Demokratie in Deutschland.* Munich: R. Piper & Co., 1965.

Däubler-Gmelin, Herta, and Marianne Müller. *Wir sind auch noch da! Ältere Frauen zwischen Resignation und Selbstbewusstsein.* Bonn: Neue Gesellschaft, 1985.

Delille, Angela, and Andrea Grohn. *Blick zurück aufs Glück: Frauenleben und Familienpolitik in den 50er Jahren.* Berlin: Elefanten Press, 1985.

———, eds. *Perlonzeit: Wie die Frauen ihr Wirtschaftswunder erlebten.* Berlin: Elefanten Press, 1985.

Denecke, Johannes. "Mutterschutz und Jugendschutz." In *Die Grundrechte: Handbuch der Theorie und Praxis der Grundrechte,* edited by Karl August Bettermann, Hans Carl Nipperdey, and Ulrich Scheuner. Vol. 3, part 1, *Die Wirtschafts- und Arbeitsverfassung.* Berlin: Duncker & Humblot, 1958.

Detje, Richard, et al. *Von der Westzone zum kalten Krieg: Restauration und Gewerkschaftspolitik im Nachkriegsdeutschland.* Hamburg: VSA, 1982.

Deutscher Bundestag, Wissenschaftliche Dienste, Abteilung Wissenschaftliche Dokumentation, ed. *Abgeordnete des Deutschen Bundestages: Aufzeichnungen und Erinnerungen.* Vol 2. Boppard am Rhein: Harald Boldt, 1983.

Deutscher Juristinnenbund, ed. *Juristinnen in Deutschland: Eine Dokumentation (1900–1984).* Munich: J. Schweitzer, 1984.

Diehl, James M. "Change and Continuity in the Treatment of German *Kriegsopfer.*" *Central European History* 18 (1985): 170–87.

Diestelkamp, Bernhard. "Kontinuität und Wandel in der Rechtsordnung, 1945 bis 1955." In *Westdeutschland 1945–1955: Unterwerfung, Kontrolle, Integration,* edited by Ludolf Herbst. Munich: R. Oldenbourg, 1986.

Diner, Dan. "Between Aporia and Apology: On the Limits of Historicizing National Socialism." In *Reworking the Past: Hitler, the Holocaust, and the Historians' Debate,* edited by Peter Baldwin. Boston: Beacon Press, 1990.

Dirks, Walter. "Soll er ihr Herr sein? Die Gleichberechtigung der Frau und die Reform des Familienrechts." *Frankfurter Hefte* 7 (1952): 825–37.

———. "Was die Ehe bedroht? Eine Liste ihrer kritischen Punkte." *Frankfurter Hefte* 6 (1951): 18–28.

Dischner, Gisela, ed. *Eine stumme Generation berichtet: Frauen der dreissiger und vierziger Jahre.* Frankfurt am Main: Fischer, 1982.

Diskant, James A. "Scarcity, Survival and Local Activism: Miners and Steelworkers, Dortmund 1945–8." *Journal of Contemporary History* 24 (1989): 547–73.

Dobkowski, Michael N., and Isidor Wallimann, eds. *Towards the Holocaust: Towards the Social and Economic Collapse of the Weimar Republic.* Westport, Conn.: Greenwood Press, 1983.

Dombois, Hans Adolf, and Friedrich Karl Schumann, eds. *Familienrechtsreform: Dokumente und Abhandlungen.* Witten-Ruhr: Luther-Verlag, 1955.

Drohsel, Petra. "Die Entlohnung der Frau nach 1945." In *"Das Schicksal Deutschlands liegt in der Hand seiner Frauen": Frauen in der deutschen Nachkriegsgeschichte,* edited by Anna-Elisabeth Freier and Annette Kuhn. Düsseldorf: Schwann, 1984.

————. *Die Lohndiskriminierung der Frauen: Eine Studie über Lohn und Lohndiskriminierung von erwerbstätigen Frauen in der Bundesrepublik Deutschland, 1945–1984.* Marburg: SP-Verlag, 1986.

Dunckelmann, Henning. *Die erwerbstätige Ehefrau im Spannungsfeld von Beruf und Konsum: Dargestellt an den Ergebnissen einer Befragung.* Tübingen: J. C. B. Mohr (Paul Siebeck), 1961.

Eckert, Roland, et al. *Familie und Familienpolitik: Zur Situation in der Bundesrepublik Deutschland.* Melle: Ernst Knoth, 1985.

Eiber, Ludwig. "Frauen in der Kriegsindustrie: Arbeitsbedingungen, Lebensumstände und Protestverhalten." In *Bayern in der NS-Zeit,* edited by Martin Broszat, Elke Fröhlich, and Anton Grossmann. Vol. 3, *Herrschaft und Gesellschaft im Konflikt,* part B. Munich: R. Oldenbourg, 1981.

Eilers, Elfriede, and Marta Schanzenbach. "Zur Nachkriegsgeschichte der Familienpolitik aus sozialdemokratischer Sicht." In *Sozialpolitik nach 1945: Geschichte und Analysen,* edited by Reinhart Bartholomäi et al. Bonn–Bad Godesberg: Neue Gesellschaft, 1977.

Einfeldt, Anne-Katrin. "Auskommen—Durchkommen—Weiterkommen: Weibliche Arbeitserfahrungen in der Bergarbeiterkolonie." In *"Die Jahre weiss man nicht, wo man die heute hinsetzen soll": Faschismus-Erfahrungen im Ruhrgebiet,* edited by Lutz Niethammer. Bonn: J. H. W. Dietz Nachf., 1983.

Eisenstein, Zillah R. *The Female Body and the Law.* Berkeley and Los Angeles: University of California Press, 1988.

Elsner, Ilse. "Der Frauenlohn in unserer Zeit." In *Die Wirtschaft braucht die Frau,* edited by Ruth Bergholtz. Darmstadt: W. W. Leske, 1956.

Elsner, Ilse, and Rüdiger Proske. "Der fünfte Stand: Eine Untersuchung über die Armut in Westdeutschland." *Frankfurter Hefte* 8 (1953): 101–11.

Enssle, Manfred J. "The Harsh Discipline of Food Scarcity in Postwar Stuttgart, 1945–1948." *German Studies Review* 10 (1987): 481–502.

Erdmenger, Klaus. "Adenauer, die Deutsche Frage und die sozialdemokratische Opposition." In *Adenauer und die Deutsche Frage,* edited by Josef Foschepoth. Göttingen: Vandenhoeck & Ruprecht, 1988.

Erhard, Ludwig. *Deutsche Wirtschaftspolitik: Der Weg der sozialen Marktwirtschaft.* Düsseldorf: Econ, 1962.

————. *Wohlstand für Alle.* 1957. Reprint, Düsseldorf: Econ, 1960.

Eschenburg, Theodor. *Jahre der Besatzung, 1945–1949.* Stuttgart: Deutsche Verlags-Anstalt, 1983.

Evans, Richard J. *The Feminist Movement in Germany, 1894–1933.* Beverly Hills: Sage Publications, 1976.

————. *Sozialdemokratie und Frauenemanzipation im deutschen Kaiserreich.* Bonn: J. H. W. Dietz Nachf., 1979.

Falter, Jürgen. "Kontinuität und Neubeginn: Die Bundestagswahl 1949 zwischen Weimar und Bonn." *Politische Vierteljahresschrift* 22 (1981): 236–63.

Familie und Sozialreform. Jahresversammlung der Gesellschaft für Sozialen Fortschritt e.V. Berlin: Duncker & Humblot, 1955.

Farquharson, John E. *The Western Allies and the Politics of Food: Agrarian Management in Postwar Germany.* Leamington Spa: Berg, 1985.

Fehrenbach, Heide. "The Fight for the 'Christian West': German Film Control, the Churches, and the Reconstruction of Civil Society in the Early Bonn Republic." *German Studies Review* 14 (1991): 39–63.

Ferree, Myra Marx. "Equality and Autonomy: Feminist Politics in the United States and West Germany." In *The Women's Movement of the United States and Western Europe: Consciousness, Political Opportunity, and Public Policy,* edited by Mary Fainsod Katzenstein and Carol McClurg Mueller. Philadelphia: Temple University Press, 1987.

Feuersenger, Marianne. *Die garantierte Gleichberechtigung: Ein umstrittener Sieg der Frauen.* Freiburg im Breisgau: Herder, 1980.

Fichter, Tilman, and Ute Schmidt. *Der erzwungene Kapitalismus: Klassenkämpfe in den Westzonen 1945–1948.* Berlin: Wagenbach, 1971.

Field, Geoffrey. "Perspectives on the Working-Class Family in Wartime Britain, 1939–1945." *International Labor and Working Class History,* no. 38 (1990): 3–28.

Fijalkowski, Jürgen. "Gastarbeiter als industrielle Reservearmee? Zur Bedeutung der Arbeitsimmigration für die wirtschaftliche und gesellschaftliche Entwicklung der Bundesrepublik Deutschland." *Archiv für Sozialgeschichte* 24 (1984): 399–456.

Fitzek, Alfons, ed. *Katholische Kirche im demokratischen Staat: Hirtenworte der deutschen Bischöfe zu wichtigen Fragen der Zeit und zu den Bundestagswahlen 1945 bis 1980.* Würzburg: Naumann, 1981.

Flechtheim, Ossip K., ed. *Dokumente zur parteipolitischen Entwicklung in Deutschland seit 1945.* Vol. 2, part 1, *Programmatik der deutschen Parteien.* Berlin: Dokumenten-Verlag Dr. Herbert Wendler & Co., 1963.

Focke, Fritz. *Sozialismus aus christlicher Verantwortung: Die Idee eines christlichen Sozialismus in der katholisch-sozialen Bewegung und in der CDU.* Wuppertal: Peter Hammer, 1978.

Forster, Karl. "Der deutsche Katholizismus in der Bundesrepublik Deutschland." In *Der soziale und politische Katholizismus: Entwicklungslinien in Deutschland 1803–1963,* edited by Anton Rauscher. Vol. 1. Munich: Günter Olzog, 1981.

Foschepoth, Josef, ed. *Adenauer und die Deutsche Frage.* Göttingen: Vandenhoeck & Ruprecht, 1988.

————. "Westintegration statt Wiedervereinigung: Adenauers Deutschlandpolitik 1949–1955." In *Adenauer und die Deutsche Frage,* edited by Josef Foschepoth. Göttingen: Vandenhoeck & Ruprecht, 1988.

————. "Zur deutschen Reaktion auf Niederlage und Besatzung." In *Westdeutschland 1945–1955: Unterwerfung, Kontrolle, Integration,* edited by Ludolf Herbst. Munich: R. Oldenbourg, 1986.

Foschepoth, Josef, and Rolf Steininger, eds. *Die britische Deutschland- und Besatzungspolitik 1945–1949*. Paderborn: Ferdinand Schöningh, 1985.

Fout, John C., ed. *German Women in the Nineteenth Century: A Social History*. New York: Holmes & Meier, 1984.

Frandsen, Dorothea, Ursula Huffmann, and Annette Kuhn, eds. *Frauen in Wissenschaft und Politik*. Düsseldorf: Schwann, 1987.

Franke, Lothar. *Das tapfere Leben: Lebensfragen alleinstehender Frauen und Mütter*. Cologne-Hoffnungsthal: Werner Scheuermann, 1957.

Frantzioch, Marion. *Die Vertriebenen: Hemmnisse, Antriebskräfte und Wege ihrer Integration in der Bundesrepublik Deutschland*. Berlin: Dietrich Reimer, 1987.

Freier, Anna-Elisabeth. "Überlebenspolitik im Nachkriegsdeutschland." In *Frauen in der deutschen Nachkriegszeit*, edited by Annette Kuhn. Vol. 2, *Frauenpolitik 1945–1949: Quellen und Materialien*. Düsseldorf: Schwann, 1986.

Freier, Anna-Elisabeth, and Annette Kuhn, eds. *"Das Schicksal Deutschlands liegt in der Hand seiner Frauen": Frauen in der deutschen Nachkriegsgeschichte*. Düsseldorf: Schwann, 1984.

Frevert, Ute. "Frauen an der 'Heimatfront.'" In *Nicht nur Hitlers Krieg: Der Zweite Weltkrieg und die Deutschen*, edited by Christoph Klessmann. Düsseldorf: Droste, 1989.

———. *Women in German History: From Bourgeois Emancipation to Sexual Liberation*. Translated by Stuart McKinnon-Evans. Oxford: Berg, 1989.

Friedan, Betty. *The Feminine Mystique*. 1963. Reprint, Harmondsworth: Penguin Books, 1965.

Friedeburg, Ludwig von. *Die Umfrage in der Intimsphäre*. Stuttgart: Ferdinand Enke, 1953.

Friese, Hildegard. *Beruf und Familie im Urteil weiblicher Lehrlinge: Eine empirische Untersuchung zur Mädchenbildung*. Hannover: Hermann Schroedel, 1967.

Frohner, Rolf, Maria von Stackelberg, and Wolfgang Eser. *Familie und Ehe: Probleme in den deutschen Familien der Gegenwart*. Bielefeld: Maria von Stackelberg, 1956.

Fromme, Friedrich Karl. *Von der Weimarer Verfassung zum Bonner Grundgesetz: Die verfassungspolitischen Folgerungen des Parlamentarischen Rates aus Weimarer Republik und nationalsozialistischer Diktatur*. Tübingen: J. C. B. Mohr (Paul Siebeck), 1960.

Fronz, Michael. "Das Bundesverfassungsgericht im politischen System der BRD: Eine Analyse der Beratungen im Parlamentarischen Rat." *Sozialwissenschaftliches Jahrbuch für Politik* 2 (1971): 629–82.

Fulbrook, Mary. "The State and the Transformation of Political Legitimacy in East and West Germany since 1945." *Comparative Studies in Society and History* 29 (1987): 211–44.

Gast, Gabriele. *Die politische Rolle der Frau in der DDR*. Düsseldorf: Bertelsmann, 1973.

Geissler, Heiner, ed. *Abschied von der Männergesellschaft*. Frankfurt am Main: Ullstein, 1986.

Gellott, Laura, and Michael Phayer. "Dissenting Voices: Catholic Women in Opposition to Fascism." *Journal of Contemporary History* 22 (1987): 91–114.

Geratewohl, Klaus. "Sonderarbeitsrecht der Frau." In *Die Wirtschaft braucht die Frau,* edited by Ruth Bergholtz. Darmstadt: W. W. Leske, 1956.

Gerhard, Ute. " 'Bis an die Wurzeln des Übels': Rechtskämpfe und Rechtskritik der Radikalen." *Feministische Studien* 3 (1984): 77–97.

―――. *Verhältnisse und Verhinderungen: Frauenarbeit, Familie und Rechte der Frauen im 19. Jahrhundert.* Frankfurt am Main: Suhrkamp, 1978.

Gersdorff, Ursula von. *Frauen im Kriegsdienst, 1914–1945.* Stuttgart: Deutsche Verlags-Anstalt, 1969.

Gimbel, John. *The American Occupation of Germany: Politics and the Military, 1945–1949.* Stanford: Stanford University Press, 1968.

Glaser, Hermann. *Kulturgeschichte der Bundesrepublik Deutschland.* Vol. 2, *Zwischen Grundgesetz und Grosser Koalition 1949–1967.* Munich: Carl Hanser, 1986.

Glass, D. V. *Population Policies and Movements in Europe.* 1940. Reprint, New York: A. M. Kelley, 1967.

Gordon, Linda. "The New Feminist Scholarship on the Welfare State." In *Women, the State, and Welfare,* edited by Linda Gordon. Madison: University of Wisconsin Press, 1990.

―――, ed. *Women, the State, and Welfare.* Madison: University of Wisconsin Press, 1990.

Gotto, Klaus. "Die deutschen Katholiken und die Wahlen in der Adenauer-Ära." In *Katholizismus im politischen System der Bundesrepublik 1949–1963,* edited by Albrecht Langer. Paderborn: Ferdinand Schöningh, 1978.

―――. "Die katholische Kirche und die Entstehung des Grundgesetzes." In *Kirche und Katholizismus 1945–1949,* edited by Anton Rauscher. Munich: Ferdinand Schöningh, 1977.

―――, ed. *Der Staatssekretär Adenauers: Persönlichkeit und politisches Wirken Hans Globkes.* Stuttgart: Ernst Klett, 1980.

―――. "Zum Selbstverständnis der katholischen Kirche im Jahre 1945." In *Politik und Konfession: Festschrift für Konrad Repgen zum 60. Geburtstag,* edited by Dieter Albrecht et al. Berlin: Duncker & Humblot, 1983.

Greeven, Heinrich, ed. *Die Frau im Beruf: Tatbestände, Erfahrungen und Vorschläge zu drängenden Fragen in der weiblichen Berufsarbeit und in der Lebenshaltung der berufstätigen Frau.* Hamburg: Im Furche, 1954.

Greven-Aschoff, Barbara. *Die bürgerliche Frauenbewegung in Deutschland, 1894–1933.* Göttingen: Vandenhoeck & Ruprecht, 1981.

Grewe, Hans. "Die arbeitsgerichtliche Rechtsprechung zum Gesetz des Landes Nordrhein-Westfalen über den Hausarbeitstag für erwerbstätige Frauen mit eigenem Hausstand." Diss., Freiburg University, 1968.

Grossmann, Atina. "Abortion and Economic Crisis: The 1931 Campaign Against Paragraph 218." In *When Biology Became Destiny: Women in Weimar and Nazi Germany,* edited by Renate Bridenthal, Atina Grossmann, and Marion Kaplan. New York: Monthly Review Press, 1984.

―――. "The New Woman and the Rationalization of Sexuality in Weimar Germany." In *Powers of Desire: The Politics of Sexuality,* edited by Ann Snitow,

Christine Stansell, and Sharon Thompson. New York: Monthly Review Press, 1984.

———. " 'Satisfaction Is Domestic Happiness': Mass Working-Class Sex Reform Organizations in the Weimar Republic." In *Towards the Holocaust: The Social and Economic Collapse of the Weimar Republic,* edited by Michael N. Dobkowski and Isidor Wallimann. Westport, Conn.: Greenwood Press, 1983.

Grum, Ulla. " 'Sie leben froher—Sie leben besser mit Constanze': Eine Frauenzeitschrift im Wandel des Jahrzehnts." In *Perlonzeit: Wie die Frauen ihr Wirtschaftswunder erlebten,* edited by Angela Delille and Andrea Grohn. Berlin: Elefanten Press, 1985.

Gruner, Isa. *Kinder in Not.* Berlin: Berthold Schulz, 1950.

Gutscher, Jörg Michael. *Die Entwicklung der FDP von ihren Anfängen bis 1961.* Meisenheim am Glan: Anton Hain, 1967.

Habermas, Jürgen. "A Kind of Settlement of Damages (Apologetic Tendencies)." *New German Critique* no. 44 (1988): 25–39.

Hackett, Amy. "Feminism and Liberalism in Wilhelmine Germany, 1890–1918." In *Liberating Women's History: Theoretical and Critical Essays,* edited by Bernice Carroll. Urbana: University of Illinois Press, 1976.

———. "The German Women's Movement and Suffrage, 1890–1914: A Study of National Feminism." In *Modern European Social History,* edited by Robert Bezucha. Lexington, Mass.: D. C. Heath, 1972.

———. "Helene Stöcker: Left-Wing Intellectual and Sex Reformer." In *When Biology Became Destiny: Women in Weimar and Nazi Germany,* edited by Renate Bridenthal, Atina Grossmann, and Marion Kaplan. New York: Monthly Review Press, 1984.

Haeberle, Erwin J. "Swastika, Pink Triangle, and Yellow Star: The Destruction of Sexology and the Persecution of Homosexuals in Nazi Germany." In *Hidden From History: Reclaiming the Gay and Lesbian Past,* edited by Martin Bauml Duberman, Martha Vicinus, and George Chauncey, Jr. New York: New American Library, 1989.

Haensch, Dietrich. *Repressive Familienpolitik: Sexualunterdrückung als Mittel der Politik.* Reinbek: Rowohlt, 1969.

Hagemann, Karen. *Frauenalltag und Männerpolitik: Alltagsleben und gesellschaftliches Handeln von Arbeiterfrauen in der Weimarer Republik.* Bonn: J. H. W. Dietz Nachf., 1990.

Handl, Johann. "Abbau von Ungleichheit im Beruf durch bessere Bildung? Eine sozialhistorische Betrachtung." In *Strukturwandel der Frauenarbeit 1880–1980,* edited by Walter Müller, Angelika Willms, and Johann Handl. Frankfurt am Main: Campus, 1983.

Harrison, Cynthia. *On Account of Sex: The Politics of Women's Issues, 1945–1968.* Berkeley and Los Angeles: University of California Press, 1988.

Hartwich, Hans-Hermann. *Sozialstaatspostulat und gesellschaftlicher Status quo.* Cologne: Westdeutscher Verlag, 1970.

Haug, Frigga. "The Women's Movement in West Germany." *New Left Review,* no. 155 (1986): 50–74.

Hausen, Karen, ed. *Frauen suchen ihre Geschichte: Historische Studien zum 19. und 20. Jahrhundert.* Munich: C. H. Beck, 1983.

————. "Mother's Day in the Weimar Republic." In *When Biology Became Destiny: Women in Weimar and Nazi Germany*, edited by Renate Bridenthal, Atina Grossmann, and Marion Caplan. New York: Monthly Review Press, 1984.

Hauser, Andrea. "Alle Frauen unter einem Hut?—Zur Geschichte des Stuttgarter Frauenausschusses." In *Frauen in der deutschen Nachkriegszeit*. Vol. 2, *Frauenpolitik 1945–1949: Quellen und Materialien*, edited by Annette Kuhn. Düsseldorf: Schwann, 1986.

————. "Frauenöffentlichkeit in Stuttgart nach 1945: Gegenpol oder hilflos im Abseits?" In *"Das Schicksal Deutschlands liegt in der Hand seiner Frauen": Frauen in der deutschen Nachkriegsgeschichte*, edited by Anna-Elisabeth Freier and Annette Kuhn. Düsseldorf: Schwann, 1984.

Heidenheimer, Arnold J. *Adenauer and the CDU: The Rise of the Leader and the Integration of the Party*. The Hague: Martinus Nijhoff, 1960.

Heimann, Siegfried. "Die Sozialdemokratische Partei Deutschlands." In *Parteien-Handbuch: Die Parteien der Bundesrepublik Deutschland 1945– 1980*, edited by Richard Stöss. Vol. 2, *FDP bis WAV*. Opladen: Westdeutscher Verlag, 1984.

Hein, Dieter. *Zwischen liberaler Milieupartei und nationaler Sammlungsbewegung: Gründung, Entwicklung und Struktur der Freien Demokratischen Partei 1945–1949*. Düsseldorf: Droste, 1985.

Heinemann, Ulrich. "Krieg und Frieden an der 'inneren Front': Normalität und Zustimmung, Terror und Opposition im Dritten Reich." In *Nicht nur Hitlers Krieg: Der Zweite Weltkrieg und die Deutschen*, edited by Christoph Klessmann. Düsseldorf: Droste, 1989.

Hellbrügge, Theodor. "Waisenkinder der Technik." *Westermanns Monatshefte* 102 (1961): 49–55.

Henicz, Barbara, and Margrit Hirschfeld. "Der Club Deutscher Frauen in Hannover." In *Frauen in der deutschen Nachkriegszeit*. Vol. 2, *Frauenpolitik 1945–1949: Quellen und Materialien*, edited by Annette Kuhn. Düsseldorf: Schwann, 1986.

————. "Die ersten Frauenzusammenschlüsse." In *Frauen in der deutschen Nachkriegszeit*. Vol. 2, *Frauenpolitik 1945–1949: Quellen und Materialien*, edited by Annette Kuhn. Düsseldorf: Schwann, 1986.

————. " 'Wenn die Frauen wüssten, was sie könnten, wenn sie wollten': Zur Gründungsgeschichte des Deutschen Frauenrings." In *Frauen in der deutschen Nachkriegszeit*. Vol. 2, *Frauenpolitik 1945–1949: Quellen und Materialien*, edited by Annette Kuhn. Düsseldorf: Schwann, 1986.

Hentschel, Volker. *Geschichte der deutschen Sozialpolitik (1880–1980): Soziale Sicherung und kollektives Arbeitsrecht*. Frankfurt am Main: Suhrkamp, 1983.

Herbert, Ulrich. *Fremdarbeiter: Politik und Praxis des "Ausländer-Einsatzes" in der Kriegswirtschaft des Dritten Reiches*. Bonn: J. H. W. Dietz Nachf., 1985.

————. *Geschichte der Ausländerbeschäftigung in Deutschland 1880 bis 1980: Saisonarbeiter, Zwangsarbeiter, Gastarbeiter*. Bonn: J. H. W. Dietz Nachf., 1986.

————. "Good Times, Bad Times: Memories of the Third Reich." In *Life in the Third Reich*, edited by Richard Bessel. New York: Oxford University Press, 1987.

———. " 'Die guten und die schlechten Zeiten': Überlegungen zur diachronen Analyse lebensgeschichtlicher Interviews." In *Die Jahre weiss man nicht, wo man die heute hinsetzen soll": Faschismus-Erfahrungen im Ruhrgebiet,* edited by Lutz Niethammer. Bonn: J. H. W. Dietz Nachf., 1983.

———. "Zur Entwicklung der Ruhrarbeiterschaft 1930 bis 1960 aus erfahrungsgeschichtlicher Perspektive." In *"Wir kriegen jetzt andere Zeiten": Auf der Suche nach der Erfahrung des Volkes in nachfaschistischen Ländern,* edited by Lutz Niethammer and Alexander von Plato. Bonn: J. H. W. Dietz Nachf., 1985.

Herbst, Ludolf, ed. *Westdeutschland 1945–1955: Unterwerfung, Kontrolle, Integration.* Munich: R. Oldenbourg, 1986.

Hermand, Jost. *Kultur im Wiederaufbau: Die Bundesrepublik Deutschland, 1945–1965.* Munich: Nymphenburger, 1986.

Herrmann, A. Hedwig. *Die ausserhäusliche Erwerbstätigkeit verheirateter Frauen: Eine sozialpolitische Studie.* Stuttgart: Ferdinand Enke, 1957.

Hewlett, Sylvia Ann. *A Lesser Life: The Myth of Women's Liberation in America.* New York: Warner Books, 1986.

Heyken, Eberhard. "Rechtsfragen des Hausarbeitstages und gleichgerichtete Massnahmen in anderen Ländern." Diss., Göttingen University, 1963.

Higonnet, Margaret Randolph, et al., eds. *Behind the Lines: Gender and the Two World Wars.* New Haven: Yale University Press, 1987.

Higonnet, Margaret R., and Patrice L.-R. Higonnet. "The Double Helix." In *Behind the Lines: Gender and the Two World Wars,* edited by Margaret Randolph Higonnet, et al. New Haven: Yale University Press, 1987.

Hinze, Edith, with the assistance of Elisabeth Knospe. *Lage und Leistung erwerbstätiger Mütter: Ergebnisse einer Untersuchung in Westberlin.* Berlin: Carl Heymanns, 1960.

Hochstein, Beatrix. *Die Ideologie des Überlebens: Zur Geschichte der politischen Apathie in Deutschland.* Frankfurt am Main: Campus, 1984.

Hockerts, Hans Günter. "Sicherung im Alter: Kontinuität und Wandel der gesetzlichen Rentenversicherung 1889–1979." In *Sozialgeschichte der Bundesrepublik Deutschland: Beiträge zum Kontinuitätsproblem,* edited by Werner Conze and M. Rainer Lepsius. Stuttgart: Klett-Cotta, 1983.

———. *Sozialpolitische Entscheidungen im Nachkriegsdeutschland: Alliierte und deutsche Sozialversicherungspolitik 1945 bis 1957.* Stuttgart: Klett-Cotta, 1980.

Hoerning, Erika M. "Frauen als Kriegsbeute: Der Zwei-Fronten-Krieg: Beispiele aus Berlin." In *"Wir kriegen jetzt andere Zeiten": Auf der Suche nach der Erfahrung des Volkes in nachfaschistischen Ländern,* edited by Lutz Niethammer and Alexander von Plato. Bonn: J. H. W. Dietz Nachf., 1985.

Hoffmann, Anton Christian, and Dietrich Kersten. *Frauen zwischen Familie und Fabrik: Die Doppelbelastung der Frau durch Haushalt und Beruf.* Munich: J. Pfeiffer, 1958.

Hohmann-Dehnhardt, Christine. "Gleichberechtigung via Rechtsnorm? Zur Frage eines Antidiskriminierungsgesetzes in der Bundesrepublik." In *Frauensituation: Veränderungen in den letzten zwanzig Jahren,* edited by Yvonne Schütze and Ute Gerhard. Frankfurt am Main: Suhrkamp, 1988.

Höhn, Elfriede. *Das berufliche Fortkommen von Frauen.* Frankfurt am Main: Norddeutsche Verlagsanstalt O. Goedel, 1964.

Hong, Young Sun. "Femininity as a Vocation: Gender and Class Conflict in the Professionalization of German Social Work." In *German Professions, 1800–1950,* edited by Geoffrey Cocks and Konrad H. Jarausch. New York: Oxford University Press, 1990.

———. "The Politics of Welfare Reform and the Dynamics of the Public Sphere: Church, Society, and the State in the Making of the Social-Welfare System in Germany, 1830–1930." Ph.D. Diss., University of Michigan, 1989.

Horkheimer, Max, ed. *Studien über Autorität und Familie.* Paris: Félix Alcan, 1936.

Horn, Wolfgang. "Demokratiegründung und Grundgesetz." *Neue politische Literatur* 21 (1976): 26–40.

Hubbard, William H. *Familiengeschichte: Materialien zur deutschen Familie seit dem Ende des 18. Jahrhunderts.* Munich: C. H. Beck, 1983.

Hudemann, Rainer. *Sozialpolitik im deutschen Südwesten zwischen Tradition und Neuordnung, 1945–1953: Sozialversicherung und Kriegsopferversorgung im Rahmen französischer Besatzungspolitik.* Mainz: v. Hase & Koehler, 1988.

Hueck, Alfred, and Hans Carl Nipperdey. *Lehrbuch des Arbeitsrechts.* Vol 1. 6th ed. Berlin: Franz Vahlen, 1959.

Hughes, Michael L. *Paying for the German Inflation.* Chapel Hill: University of North Carolina Press, 1988.

Hülsmann, Paul. *Die berufstätige Frau: Arbeitsmedizinische Leitsätze.* Stuttgart: Georg Thieme, 1962.

Hurwitz, Harold. *Die politische Kultur der Bevölkerung und der Neubeginn konservativer Politik.* Cologne: Wissenschaft und Politik, 1983.

Huss, Marie-Monique. "Pronatalism in the Inter-War Period in France." *Journal of Contemporary History* 25 (1990): 39–68.

Huster, Ernst-Ulrich, et al. *Determinanten der westdeutschen Restauration 1945–1949.* Frankfurt am Main: Suhrkamp, 1972.

Jacobmeyer, Wolfgang. *Vom Zwangsarbeiter zum heimatlosen Ausländer: Die Displaced Persons in Westdeutschland 1945–1951.* Göttingen: Vandenhoeck & Ruprecht, 1985.

Jacobsohn, Christa. "Familiengerechte Frauenarbeit—ein gesamtgesellschaftliches Zeitproblem." Diss., Free University, Berlin, 1961.

Jaide, Walter. "Selbsterzeugnisse jugendlicher Industriearbeiterinnen." In *Die junge Arbeiterin: Beiträge zur Sozialkunde und Jugendarbeit,* edited by Gerhard Wurzbacher, et al. Munich: Juventa-Verlag, 1958.

Jansen, Mechtild. "Der Einfluss der Frauenbewegung auf die politische Kultur der Bundesrepublik." *Blätter für deutsche und internationale Politik* 31 (1986): 289–305.

———. "Frauen und Politik: Die 'neue' Frauenpolitik der Bundesrepublik und das Agieren der Frauenbewegung." In *FrauenWiderspruch: Alltag und Politik,* edited by Mechtild Jansen. Cologne: Pahl-Rugenstein, 1987.

Janssen-Jurreit, Marielouise. *Sexismus: Über die Abtreibung der Frauenfrage.* Munich: Carl Hanser, 1976.

Jay, Martin. *The Dialectical Imagination: A History of the Frankfurt School and the Institute of Social Research, 1923–1950.* Boston: Little, Brown & Co., 1973.

Jellonnek, Burkhard. *Homosexuelle unter dem Hakenkreuz: Die Verfolgung von Homosexuellen im Dritten Reich.* Paderborn: Ferdinand Schöningh, 1990.

Jenkins, Eva. "Teilzeitarbeit: Eine Sackgasse." In *Vom Nutzen weiblicher Lohnarbeit,* edited by Gerlinde Seidenspinner et al. Opladen: Leske & Budrich, 1984.

Jenson, Jane. "Both Friend and Foe: Women and State Welfare." In *Becoming Visible: Women in European History,* edited by Renate Bridenthal, Claudia Koonz, and Susan Stuard. 2d ed. Boston: Houghton Mifflin, 1987.

———. "The Liberation and New Rights for French Women." In *Behind the Lines: Gender and the Two World Wars,* edited by Margaret R. Higonnet et al. New Haven: Yale University Press, 1987.

———. "Representations of Gender: Policies to 'Protect' Women Workers and Infants in France and the United States before 1914." In *Women, the State, and Welfare,* edited by Linda Gordon. Madison: University of Wisconsin Press, 1990.

Jessen, Arnd. "Der Aufwand für Kinder in der Bundesrepublik im Jahre 1954: Eine statistische Untersuchung." In *Familie und Sozialreform.* Jahresversammlung der Gesellschaft für Sozialen Fortschritt e.V. Berlin: Duncker & Humblot, 1955.

———. *Was kostet dein Kind? Ein Vorschlag zur Einführung allgemeiner staatlicher Kinderbeihilfen.* Berlin: R. v. Decker's Verlag, n.d. [1937].

Jochum, Maria. "Frauenfrage 1946." *Frankfurter Hefte* 1 (1946): 24–31.

John, Michael. *Politics and the Law in Late Nineteenth-Century Germany: The Origins of the Civil Code.* Oxford: Clarendon Press, 1989.

Junker, Reinhold. *Die Lage der Mütter in der Bundesrepublik Deutschland: Ein Forschungsbericht.* Part I, *Mütter in Vollfamilien,* Vol. 1, *Belastungen und Folgen.* Cologne: Eigenverlag des deutschen Vereins für öffentliche und private Fürsorge, 1965.

Jurczyk, Karin. *Frauenarbeit und Frauenrolle: Zum Zusammenhang von Familienpolitik und Frauenerwerbstätigkeit in Deutschland von 1918–1975.* 3d ed. Frankfurt am Main: Campus, 1978.

Kamerman, Sheila B., and Alfred J. Kahn, eds. *Family Policy: Government and Families in Fourteen Countries.* New York: Columbia University Press, 1978.

Kamerman, Sheila B., Alfred J. Kahn, and Paul Kingston. *Maternity Policies and Working Women.* New York: Columbia University Press, 1983.

Kaplan, Marion A. "Jewish Women in Nazi Germany: Daily Life, Daily Struggles, 1933–1939." *Feminist Studies* 16 (1990): 579–606.

———. "Sisterhood under Siege: Feminism and Anti-Semitism in Germany, 1904–1938." In *When Biology Became Destiny: Women in Weimar and Nazi Germany,* edited by Renate Bridenthal, Atina Grossmann, and Marion Kaplan. New York: Monthly Review Press, 1984.

Kaplan, Temma. *Red City, Blue Period: Social Movements in Picasso's Barcelona.* Berkeley and Los Angeles: University of California Press, 1992.

———. "Women and Communal Strikes in the Crisis of 1917–1922." In *Becoming Visible: Women in European History*, edited by Renate Bridenthal, Claudia Koonz, and Susan Stuard. 2d ed. Boston: Houghton Mifflin, 1987.

Karbe, Agnes, and Maria Tritz. *Das Mädchen im Betrieb*. N.p., n.d. [1957].

Katzenstein, Peter J. *Policy and Politics in West Germany: The Growth of a Semisovereign State*. Philadelphia: Temple University Press, 1987.

Kaufmann, Doris. "Vom Vaterland zum Mutterland: Frauen im katholischen Milieu der Weimarer Republik." In *Frauen suchen ihre Geschichte: Historische Studien zum 19. und 20. Jahrhundert*, edited by Karin Hausen. Munich: C. H. Beck, 1983.

Kay, Herma Hill. "Equality and Difference: The Case of Pregnancy." *Berkeley Women's Law Journal* 1 (1985): 1–38.

———. "Models of Equality." *University of Illinois Law Review* (1985): 39–88.

Kershaw, Ian. *Popular Opinion and Political Dissent in the Third Reich: Bavaria, 1933–1945*. Oxford: Clarendon Press, 1983.

Kessler-Harris, Alice. "The Debate over Equality for Women in the Work Place: Recognizing Differences." *Women and Work: An Annual Review* 1 (1985): 141–61.

———. *Out to Work: A History of Wage-Earning Women in the United States*. New York: Oxford University Press, 1982.

Kitzinger, U. W. *German Electoral Politics: A Study of the 1957 Campaign*. Oxford: Clarendon Press, 1960.

Klaas, Helmut, ed. *Die Entstehung der Verfassung für Rheinland-Pfalz: Eine Dokumentation*. Boppard am Rhein: Harald Boldt, 1978.

Kleiber, Lore. " 'Wo ihr seid, da soll die Sonne scheinen!'—Der Frauenarbeitsdienst am Ende der Weimarer Republik und im Nationalsozialismus." In *Mutterkreuz und Arbeitsbuch: Zur Geschichte der Frauen in der Weimarer Republik und im Nationalsozialismus*, edited by Frauengruppe Faschismusforschung. Frankfurt am Main: Fischer, 1981.

Klessmann, Christoph. *Die doppelte Staatsgründung: Deutsche Geschichte 1945–1955*. Göttingen: Vandenhoeck & Ruprecht, 1982.

———. "Untergänge-Übergänge: Gesellschaftsgeschichtliche Brüche und Kontinuitätslinien vor und nach 1945." In *Nicht nur Hitlers Krieg: Der zweite Weltkrieg und die Deutschen*, edited by Christoph Klessmann. Düsseldorf: Droste, 1989.

———. *Zwei Staaten, eine Nation: Deutsche Geschichte 1955–1970*. Göttingen: Vandenhoeck & Ruprecht, 1988.

Klinksiek, Dorothee. *Die Frau im NS-Staat*. Stuttgart: Deutsche Verlags-Anstalt, 1982.

Klotzbach, Kurt. *Der Weg zur Staatspartei: Programmatik, praktische Politik und Organisation der deutschen Sozialdemokratie 1945 bis 1965*. Bonn: J. H. W. Dietz Nachf., 1982.

Kolinsky, Eva. *Women in West Germany: Life, Work and Politics*. Oxford: Berg, 1989.

Köllmann, Wolfgang. "Die Bevölkerungsentwicklung der Bundesrepublik." In *Sozialgeschichte der Bundesrepublik Deutschland: Beiträge zum Kontinuitätsproblem*, edited by Werner Conze and M. Rainer Lepsius. Stuttgart: Klett-Cotta, 1983.

Kommers, Donald P. *The Constitutional Jurisprudence of the Federal Republic of Germany.* Durham: Duke University Press, 1989.

———. *Judicial Politics in West Germany: A Study of the Federal Constitutional Court.* Beverly Hills: Sage Publications, 1976.

König, Gudrun. " 'Man hat vertrennt, vertrennt und wieder vertrennt': Erinnerungen an den Nachkriegsalltag." In *"Das Schicksal Deutschlands liegt in der Hand seiner Frauen": Frauen in der deutschen Nachkriegsgeschichte,* edited by Anna-Elisabeth Freier and Annette Kuhn. Düsseldorf: Schwann, 1984.

Koonz, Claudia. *Mothers in the Fatherland: Women, the Family, and Nazi Politics.* New York: St. Martin's, 1987.

Korte, Hermann. "Bevölkerungsstruktur und -entwicklung." In *Die Bundesrepublik Deutschland: Geschichte in drei Bänden,* edited by Wolfgang Benz. Vol. 2, *Gesellschaft.* Frankfurt am Main: Fischer, 1983.

———. *Eine Gesellschaft im Aufbruch: Die Bundesrepublik in den sechziger Jahren.* Frankfurt am Main: Suhrkamp Taschenbuch, 1987.

Kramer, Sylvia, as told by Ruth Nebel. "The Story of Ruth." In *When Biology Became Destiny: Women in Weimar and Nazi Germany,* edited by Renate Bridenthal, Atina Grossmann, and Marion Kaplan. New York: Monthly Review Press, 1984.

Krauss, Marita. " '. . . es geschahen Dinge, die Wunder ersetzten': Die Frau im Münchner Trümmeralltag." In *Trümmerleben: Texte, Dokumente, Bilder aus den Münchner Nachkriegsjahren,* edited by Friedrich Prinz and Marita Krauss. Munich: Deutscher Taschenbuch, 1985.

Kroeber-Keneth, L. *Frauen unter Männern: Grenzen und Möglichkeiten der arbeitenden Frau.* Düsseldorf: Econ Verlag, 1955.

Kröger, Peter. "Entwicklungsstadien der Bestrafung der widernatürlichen Unzucht und kritische Studie zur Berechtigung der §§ 175, 175a, 175b StGB de lege ferenda." Diss., Free University, Berlin, 1957.

Kropholler, Jan. *Gleichberechtigung durch Richterrecht: Erfahrungen im Familienrecht—Perspektive im internationalen Privatrecht.* Bielefeld: Ernst und Werner Gieseking, 1975.

Krüger, Hildegard. "Gedanken zur Familienrechtsreform." *Hochland* 44 (1952): 542–51.

Krüger, Hildegard, Ernst Breetzke, and Kuno Nowack. *Gleichberechtigungsgesetz.* Munich: C. H. Beck, 1958.

Kuhn, Annette, ed. *Frauen in der deutschen Nachkriegszeit.* Vol. 2, *Frauenpolitik 1945–1949: Quellen und Materialien.* Düsseldorf: Schwann, 1986.

———. "Frauen suchen neue Wege der Politik." In *Frauen in der deutschen Nachkriegszeit,* vol. 2, *Frauenpolitik 1945–1949: Quellen und Materialien,* edited by Annette Kuhn. Düsseldorf: Schwann, 1986.

———. "Power and Powerlessness: Women after 1945, or the Continuity of the Ideology of Femininity." *German History* 7 (1989): 34–46.

———. "Die vergessene Frauenarbeit in der Nachkriegszeit." In *"Das Schicksal Deutschlands liegt in der Hand seiner Frauen": Frauen in der deutschen Nachkriegsgeschichte,* edited by Anna-Elisabeth Freier and Annette Kuhn. Düsseldorf: Schwann, 1984.

Kuhn, Anette [*sic*], and Doris Schubert, eds. *Frauen in der Nachkriegszeit und im Wirtschaftswunder 1945–1960*. Frankfurt am Main: Hans Mousiol, 1980.

Kühn, Evelyn. "Die Entwicklung und Diskussion des Ehescheidungsrechts in Deutschland: Eine sozialhistorische und rechtssoziologische Untersuchung." Diss., Hamburg University, 1974.

Kuhrig, Herta, and Wulfram Speigner. "Gleichberechtigung der Frau: Aufgaben und ihre Realisierung in der DDR." In *Wie emanzipiert sind die Frauen in der DDR?*, edited by Herta Kuhrig and Wulfram Speigner. Cologne: Pahl-Rugenstein, 1979.

Lafeber, Walter, ed. *The Origins of the Cold War, 1941–1947: A Historical Problem with Interpretations and Documents*. New York: Wiley, 1971.

Land, Hilary. "Eleanor Rathbone and the Economy of the Family." In *British Feminism in the Twentieth Century*, edited by Harold L. Smith. Hants: Edward Elgar, 1990.

———. "Who Still Cares about the Family? Recent Developments in Income Maintenance, Taxation and Family Law." In *Women's Welfare, Women's Rights*, edited by Jane Lewis. London: Croom Helm, 1983.

Lange, Max Gustav, et al. *Parteien in der Bundesrepublik: Studien zur Entwicklung der deutschen Parteien bis zur Bundestagswahl 1953*. Stuttgart: Ring, 1955.

Langer, Ingrid. "In letzter Konsequenz . . . Uranbergwerk! Die Gleichberechtigung in Grundgesetz und Bürgerlichem Gesetzbuch." In *Perlonzeit: Wie die Frauen ihr Wirtschaftswunder erlebten*, edited by Angela Delille and Andrea Grohn. Berlin: Elefanten Press, 1985.

———. "Die Mohrinnen hatten ihre Schuldigkeit getan . . . Staatlich-moralische Aufrüstung der Familien." In *Die fünfziger Jahre: Beiträge zu Politik und Kultur*, edited by Dieter Bähnsch. Tübingen: Gunter Narr, 1985.

Laurien, Ingrid. " 'Wie kriege ich einen Mann'? Zum weiblichen Leitbild und zur Rolle der Frau in den Fünfziger Jahren." *Sozialwissenschaftliche Informationen* 15 (1986): 32–44.

Lautmann, Rüdiger. " 'Hauptdevise: bloss nicht anecken': Das Leben homosexueller Männer unter dem Nationalsozialismus." In *Terror und Hoffnung in Deutschland 1933–1945: Leben im Faschismus*, edited by Johannes Beck, et al. Reinbek bei Hamburg: Rowohlt, 1980.

Lehmann, Albrecht. *Gefangenschaft und Heimkehr: Deutsche Kriegsgefangene in der Sowjetunion*. Munich: C. H. Beck, 1986.

Lehr, Ursula. *Die Frau im Beruf: Eine psychologische Analyse der weiblichen Berufsrolle*. Frankfurt am Main: Athenäum, 1969.

Leibholz, Gerhard, and Hermann von Mangoldt, eds. *Entstehungsgeschichte der Artikel des Grundgesetzes. Jahrbuch des öffentlichen Rechts der Gegenwart*, n.s. 1 (1951). Tübingen: J. C. B. Mohr (Paul Siebeck), 1951.

Lepsius, M. Rainer. "Die Entwicklung der Soziologie nach dem zweiten Weltkrieg." In *Deutsche Soziologie seit 1945: Entwicklungsrichtungen und Praxisbezug*, edited by Günther Lüschen. Cologne: Westdeutscher Verlag, 1979.

Lewis, Jane. "Dealing with Dependency: State Practices and Social Realities, 1870–1945." In *Women's Welfare, Women's Rights*, edited by Jane Lewis. London: Croom Helm, 1983.

———. "Models of Equality for Women: The Case of State Support for Children in Twentieth-Century Britain." In *Maternity and Gender Policies: Women and the Rise of the European Welfare States, 1880s–1950s,* edited by Gisela Bock and Pat Thane. London: Routledge, 1991.

———, ed. *Women's Welfare, Women's Rights.* London: Croom Helm, 1983.

Liljeström, Rita. "Sweden." In *Family Policy: Government and Families in Fourteen Countries,* edited by Sheila B. Kamerman and Alfred J. Kahn. New York: Columbia University Press, 1978.

Limbach, Jutta. "Die Entwicklung des Familienrechts seit 1949." In *Wandel und Kontinuität der Familie in der Bundesrepublik Deutschland,* edited by Rosemarie Nave-Herz. Stuttgart: Ferdinand Enke, 1988.

Löwenthal, Richard, and Hans-Peter Schwarz, eds. *Die zweite Republik: 25 Jahre Bundesrepublik Deutschland—eine Bilanz.* Stuttgart: Seewald, 1974.

Lübbe, Hermann. "Der Nationalsozialismus im deutschen Nachkriegsbewusstsein," *Historische Zeitschrift* 236 (1983): 579–99.

Lüders, Marie-Elisabeth. *Fürchte dich nicht: Persönliches und Politisches aus mehr als 80 Jahren, 1878–1962.* Cologne: Westdeutscher Verlag, 1963.

Ludwig-Bühler, Ulrike. "Im NS-Musterbetrieb: Frauen in einem Textilunternehmen an der Schweizer Grenze." In *"Wir kriegen jetzt andere Zeiten": Auf der Suche nach der Erfahrung des Volkes in nachfaschistischen Ländern,* edited by Lutz Niethammer and Alexander von Plato. Bonn: J. H. W. Dietz Nachf., 1985.

Mabry, Hannelore. *Unkraut ins Parlament: Die Bedeutung weiblicher parlamentarischer Arbeit für die Emanzipation der Frau.* Lollar über Giessen: Andreas Achenbach, 1974.

McDougall, Mary Lynn. "Protecting Infants: The French Campaign for Maternity Leaves, 1890s–1913." *French Historical Studies* 13 (1983): 79–105.

Mackenroth, Gerhard. *Bevölkerungslehre: Theorie, Soziologie und Statistik der Bevölkerung.* Berlin: Springer-Verlag, 1953.

———. "Die Reform der Sozialpolitik durch einen deutschen Sozialplan." *Schriften des Vereins für Sozialpolitik,* n.s. 4 (1952): 40–76.

Macnicol, John. *The Movement for Family Allowances, 1919–1945: A Study in Social Policy Development.* London: Heineman, 1980.

Mai, Gunther. *Westliche Sicherheitspolitik im Kalten Krieg: Der Korea-Krieg und die deutsche Wiederbewaffnung 1950.* Boppard am Rhein: Harald Boldt, 1977.

Maier, Hans. "Die Kirchen." In *Die zweite Republik: 25 Jahre Bundesrepublik Deutschland—eine Bilanz,* edited by Richard Löwenthal and Hans-Peter Schwarz. Stuttgart: Seewald, 1974.

———. "Der politische Weg der deutschen Katholiken nach 1945." In *Deutscher Katholizismus nach 1945: Kirche, Gesellschaft, Geschichte,* edited by Hans Maier. Munich: Kösel-Verlag, 1964.

Mangoldt, Hermann von. *Das Bonner Grundgesetz.* With an introduction by Gerhard Leibholz. Berlin: Franz Vahlen, 1953.

Marshall, Barbara. "German Attitudes to British Military Government 1945–1947." *Journal of Contemporary History* 15 (1980): 655–84.

Martin, Bernd, and Alan S. Milward, eds. *Agriculture and Food Supply in the Second World War.* Ostfildern: Scripta Mercaturae, 1985.

Martiny, Anke. "Von der Trümmerfrau zur Quotenfrau: Vierzig Jahre Gleichberechtigung im Lichte und im Schatten der Verfassung." *Blätter für deutsche und internationale Politik* 34 (1989): 69–75.

Mason, Timothy W. *Sozialpolitik im Dritten Reich: Arbeiterklasse und Volksgemeinschaft.* 2d ed. Opladen: Westdeutscher Verlag, 1978.

———. "Women in Germany, 1925–1940: Family, Welfare and Work, Part I." *History Workshop,* no. 1 (1976): 73–113.

———. "Women in Germany, 1925–1940: Family, Welfare and Work, Part II." *History Workshop,* no. 2 (1976): 5–32.

Maxson, Rhea. *The Woman Worker in Germany.* Mehlem: Office of the United States High Commissioner for Germany, 1952.

May, Elaine Tyler. *Homeward Bound: American Families in the Cold War Era.* New York: Basic Books, 1988.

Mayer, A. "Doppelberuf der Frau als Gefahr für Familie, Volk und Kultur." *Münchener medizinische Wochenzeitschrift* 98 (1956): 649–51, 692–95.

———. *Emanzipation, Frauentum, Muttertum, Familie und Gesellschaft.* Stuttgart: Ferdinand Enke, 1962.

Mayer, Karl Ulrich. "German Survivors of World War II: The Impact on the Life Course of the Collective Experience of Birth Cohorts." In *Social Structures and Human Lives,* edited by Matilda White Riley in association with Bettina J. Huber and Beth B. Hess. Beverly Hills: Sage Publications, 1988.

———. "Sozialhistorische Materialien zum Verhältnis von Bildungs- und Beschäftigungsstruktur bei Frauen." In *Bildungsexpansion und betriebliche Beschäftigungspolitik: Aktuelle Entwicklungstendenzen im Vermittlungszusammenhang von Bildung und Beschäftigung,* edited by Ulrich Beck, Karl H. Hörning, and Wilke Thomssen. Frankfurt am Main: Campus, 1980.

Menck, Clara. "The Problem of Reorientation." In *The Struggle for Democracy in Germany,* edited by Gabriel A. Almond. Chapel Hill: University of North Carolina Press, 1949.

Mensing, Hans Peter, ed. *Adenauer Briefe 1945–1951.* Berlin: Wolf Jobst Siedler, 1985.

Merkl, Ina. *. . . und Du, Frau an der Werkbank: Die DDR in den 50er Jahren.* Berlin: Elefanten Press, 1990.

Merkl, Peter H. *The Origin of the West German Republic.* New York: Oxford University Press, 1963.

———, ed. *The Federal Republic at Forty.* New York: New York University Press, 1989.

Merritt, Anna J., and Richard L. Merritt. *Public Opinion in Occupied Germany: The OMGUS Surveys, 1945–1949.* Urbana: University of Illinois Press, 1970.

Metzger, Wolfgang. "Der Auftrag des Elternhauses." In *Familie im Umbruch,* edited by Ferdinand Oeter. Gütersloh: Gerd Mohn, 1960.

Meyer, Birgit. "Viel bewegt—auch viel erreicht? Frauengeschichte und Frauenbewegung in der Bundesrepublik." *Blätter für deutsche und internationale Politik* 34 (1989): 832–42.

Meyer, Sibylle, and Eva Schulze. " 'Alleine war's schwieriger und einfacher zugleich': Veränderungen gesellschaftlicher Bewertung und individueller Erfahrung alleinstehender Frauen in Berlin 1943–1955." In *Das Schicksal Deutschlands liegt in der Hand seiner Frauen": Frauen in der deutschen Nachkriegsgeschichte,* edited by Anna-Elisabeth Freier and Annette Kuhn. Düsseldorf: Schwann, 1984.

———. " 'Als wir wieder zusammen waren, ging der Krieg im Kleinen weiter': Frauen, Männer und Familien in Berlin der vierziger Jahre." In *Wir kriegen jetzt andere Zeiten": Auf der Suche nach der Erfahrung des Volkes in nachfaschistischen Ländern,* edited by Lutz Niethammer and Alexander von Plato. Bonn: J. H. W. Dietz Nachf., 1985.

———. *Von Liebe sprach damals keiner: Familienalltag in der Nachkriegszeit.* Munich: C. H. Beck, 1985.

———. *Wie wir das alles geschafft haben: Alleinstehende Frauen berichten über ihr Leben nach 1945.* Munich: C. H. Beck, 1985.

Meyer-Harter, Renate. *Die Stellung der Frau in der Sozialversicherung: Lageanalyse und Reformmöglichkeit.* Berlin: Duncker & Humblot, 1974.

Michel, Sonya, and Seth Koven. "Womanly Duties: Maternalist Politics and the Origins of Welfare States in France, Germany, Great Britain, and the United States, 1880–1920." *American Historical Review* 95 (1990): 1076–1108.

Miller, Max. "Kollektive Erinnerungen und gesellschaftliche Lernprozesse: Zur Struktur sozialer Mechanismen der Vergangenheitsbewältigung." In *Antisemitismus in der politischen Kultur nach 1945,* edited by Werner Bergmann and Rainer Erb. Opladen: Westdeutscher Verlag, 1990.

Miller, Susanne. "Die SPD vor und nach Godesberg." In *Die zweite Republik: 25 Jahre Bundesrepublik Deutschland—eine Bilanz,* edited by Richard Löwenthal and Hans-Peter Schwarz. Stuttgart: Seewald, 1974.

———. *Die SPD vor und nach Godesberg.* Bonn: Verlag Neue Gesellschaft, 1974.

Mink, Gwendolyn. "The Lady and the Tramp: Gender, Race, and the Origins of the American Welfare State." In *Women, the State, and Welfare,* edited by Linda Gordon. Madison: University of Wisconsin Press, 1990.

Mitchell, Juliet. *Psychoanalysis and Feminism.* New York: Vintage, 1974.

Mitscherlich, Alexander. *Auf dem Weg zur vaterlosen Gesellschaft: Ideen zur Sozialpsychologie.* 1963. Reprint, Munich: R. Piper & Co., 1973.

———. "Der unsichtbare Vater: Ein Problem für Psychoanalyse und Soziologie." *Kölner Zeitschrift für Soziologie und Sozialpsychologie* 7 (1955): 188–201.

Mitscherlich, Alexander, and Margarete Mitscherlich. *Die Unfähigkeit zu trauern: Grundlagen kollektiven Verhaltens.* Munich: R. Piper & Co., 1967.

Möding, Nora. " 'Ich muss irgendwo engagiert sein—fragen Sie mich bloss nicht, warum': Überlegungen von Mädchen in NS-Organisationen." In *Wir kriegen jetzt andere Zeiten": Auf der Suche nach der Erfahrung des Volkes in nachfaschistischen Ländern,* edited by Lutz Niethammer and Alexander von Plato. Bonn: J. H. W. Dietz Nachf., 1985.

———. "Kriegserfahrungen von Frauen und ihre Verarbeitung." In *Über Leben im Krieg: Kriegserfahrungen in einer Industrieregion 1939–1945,* edited by Ulrich Borsdorf and Mathilde Jamin. Reinbek bei Hamburg: Rowohlt, 1989.

————. "Die Stunde der Frauen? Frauen und Frauenorganisationen des bürgerlichen Lagers." In *Von Stalingrad zur Währungsreform: Zur Sozialgeschichte des Umbruchs in Deutschland,* edited by Martin Broszat, KlausDietmar Henke, and Hans Woller. Munich: R. Oldenbourg, 1988.

Möller, Hans, ed. *Zur Vorgeschichte der deutschen Mark: Die Währungsreformpläne 1945–1948.* Tübingen: J. C. B. Mohr (Paul Siebeck), 1961.

Molitor, Erich. "Die arbeitsrechtliche Bedeutung des Art. 3 des Bonner Grundgesetzes." *Archiv für die civilistische Praxis* 151 (1950/51): 385–415.

Mooser, Josef. "Abschied von der 'Proletarität.'" In *Sozialgeschichte der Bundesrepublik Deutschland: Beiträge zum Kontinuitätsproblem,* edited by Werner Conze and M. Rainer Lepsius. Stuttgart: Klett-Cotta, 1983.

————. *Arbeiterleben in Deutschland, 1900–1970: Klassenlagen, Kultur und Politik.* Frankfurt am Main: Suhrkamp, 1984.

Morsey, Rudolf. "Adenauer und Kardinal Frings 1945–1949." In *Politik und Konfession: Festschrift für Konrad Repgen zum 60. Geburtstag,* edited by Dieter Albrecht, et al. Berlin: Duncker & Humblot, 1983.

————. "Helene Weber (1881–1962)." In *Zeitgeschichte in Lebensbildern,* edited by Jürgen Aretz, Rudolf Morsey, and Anton Rauscher. Vol. 3, *Aus dem deutschen Katholizismus des 19. und 20. Jahrhunderts.* Mainz: MatthiasGrünewald, 1979.

————. "Katholizismus und Unionsparteien in der Ära Adenauer." In *Katholizismus im politischen System der Bundesrepublik 1949–1963,* edited by Albrecht Langer. Paderborn: Ferdinand Schöningh, 1978.

————. "Die Rhöndorfer Weichenstellung vom 21. August 1949." *Vierteljahrshefte für Zeitgeschichte* 28 (1980): 508–42.

Müchler, Günter. *CDU/CSU: Das schwierige Bündnis.* Munich: Ernst Vögel, 1976.

Mugdan, Benno. *Die gesamten Materialien zum bürgerlichen Gesetzbuch für das deutsche Reich.* Vol. 4, *Familienrecht.* 1899; reprint, Aalen: Scientia, 1979.

Müller, Albert. "Ideologische Elemente, Ungereimtes und Widersprüchliches in der bevölkerungs- und familienpolitischen Diskussion." In *Geburtenrückgang: Risiko oder Chance,* edited by Rainer Silkenbeumer. Hannover: Fackelträger, 1979.

Müller, Walter, Angelika Willms, and Johann Handl, eds. *Strukturwandel der Frauenarbeit 1880–1980.* Frankfurt am Main: Campus, 1983.

Müller-Freienfels, Wolfram. "Zur Kodifikation des Familienrechts." In *Seminar: Familie und Familienrecht,* vol. 1, edited by Spiros Simitis and Gisela Zenz. Frankfurt am Main: Suhrkamp, 1975.

Müller-Schwefe, Hans-Rudolf. *Die Welt ohne Väter: Gedanken eines Christen zur Krise der Autorität.* Hamburg: Furche, 1957.

Münke, Stephanie. *Die Armut in der heutigen Gesellschaft: Ergebnisse einer Untersuchung in Westberlin.* Berlin: Duncker & Humblot, 1956.

————. "Frauenarbeit in der Sowjetzone." In *Die Wirtschaft braucht die Frau,* edited by Ruth Bergholtz. Darmstadt: W. W. Leske, 1956.

Mushaben, Joyce M. "Feminism in Four Acts: The Changing Political Identity of Women in the Federal Republic of Germany." In *The Federal Republic at Forty,* edited by Peter H. Merkl. New York: New York University Press, 1989.

Myrdal, Alva. *Nation and Family: The Swedish Experiment in Democratic Family and Population Policy.* 1941. Reprint, Cambridge, Massachusetts: M.I.T. Press, 1968.

Nahm, Peter Paul. *Der Lastenausgleich.* Stuttgart: W. Kohlhammer, 1961.

———. "Lastenausgleich und Integration der Vertriebenen und Geflüchteten." In *Die zweite Republik: 25 Jahre Bundesrepublik Deutschland—eine Bilanz,* edited by Richard Löwenthal and Hans-Peter Schwarz. Stuttgart: Seewald, 1974.

Naimark, Norman. " 'About the Russians and About Us': The Question of Rape and Soviet-German Relations in the East Zone" (manuscript).

Narr, Wolf-Dieter. *CDU-SPD: Programm und Praxis seit 1945.* Stuttgart: W. Kohlhammer, 1969.

Naujeck, Kurt. *Die Anfänge des sozialen Netzes 1945–1952.* Bielefeld: B. Kleine, 1984.

Nave-Herz, Rosemarie, ed. *Wandel und Kontinuität der Familie in der Bundesrepublik Deutschland.* Stuttgart: Ferdinand Enke, 1988.

Neidthardt, Friedhelm. "Germany." In *Family Policy: Government and Families in Fourteen Countries,* edited by Sheila Kamerman and Alfred J. Kahn. New York: Columbia University Press, 1978.

Nell-Breuning, Oswald von. "Kommerzialisierte Gesellschaft." *Stimmen der Zeit,* no. 158 (1956): 32–45.

Niclauss, Karlheinz. *Demokratiegründung in Westdeutschland: Die Entstehung der Bundesrepublik 1945–1949.* Munich: R. Piper & Co., 1974.

Niedhardt, Gottfried, and Normen Altmann. "Zwischen Beurteilung und Verurteilung: Die Sowjetunion im Urteil Konrad Adenauers." In *Adenauer und die Deutsche Frage,* edited by Josef Foschepoth. Göttingen: Vandenhoeck & Ruprecht, 1988.

Niehuss, Merith. "Zur Sozialgeschichte der Familie in Bayern." *Zeitschrift für bayerische Landesgeschichte* 51 (1988): 917–36.

Niethammer, Lutz. "Heimat und Front: Versuch, zehn Kriegserinnerungen aus der Arbeiterklasse des Ruhrgebietes zu verstehen." In *"Die Jahre weiss man nicht, wo man die heute hinsetzen soll": Faschismus-Erfahrungen im Ruhrgebiet,* edited by Lutz Niethammer. Bonn: J. H. W. Dietz Nachf., 1983.

———, ed. *"Hinterher merkt man, dass es richtig war, dass es schiefgegangen ist": Nachkriegs-Erfahrungen im Ruhrgebiet.* Bonn: J. H. W. Dietz Nachf., 1983.

———, ed. *"Die Jahre weiss man nicht, wo man die heute hinsetzen soll": Faschismus-Erfahrungen im Ruhrgebiet.* Bonn: J. H. W. Dietz Nachf., 1983.

———. " 'Normalisierung' im Westen: Erinnerungsspuren in die 50er Jahre." In *Ist der Nationalsozialismus Geschichte? Zur Historisierung und Historikerstreit,* edited by Dan Diner. Frankfurt am Main: Fischer, 1987.

———. "Privat-Wirtschaft: Erinnerungsfragmente einer anderen Umerziehung." In *"Hinterher merkt man, dass es richtig war, dass es schiefgegangen ist": Nachkriegs-Erfahrungen im Ruhrgebiet,* edited by Lutz Niethammer. Bonn: J. H. W. Dietz Nachf., 1983.

———. "Zum Wandel der Kontinuitätsdiskussion." In *Westdeutschland 1945– 1955: Unterwerfung, Kontrolle, Integration,* edited by Ludolf Herbst. Munich: R. Oldenbourg, 1986.

Niethammer, Lutz, and Franz Brüggemeier. "Wie wohnten Arbeiter im Kaiserreich?" *Archiv für Sozialgeschichte* 16 (1976): 61–134.

Niethammer, Lutz, and Alexander von Plato, eds. *"Wir kriegen jetzt andere Zeiten": Auf der Suche nach der Erfahrung des Volkes in nachfaschistischen Ländern.* Bonn: J. H. W. Dietz Nachf., 1985.

Niggemann, Heinz. *Emanzipation zwischen Sozialismus und Feminismus: Die sozialdemokratische Frauenbewegung im Kaiserreich.* Wuppertal: Peter Hammer, 1981.

Nipperdey, H. C. *Gleicher Lohn der Frau für gleiche Leistung: Rechtsgutachten erstattet dem Bundesvorstand des Deutschen Gewerkschaftsbundes.* Cologne: Bund, 1951.

Noelle, Elisabeth, and Erich Peter Neumann. *The Germans: Public Opinion Polls, 1947–1966,* trans. Gerard Finan. 1967. Reprint, Westport, Ct.: Greenwood Press, 1981.

———. *Jahrbuch der öffentlichen Meinung, 1947–1955.* Allensbach: Verlag für Demoskopie, 1955.

Nolan, Mary. " 'Housework Made Easy': The Taylorized Housewife in Weimar Germany's Rationalized Economy." *Feminist Studies* 16 (1990): 549–77.

———. "Proletarischer Anti-Feminismus: Dargestellt am Beispiel der SPD-Ortsgruppe Düsseldorf, 1890–1914." In *Frauen und Wissenschaft: Beiträge zur Berliner Sommeruniversität für Frauen, Juli 1976.* Berlin: Courage, 1977.

Noll, Heinz-Herbert. "Soziale Indikatoren für Arbeitsmarkt und Beschäftigungsbedingungen." In *Lebensbedingungen in der Bundesrepublik: Sozialer Wandel und Wohlfahrtsentwicklung,* edited by Wolfgang Zapf. Frankfurt am Main: Campus, 1978.

Nyssen, Elke, and Sigrid Metz-Göckel. " 'Ja, die waren ganz einfach tüchtig'— Was Frauen aus der Geschichte lernen können." In *"Das Schicksal Deutschlands liegt in der Hand seiner Frauen": Frauen in der deutschen Nachkriegsgeschichte,* edited by Anna-Elisabeth Freier and Annette Kuhn. Düsseldorf: Schwann, 1984.

Obertreis, Gesine. *Familienpolitik in der DDR 1945–1980.* Opladen: Leske & Budrich, 1986.

Oeter, Ferdinand. "Frondienstpflicht der Familie?" *Frankfurter Hefte* 8 (1953): 438–44.

———. *Soziale Sicherheit für Deutschland.* Giessen: Ärzte-Verlag, 1950.

Offen, Karen. "Body Politics: Women, Work and the Politics of Motherhood in France, 1920–1950." In *Maternity and Gender Policies: Women and the Rise of the European Welfare States, 1880s–1950s,* edited by Gisela Bock and Pat Thane. London: Routledge, 1991.

———. "Defining Feminism: A Comparative Historical Approach." *Signs* 14 (1988): 119–57.

Ohlander, Ann-Sofie. "The Invisible Child? The Struggle for a Social Democratic Family Policy in Sweden, 1900–1960s." In *Maternity and Gender*

Policies: Women and the Rise of the European Welfare States, 1880s–1950s,
edited by Gisela Bock and Pat Thane. London: Routledge, 1991.

Oppens, Edith. "Ruhelose Welt." In *Die Frau in unserer Zeit,* edited by Edith
Oppens et al. Oldenburg: Gerhard Stalling, 1954.

Oppens, Edith, et al., eds. *Die Frau in unserer Zeit.* Oldenburg: Gerhard Stalling, 1954.

Ortlieb, Heinz-Dietrich. "Glanz und Elend des deutschen Wirtschaftswunders."
In *Bestandsaufnahme: Eine deutsche Bilanz 1962,* edited by Hans Werner
Richter. Munich: Kurt Desch, 1962.

Osterkamp, Karl, and Heinz Beykirch. "Soziallohn oder Kinderbeihilfen." *Mitteilungen des wirtschaftswissenschaftlichen Instituts der Gewerkschaften* 4
(October 1951): 4–10.

Ostner, Ilona. *Beruf und Hausarbeit: Die Arbeit der Frau in unserer Gesellschaft.* 3d ed. Frankfurt am Main: Campus, 1978.

Otto, Volker. *Das Staatsverständnis des Parlamentarischen Rates: Ein Beitrag
zur Entstehungsgeschichte des Grundgesetzes für die Bundesrepublik
Deutschland.* Düsseldorf: Rheinisch-Bergische Druckerei- und Verlagsgesellschaft, 1971.

Pateman, Carole. "The Patriarchal Welfare State." In *Democracy and the Welfare State,* edited by Amy Gutman. Princeton: Princeton University Press,
1988.

Pedersen, Susan Gay. "The Failure of Feminism in the Making of the British
Welfare State." *Radical History Review,* no. 43 (1989): 86–110.

———. "Gender, Welfare, and Citizenship in Britain during the Great War."
American Historical Review 95 (1990): 983–1006.

———. "Social Policy and the Reconstruction of the Family in Britain and
France, 1900–1945." Ph.D. diss., Harvard University, 1989.

Peukert, Detlev J. K. *Inside Nazi Germany: Conformity, Opposition, and Racism in Everyday Life,* trans. Richard Deveson. New Haven: Yale University
Press, 1987.

Pfeil, Elisabeth. *Die Berufstätigkeit von Müttern: Eine empirisch-soziologische
Erhebung an 900 Müttern aus vollständigen Familien.* Tübingen: J. C. B.
Mohr (Paul Siebeck), 1961.

———. *Die 23jährigen: Eine Generationsuntersuchung am Geburtenjahrgang
1941.* Tübingen: J. C. B. Mohr (Paul Siebeck), 1968.

Pfetsch, Frank R. "Die Gründergeneration der Bundesrepublik: Sozialprofil und
politische Orientierung." *Politische Vierteljahresschrift* 27 (1986): 237–51.

Phayer, Michael. *Protestant and Catholic Women in Nazi Germany.* Detroit:
Wayne State University Press, 1990.

Pirker, Theo. *Die SPD nach Hitler: Die Geschichte der Sozialdemokratischen
Partei Deutschlands 1945–1964.* Munich: Rütten & Loening, 1965.

———. *Die verordnete Demokratie: Grundlagen und Erscheinungen der Restauration.* Berlin: Olle und Wolter, 1977.

Planken, Helgard. *Die soziale Sicherung der nicht-erwerbstätigen Frau.* Berlin:
Duncker & Humblot, 1961.

Plato, Alexander von. "Fremde Heimat: Zur Integration von Flüchtlingen und
Einheimischen in die Neue Zeit." In *"Wir kriegen jetzt andere Zeiten": Auf*

der Suche nach der Erfahrung des Volkes in nachfaschistischen Ländern, edited by Lutz Niethammer and Alexander von Plato. Bonn: J. H. W. Dietz Nachf., 1985.

Pore, Renate. *A Conflict of Interest: Women in German Social Democracy, 1919–1933*. Westport, Conn.: Greenwood Press, 1981.

Pridham, Geoffrey. *Christian Democracy in Western Germany: The CDU/ CSU in Government and Opposition, 1945–1976*. London: Croom Helm, 1977.

Prinz, Friedrich, and Marita Krauss, eds. *Trümmerleben: Texte, Dokumente, Bilder aus den Münchner Nachkriegsjahren*. Munich: Deutscher Taschenbuch, 1985.

Proctor, Robert. *Racial Hygiene: Medicine under the Nazis*. Cambridge: Harvard University Press, 1988.

Proske, Rüdiger. "Die Familie 1951: Eine Beschreibung ihrer wichtigsten Merkmale." *Frankfurter Hefte* 6 (1951): 179–90, 264–74.

Pross, Helge. *Abtreibung: Motive und Bedenken*. Stuttgart: W. Kohlhammer, 1971.

———. "Die gesellschaftliche Stellung der Frau in Westdeutschland." *Deutsche Rundschau* 81 (1958): 26–33.

———. *Gleichberechtigung im Beruf? Eine Untersuchung mit 7000 Arbeitnehmerinnen in der EWG*. Frankfurt am Main: Athenäum, 1973.

———. *Kapitalismus und Demokratie: Studien über westdeutsche Sozialstrukturen*. Frankfurt am Main: Athenäum, 1972.

———. *Über die Bildungschancen von Mädchen in der Bundesrepublik*. Frankfurt am Main: Suhrkamp, 1969.

———. *Die Wirklichkeit der Hausfrau: Die erste repräsentative Untersuchung über nichterwerbstätige Ehefrauen: Wie leben sie? Wie denken sie? Wie sehen sie sich selbst?* Reinbek: Rowohlt, 1976.

Protzner, Wolfgang. "Vom Hungerwinter bis zum Beginn der 'Fresswelle.' " In *Vom Hungerwinter zum kulinarischen Schlaraffenland: Aspekte einer Kulturgeschichte des Essens in der Bundesrepublik Deutschland*, edited by Wolfgang Protzner. Stuttgart: Steiner-Verlag-Wiesbaden, 1987.

Quataert, Jean H. *Reluctant Feminists in German Social Democracy, 1885–1917*. Princeton: Princeton University Press, 1979.

———. "Social Insurance and the Family Work of Oberlausitz Home Weavers in the Late Nineteenth Century." In *German Women in the Nineteenth Century: A Social History*, edited by John C. Fout. New York: Holmes & Meier, 1984.

———. "A Source Analysis in German Women's History: Factory Inspectors' Reports and the Shaping of Working-Class Lives, 1878–1914." *Central European History* 16 (1983): 99–121.

Questiaux, Nicole, and Jacques Fournier. "France." In *Family Policy: Government and Families in Fourteen Countries*, edited by Sheila B. Kamerman and Alfred J. Kahn. New York: Columbia University Press, 1978.

Ramm, Thilo. *Familienrecht*. Vol. 1, *Recht der Ehe*. Munich: C. H. Beck, 1985.

Rationalisierungs-Kuratorium der deutschen Wirtschaft, ed. *Frauenarbeit: Ergebnisse einer Befragung*. N.p., n.d. [1959].

Rauscher, Anton, ed. *Kirche und Katholizismus 1945–1949*. Munich: Ferdinand Schöningh, 1977.

Rausing, Lisbet. "The Population Question: The Debate of Family Welfare Reforms in Sweden, 1930–38." *Europäische Zeitschrift für politische Ökonomie* 2 (1986): 521–56.

Reich-Hilweg, Ines. *Männer und Frauen sind gleichberechtigt*. Frankfurt am Main: Europäische Verlagsanstalt, 1979.

Reinecke, Dietrich, and Elisabeth Schwarzhaupt. *Die Gleichberechtigung von Mann und Frau nach dem Gesetz vom 18. Juni 1957*. Stuttgart: W. Kohlhammer, 1957.

Richebächer, Sabine. *Uns fehlt nur eine Kleinigkeit: Deutsche proletarische Frauenbewegung 1890–1914*. Frankfurt am Main: Fischer, 1982.

Richter, Charlotte. *Frauenarbeitsnot in Duisburg*. Duisburg: n.p., 1951.

Riedmüller, Barbara. "Frauen haben keine Rechte: Zur Stellung der Frau im System sozialer Sicherheit." In *Die armen Frauen: Frauen und Sozialpolitik*, edited by Ilona Kickbusch and Barbara Riedmüller. Frankfurt am Main: Suhrkamp, 1984.

Riley, Denise. *War in the Nursery: Theories of the Child and Mother*. London: Virago, 1983.

Rodnick, David. *Postwar Germans: An Anthropologist's Account*. New Haven: Yale University Press, 1948.

Röhrich, Wilfried. *Die Demokratie der Westdeutschen: Geschichte und politisches Klima einer Republik*. Munich: C. H. Beck, 1988.

Roesler, Jörg. "The Black Market in Post-war Berlin and the Methods Used to Counteract it." *German History* 7 (1989): 92–107.

Rosenbaum, Heidi. *Familie als Gegenstruktur zur Gesellschaft*. Stuttgart: Ferdinand Enke, 1973.

———. *Formen der Familie: Untersuchungen zum Zusammenhang von Familienverhältnissen, Sozialstruktur und sozialem Wandel in der deutschen Gesellschaft des 19. Jahrhunderts*. Frankfurt am Main: Suhrkamp, 1982.

Rosenthal, Gabriele, ed., with the assistance of Christiane Grote. *"Als der Krieg kam, hatte ich mit Hitler nichts mehr zu tun": Zur Gegenwärtigkeit des "Dritten Reiches" in Biographien*. Opladen: Leske & Budrich, 1990.

Rothenberger, Karl-Heinz. *Die Hungerjahre nach dem Zweiten Weltkrieg: Ernährungs- und Landwirtschaft in Rheinland-Pfalz 1945–1950*. Boppard am Rhein: Harald Boldt, 1980.

Rückert, Gerd-Rüdiger. "Die Kinderzahl der Ehen in der Bundesrepublik Deutschland im Intergenerationenvergleich." In *Soziale Strukturen und individuelle Mobilität: Beiträge zur sozio-demographischen Analyse der Bundesrepublik Deutschland*, edited by Heinrich Tegtmeyer. Boppard am Rhein: Harald Boldt, 1979.

Rüdenhausen, Adelheid Gräfin Castell zu. " 'Nicht mitzuleiden, mitzukämpfen sind wir da!' Nationalsozialistische Volkswohlfahrt im Gau Westfalen-Nord." In *Die Reihen fast geschlossen: Beiträge zur Geschichte des Alltags unterm Nationalsozialismus*, edited by Detlev Peukert, Jürgen Reulecke, with assistance of Adelheid Gräfin zu Castell Rüdenhausen. Wuppertal: Peter Hammer, 1981.

Ruggie, Mary. *The State and Working Women: A Comparative Study of Britain and Sweden.* Princeton: Princeton University Press, 1984.

Ruhl, Klaus-Jörg. *Frauen in der Nachkriegszeit 1945–1963.* Munich: Deutscher Taschenbuch Verlag, 1988.

———. *Unsere verlorenen Jahre: Frauenalltag in Kriegs- und Nachkriegszeit 1939–1949 in Berichten, Dokumenten und Bildern.* Darmstadt: Luchterhand, 1985.

Rupieper, Hermann-Josef. *Der besetzte Verbündete: Die amerikanische Deutschlandpolitik 1949–1955.* Opladen: Westdeutscher Verlag, 1991.

Rupp, Leila. " 'I Don't Call that *Volksgemeinschaft*': Women, Class and War in Nazi Germany." In *Women, War, and Revolution,* edited by Carol R. Berkin and Clara M. Lovett. New York: Holmes & Meier, 1980.

———. *Mobilizing Women for War: German and American War Propaganda, 1939–1945.* Princeton: Princeton University Press, 1978.

Rupp, Leila, and Verta Taylor. *Survival in the Doldrums: The American Women's Rights Movement, 1945 to the 1960s.* New York: Oxford University Press, 1987.

Rusinek, Bernd-A. " 'Maskenlose Zeit': Der Zerfall der Gesellschaft im Krieg." In *Über Leben im Krieg: Kriegserfahrungen in einer Industrieregion 1939–1945,* edited by Ulrich Borsdorf and Mathilde Jamin. Reinbek bei Hamburg: Rowohlt, 1989.

Rytlewski, Ralf, and Manfred Opp de Hipt. *Die Bundesrepublik Deutschland in Zahlen, 1945/49–1980: Ein sozialgeschichtliches Arbeitsbuch.* Munich: C. H. Beck, 1987.

Sachsse, Christoph. *Mütterlichkeit als Beruf: Sozialarbeit, Sozialreform und Frauenbewegung 1871–1929.* Frankfurt am Main: Suhrkamp, 1986.

Sachsse, Christoph, and Florian Tennstedt. "Familienpolitik durch Gesetzgebung: Die juristische Regulierung der Familie." In *Staatliche Sozialpolitik und Familie,* edited by Franz-Xaver Kaufmann. Munich: R. Oldenbourg, 1982.

Salzmann, Bruno. "Fruchtbarkeitswandel und die Rolle der Politik." In *Beiträge aus der bevölkerungswissenschaftlichen Forschung: Festschrift für Hermann Schubnell,* edited by Sabine Rupp and Karl Schwarz. Boppard am Rhein: Boldt, 1983.

Salzmann, Rainer, ed. *Die CDU/CSU im Parlamentarischen Rat: Sitzungsprotokolle der Unionsfraktion.* Stuttgart: Klett-Cotta, 1981.

Schäfer, Hans Dieter. *Das gespaltene Bewusstsein: Deutsche Kultur und Lebenswirklichkeit 1933–1945.* Munich: Carl Hanser, 1981.

Schaffner, Bertram. *Father Land: A Study of Authoritarianism in the German Family.* New York: Columbia University Press, 1948.

Scheffler, Erna. *Die Stellung der Frau in Familie und Gesellschaft im Wandel der Rechtsordnung seit 1918.* Frankfurt am Main: Alfred Metzner, 1970.

———. "Die Stellung der Frau in Familie und Gesellschaft im Wandel der Rechtsordnung seit 1918." In *Frauen in Wissenschaft und Politik,* edited by Dorothea Frandsen, Ursula Huffmann, and Annette Kuhn. Düsseldorf: Schwann, 1987.

Schelsky, Helmut. *Auf der Suche nach der Wirklichkeit: Gesammelte Aufsätze.* Düsseldorf: Eugen Diedrichs, 1965.

————. "Die Aufgaben einer Familiensoziologie in Deutschland." *Kölner Zeitschrift für Soziologie und Sozialpsychologie* 2 (1949/50): 218–47.

————. "Die gelungene Emanzipation." *Merkur* 9 (1955): 360–70.

————. "Die gegenwärtige Problemlage der Familiensoziologie." In *Soziologische Forschung in unserer Zeit*, edited by Karl Gustav Specht. Cologne: Westdeutscher Verlag, 1951.

————. "Die Jugend in der industriellen Gesellschaft und die Arbeitslosigkeit." In *Arbeitslosigkeit und Berufsnot der Jugend*, vol. 2, edited by Helmut Schelsky. Cologne: Bund, 1952.

————. *Soziologie der Sexualität: Über die Beziehungen zwischen Geschlecht, Moral und Gesellschaft.* Hamburg: Rowohlt, 1955.

————. *Wandlungen der deutschen Familie in der Gegenwart: Darstellung und Deutung einer empirisch-soziologischen Tatbestandsaufnahme.* 4th ed. Stuttgart: Ferdinand Enke, 1960.

Scherpe, Klaus, ed. *In Deutschland unterwegs: Reportagen, Skizzen, Berichte 1945–1948.* Stuttgart: Phillipp Reclam jun., 1982.

Schewick, Burkhard van. *Die katholische Kirche und die Entstehung der Verfassungen in Westdeutschland 1945–1950.* Mainz: Matthias-Grünewald, 1980.

Schildt, Axel. "Gründerjahre: Zur Entwicklung der westdeutschen Gesellschaft in der 'Ära Adenauer.' " *Blätter für deutsche und internationale Politik* 34 (1989): 22–36.

Schildt, Axel, and Arnold Sywottek. " 'Wiederaufbau' und 'Modernisierung': Zur westdeutschen Gesellschaftsgeschichte in den fünfziger Jahren." *Aus Politik und Zeitgeschichte: Beilage zur Wochenzeitung Das Parlament* B 6–7 (1989): 18–32.

Schilling, Heinz-Dieter, ed. *Schwule und Faschismus.* Berlin: Elefanten Press, 1983.

Schillinger, Reinhold. *Der Entscheidungsprozess beim Lastenausgleich 1945–1952.* St. Katharinen: Scripta Mercaturae, 1985.

Schmidt, Eberhard. *Die verhinderte Neuordnung 1945–1952.* Frankfurt am Main: Europäische Verlagsanstalt, 1970.

Schmidt, Margot. "Im Vorzimmer: Arbeitsverhältnisse von Sekretärinnen und Sachbearbeiterinnen bei Thyssen nach dem Krieg." In *"Hinterher merkt man, dass es richtig war, dass es schiefgegangen ist": Nachkriegs-Erfahrungen im Ruhrgebiet*, edited by Lutz Niethammer. Bonn: J. H. W. Dietz Nachf., 1983.

Schmidt-Harzbach, Ingrid. "Eine Woche im April. Berlin 1945: Vergewaltigung als Massenschicksal." *Feministische Studien* 2 (1984): 51–62.

Schmollinger, Horst W. "Die Deutsche Partei." In *Parteien-Handbuch: Die Parteien der Bundesrepublik Deutschland 1945–1980*, edited by Richard Stöss. Vol. 1, *AUD bis EFP.* Opladen: Westdeutscher Verlag, 1983.

Schmucker, Helga. "Auswirkungen des generativen Verhaltens der Bevölkerung auf die Lage der Familie und auf die Wirtschaft." In *Die ökonomischen Grundlagen der Familie in ihrer gesellschaftlichen Bedeutung*, edited by Gesellschaft für sozialen Fortschritt. Berlin: Duncker & Humblot, 1960.

Schoenbaum, David. *Hitler's Social Revolution: Class and Status in Nazi Germany, 1933–1939.* Garden City, New York: Anchor Books, 1966.

Schoppmann, Claudia. *Nationalsozialistische Sexualpolitik und weibliche Homosexualität.* Pfaffenweiler: Centaurus, 1991.

Schöpp-Schilling, Hanna Beate. "Federal Republic of Germany." In *Women Workers in Fifteen Countries: Essays in Honor of Alice Hanson Cook,* edited by Jennie Farley. Ithaca: ILR Press, 1985.

Schrecker, Margarete. *Die Entwicklung der Mädchenberufsschule.* Weinheim: Julius Beltz, 1963.

Schreiber, Wilfrid. *Existenzsicherheit in der industriellen Gesellschaft: Vorschläge zur "Sozialreform".* Cologne: J. P. Bachem, 1955.

———. *Kindergeld im sozio-ökonomischen Prozess: Familienlastenausgleich als Prozess zeitlicher Kaufkraft-Umschichtung im Individual-Bereich.* Cologne: W. Kohlhammer, 1964.

Schröder, Hans-Jürgen. "Kanzler der Alliierten? Die Bedeutung der USA für die Aussenpolitik Adenauers." In *Adenauer und die Deutsche Frage,* edited by Josef Foschepoth. Göttingen: Vandenhoeck & Ruprecht, 1988.

Schubert, Doris. *Frauen in der deutschen Nachkriegszeit.* Vol. 1, *Frauenarbeit 1945–1949: Quellen und Materialien.* Düsseldorf: Schwann, 1984.

———. " 'Frauenmehrheit verpflichtet': Überlegungen zum Zusammenhang von erweiterter Frauenarbeit und kapitalistischem Wiederaufbau in Westdeutschland." In *"Das Schicksal Deutschlands liegt in der Hand seiner Frauen": Frauen in der deutschen Nachkriegsgeschichte,* edited by Anna-Elisabeth Freier and Annette Kuhn. Düsseldorf: Schwann, 1984.

Schubert, Friedel. *Die Frau in der DDR: Ideologie und konzeptionelle Ausgestaltung ihrer Stellung in Beruf und Familie.* Opladen: Leske & Budrich, 1980.

Schubert, Klaus von. *Wiederbewaffnung und Westintegration: Die innere Auseinandersetzung um die militärische und aussenpolitische Orientierung der Bundesrepublik, 1950–1952.* Stuttgart: Deutsche Verlags-Anstalt, 1970.

Schubert, Werner. *Die Projekte der Weimarer Republik zur Reform des Nichtehelichen-, des Adoptions- und des Ehescheidungsrechts.* Paderborn: Ferdinand Schöningh, 1986.

Schubnell, Hermann. *Der Geburtenrückgang in der Bundesrepublik Deutschland: Die Entwicklung der Erwerbstätigkeit von Frauen und Müttern.* Stuttgart: W. Kohlhammer, 1973.

Schüddekopf, Charles, ed. *Der alltägliche Faschismus: Frauen im Dritten Reich.* Bonn: J. H. W. Dietz Nachf., 1981.

Schulz, Gerhard. "Die CDU: Merkmale ihres Aufbaues." In *Parteien in der Bundesrepublik: Studien zur Entwicklung der deutschen Parteien bis zur Bundestagswahl 1953,* edited by Max Gustav Lange et al. Stuttgart: Ring-Verlag, 1955.

Schulze, Rainer, Doris von der Brelie-Lewien, and Helga Grebing, eds. *Flüchtlinge und Vertriebene in der westdeutschen Nachkriegsgeschichte: Bilanzierung der Forschung und Perspektiven für die künftige Forschungsarbeit.* Hildesheim: August Lax, 1987.

Schulze, Ursel. "Ausbildung und Stellung der Frau in den kaufmännischen Berufen." In *Die Wirtschaft braucht die Frau,* edited by Ruth Bergholtz. Darmstadt: W. W. Leske, 1956.

Schupetta, Ingrid. *Frauen- und Ausländererwerbstätigkeit in Deutschland von 1939 bis 1945*. Cologne: Pahl-Rugenstein, 1983.

Schütze, Yvonne. *Die gute Mutter: Zur Geschichte des normativen Musters "Mutterliebe"*. Bielefeld: B. Kleine, 1986.

———. "Mütterliche Erwerbstätigkeit und wissenschaftliche Forschung." In *Frauensituation: Veränderungen in den letzten zwanzig Jahren*, edited by Yvonne Schütze and Ute Gerhard. Frankfurt am Main: Suhrkamp, 1988.

Schütze, Yvonne, and Ute Gerhard, eds. *Frauensituation: Veränderungen in den letzten zwanzig Jahren*. Frankfurt am Main: Suhrkamp, 1988.

Schwarz, Hans-Peter. *Adenauer*. Vol. 1, *Der Aufstieg: 1876–1952*. Stuttgart: Deutsche Verlags-Anstalt, 1986.

———. *Die Ära Adenauer: Gründerjahre der Republik, 1949–1957*. Stuttgart: Deutsche Verlags-Anstalt, 1981.

Schweitzer, Rosemarie von, and Helge Pross, eds. *Die Familienhaushalte im wirtschaftlichen und sozialen Wandel: Rationalverhalten, Technisierung, Funktionswandel der Privathaushalte und das Freizeitbudget der Frau*. Göttingen: Otto Schwarz & Co., 1976.

Scott, Joan Wallach. "Rewriting History." In *Behind the Lines: Gender and the Two World Wars*, edited by Margaret R. Higonnet, et al. New Haven: Yale University Press, 1987.

———. "Women in History: The Modern Period." *Past & Present*, no. 101 (1983): 141–57.

Seeler, Angela. "Ehe, Familie und andere Lebensformen in den Nachkriegsjahren im Spiegel der Frauenzeitschriften." In *"Das Schicksal Deutschlands liegt in der Hand seiner Frauen": Frauen in der deutschen Nachkriegsgeschichte*, edited by Anna-Elisabeth Freier and Annette Kuhn. Düsseldorf: Schwann, 1984.

Seidenspinner, Gerlinde, et al. *Vom Nutzen weiblicher Lohnarbeit*. Opladen: Leske Verlag & Budrich, 1984.

Die Sexualität des Heimkehrers: Vorträge gehalten auf dem 4. Kongress der Deutschen Gesellschaft für Sexualforschung in Erlangen 1956. Stuttgart: Ferdinand Enke, 1957.

Shaffer, Harry G. *Women in the Two Germanies: A Comparative Study of a Socialist and a Non-Socialist Society*. New York: Pergamon, 1981.

Sierks, Jan. "Löst die analytische Arbeitsplatzbewertung die Lohngleichheit von Mann und Frau?" In *Die Wirtschaft braucht die Frau*, edited by Ruth Bergholtz. Darmstadt: W. W. Leske, 1956.

Silkenbeumer, Rainer. "Familie ist Trumpf—statt eines Vorworts." In *Geburtenrückgang: Risiko oder Chance*, edited by Rainer Silkenbeumer. Hannover: Fackelträger, 1979.

Simitis, Spiros, and Gisela Zenz, eds. *Seminar: Familie und Familienrecht*. 2 vols. Frankfurt am Main: Suhrkamp, 1975.

Sklar, Kathryn Kish. "A Call for Comparisons." *American Historical Review* 95 (1990): 1109–14.

Smart, Carol. *The Ties That Bind: Law, Marriage and the Reproduction of Patriarchal Relations*. London: Routledge & Kegan Paul, 1984.

Smith, Arthur L. *Heimkehr aus dem Zweiten Weltkrieg: Die Entlassung der deutschen Kriegsgefangenen.* Trans. Rainer Michael Gottlob. Stuttgart: Deutsche Verlags-Anstalt, 1985.

Sommerkorn, Ingrid N. "Die erwerbstätige Mutter in der Bundesrepublik: Einstellungs- und Problemveränderungen." In *Wandel und Kontinuität der Familie in der Bundesrepublik Deutschland,* edited by Rosemarie Nave-Herz. Stuttgart: Ferdinand Enke, 1988.

Sommeruniversität für Frauen e.V. Berlin, ed. *Frauen als bezahlte und unbezahlte Arbeitskräfte: Beiträge zur Berliner Sommeruniversität für Frauen, Oktober 1977.* Berlin: Oktoberdruck, 1978.

Sons, Hans-Ulrich. *Gesundheitspolitik während der Besatzungszeit: Das öffentliche Gesundheitswesen in Nordrhein-Westfalen, 1945–1949.* Wuppertal: Peter Hammer, 1983.

Sörgel, Werner. *Konsensus und Interessen: Eine Studie zur Entstehung des Grundgesetzes für die Bundesrepublik Deutschland.* Stuttgart: Ernst Klett, 1969.

Späth, Anna. "Vielfältige Forderungen nach Gleichberechtigung und 'nur' ein Ergebnis: Artikel 3 Absatz 2 GG." In *"Das Schicksal Deutschlands liegt in der Hand seiner Frauen": Frauen in der deutschen Nachkriegsgeschichte,* edited by Anna-Elisabeth Freier and Annette Kuhn. Düsseldorf: Schwann, 1984.

Speck, Otto. *Kinder erwerbstätiger Mütter: Ein soziologisch-pädagogisches Gegenwartsproblem.* Stuttgart: Ferdinand Enke, 1956.

Sperr, Monika. *Schlager: Das grosse Schlager-Buch, Deutsche Schlager 1800–Heute.* Munich: Rogner & Bernhard, 1978.

Spotts, Friedrich. *The Churches and Politics in Germany.* Middletown, Conn.: Wesleyan University Press, 1973.

Stammen, Theo. "Das alliierte Besatzungsregime in Deutschland." In *Vorgeschichte der Bundesrepublik Deutschland: Zwischen Kapitulation und Grundgesetz,* edited by Josef Becker, Theo Stammen, and Peter Waldmann. Munich: Wilhelm Fink, 1979.

Steinbach, Lothar, ed. *Ein Volk, ein Reich, ein Glaube? Ehemalige Nationalsozialisten und Zeitzeugen berichten über ihr Leben im Dritten Reich.* Bonn: J. H. W. Dietz Nachf., 1983.

Steininger, Rolf. *Deutsche Geschichte 1945–1961: Darstellung und Dokumente in zwei Bänden.* Vol. 1. Frankfurt am Main: Fischer, 1983.

Stephenson, Jill. " 'Emancipation' and its Problems: War and Society in Württemberg 1939–45," *European Studies Quarterly* 17 (1987): 345–65.

———. " 'Reichsbund der Kinderreichen': The League of Large Families in the Population Policy of Nazi Germany." *European Studies Review* 9 (1979): 351–75.

———. "War and Society in Württemberg, 1939–1945: Beating the System," *German Studies Review* 9 (1985): 89–105.

———. *Women in Nazi Society.* New York: Barnes and Noble, 1975.

———. "Women's Labor Service in Nazi Germany." *Central European History* 15 (1982): 241–65.

Stewart, Mary Lynn. *Women, Work, and the French State: Labour Protection and Social Patriarchy, 1879–1919.* Kingston: McGill University Press, 1989.

Stoehr, Irene. "Housework and Motherhood: Debates and Policies in the Women's Movement in Imperial Germany and the Weimar Republic." In *Maternity and Gender Policies: Women and the Rise of the European Welfare States, 1880s–1950s*, edited by Gisela Bock and Pat Thane. London: Routledge, 1991.

———. " 'Organisierte Mütterlichkeit': Zur Politik der deutschen Frauenbewegung um 1900." In *Frauen suchen ihre Geschichte: Historische Studien zum 19. und 20. Jahrhundert*, edited by Karin Hausen. Munich: C. H. Beck, 1982.

Stolten, Inge, ed. *Das alltägliche Exil: Leben zwischen Hakenkreuz und Währungsreform*. Bonn: J. H. W. Dietz Nachf., 1982.

———, ed. *Der Hunger nach Erfahrung: Frauen nach 1945*. Frankfurt am Main: Fischer, 1983.

Stöss, Richard, ed. *Parteien-Handbuch: Die Parteien der Bundesrepublik Deutschland 1945–1980*. 2 vols. Opladen: Westdeutscher Verlag, 1983–84.

Strecker, Gabriele. *Gesellschaftspolitische Frauenarbeit in Deutschland: 20 Jahre Deutscher Frauenring*. Opladen: Leske, 1970.

———. *Überleben ist nicht genug: Frauen 1945–1950*. Freiburg im Breisgau: Herder, 1981.

Stümke, Hans-Georg. *Homosexuelle in Deutschland: Eine politische Geschichte*. Munich: C. H. Beck, 1989.

Stümke, Hans-Georg, and Rudi Finkler. *Rosa Winkel, Rosa Listen: Homosexuelle und "gesundes Volksempfinden" von Auschwitz bis heute*. Reinbek: Rowohlt, 1981.

Szepansky, Gerda, ed. *"Blitzmädel," "Heldenmütter," "Kriegerwitwe": Frauenleben im zweiten Weltkrieg*. Frankfurt am Main: Fischer, 1986.

———. *Frauen leisten Widerstand: 1933–1945 (Lebensgeschichten nach Interviews und Dokumenten)*. Frankfurt am Main: Fischer Taschenbuch, 1983.

Tenbruck, Friedrich H. "Alltagsnormen und Lebensgefühle in der Bundesrepublik." In *Die zweite Republik: 25 Jahre Bundesrepublik Deutschland—eine Bilanz*, edited by Richard Löwenthal and Hans-Peter Schwarz. Stuttgart: Seewald, 1974.

Thane, Pat. "Visions of Gender in the Making of the British Welfare State: The Case of Women in the British Labour Party and Social Policy, 1906–1945." In *Maternity and Gender Policies: Women and the Rise of the European Welfare States, 1880s–1950s*, edited by Gisela Bock and Pat Thane. London: Routledge, 1991.

Theuerkauf, Emmy, and Thea Harmuth. *Mutterschutzgesetz: Gesetz zum Schutze der erwerbstätigen Mutter*. Cologne: Bund, 1952.

Thönnessen, Werner. *The Emancipation of Women: The Rise and Decline of the Women's Movement in German Social Democracy 1863–1933*. Trans. by Joris de Bres. London: Pluto Press, 1973.

Thurnwald, Hilde. *Gegenwartsprobleme Berliner Familien: Eine soziologische Untersuchung an 498 Familien*. Berlin: Weidmannsche Verlagsbuchhandlung, 1948.

Townsend, Colin, and Eileen Townsend. *War Wives: A Second World War Anthology*. London: Grafton, 1989.

Trittel, Günter J. *Hunger und Politik: Die Ernährungskrise in der Bizone (1945–1949)*. Frankfurt am Main: Campus, 1990.

Tritz, Maria. *Die Frauenerwerbsarbeit in der Bundesrepublik*. Stuttgart: W. Kohlhammer, 1961.

Tröger, Annemarie. "Between Rape and Prostitution: Survival Strategies and Chances of Emancipation for Berlin Women after World War II." In *Women in Culture and Politics: A Century of Change*, edited by Judith Friedlander et al. Bloomington: Indiana University Press, 1986.

———. "The Creation of a Female Assembly-Line Proletariat." In *When Biology Became Destiny: Women in Weimar and Nazi Germany*, edited by Renate Bridenthal, Atina Grossmann, and Marion Kaplan. New York: Monthly Review Press, 1984.

———. "German Women's Memories of World War II." In *Behind the Lines: Gender and the Two World Wars*, edited by Margaret R. Higonnet et al. New Haven: Yale University Press, 1987.

Tuma, Nancy B., and Johannes Huinink. "Post-War Fertility Patterns in the Federal Republic of Germany." In *Applications of Event History Analysis in Life Course Research*, edited by Karl Ulrich Mayer and Nancy Brandon Tuma. Berlin: Max-Planck-Institut für Bildungsforschung, 1987.

Turner, Ian D., ed. *Reconstruction in Post-War Germany: British Occupation Policy and the Western Zones, 1945–55*. Oxford: Berg, 1989.

Uertz, Rudolf. *Christentum und Sozialismus in der frühen CDU: Grundlagen und Wirkungen der christlich-sozialen Ideen in der Union 1945–1949*. Stuttgart: Deutsche Verlags-Anstalt, 1981.

Ungern-Sternberg, Roderich von. "Ehe und Ehezerrüttung, Geburten, Bevölkerungsgrösse und Eliteschwund," *Schmollers Jahrbuch* 73 (1953): 575–615.

———. "Mutterschaft und weibliche Berufstätigkeit." *Stimmen der Zeit*, no. 159 (1956/57): 341–47.

Ungern-Sternberg, Roderich von, and Hermann Schubnell. *Grundriss der Bevölkerungswissenschaft (Demographie)*. Stuttgart: Piscator-Verlag, 1950.

Usslar, Otto von. "Massnahmen und Forderungen zum wirtschaftlichen Ausgleich der Familienlasten unter Berücksichtigung der Bevölkerungswissenschaft." Diss., Hamburg University, 1955.

Voegeli, Wolfgang, and Barbara Willenbacher. "Die Ausgestaltung des Gleichberechtigungssatzes im Eherrecht." *Zeitschrift für Rechtssoziologie* 5 (1984): 235–59.

Vogel, Angela. "Familie." In *Die Bundesrepublik Deutschland: Geschichte in drei Bänden*, edited by Wolfgang Benz. Vol. 2, *Gesellschaft*. Frankfurt am Main: Fischer, 1983.

———. "Frauen und Frauenbewegung." In *Die Bundesrepublik Deutschland: Geschichte in drei Bänden*, edited by Wolfgang Benz. Vol. 2, *Gesellschaft*. Frankfurt am Main: Fischer, 1983.

Vogel, Lise. "Debating Difference: Feminism, Pregnancy, and the Workplace." *Feminist Studies* 16 (1990): 9–32.

Vogelheim, Elisabeth. "Women in a Changing Workplace: The Case of the Federal Republic of Germany." In *Feminization of the Labor Force: Paradoxes and Promises*, edited by Jane Jenson, Elisabeth Hagen, and Ceallaigh Reddy. New York: Oxford University Press, 1988.

Volz, Gunther. "Trümmermode und New Look: Kleidung und Mode in München 1945–1949." In *Trümmerleben: Texte, Dokumente, Bilder aus den Münchner Nachkriegsjahren*, edited by Friedrich Prinz and Marita Krauss. Munich: Deutscher Taschenbuch, 1985.

Weber, Marianne. *Ehefrau und Mutter in der Rechtsentwicklung: Eine Einführung*. Tübingen: J. C. B. Mohr (Paul Siebeck), 1907.

Weinbaum, Batya, and Amy Bridges. "The Other Side of the Paycheck: Monopoly Capital and the Structure of Consumption." In *Capitalist Patriarchy and the Case for Socialist Feminism*, edited by Zillah R. Eisenstein. New York: Monthly Review Press, 1979.

Weindling, Paul. *Health, Race and German Politics Between National Unification and Nazism*. Cambridge: Cambridge University Press, 1989.

Wengst, Udo. *Beamtentum zwischen Reform und Tradition: Beamtengesetzgebung in der Gründungsphase der Bundesrepublik Deutschland, 1945–1953*. Düsseldorf: Droste, 1988.

Weyer, Johannes. *Westdeutsche Soziologie 1945–1960: Deutsche Kontinuität und nordamerikanischer Einfluss*. Berlin: Duncker & Humblot, 1984.

Weyrather, Irmgard. *"Ich bin noch aus dem vorigen Jahrhundert": Frauenleben zwischen Kaiserreich und Wirtschaftswunder*. Frankfurt am Main: Fischer, 1985.

Wieck, Hans Georg. *Die Entstehung der CDU und die Wiedergründung des Zentrums im Jahre 1945*. Düsseldorf: Droste, 1953.

Wiggershaus, Renate. *Geschichte der Frauen und der Frauenbewegung in der Bundesrepublik Deutschland und in der Deutschen Demokratischen Republik nach 1945*. Wuppertal: Peter Hammer, 1979.

Wildt, Michael. *Der Traum vom Sattwerden: Hunger und Protest, Schwarzmarkt und Selbsthilfe*. Hamburg: VSA, 1986.

Willenbacher, Barbara. "Thesen zur rechtlichen Stellung der Frau." In *Frauensituation: Veränderungen in den letzten zwanzig Jahren*, edited by Ute Gerhard and Yvonne Schütze. Frankfurt am Main: Suhrkamp, 1988.

———. "Zerrüttung und Bewährung der Nachkriegsfamilie." In *Von Stalingrad zur Währungsreform: Zur Sozialgeschichte des Umbruchs in Deutschland*, edited by Martin Broszat, Klaus-Dietmar Henke, and Hans Woller. Munich: R. Oldenbourg, 1988.

Williams, Wendy W. "Equality's Riddle: Pregnancy and the Equal Treatment/Special Treatment Debate." *New York University Review of Law and Social Change* 13 (1984–85): 325–80.

Willms, Angelika. *Die Entwicklung der Frauenerwerbstätigkeit im Deutschen Reich: Eine historisch-soziologische Studie*. Institut für Arbeitsmarkt- und Berufsforschung der Bundesanstalt für Arbeit, BeitrAB 50. Nuremberg: F. Willmy, 1980.

———. "Grundzüge der Entwicklung der Frauenarbeit von 1880 bis 1980." In *Strukturwandel der Frauenarbeit 1880–1980*, edited by Walter Müller, Angelika Willms, and Johann Handl. Frankfurt am Main: Campus, 1983.

———. "Segregation auf Dauer? Zur Entwicklung der Verhältnisse von Frauenarbeit und Männerarbeit in Deutschland, 1882–1980." In *Strukturwandel der Frauenarbeit 1880–1980,* edited by Walter Müller, Angelika Willms, and Johann Handl. Frankfurt am Main: Campus, 1983.

Willms-Herget, Angelika. *Frauenarbeit: Zur Integration der Frauen in den Arbeitsmarkt.* Frankfurt am Main: Campus, 1985.

Winkler, Dörte. "Die amerikanische Sozialisierungspolitik in Deutschland, 1945–1948." In *Politische Weichenstellungen im Nachkriegsdeutschland 1945–1953,* edited by Heinrich August Winkler. Göttingen: Vandenhoeck & Ruprecht, 1979.

———. *Frauenarbeit im "Dritten Reich".* Hamburg: Hoffmann und Campe, 1977.

Winkler, Heinrich August, ed. *Politische Weichenstellungen im Nachkriegsdeutschland 1945–1953.* Göttingen: Vandenhoeck & Ruprecht, 1979.

Wirth, Dieter. "Die Familie in der Nachkriegszeit: Desorganisation oder Stabilität?" In *Vorgeschichte der Bundesrepublik Deutschland: Zwischen Kapitulation und Grundgesetz,* edited by Josef Becker, Theo Stammen, and Peter Waldmann. Munich: Wilhelm Fink, 1979.

Woycke, James. *Birth Control in Germany, 1871–1933.* London: Routledge, 1988.

Wurzbacher, Gerhard. *Leitbilder gegenwärtigen deutschen Familienlebens.* 3d ed. Stuttgart: Ferdinand Enke, 1958.

Zahn-Harnack, Agnes von. "Um die Ehe (1946)." In *Agnes von Zahn-Harnack: Schriften und Reden 1914 bis 1950,* edited by Marga Anders and Ilse Reiche. Tübingen: Hopfer, 1964.

Zeiger, Ivo. "Gleichberechtigung der Frau." *Stimmen der Zeit,* no. 150 (1951/52): 113–22, 176–86.

Zieger, Gottfried. "Die Entwicklung des Familienrechts in der DDR mit Berlin (Ost)." In *Das Familienrecht in beiden deutschen Staaten: Rechtsentwicklung, Rechtsvergleich, Kollisionsprobleme.* Cologne: Carl Heymanns Verlag, 1983.

Zöllner, Detlev. "Germany." In *The Evolution of Social Insurance, 1881–1981: Studies of Germany, France, Great Britain, Austria and Switzerland,* edited by Peter A. Köhler and Hans A. Zacher. New York: St. Martin's Press, 1982.

Index

Abortion: and consumer society, 140; in immediate postwar period, 10, 32, 33; in Nazi period, 16; in post-Adenauer era, 224; in Weimar Republic, 241n96

Achinger, Hans, 121–22, 133, 136

Adenauer, Konrad, 44, 64, 70, 78, 224; anticommunism of, 102–3, 104; on birth rate, 125, 216; Catholic background of, 105; and criminal code reform, 221–22; and elections, 82, 211; and patriarchal family law, 92, 93, 95–99, 102–8, 186–87, 198, 200; SPD criticized by, 80–81, 82; and West German rearmament, 104; woman appointed to cabinet by, 221–22, 288n18

Adorno, Theodor, 136, 226, 267n91

Affirmative-action programs, 71

Agriculture, 19, 151, 155, 156, 160, 163, 216, 217

Albers, Willi, 268n100

Allied forces. See Bomb attacks; Occupation

American Association of University Women, 74

Anticommunism: and CDU/CSU coalition, 68–69, 72, 78, 103, 105, 126, 218, 224; and Christianity, 103, 104; and family policy, 6, 68–69, 72, 78, 89, 102–3, 104, 105, 214, 218; German Democratic Republic as target of, 78, 119, 197–98, 211, 218, 224, 268n99; historical antecedents of,

218; and patriarchy, 104, 105; and Social Democratic party (SPD), 105, 199. See also Cold War

Arndt, Adolf, 88, 98–99

Association of Female Salaried Employees, 84, 199

Augstein, Rudolph, 211

Authoritarianism, 36, 48, 77, 119, 197

Bähnisch, Theanolte, 82–83, 93, 248n57

Basic Law: and Bundestag debates, 86, 98, 181, 187, 202–7; drafted by Parliamentary Council, 40, 45–46, 50, 54, 61, 205, 213; and economic assistance to families, 134; equal rights provision of, 40, 46, 50–54, 61, 70–71, 74–75, 147, 157, 159, 179, 184, 187, 191, 192, 195, 196, 207, 221; and family, 40–41, 65, 69, 70, 74, 83, 86, 93, 95, 98, 112, 186, 187, 190, 202–6; and governmental structure, 40, 182; and homosexuality, 190–91, 192; judicial interpretation of, 80, 99, 181–96, 204–7; legislation of sociocultural order avoided in, 54, 62; and marriage, 40–41, 61, 70, 75, 86, 112, 179, 186, 190; and motherhood, 40–41, 61, 70, 74, 75, 179, 205–6; and parental rights, 69, 70, 93, 95, 101, 190, 204–7; and protective legislation, 157, 158, 159; and public opinion, 41; and recognition of sexual difference, 73–74, 134, 155, 187, 195, 196,

333

tion, 64; and domestic labor, 88; and economic assistance to families, 112–16, 126–29; and economic policy, 44, 78, 114, 212; electoral representation of, 43, 80–82, 100–101, 211, 221; and equal rights, 51–52, 54, 55–57, 91, 92, 97, 99, 102, 106, 108, 159, 205; and family policy, 3, 41, 65–66, 68, 69, 72, 78, 81, 88–96, 102, 103, 112, 115, 138, 197, 199–200, 202–3; and marriage, 41, 65, 66, 72, 88–89, 197; middle-class representation in, 43, 89, 159; and motherhood, 41; and natural law, 64, 67, 72; and parental rights, 69–70, 101; in Parliamentary Council, 41, 42, 44, 51–57, 61–70, 72, 205; and Protestantism, 43, 44, 81, 93–94; and recognition of sexual difference, 52, 53, 155, 184, 202; and separation of church and state, 44; and sexual division of labor, 87; upper-class representation in, 43; and wage differentials based on gender, 53; and wage labor performed by women, 66, 90–91, 112, 159; women's caucus in, 93, 105, 221; working-class representation in, 43, 53

Center party: in Bundestag, 81; and Catholic Church, 17, 43, 45, 49, 53, 116; and economic policy, 116; and family policy, 65, 69, 71, 116; in Parliamentary Council, 45, 62–63; and pronatalism, 116; in Weimar Republic, 49, 63, 65, 81

Children: and day-care facilities, 175; illegitimate, 32, 66–67, 69, 70; latch-key, 139, 216; legal status of, 66, 67, 68, 69; and Nazi loan program, 15–17; Nazi organization of, 70; and parental authority, 93, 186, 189–90, 198, 201–2, 204, 206. *See also* "Money-for-children" program

Christian Democratic Union. *See* CDU/CSU coalition

Christianity: and anticommunism, 103, 104; and capitalism, 78, 103; and collectivism, 64–65, 89; and democracy, 43–44, 126; family ideal of, 65–68, 72, 78, 79, 81, 89, 92–98, 182; and Law for Protection of Mothers, 168; and liberalism, 101, 102; and National Socialist state, 43, 63, 64–65; and natural law, 64, 67–68, 72; and patriarchy, 93, 95, 98, 102, 105, 186; and religious schools,

69, 70; and secularization, 64; and socialism, 78, 101, 102

Christian Social Union. *See* CDU/CSU coalition

Churchill, Winston, 21

Civil Code, 95, 126, 134, 136; and equal rights, 47–49, 51, 54, 55, 61, 79, 86, 147, 220; and family, 4, 47–48, 61, 79, 86, 92, 107, 108; and marriage, 4, 47, 48–49, 61, 79, 86, 92, 107, 108, 201; patriarchal order enforced by, 47, 48, 61, 86, 92, 95, 116, 184; and property rights, 47, 86, 107; and reform deliberations in Bundestag, 86, 98, 102, 104, 111, 146–47, 181; and reform deliberations in court system, 181, 182–85; and reform deliberations in Parliamentary Council, 47, 48–51, 51, 54, 55, 61, 79, 183; and wage labor performed by women, 48–49, 147, 201

Civil service, 84, 90

Class structure: and economic assistance to families, 122–23, 141; and family type, 107, 119; and feminism, 118–19; and legislative protection for working women, 160; mitigated by consumerism, 140; and Nazi labor mobilization, 20; obsolescence of, 119–20, 140–41, 224; and wartime shortages, 19; and women's organizations, 58–59, 83, 118. *See also* Bourgeoisie; Middle class; Petite bourgeoisie; Working class

Cold War, 6, 37, 39, 72, 78, 104, 161, 214, 218, 224

Collectivism, 64–65, 89, 104, 126

Communism: containment of, 6, 68; and equal rights, 49, 57, 71, 92, 106, 199; and family policy, 71–72, 78, 89, 119, 129, 138, 176, 268n99; identified with atheism, 43, 63; perceived threat of, 4, 34, 35, 68, 72, 102–3, 104, 105; and recognition of sexual difference, 97. *See also* Anticommunism

Communist Manifesto, 60

Communist party, West German (KPD): in Bundestag, 81, 85; electoral representation of, 42–43, 81, 100; and equal rights, 92; and family, 92; in Parliamentary Council, 45, 73; prohibition of, 211; and recognition of sexual difference, 155; and wage differentials based on gender, 53, 85; working-class representation in, 42, 45

Compositor: BookMasters, Inc.
Text: 10/13 Sabon
Display: Sabon
Printer: BookCrafters, Inc.
Binder: BookCrafters, Inc.